THE HOOK PENINSULA

COUNTY WEXFORD

Billy Colfer

CORK UNIVERSITY PRESS

Irish Rural Landscapes: Volume II
The Hook Peninsula, County Wexford

General Editors:
F. H. A. Aalen
Kevin Whelan
Matthew Stout

First published by
Cork University Press,
Crawford Business Park,
Crosses Green,
Cork,
Ireland

The Hook Peninsula received financial
assistance from Wexford County Council.

British Library Cataloguing in Publication Data
A CIP catalogue record for this book is available from the British
Library.

ISBN 1 85918 378 6

Colour Reproduction by Keystrokes, Dublin
Printed in China through Phoenix Offset

CONTENTS

PREFACE AND ACKNOWLEDGEMENTS

Just before the outbreak of the second World War, I was brought as a newly-born infant from London, where my parents had met and married, to my father's native Hook. I grew up in the secluded confines of the peninsula immersed in a community where the older ways still held sway, although on the verge of sweeping changes. As children, we were part of the environment, instinctively absorbing knowledge about land, rock and sea as we roamed the headland. Because of the intimate nature of the community, there was interaction between all age groups and the younger generation learned by observing and participating in the seasonal activities of fishing and farming which dictated the rhythm of the year. Events which required the involvement of a *meitheal*, or team, were of special interest, particularly the threshing of the corn at harvest time, collecting seaweed, and hauling the bigger boats up the slipway at Slade for repairs, usually done by every able-bodied man available after mass on Sunday morning.

Occasional visits to my mother's home in Tipperary necessitated a long train journey from Campile to Laffan's Bridge, where we were met by my grandmother in the ass and cart. Counting sheep with my grandfather on the Slieve Ardagh Hills and saving turf on the Duravella Bog provided an experience of an entirely different landscape, which placed our own peninsular environment in perspective. When he first visited my mother, my Tipperary grandfather's shocked comment 'My poor child, is this where you're living?' expressed his reaction to the exposed maritime landscape of the Hook in contrast to the midland mix of rolling hills, green fields and brown bogs of his own place.

I have often wondered why and when my attachment for the Hook deepened into an intellectual interest in its landscape and society. Growing up in the shadow of Slade Castle had a subliminal influence; I watched workmen carrying out conservation work when the Castle was taken over by the O.P.W. in the late 1940s. I remember being fascinated by the class in local history taught (rather remarkably, at the time) in Loftus Hall N.S. by teacher Kathleen Walsh (later Mrs Conway) for which I was requisitioned to provide illustrations, being regarded as having some aptitude for drawing.

After primary school, I left the Hook to become a boarder in St Peter's College, Wexford, then a student at St Pats, Drumcondra, and finally a teacher in Wexford town, and for the next forty years my visits to the Hook were confined to extended holiday periods. In the early 1970s, however, I began to collect local folklore and place-names, initiating a process that would ultimately lead to the publication of this volume, celebrating the evolution of this small but unique part of the Irish landscape. This study complements the *Atlas of the Irish Rural Landscape* and is the second of a Landscape Series that will focus in detail on different regions in Ireland.

I must record my gratitude to many individuals, organisations, friends and family for assistance in preparing this publication. My mentor and friend Professor Terry Barry, Trinity College Dublin, guided me through two stints in his department, leading to the acquisition of an academic background which assisted in the undertaking of a project of this nature. I wish to acknowledge the influence and encouragement of the Wexford Historical Society, of which I am a long-time member. I am grateful to Adrian Doyle of Wexford County Council for his support; also Wexford County Librarian, Fionnuala Hanrahan, and her staff, particularly Jarlath Glynn, Celestine Rafferty, Michael Dempsey and Gráinne Doran, for unfailing help and patience. The original digital images used in this book are now housed in Wexford County Library. I would like to thank Eamonn Murphy and Frank Kearney of Keystrokes for the professionalism with which they generated these images.

Kevin Redmond and Maeve O'Brien in Wexford County Council Planning Office were also of assistance. I wish to acknowledge the assistance of staff in: the National Library of Ireland; The National Museum of Ireland, particularly Mary Cahill; the National Archive; the Royal Irish Academy, especially Siobhán O'Rafferty; the Royal Society of Antiquaries, particularly Colette Ellison; Matthew Parkes of the Geological Survey of Ireland; Eugene Ryan of Teagasc; Jim Hurley for discussions on the natural environment; Mairéad Timmins for information on the Saltmills explosion; Marcella Senior, TCD, and Brendan Dempsey, photo-archivist, TCD; Connie Kelleher of the Underwater Unit, Department of Environment, Heritage and Local Government (formerly known as Dúchas), for underwater photographs. A special thanks to Tony Roche, photo-archivist with D.EHLG, for his patience and assistance and Helena Campbell for GIS assistance.

I would like to acknowledge the support of many individuals, many of them valued friends: Tom and Eileen Neville for years of discussion and enthusiasm for my work on the Hook; fellow researcher Ned Culleton whose advice and experience have always been invaluable; Bernard Browne who is always generous with his wide knowledge of sources and publications; the late Rory Murphy whose enthusiasm and help was always a source of inspiration; Hilary Murphy for many discussions on family history; Petra Coffey for her detailed knowledge of the Du Noyer drawings; Geraldine Stout for comparisons with the Boyne valley; Daithí and Mary Nevins for unfailing interest and encouragement; Pierce and Valerie McAuliffe for support over many years, and Ben Murtagh for discussions on Fethard Castle and the Tower of Hook.

Over the years I have had helpful discussions on matters relating to the Hook with various people from the locality; these included the late Tommy Murphy, Charlie Colfer, Tux Tweedy, Peggy Colfer, Thomas Colfer, Bunny Power, Aidan Devereux and Barbara Kelly. A special word of appreciation to Dermot Hearne, Noel Morris and John O'Brien of the 'Wednesday Four,' who help to keep my work up to par!

I wish to thank the many people who allowed illustrations to be reproduced: John Ironside for the cover photograph; Killian Mullarney for his bird sketches; David Lloyd for the use of the Colclough portraits; Jimmy and Breda FitzGibbon for historic photographs and a Tony O'Malley drawing; Sir David Davis; James O'Halloran of James Adam Showrooms for permission to reproduce a Tony O'Malley painting; Kathleen Delaney for permission to use her artwork commissioned by Wexford County Council; Bob Howlett of Shelburne Co-op/Glanbia; Niall Byrne, Mairéad Furlong and Mary Byrne. Those who gave individual illustrations are acknowledged on the appropriate pages.

I am fortunate in having the backing of two friends in the preparation of this book: the help given by Kevin Whelan, director of the Keough–Notre Dame Centre, a generous supporter of my work over many years, has been indispensable; the technological skill of Matthew Stout is evident in the design of the book and the preparation of maps.

I have always had the complete backing of my family in any project I wished to undertake and this one has been no exception. A special thanks to Paul and Helen; Eoin, Jackie, Finn and Seán; Donal, Eamonn, Niall and Lisa. A particular word of appreciation to Eoin for technical support. As always, my wife Noreen has given me unstinted encouragement and we have enjoyed many leisurely field-trips together in researching this publication.

Finally, I wish to thank my editors, F. H. A. Aalen, Matthew Stout and Kevin Whelan, and Cork University Press, particularly Caroline Somers, Michael Collins and former publisher Sara Wilbourne, for commissioning this book.

Billy Colfer

FROM THE EDITORS OF *IRISH RURAL LANDSCAPES*

The *Atlas of the Irish Rural Landscape* was published in 1997 to heighten awareness of the cultural landscape. Beyond a superficial appreciation of 'scenery', the landscape rarely impinged on Irish national consciousness. Its ubiquity seemed to camouflage it, despite its centrality in our daily lives. The *Atlas* was designed to allow Irish people to see their landscape, rather than merely look at it. It sought to increase the legibility of the landscape, making the familiar exotic, lifting the lid of the present surface to show the buried layers beneath. It excavated the hidden layers in the landscape, demonstrating its remarkable longevity.

Seen in this way, the cultural landscape acquired a fascination and a resonance which heightened its aesthetic allure. The *Atlas* appeared at the height of the Tiger years, and its emphasis on the fragility of the landscape struck a chord at a moment of momentous transformation in the nature of Irish society. Irish people appreciated that a wider understanding of the landscape was needed to develop sensitive policies, and that the landscape itself had to be recognised and safeguarded as a central component of the national heritage.

The *Atlas* authors also highlighted the dynamism of the landscape, and the cumulative ways in which it has evolved as a shared creation of the myriad generations of Irish people. In that sense the Irish landscape is the most democratic of documents, bearing the imprints of all social strata. It is also the most pluralist, as it retains the stories of the diverse groups who occupied it. A popular section of the *Atlas* comprised six short case-studies which amply demonstrated that diversity across a distinct series of regions – The Hook in Wexford, Lecale in Down, The Burren in Clare, The Bend of the Boyne in Meath, The Ring of Gullion in south Armagh and Connemara in west Galway. It was always our intention to expand these studies (and commission others) into full-length volumes, modelled on the style and philosophy of the *Atlas*. The warm critical and popular reception of the original *Atlas* (reprinted five times) encouraged us to proceed with the series, and Geraldine Stout's *Newgrange and the Bend of the Boyne* appeared in 2002. The success of that volume (reprinted in 2003) has demonstrated that the local has a universal appeal.

Billy Colfer's *The Hook Peninsula* continues the series. These two volumes on the Boyne and the Hook brilliantly develop the thematic concerns of the original *Atlas* volume: the landscape as a reciprocal relationship between nature and culture; the variety of regional landscape as a reflection of cultural diversity; the challenge to the inherited landscape by increasingly intrusive and pervasive forces for change; the appreciation of landscape as dynamic and evolving, and the need for changes to be introduced in sympathy with the inherited grain of the landscape. Billy Colfer's *Hook* is written by a sympathetic insider who has also acquired an objective and detached eye. The book integrates the landscape and the archival record in an accomplished performance. The compact and highly distinctive peninsula makes for a compelling case-study, with Colfer carefully stitching the local story into a wider narrative. An eye for detail and an intuitive understanding of the local community create a vivid narrative, while Colfer's obvious love for the place infuses the volume with an underlying passion all the more moving for being understated. In these beautiful pages, the landscape of the Hook Peninsula has been given a radiant treatment. Has the landscape of any other small region in the world been treated so marvellously?

F. H. A. Aalen
Matthew Stout
Kevin Whelan

Dedicated to the memory of my parents, Willie and Jenny

The Peninsula

When you have nothing more to say, just drive
For a day all round the peninsula.
The sky is tall as over a runway,
The land without marks, so you will not arrive

But pass through, though always skirting landfall.
At dusk, horizons drink down sea and hill,
The ploughed field swallows the whitewashed gable
And you're in the dark again. Now recall

The glazed foreshore and silhouetted log,
That rock where breakers shredded into rags,
The leggy birds stilted on their own legs,
Islands riding themselves out into the fog

And drive back home, still with nothing to say
Except that now you will uncode all landscapes
By this: things founded clean on their own shapes,
Water and ground in their extremity.

Seamus Heaney

THE HOOK PENINSULA

The tapering promontory of the Hook, located in the barony of Shelburne in the south-western corner of county Wexford, forms the eastern boundary of Waterford Harbour. Although this study, as the title suggests, focuses specifically on the peninsula, a larger area between the estuaries of Waterford Harbour and Bannow Bay (generally regarded as the Hook region) is included. This triangular district narrows from a fifteen kilometre base in the north to the tapering point of Hook, fifteen kilometres to the south. Because of its peninsular character, the Hook has always been considered remote and isolated; yet its association with Waterford Harbour has given the region strategic importance, particularly evident in the medieval period.

Remoteness by land and accessibility by sea have had a marked impact on the evolution of landscape and settlement, contributing to the development of cultural identity and continuity. The traditional use of the estuary as a political and ecclesiastical boundary further isolated the Hook as a frontier area. The significance of the harbour, with its three 'sister rivers', the Barrow, Nore and Suir, has been recognised since earliest times. Known in Irish as Comar na dTrí nUisce (the confluence of three rivers), or Loch Dá Chaoch (the loch of the two sources), the harbour has been used as a gateway to south-east Ireland by successive waves of newcomers, including the Vikings (who gave it its present name), the Anglo-Normans and the English.

JOHN IRONSIDE

Fig. 1 This view, taken from 3,000m looking towards the north-east, dramatically illustrates the peninsular, rock-bound topography of the Hook, its threat to shipping emphasised by the imposing medieval lighthouse. The regular estate field-system of Loftus Hall in the middle distance contrasts sharply with the small fields and fragmented holdings associated with the farmhouse cluster of Churchtown in the left foreground. In the right foreground, the townland of Slade replicates the contrasting field patterns. The manorial village of Slade, with its tower house, developed at the only natural landing-place on the peninsula, beside a small bay sheltered from the prevailing south-westerly winds. In the far distance, the promontory of Baginbun and the island of Bannow are visible, both sites associated with the arrival of the Anglo-Normans in the late twelfth century.

*The first the gentle Suire, that making way
By sweet Clonmel, adorns rich Waterford;
The next the stubborn Nore, whose waters gray
By fair Kilkenny, and Rosponte board.
The third the goodly Barrow, which doth hoard,
Great heaps of salmon in his dreary bosom;
All which long sundered do at last accord
To join in one e'er to the sea they come,
So flowing all from one, all one at last become.*

Fig. 2 In the sixteenth century, the significance of the harbour with its river system was celebrated by Edmund Spenser in his epic poem *The Faerie Queene* (1589), B. 4. Cant. II, v. 43.

INTRODUCTION

The importance of Waterford Harbour as a trade route inevitably influenced the growth of settlement in the adjoining district. In the medieval period, the foundation of key ports on its tributary rivers made the protection of the harbour a priority. Security requirements in the late twelfth century were partly responsible for the granting of the land bordering Waterford Harbour in the Hook region to high-profile religious orders: the Cistercians at Dunbrody and the Templars at Templetown. In the early thirteenth century, the volume of shipping using the harbour led to the building of a unique tower at the tip of the peninsula as a lighthouse and navigation aid. In the late sixteenth century, the construction of Duncannon Fort, positioned to control access to the harbour and its ports, was motivated by security and economic concerns. The *Civil Survey*, compiled in the 1650s, emphasised the commercial significance of the harbour and its river system:

> Those three incomparable sisters commonly called the three famous rivers of Barrow, Nore and Suir, whose lovely embracements makes the harbour deep and spatious, safe for navigation which plentifully enricheth the several parts of this nation by traffic and commerce, with shipping both foreign and domestic.[1]

The granting of the region to three religious foundations in the medieval period established the fundamental matrix for subsequent social and landscape organisation, giving a cohesiveness and distinctive character to the settlement pattern. This was particularly true for the Cistercian estates, which, in theory at least, created a *tabula rasa* by removing all lay people from the monastic lands. The three secular estates which evolved from the church lands in the sixteenth century inherited existing land divisions and tenants and, in turn, added a new layer of occupants and infrastructure. These two principal periods of colonisation and change in land

ownership led to a three-tiered society made up of Irish, Old English and New English. By the mid-nineteenth century, the Hook had one of the highest densities of Old English family names in Ireland.[2] Similarly, the high ratio of Irish and English place-names with cultural elements is the product of this distinctive settlement history.

While development on the estates over three centuries was broadly similar, there were also marked differences. These included location, natural resources, the introduction of new tenants and the social and political philosophy of the landlord. Based on a hierarchical class structure which generated concern about tenurial rights, the estate system encouraged psychological dependence while providing a basic economic and social structure. The impact on the psyche of Hook people must have been heightened by the erection of an impressive gateway at Porters Gate, on the neck of the peninsula, as an entrance to the Loftus demesne lands. Although the gateway was removed seventy years ago, the site is still referred to as 'the piers'; an indication that the gate, as well as being an actual barrier, created a subliminal division between 'insiders' and 'outsiders.' The disintegration of the estate system and revolution in land ownership at the end of the nineteenth century introduced considerable social change. People whose ancestors had been tenants for generations became owners of their traditional family farms; an

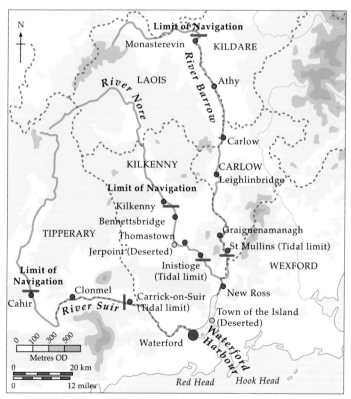

Fig. 3 Waterford Harbour with its river system provides access by boat to many of the principal towns in the south-east of Ireland.

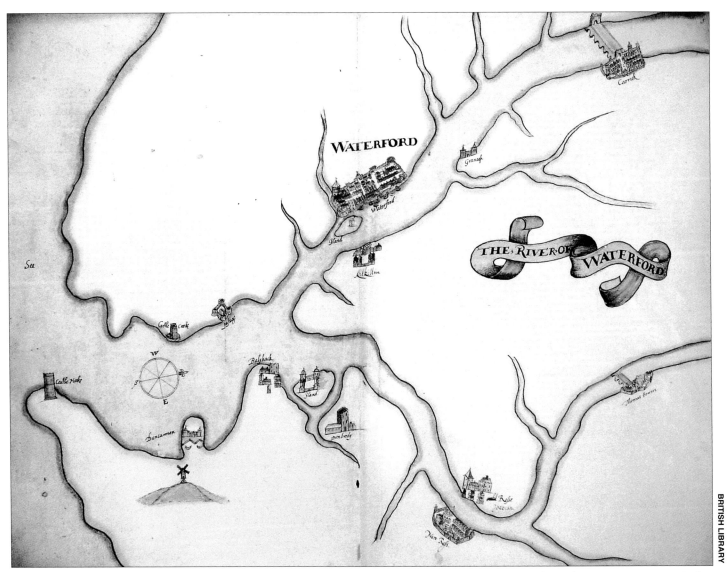

Fig. 4 The strategic and economic value of the estuary with its river system led to the production of a series of charts showing settlements and other coastal features. This early seventeenth-century map has vignettes of the walled towns of Waterford and Carrick on the River Suir, and Thomastown, Rosbercon and New Ross on the River Barrow. The recently constructed forts at Duncannon and Passage are also shown. Prominent landmarks, such as churches, castles and windmills, are included because of their use by mariners as navigational aids. The lighthouse is called Castle Hooke, as by the early seventeenth century the peninsula was no longer called Rinn Dubháin but was known as The Hook, an Old English word for a projecting piece of land.

increase in emigration was also inevitable as the various traditional occupations which supported a labouring class on the estate were no longer viable. In spite of the highly organised nature of the estate system, the secluded, cul-de-sac nature of the Hook allowed older landscape and cultural features to survive the intrusive forces of change, particularly on the Loftus lands in the south of the region; the resultant landscape and society are remarkable palimpsests of complex origin.

The physical attributes of the peninsula itself had a fundamental impact on the growth of settlement; decisions which resulted in landscape changes were inevitably influenced by location, topography, geology and soil quality. In a region with such extensive maritime connections, the sea obviously played a prominent role in people's lives, especially along the coastal strip. The need to exploit the rich off-shore fishing grounds, for commercial as well as subsistence purposes, led to the construction of six small harbours, which were also engaged in low-level commercial activity. The opportunities for employment offered by the sea were taken up by many who broadened their horizons by sailing the world. Derelict houses in the region are reminders of many others who left by sea, not as sailors but as emigrants, whose descendants periodically return seeking their ancestral origins.

The Tower of Hook from Doornogue Point

B. COLFER

LANDSCAPE AND ENVIRONMENT

Physically part of the south county Wexford lowland plain, the Hook, for the most part, lies under 60 metres in elevation, except for some low hills to the north between Ramsgrange and Campile. Landscape and environment fundamentally affected the development of the region; the location beside a major estuary and busy shipping lanes was of vital significance. Natural resources, on land and sea, influenced the selection, nature and development of population centres as well as the occupations and lifestyles of the inhabitants. The bedrock has been exploited as a valuable economic asset for building and other purposes. The covering of soil, mainly of glacial origin, deposited over the rocks has largely determined the quality of land and its potential for farming, which in turn inevitably dictated the subsequent growth of settlement and society.

B. COLFER

Fig. 1 Old Red Sandstone cliffs at Carnivan, with thrift, birds-foot trefoil and kidney vetch in the foreground. The low-lying point of Hook can be seen on the far horizon. The deposit of white droppings on the nearest rock mark it as a favourite roost for seabirds, particularly shags and cormorants.

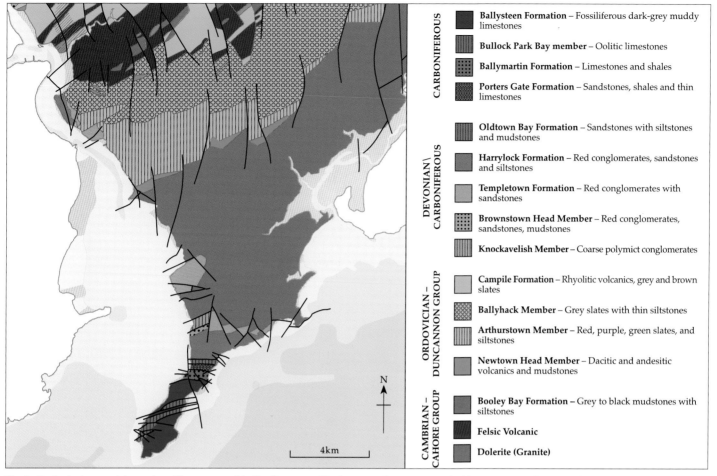

CARBONIFEROUS

Ballysteen Formation – Fossiliferous dark-grey muddy limestones

Bullock Park Bay member – Oolitic limestones

Ballymartin Formation – Limestones and shales

Porters Gate Formation – Sandstones, shales and thin limestones

DEVONIAN\ CARBONIFEROUS

Oldtown Bay Formation – Sandstones with siltstones and mudstones

Harrylock Formation – Red conglomerates, sandstones and siltstones

Templetown Formation – Red conglomerates with sandstones

Brownstown Head Member – Red conglomerates, sandstones, mudstones

Knockavelish Member – Coarse polymict conglomerates

ORDOVICIAN – DUNCANNON GROUP

Campile Formation – Rhyolitic volcanics, grey and brown slates

Ballyhack Member – Grey slates with thin siltstones

Arthurstown Member – Red, purple, green slates, and siltstones

Newtown Head Member – Dacitic and andesitic volcanics and mudstones

CAMBRIAN – CAHORE GROUP

Booley Bay Formation – Grey to black mudstones with siltstones

Felsic Volcanic

Dolerite (Granite)

N

4km

Fig. 2 Geological map of the region. The topographically distinctive Hook peninsula is comprised of limestone, sandstone and Old Red Sandstone.

GEOLOGY

The Hook rocks are primarily sedimentary in nature, deposited under the margins of an ocean which covered the region for millions of years.[1] The oldest rocks belong to the Cahore Group of the Cambrian period, deposited in a marine basin 570 to 510 million years ago by earthquake-generated currents which carried large quantities of sand and mud. These sedimentary rocks are represented in the region by the Booley Bay Formation, which constitutes the main bedrock mass in the area. This series is dominated by mudstones and siltstones with subordinate greywacke sandstones (grey or green with a high proportion of mud). The siltstones may be only a millimetre or two thick and closely spaced, giving the rocks a pin-striped appearance. Occasional black mudstones, up to two metres thick, represent long quiescent intervals between periods of earthquake activity. These rocks, forming striking cliffs between Fethard Dock and Baginbun Head and between Duncannon and Templetown Bay, are best examined at Booley Bay and Dollar Bay. Fossils from this period, of rigid-bodied, sedentary organisms, have been found at Booley Bay in recent times.[2]

North of the Booley Bay Formation, the sedimentary rocks of the Campile Formation were deposited during the Ordovician period, 510 to 438 million years ago. Isolated volcanic rocks occur within the Campile Formation, which consists principally of mudstones with occasional grey and brown slates. The Ballyhack Member, composed of grey slates and thin siltstones, and the Arthurstown Member, containing red, purple and green slates and siltstones, constitute sub-divisions of the Campile Formation.

Old Red Sandstone

In the Hook, the Devonian period (410 to 355 million years ago) was a period of rapid erosion and deposition under semi-desert conditions in an area which had once been an ocean. This period saw the deposition of a succession of fluviatile red beds of locally derived pebble and cobble conglomerates, sandstones and mudstones. The beds of Old Red Sandstone survive only in separated outliers in the Hook and can be seen in the red conglomerates, sandstone and siltstone of the Herrylock Formation; the red conglomerates and sandstones of the Templetown Formation and the sandstones with siltstones and

B. COLFER

Fig. 3 Old Red Sandstone cliffs at Herrylock on the west coast of the peninsula. This rock type also occurs at Broomhill, Carnivan, Arthurstown and Ballyhack. For centuries, it was used by local stone masons to manufacture millstones, troughs and other objects.

mudstones of the Oldtown Bay Formation. Small outcrops occur at Arthurstown and Ballyhack. The entire succession is well displayed along the west of the Hook peninsula, between Templetown Bay and Boyces (Lumsden's) Bay. The lowest beds, belonging to the Templetown Formation, are predominantly quartz conglomerates with a small proportion of red sandstone overlying rocks of the Booley Bay Formation. The Templetown Formation is succeeded to the south by the Herrylock Formation, which shows a change to interbedded quartz conglomerates, fining up to red sandstones and siltstones with occasional grey mudstones. The coarser-grained rock types represent river channels meandering over a floodplain, which in turn is indicated by the finer-grained siltstones and mudstones. The upper beds of the Old Red Sandstone, the Oldtown Bay Formation, represent deposition on a coastal plain, characterised by large-scale, cross-bedded grey sandstones. There are no conglomerates; instead there are thin-bedded pebbly and granule-rich sandstones with minor mudstones and sandstones. The overall appearance of the formation is

B. COLFER

Fig. 4 The junction of siltstones and Old Red Sandstone at a bay known as Liu na Scooth, on the shore of Waterford Harbour in Templetown.

grey in colour and it passes up gradually to the marine sandstones of the Porters Gate Formation.

Near-shore sandstone and shales

Immediately south of the Old Red Sandstone, the grey calcereous sandstones, thin marine limestones and mudstones of the Porters Gate Formation, laid down during early Carboniferous times (355 to 290 million years ago), record the change to a marine environment. The Porters Gate Formation is best seen south of Sandeel Bay, at Woarwoy Bay and Lyraun. This formation (about 40m thick) records a series of shallow-water beach sandstones, tidally influenced sandstones and mudstones, and the first shallow-water limestones, followed by sub-tidal mudstones. With increasing depth

B. COLFER

Fig. 5 Dramatic rock folding at Templetown Bay, caused by slump deformation in the thinly interbedded mudstones and siltstones, deposited in an ocean in the Cambrian period c. 550 million years ago.

of water, and consequently calmer conditions, came various shellfish (brachiopods, bivalves), other invertebrates (crinoids, corals) and fish, whose fossil teeth can be seen in this formation.

Carboniferous Limestones

As the early Carboniferous sea gradually advanced northwards, successive depth-related sediments were deposited. South of the Porters Gate Formation, there is a gradual transition into the overlying limestone and shale succession of the 70 metres thick Ballymartin Formation with its much more diverse fossil fauna. This series, deposited in deeper sub-tidal conditions, consists of interbedded dark-grey muddy limestones and calcareous shaley mudstones. The presence of so much mud indicates that a land source, probably the Leinster Massif, was being

GEOLOGICAL SURVEY OF IRELAND

Fig. 6 *Junction of lower limestone, Co. Wexford,* a painting by G. Du Noyer c.1850. The location is near Sandeel Bay on the east coast of the peninsula in the townland of Houseland. The fishermen shown in the background indicates that, in summer, boats were kept at suitable locations around the coast.

eroded to supply the non-carbonate material. This series is exposed in the cliffs between Lyraun and Brecaun Church.

The remainder of the point of Hook consists of the Ballysteen Formation, comprising well-bedded relatively clean limestones. It passes gradually up into finer-grained and more muddy limestones. The formation represents carbonate sands and gravels produced primarily from the remains of crinoids and fragments of other calcareous shellfish and corals which lived in the warm, shallow tropical sea. The limestone, with a wide variety of fossils, can be seen in the vicinity of Hook Lighthouse.[3] The formation is bisected by a band of dolomitised oolitic (composed of small rounded granules) limestone, known as the Bullockpark Bay Member, which crosses the peninsula from Bullockpark to Churchtown (dolomite is a sedimentary rock with a crystalline structure and hexagonal characteristics). This formation was caused by a temporary shallowing of the sea and represents carbonate sand banks that accumulated above the wave base. It can be seen, with abundant trace fossils, in the cliffs around Doornogue Point. A number of deep fissures

(known locally as chans) have been formed by the action of the sea on faults in the bedrock along the coastline. The principal ones occur at Conigear, Black Chan and Bullock Park on the east coast, at Piper's Hole beside the lighthouse, and at Pursheen and the Long Chan near Doornogue Point.

B. COLFER

Fig. 7 View of limestone rocks from the top of Hook Lighthouse. Wave action creates fissures and clefts (known locally as 'chans' or 'guts') by removing softer material in faults in the bedrock.

HOOK PENINSULA FOSSILS

Well-organised life forms existed on earth by 1000 million years ago. Individual animals and plants gradually evolved and their hard parts changed and developed. As successive rocks were deposited, some of these hard parts were preserved in them as fossils. Rocks can be dated if the fossils in the different layers can be placed in an evolutionary sequence. The oldest fossils in the Hook region, called *Ediacaria booleyi and Nimbia occlusa,* have been found at Booley Bay on the west coast of the peninsula. These rigid-bodied, sedentary organisms belong to the Cambrian period, c. 550 million years ago, when the fragment of earth now called Ireland was in the southern hemisphere, covered by a wide ocean. The profusion of marine fossils at Hook Head were deposited c. 350 million years ago during the Carboniferous period when a tropical sea flooded over the land. These include corals, brachiopods with paired calcareous shells like the modern cockle, trilobites or jointed animals with hard outer coats, and crinoids, which are members of a group that includes sea urchins.

Ediacaria booleyi, a rigid-bodied, sedentary organism; found at Booley Bay.

Colonial coral; found at Hook Head.

Crinoid stems and brachiopods; found at Hook Head.

A solitary coral; found at Hook Head.

A section of crinoid stem; found at Hook Head.

A bed of brachiopods; found at Hook Head.

B. COLFER

Fig. 8 A painting by G. Du Noyer, c. 1850, of a sea arch, known locally as 'Solomon's Boat,' created by the action of the waves on the limestone rock just south of the village of Slade. The feature survives in substantially the same form at the present time.

Fig. 9 This inlet, known as Conigear, about 500m north of the lighthouse on the east coast of the headland, was formed by the removal of material by wave action from a fault in the limestone bedrock.

THE ICE AGE

About two million years ago, climate fluctuated between heat and cold, resulting in higher sea levels during warm spells due to melting ice-caps.[4] Evidence for these higher sea levels is provided by 'raised beaches' along the south Wexford coast. These consist of a layer of beach pebbles and sand occurring well above the height of the present sea level. An excellent example can be seen on the seashore at Grange beach just north of Fethard. During cold periods, glaciers moved across the land, depositing a layer of glacial drift containing material ranging from large boulders to fine clay. Glacial deposits and features in the Hook are legacies of the most recent Quaternary events which ended 10,000 years ago. Glacial deposits from the midlands covered the Hook and deposited a level blanket of drift over the underlying bedrock. Granite erratics picked up by the ice as it moved from the midlands across the Blackstairs Mountains into south-west Wexford can be seen in sections of glacial drift in the area. The surface is

PRIVATE COLLECTION

Fig. 10 A c. 1870 photograph taken of a sea arch, known as 'the Hole of Ingard,' in the shale cliffs near Fethard. The arch fell in 1907.

B . COLFER

Fig. 11 A 'blow-hole' at Conigear on the eastern cliff about five hundred metres from the lighthouse. Blow-holes are formed by the pneumatic action of air being forced by wave power through clefts in the rock, expanding the fissure to form a cave and creating a vent on the cliff top which produces a geyser-like effect during a storm. The cave eventually collapses, leaving the distinctive crevice known locally as a chan.

remarkably level over large areas as the ice deposited material on the uneven bedrock and left an even surface in its wake. The till is often inadequately drained due to the compacting action of the ice.

As no part of the region is far from the sea, there are no rivers of note except for the Owenduff, which forms the north-east boundary of the region. There are five principal drainage systems in the north of the area, based on three streams flowing east and two flowing west. The Taulaght, Tintern and Poulfur streams empty into Bannow Bay while the Campile and Duncannon streams flow from the high ground around Campile into the Waterford estuary.

Soils
The soils of the region were formed from the glacial drift deposited during the Ice Age by the movement of glaciers from the north-west.[5] Soil quality was also influenced to a considerable degree by the nature of the underlying bedrock. The dominant soils in the area are freely drained and have a wide use range for cultivated crops, pasture and forestry. These soils consist of the well-drained brown earth of the Clonroche Association to the north of the area, based on glacial drift of predominantly shale origin with some granite; the freely drained brown earths of the Broomhill Association, predominantly of Old Red Sandstone derivation; and the freely drained Grey-Brown Podzolics of the southern Hook Head Association, predominantly of limestone composition. Because of imperfect drainage and heavy texture, the Fethard Association has a somewhat limited use range and within this association the Ballinruan Series, because of a serious drainage problem, has a limited use range, being of moderate suitability for pasture and forestry. Within the Clonroche Association, the Kilpierce Series is similarly classified, because of a serious drainage problem.

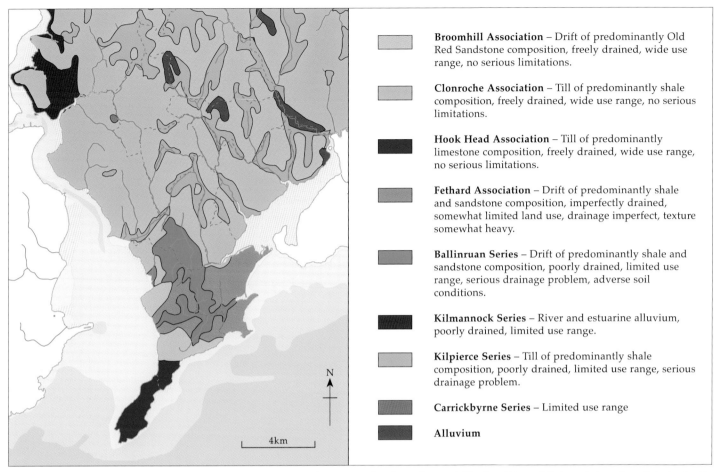

Broomhill Association – Drift of predominantly Old Red Sandstone composition, freely drained, wide use range, no serious limitations.

Clonroche Association – Till of predominantly shale composition, freely drained, wide use range, no serious limitations.

Hook Head Association – Till of predominantly limestone composition, freely drained, wide use range, no serious limitations.

Fethard Association – Drift of predominantly shale and sandstone composition, imperfectly drained, somewhat limited land use, drainage imperfect, texture somewhat heavy.

Ballinruan Series – Drift of predominantly shale and sandstone composition, poorly drained, limited use range, serious drainage problem, adverse soil conditions.

Kilmannock Series – River and estuarine alluvium, poorly drained, limited use range.

Kilpierce Series – Till of predominantly shale composition, poorly drained, limited use range, serious drainage problem.

Carrickbyrne Series – Limited use range

Alluvium

Fig. 12 The soils of the Hook region fall into six categories. Most of the land, in the Clonroche, Hook Head and Broomhill Associations, is well drained with a wide use range. Land in the imperfectly drained Fethard Association, including the Ballinruan series, and in the scattered patches of the Kilpierce series, is less productive. The quality of the land had a direct bearing on settlement. In the medieval period, the Cistercian estates of Dunbrody and Tintern, and the Templar manor of Kilcloggan, were located, for the most part, on the better quality soils.

B. COLFER

Fig. 13 Glacial till on the cliffs near Brecaun church on the east coast of the peninsula. During the Ice Age, an even blanket of till was spread over the bedrock. Places like the one shown above, where the rock is low-lying, with a deep covering of clay, are more susceptible to erosion by wave action.

The Blackcap, a common autumn migrant.

Manx Shearwater.

The Great Skua is frequently seen off-shore.

The Firecrest is a regular scarce migrant in October.

The Hobby is a rare European visitor.

Dartford Warbler, seventh Irish record at Hook Head, October 1995.

Guillemots.

The Merlin, a regular visitor to the Hook in autumn, feeds on small migrant birds.

Storm Petrels

KILLIAN MULLARNEY

Fig. 14 The migrant birds attracted to the Hook peninsula as a point of arrival and departure in spring and autumn, as well as a variety of seabirds, are of particular interest to ornithologists. The examples shown here, some of them rare migrants, were observed and drawn in the Hook by the internationally renowned, Wexford-based ornithological artist Killian Mullarney, illustrator of the standard reference Collins *Bird Guide*.

WILDLIFE HABITATS

The intensification of agriculture in the area has reduced wildlife haunts. Surviving habitats of significance are mostly located on wetlands and the sea coast. The south Wexford coast, supporting a unique cluster of natural heritage sites, is one of the outstanding coastal heritage features in Ireland and Europe. Of fourteen proposed Natural Heritage Areas (NHAs) designated along this coastline, six are located in the Hook region.[6]

Hook Head

Natural attractions at the Hook include fossils and other geological features. Marine life can be observed in rock pools on the foreshore and in shallow inshore waters. The prominent headland acts as a departure point in autumn for birds heading south and as a point of arrival for tired migrants in spring, many of them attracted by the lighthouse at night. Early in the year, seabirds, particularly manx shearwaters, auks, gannets, skuas, scoters and divers, migrating from the Atlantic to breeding colonies on the Irish Sea and further north can be observed from the point. Late in the year, these birds make the return journey to the Atlantic and in addition rare species such as sooty shearwaters and black terns are sometimes seen. The most numerous land bird migrants include wheatears, whinchats, swallows, sand martins, willow warblers and chiffchaffs. In autumn, these arrive in large numbers and are later replaced by migrating skylarks, chaffinches and starlings, among other species. The most distinctive non-migrant found at Hook Head is the chough, a member of the crow family, easily recognised by its vivid red legs and beak and characteristic behaviour. The point of Hook is also well placed for

Fig. 16 The Leap Rock at Baginbun Head, painted by G. Du Noyer in 1850. Because of its bird life, Baginbun is designated as an NHA.

observing other forms of wildlife: grey seals can usually be seen in small numbers, particularly during the winter months, and occasionally passing porpoises and dolphins and even whales can be viewed from the headland. During the winter of 2003–4, a number of fin and minke whales, attracted by large shoals of herring and sprat in Waterford Harbour, remained in the waters off the Hook for several weeks. Recently, perhaps due to the effects of global warming, sightings of sun-fish, normally found in tropical seas, have been reported from the waters around the peninsula.

Baginbun Head

The cliffs at Baginbun are composed of Old Red Sandstone and older siltstones, mudstones and shales. The holes and ledges of the cliffs provide homes for numerous birds. Depending on the season, many of the following birds can be seen: fulmar, cormorant, peregrine, herring gull, guillemot, wheatear, chough and raven.

Tintern Abbey

In recent years, roosts of breeding bats have been recorded in the buildings at Tintern Abbey, including a nationally significant colony of whiskered bats. The Tintern River flows through secluded woodland west of the abbey. The estuary of the river supports teal, black-tailed godwit and redshank.

Fethard Saltmarsh

This saltmarsh, regularly flooded by the sea, is developing behind the sand spit known as the Little Burrow. It

Fig. 15 Thrift or Sea Pink, shown here at Pursheen in Churchtown, decorates the cliff edges in early summer. Hook Head is an NHA of international importance for its plants, animals and geology. It is also a designated Area of Outstanding Landscape Importance.

B. COLFER

Fig. 17 Woodland along the Tintern river which flows into Bannow Bay at Saltmills. Tintern Abbey was located beside the stream, which was used to power a number of mills. The pungent wild garlic which grows profusely in the wood may have originated in the monks' garden.

Fig. 18 Fethard saltmarsh, located on an inlet just south of the village, is classified as an NHA because of the rare and protected plants which it contains.

supports a community of salt-tolerant plants growing on tidal mud in sheltered conditions. Some of these rare and protected plants are not found elsewhere in Ireland. Herons, shelduck, brent geese and other birds frequent the marsh and can be conveniently viewed from the public road which crosses the marsh on a causeway.

Wood Village

This site consists of a 700 metre stretch of soft cliff extending along the shoreline from Wood Village to Windy Gap in the townland of Grange. The section contains an ascending sequence of the following features: at the base, a wave-cut platform of a former shoreline, cut in folded siltstones; a fossil raised beach; an overlying mass of earth called 'head'; and, on top, material known as 'till,' deposited by melting ice sheets which moved from the north-west during the last Ice Age. This section is regarded as one of the finest examples of this kind of deposit in western Europe.

Bannow Bay

Bannow Bay is an extensive, shallow estuary fed by two small rivers, the Corock and the Owenduff. The mouth of the bay is obstructed by offshore sand and gravel bars. The estuary is fringed by a narrow strip of saltmarsh which contains stands of cord-grass. About three-quarters of the bay is stripped at low water, exposing extensive expanses of mudflats and sandflats. In winter, the bay holds 20,000 wintering wildfowl, including internationally significant numbers of the European population of the pale-bellied

Fig. 19 The cliff at Wood Village in Grange is an NHA of international importance for its glacial features, particularly the raised beach at (A).

B. COLFER

Fig. 20 Mute swans and mallard duck on a pond and miniature wetland in Porters Gate townland.

ALYN WALSH

Fig. 21 Small numbers of choughs, a member of the crow family but with distinctive red beak and legs, frequent isolated cliffs around the Hook.

BERNIE COLFER

Fig. 22 Whales and particularly dolphins are often sighted in the waters off the Hook, although not as frequently as in former years. In 1957, Nan Colfer and daughter Bernie were photographed while viewing about forty pilot whales which beached and died on the Little Burrow at Fethard.

B. COLFER

Fig. 23 A natural meadow in Slade townland, containing a profusion of wild flowers including poppies and ox-eye daisies. In season, road verges throughout the region provide a vital habitat for wildflowers such as meadow-sweet, purple loosestrife, rosebay willow herb and primrose.

GILLIAN BARRETT

Fig. 24 This aerial perspective (north is to the left of the picture) shows the narrow entrance to Bannow Bay between the townland of Grange, south of the Poulfur inlet, and Bannow Island, now connected to the mainland by a sandspit. The island was the site of the first Anglo-Norman landing in Ireland in 1169. The south Wexford coast extends into the distance to Kilmore Quay and Carnsore. Bannow Bay with its sand dune system and saltmarshes is an NHA of international significance for its bird and plant life. The bay is an EU Important Bird Area (IBA) and CORINE Biotope site because of its concentrations of wintering wildfowl. The Big Burrow, a sand spit shown here across the mouth of the bay, was largely eroded in the late 1990s.

variant of the brent goose and concentrations of duck including shelduck, wigeon and teal. The major wading species occurring in significant numbers are oystercatcher, golden plover, lapwing, knot, dunlin, godwit, curlew and redshank. The little tern breeds irregularly in summer. The plant communities supported by the saltmarsh and surrounding lands contain protected and rare wild flowers.

Over many millennia, geological and climatic forces have combined to create the diverse topography of the Hook. Located at the interface of land, river and sea, the peninsula provides an environment which is both visually and economically attractive. The exploitation of the region's potential by successive incoming groups is recorded in the complex palimpsest of the modern landscape.

PREHISTORIC AND EARLY CHRISTIAN LANDSCAPES

An understanding of early settlement and society depends on the survival of archaeological monuments and the recovery of objects of cultural significance. Every site is vital, but an analysis of the distribution of monuments adds greatly to an appreciation of past socio-cultural activity. In spite of the advantages offered by Waterford Harbour as a gateway for incoming groups, the Hook has relatively few surviving monuments from the prehistoric era, possibly because the access to the interior provided by the three rivers encouraged newcomers to penetrate further inland. Over the past millennium, the productive soils of the region have been subjected to intensive arable cultivation and the scarcity of surviving sites may be due to removal by landowners wishing to maximise their arable land. This scenario is strongly supported by an examination of the ringforts in the region. Of fifty known examples, only fifteen survive in various stages of preservation. The archaeological survey for county Wexford facilitates a better understanding of the cultural landscape. A growing focus on the value of heritage has led to a greater awareness of the intrinsic value of archaeological monuments as vital cultural elements of Irish life. As the pace of development accelerates, the archaeological record becomes more vulnerable and there is a risk that sites may be removed without investigation. Priority should be given to the conservation of monuments, as they provide a testimony to the changing lifestyles of previous generations.

B. COLFER

Fig. 1 In Loftus Hall townland, an enigmatic, low circular mound, about 20 metres in diameter, surrounded by a ditch and low bank, may be a Bronze Age burial mound. The nature of the associated linear earthwork (now removed) has not been established, although there has been some speculation that it could be a cursus type monument. The pipe carrying water to Loftus Hall from the reservoir at Herrylock runs between the parallel banks.

Fig. 2 Settlement activity in the Hook region during the Bronze Age is indicated by the stray find c. 1990, on the cliff-top near Hook Lighthouse, of a chert arrow-head dated to c. 1800 BC.

BRONZE AGE

Despite its apparently advantageous coastal location, no evidence has yet emerged to indicate mesolithic or neolithic settlement activity in the Hook. Although evidence is meagre for Bronze Age occupation, the period is represented by sites with a northern concentration. A low mound surrounded by a ditch and bank in the townland of Loftus Hall on the Hook may be a Bronze Age ring barrow or burial mound.[1] An enigmatic double-bank linear feature, formerly associated with the mound but removed in the 1980s, poses questions which have not been resolved. Bronze Age activity on the headland has been indicated by the recent stray find of an arrow-head dating to c. 1800 BC on the cliff edge near the lighthouse. A cist burial and two urn burials have been found in Ballyvelig, where there is also a Bronze Age cooking place, or fulacht fiadh. The grouping of fulachta fiadh is a recurrent feature; at Battlestown, for example, there is a cluster of eight.[2] These ancient cooking sites, dated to between 1900 BC and 1400 BC, provide the most substantial evidence for Bronze Age activity in the region. These sites are not confined to Ireland but are found throughout northern Europe and Britain, where they are referred to as 'burnt mounds.' The method of cooking involved dropping heated stones into a water-filled trough until it was brought to the boil. The food was then placed in the water to cook, more hot stones being added to maintain the correct temperature. The shattered stones were thrown into a pile surrounding the trough on three sides. This eventually created the typical horseshoe-shaped mound of burnt stones by which these sites are identified.

IRON AGE

A Celtic Iron Age civilisation emerged in Europe in the middle of the first millennium BC and eventually extended from the Atlantic to the Black Sea.[3] This La Tène

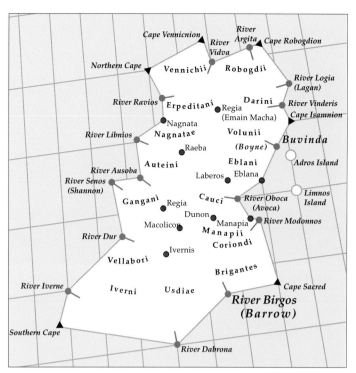

Fig. 3 The importance of the Waterford estuary and river system as an Iron Age trade route was shown by the inclusion of the river Barrow (Birgos) on a second-century 'map' by the Greek geographer Ptolemy.

culture, so named after a site in Switzerland, dominated Europe until ultimately falling before the expanding Roman empire. Untouched by Rome, the Celts of Ireland and Britain survived for many centuries longer. This period saw the emergence of small kingdoms in Ireland defended by hilltop forts and linear earthworks. Towards the end of the Iron Age, the Irish Sea was a much-travelled highway, facilitating extensive contacts between communities on both sides. Coastal promontory forts belong to this cultural zone, many of them developed as trading centres during the Roman period. These forts were

Fig. 4 Trading activities may have resulted in the construction of the promontory fort of Dún Domhnall on a secondary headland at Baginbun, where there is an excellent landing beach sheltered from the prevailing south-westerly winds as well as deep-water anchorage close to shore.

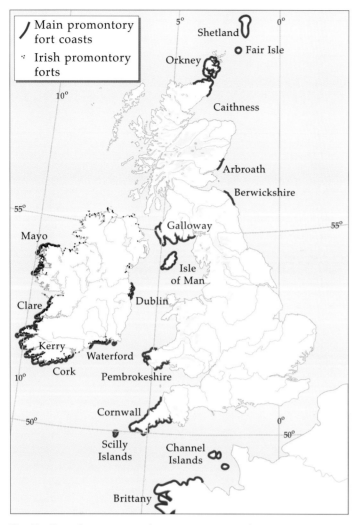

Fig. 5 Coastal promontory forts are concentrated in western Europe, suggesting a shared building tradition. Their use as trade centres is indicated by the discovery of archaeological evidence in county Dublin, for sustained contact between Ireland and the Roman world.

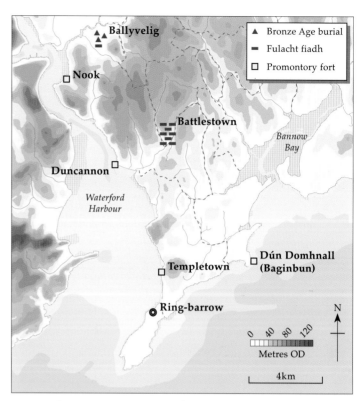

Fig. 6 Prehistoric sites. Apart from the possible ring-barrow on the point of Hook, known Bronze Age sites are concentrated to the north of the region. The Iron Age is represented by four coastal promontory forts.

usually constructed by building a defensive earthwork across the neck of cliff-bound sea promontories. At the end of the first century AD, the Roman historian Tacitus wrote of Ireland: 'The interior parts are little known, but through commercial intercourse and the merchants there is better knowledge of the harbours and approaches.'[4] In the mid-second century AD, Ptolemy, a Greek geographer living in Alexandria, produced a list of known places in Ireland based on accounts of merchants and mariners. This 'map' identifies sites of coastal promontory forts along the east coast of Ireland, some of which have produced evidence for Roman contacts. The Barrow (Birgos) features in this source, indicating that the estuary was known as a centre of commercial activity at that time.[5]

Although evidence for Iron Age settlement in county Wexford is meagre, four coastal promontory forts associated with the period are located in the Hook region.[6] The siting of three Iron Age forts on the shores of

Waterford Harbour emphasises the function of the estuary as a trading centre. Extensive ramparts survive at Nook, just north of Ballyhack, and a small site on the cliff at Templetown known as 'the Raheens' is also classified as a promontory fort. The Celtic name of the strategically placed rocky headland of Duncannon (Conan's fort) is a strong indication that it was fortified during the Iron Age period. Conan may have been a member of the legendary Celtic warriors known as the Fianna, whose leader, Fionn Mac Cumhaill, was traditionally associated with the Hook.[7] On the Waterford side of the estuary, the place-name Dunmore (dún mór: the big fort) may also indicate an Iron Age coastal fortification. On the east coast of the peninsula, the remains of a promontory fort, originally called Dún Domhnall (Domhnall's fort), survive on the headland of Baginbun, just south of Fethard. Baginbun dominates the entrance to Bannow Bay and the fort was presumably associated with trading activities in the estuary. The element dún (fort) in the inland townland names of Dunbrody and Dungulph suggests the former presence of settlement activity, although no archaelogical evidence has yet been identified. These sites indicate the presence of an Iron Age society in the locality c. 500 BC to 500 AD and an awareness of the strategic significance of the headland and a considerable level of commercial activity in the two estuaries, particularly Waterford Harbour.

B. COLFER

Fig. 7 The element *dún* (fort) in the name Duncannon is a strong indication that the promontory was the site of an Iron Age fort. The promontory was well positioned as a trading centre as it is located beside the deep-water channel which, as the picture shows, is still used by shipping

EARLY CHRISTIAN SETTLEMENT

A combination of factors led to radical change in Irish society and landscape from the fifth century onwards. The introduction of Christianity, leading to closer contacts with the continent and the introduction of recent technological advances, was central to these changes. There is evidence for a substantial increase in pasture and arable farming, while the introduction of a new type of plough and the horizontal mill improved Irish food production, allowing an increase in population levels. This economic and demographic expansion led to the construction of thousands of ringforts (raths), enclosing single farmsteads involved in a predominantly pastoral economy, accompanied by complementary unenclosed settlement.[8] Some crops were grown in irregular fields, some of which can still be identified. Ringforts vary in size but most are small circular enclosures, about 30 metres in diameter, usually consisting of an earthen bank and outer fosse which originally enclosed a house and farm buildings, and presumably, were used to protect the livestock in times of danger.[9] The vast majority of ringforts were constructed during the early historic period,

specifically from the beginning of the seventh century to the end of the ninth century AD. The ringfort is the most common archaeological feature in the Irish landscape, with at least 45,000 sites identified from various sources.[10]

In the Early Christian era, the minor kingdom in which the Hook was located was called Síl mBrain, now

B. COLFER

Fig. 8 This bivallate ringfort in the townland of Monacahee is believed to have been re-used as the site for the medieval church of Rathroe. Remains of a rectangular building survive in the interior.

GILLIAN BARRETT

Fig. 9 The cropmarks shown in this aerial view (looking north) of Ballyvaroge townland indicates the former existence of a complex of earthworks in a valley overlooking the Tintern river. It is possible that some may be relatively modern, but one, and possibly two, circular enclosures (presumably ringforts) can be identified as well as a later, sub-rectangular feature with an entrance on the west side. The identification of cropmarks of removed earthworks has been greatly advanced by a programme of superb aerial photography undertaken by Gillian Barrett.

GILLIAN BARRETT

Fig. 10 Evidence for removed earthworks can often be provided by aerial photography, which identifies colour variation in the growth of vegetation. The former existence of a ringfort in Ramsgrange townland is indicated by the circular crop marks which are visible from the air.

represented by the barony of Shelburne. Possibly due to an expanding population, the Hook provides more substantial indications for settlement during this period, principally evidence for forty-five ringforts. Thirteen of these survive, in various stages of preservation; the remainder have been identified from aerial photography and cartographic sources.[11] The removal of ringforts from the landscape has probably been a continuous process, accelerated in recent times by the availability of earth-moving machinery. The absence of surviving sites on the core Cistercian lands of Dunbrody and Tintern, and the Templar/Hospitaller lands of Templetown, combined with evidence for the former existence of ringforts on these lands, suggest that the original religious owners or their lay successors removed ringforts from the landscape. There was a tradition on the Colclough estate that the removal of a rath in the seventeenth century had brought bad luck to the family.[12] Of forty-five recorded ringforts, thirty-eight (84%) are in townlands with Irish names. As these constitute about 60 per cent of the townlands in the area, the ringforts were not removed to the same extent in townlands where the native Irish remained predominant.

Ecclesiastical centres

The principal Early Christian monastic site in the region was at Kilmokea on Great Island, formerly an island in the river Barrow but subsequently joined to the mainland by late nineteenth-century land reclamation. The seven hectare circular site was enclosed by an earthen bank and fosse, substantial parts of which survive.[13] There are two bullán stones in the enclosure. The function of these stones with hollowed-out basins, commonly associated with Early Christian ecclesiastical sites, is not known, but they presumably were of ceremonial significance. The smallest

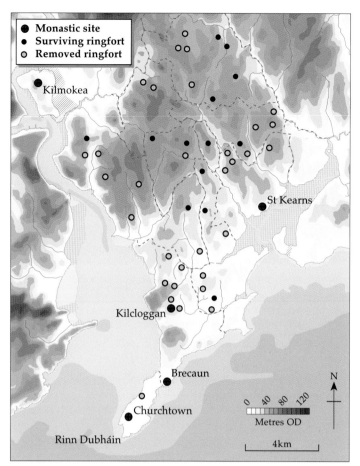

Fig. 11 Ringforts and ecclesiastical centres. Of forty-five ringforts recorded in the region, only thirteen survive in various states of preservation. The low number of ringforts on medieval church estates suggest a policy of removal by the monks or their lay successors.

high cross in Ireland is located at the church site in the enclosure.[14] The remains of a horizontal mill dating to the Early Christian period was discovered in the enclosure in the 1970s.[15] Although the extensive remains at Kilmokea are an indication of its former status, the monastery is not mentioned in the historic record, apart from a single reference in 1399 to 'the chapel of St Macethe di Island.'[16]

Four other sites in the region are believed to have Early Christian origins, but none were of major importance. The remains of a church, with associated bullán stone, at St Kearns on the shore of Bannow Bay, is associated with the saint of that name. Three Welsh monks of the same family were responsible for fifth-century foundations in the Hook: Dubhán at Churchtown, Alloc at Kilcloggan, and Brecaun on the cliffs at Porters Gate.[17] Dubhán gave his name to the promontory, which was known as Rinn Dubháin until the late Middle Ages when it became known as the Hook, an old English word for a narrow headland.[18] Coincidentally, the name Dubhán is also the Irish word for a fishing hook. A spring, known as Duffin's well, near the cliff edge may preserve the name Dubhán in

GILLIAN BARRETT

Fig. 12 Kilmokea (Cill Machethe) monastic enclosure. Although there are no historical records relating to this seven hectare site, it must have been of considerable significance. Located on Great Island (no longer an island due to reclamation), the monastery controlled the ferry crossing to Ossory. This perspective shows the island's strategic location at the top of Waterford Harbour. The diamond-shaped field at the left of the picture was originally a large moated site from the Anglo-Norman period. The low-lying ground at left-centre marks the location of the east channel which, before reclamation, created the island (formerly called Miléadach). Other landscape features include the railway, the Barrow bridge and the power station.

B. COLFER

Fig. 13 The remains of a horizontal mill found at Kilmokea were dated to the Early Christian period. The wooden chute that delivered water to power the mill-wheel (A) and a mill-stone with concentric grooves on its surface (B) were retained at the site of the find.

B. COLFER

Fig. 14 Early Christian stone artefacts have been found at the church site.

PETER HARBINSON AND PADDY HEALY

Fig. 15 The smallest high cross in Ireland (56cm high) is located at the church site at the centre of the enclosure.

Fig. 16 The medieval nave and chancel parish church of Hook incorporates elements of the Early Christian foundation of St Dubhán. This drawing by G. Du Noyer, c. 1850, shows the original east wall (now in the centre of the church) with remains of antae (projections of the side walls beyond the gable) and evidence for a round-headed window in the early gable, in which a doorway was inserted to give access to the later chancel.

a corrupt form. The surviving medieval parish church of Hook at Churchtown, where there is a suggestion of a circular enclosure, incorporates parts of Dubhán's Early Christian structure. These include remains of antae (projections of the side walls beyond the gables) and a small round-headed window in the east gable, which prove the church to be of early origin; it is the earliest surviving church in county Wexford.[19] A persistent tradition claims that the monks of Dubhán's monastery kept a warning beacon for shipping at the tip of the headland as an act of practical Christianity.

Evidence for Alloc's foundation survives in the place-name Kilcloggan (pronounced Kiloggan; i.e. cill Allocan: the church of Alloc). A well in the townland called Toberluke, a corruption of tobar Alloc (Alloc's well), provides a further connection. Parts of Kilcloggan church may have been incorporated into the dwelling-house beside the castle. The church on the site of Brecaun's foundation has almost disappeared due to coastal erosion. A recent excavation found evidence for an earlier stone church, also partly eroded, and surrounding ditch. The site

of the original structure, possibly of wood, has disappeared into the sea. Fragments of an ogham stone, found at the church in 1835 and 1929 and now in the National Museum, place the foundation in the early years of the Christian era. Another small fragment of possibly

Fig. 17 A bullán stone on the site of St Kearn's church on the west shore of Bannow Bay. Usually associated with Early Christian church sites, the original purpose of these basin stones remains enigmatic.

B. COLFER

Fig. 18 The Early Christian origin of St Brecaun's church was established by an archaeological excavation in 1988. The early church has disappeared due to coastal erosion; the remains, probably medieval in origin, are under constant threat. The west gable has fallen since this photograph was taken in 1988.

the same ogham stone was recovered during the archaeological excavation of the site in 1988.[20] Like promontory forts, ogham stones, also found in Wales, reflect cultural contact around the Irish Sea and the advent of literacy with the arrival of Christianity.

Fethard church, still serving as a place of worship, incorporates elements of an Early Christian foundation associated with a pre-Norman episcopal manor. An early origin is suggested by its dedication to St Mogue (synonymous with Aidan), the first bishop of Ferns, an

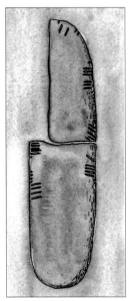

N.M.I.

Ogham inscriptions

• **One stone**

• **Group of stones**

10°

5°

50°

Fig. 19 The earliest writing in Ireland, inscribed on standing stones in an alphabet known as ogham, dates from c. 300 AD and was used for several centuries. Ogham inscriptions, densest in Munster and south Wales, indicate contacts between the two communities. Historically, the sea has facilitated contact between the regions. For example, in the Early Christian period, monks from Wales established foundations in the Hook and elsewhere in the county and in the late twelfth century the initial groups of Anglo-Normans sailed from Pembroke to Wexford. Many of the Welsh surnames that arrived at that time are now regarded as typically Wexford. The association of Tintern de Voto with Tintern Abbey on the river Wye formed another connection. In modern times, the link is typified by the ferries that operate from Rosslare to Fishguard and Pembroke.

Fig. 20 Parts of an ogham stone (now in the National Museum) discovered at Brecaun church place the foundation in the Early Christian period. The inscription has been deciphered as *Sedan (i maqqi cat) tabbot avvi Dercmasoc.* (Sedan son of Cattabott descended from Derc Mosach).

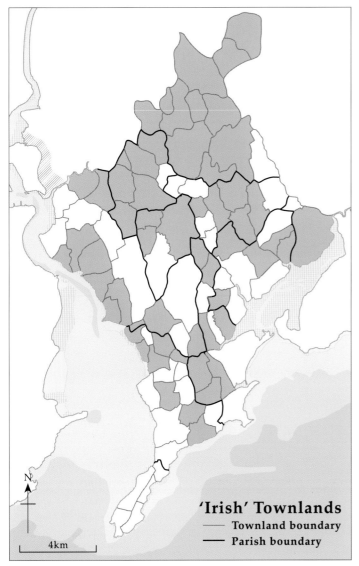

'Irish' Townlands
— Townland boundary
— Parish boundary

4km

Fig. 21   The townland system represents one of the most pervasive survivals from the Early Christian period. Of eighty-five townlands in the region, forty-five (52%) have Irish names. The distribution of place-names allows tentative observations to be made about settlement patterns. There is some correlation between place-names and soil, as townlands with English names are concentrated on the best soils close to Waterford Harbour. On the poorer quality soils of the Fethard series, however, Irish names predominate. Townland names containing the elements móin (bog) and currach (moor) retained their Irish names; for example, Monacahee and Curraghmore. Following the arrival of the Anglo-Normans, the English-speaking settlers concentrated on the best land close to the estuary; by contrast the Irish who remained on the manors occupied less productive land and more peripheral locations. Irish place-names form definite groupings, indicating that the Irish population remained strongest in peripheral locations on the various land-grants. The distribution of ringforts reinforces this point: they are almost completely absent from the heartland of the Dunbrody and Templar estates, perhaps indicating a policy of removal on some church lands.

indication that it may be the oldest church still in use in the county. Further north, a circular church site at the episcopal manor of Kinnagh also points to a pre-Norman origin. The lands of Tintern Abbey were divided in two by the parish of Kinnagh, further proof that the episcopal manor pre-dated the grant of land to the Cistercians.

Townlands

The townland network provides the most pervasive landscape survival from the Gaelic era. Most townlands, many retaining their Gaelic names, are believed to pre-date the arrival of the Anglo-Normans. Names such as Fethard (fiodh ard: high wood) and Curraghmore (currach mór: big moor) convey topographical information. Other names contain elements relating to former settlement activity: Bally (baile: place/home); Dun (dún: fort); Kil (cill: church); Rath (rath: ringfort). Some names record social or cultural activity: Taulaght (támhlacht: a plague burial ground), for example, on the shore of Bannow Bay, where a mound containing human bones was found, is a record of an enigmatic event which must have been of great significance. The early Irish practice of moving herds to the buaile (summer milking place), or transhumance, is referenced in Boley (Owenduff parish) and Booley (Templetown parish) and in the name Booley Hill near Fethard.[21]

THE VIKINGS

First appearing off the coast at the end of the eighth century, the Scandinavian Vikings played a vital role in Irish affairs for four hundred years, initially as raiders but later as traders and town builders. Although there is no direct indication of a Viking presence in the Hook, place-name evidence suggests that they frequented the adjacent

Fig. 22   Place-names of Norse provenance in county Wexford have a predominantly coastal orientation, reflecting the sea-faring ethos of the Norse and their control of the littoral. Inland, the names are concentrated in the southern baronies of Forth and Bargy, a strong indication that this region was controlled by the Norse of Wexford town.

Fig. 23 A hoard of Viking silver found at 'Blackcastle' in county Wexford may have been found near the tower house in Clonmines, as this is the only castle in the county which is known by that name.

sea routes. A cluster of Norse place-names around Bannow Bay, mostly coastal, provide convincing evidence for a Viking presence.[22] The name Bannow itself (originally Bannoe) is a combination of the Gaelic word *bann*, a river, and the Norse *-oe* or *-ee*, an island (also found in Saltee Island); i.e. the island in the river. The name of the Keeragh Islands (formerly written Keeroe) falls into the same category. Selskar Rock contains the element *skar*, meaning a rock (also found in Tuskar); the estuary itself was originally known as the Scar. Nearby, the headland of Baginbun may have originated as Bec an Bann, from the Norse word *bec*, a promontory, and bann (i.e. the promontory at the rivermouth). At the head of Bannow Bay, the townland of Arklow, like the town of the same name, implies pure Norse origin. The name consists of the Norse personal name Arkill with the Norse word *lo*, a swamp or low-lying meadow near water, a perfect description in this instance,

as Arklow adjoins the marshy valley of the Owenduff river. The place-name Arklow is the only indication of an actual Viking settlement around Bannow Bay. As the demand for silver increased in tenth-century Europe, they may have attempted to exploit the silver deposits on the eastern shore of the bay.[23] A Viking silver hoard of seventeen ingots was discovered at 'Blackcastle near Wexford'; the only known Blackcastle in the county is located at Clonmines at the head of Bannow Bay.[24]

The great estuary with its river system to the west of the Hook, known in Irish as Cumar na dTᵒrí nUisce (the confluence of three rivers), was used extensively by the Vikings. They called the estuary *Vadra fiord* (weather fiord), an acknowledgement that it was the only secure shelter between Carlingford Lough and Cork Harbour for a large fleet in stormy weather. The town established by the Vikings on the Suir early in the tenth century became known by the same name, which in time was anglicised as Waterford.[25] There was also an inland Viking settlement at St Mullins on the Barrow.[26] The land opposite the Hook, on the west shore of the estuary, became known as Gaultír (the land of the foreigners), an indication that there was a rural Viking population living there who supplied the town of Waterford with essential food supplies. A Viking Age coin hoard, dating to c. 1050, found at Dunbrody beside Waterford Harbour, reflects the function of the estuary as a trade route.[27] It could also relate to trading activities with the adjacent monastic centre of Kilmokea, situated at a strategic ferry crossing on the road linking the Norse towns of Wexford and Waterford. In the mid seventeenth-century *Civil Survey*, the rocky headland above Ballyhack was referred to as Skeroirke, which possibly contains *skar*, the Norse word for a rock.

ncannon Fort and Waterford Harbour from 'The Spring' above Dollar Bay

B. COLFER

MANOR AND MONASTERY: THE MEDIEVAL LANDSCAPE

The arrival of the Anglo-Normans in the late twelfth century was a crucial watershed in the evolution of Irish culture and society.[1] Arriving initially as mercenaries in the service of Diarmait Mac Murchada (Dermot MacMurrough), deposed king of Uí Chennselaig and Leinster, the ambitious knights, welcoming the opportunity to acquire new possessions, quickly seized the initiative and took control of eastern and southern Ireland. Military control was followed by the imposition of a hierarchical land-holding system known as feudalism and the introduction of settlers from England and Wales. The subsequent imposition of Anglo-Norman structures on Gaelic Ireland created a complex society and a wide range of settlement features. During the thirteenth century, Anglo-Norman settlement in Ireland expanded rapidly, particularly in the south and east, but in the following centuries a determined Irish revival forced the colonists to consolidate in a limited Pale area around Dublin.

The progress of Anglo-Norman settlement in county Wexford can be seen as a paradigm for the country as a whole.[2] Initially, most of the county was occupied by the newly arrived English settlers, but, by the end of the fourteenth century, weakened by warfare, famine and plague and under pressure from the resurgent Irish, the colonists had been forced to abandon the north of the county. They were subsequently mostly confined to an English Pale in the south of the county, consisting principally of the baronies of Forth and Bargy, protected by the natural barriers of Forth Mountain and the Corock and Owenduff rivers. The failure of English settlement in the north of the county led to a dramatic contrast in the growth of settlement in the Gaelic north and English south. Significantly, the defensive earthworks built by the settlers were concentrated in the intermediate frontier territory. The emergence of a distinctive settlement and administrative patterns in both areas, expressed in a variety of ways, influenced succeeding developments and is echoed in the modern landscape.

The medieval parish structure evolved in tandem with manorial organisation. The large northern parishes, created by a scattered population on sprawling manors, contrast with the complex of small, sometimes diminutive, parishes corresponding to the compact, densely populated manors in the south. Similar influences led to a marked contrast in the size of townlands. The southern concentration of medieval villages, parish churches and the later tower houses are further indications of the contrast between the Gaelic and English regions in the county. The large ecclesiastical estates established by the Anglo-Normans in the Hook region, following confiscation by the crown in the sixteenth century, became lay estates which survived until the twentieth century. The most remarkable testament to the resilience and endurance of the colonists comes from their descendants, whose surnames continue to be prevalent, particularly in the south of the county.

Fig. 1 The Bayeux Tapestry records the arrival of the Normans in England in 1066 and their victory at the Battle of Hastings. Just over a century later, they used the same military expertise to exert control over much of Ireland, after establishing a base in the south-east of the island.

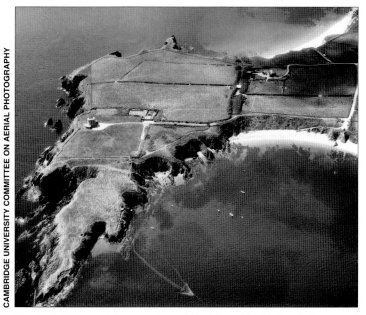

CAMBRIDGE UNIVERSITY COMMITTEE ON AERIAL PHOTOGRAPHY

Fig. 2 A 1950s aerial perspective of Baginbun Head, site of the second Anglo-Norman landing in Ireland. The sheltered landing beach and the existence of the Iron Age promontory fort of Dún Domhnall probably influenced Raymond le Gros to land here in May 1170 with about one hundred men. They may have occupied the existing fort pending the construction of a double rampart across the neck of the headland.

At the creeke of Baginbun,
Ireland was lost and won.

THE ANGLO-NORMANS

South-west Wexford was directly involved in the initial phases of Anglo-Norman activity in Ireland.[3] Following the first landing at Bannow Island in 1169 and the capture of the Norse town of Wexford, Diarmait Mac Murchada (Dermot MacMurrough) granted extensive lands to Hervey de Montmorency, including the barony of Shelburne, in which the Hook is located.[4] In May 1170, another small group of Anglo-Normans, under the leadership of Raymond le Gros, landed at the promontory of Baginbun just south of Fethard, where good anchorage and a sheltered beach provided ideal landing conditions. The Iron Age promontory fort of Dún Domhnaill, which occupied a secondary headland, may also have been an attraction, as it provided immediate protection in case of attack. Raymond was quickly joined by de Montmorency, in whose newly acquired lands Baginbun was located, with three knights. Raymond constructed a campaign fort – a double bank of clay, surmounted by a wooden palisade – across the neck of the headland. Extensive surviving earthworks at Baginbun represent the remains of this fortification. The small band of Anglo-Normans was attacked by a much larger force of Norsemen from Waterford and Irish from the Déisi but by using a herd of cattle to disorganise the attacking force the Anglo-Normans emerged completely victorious. Seventy of the

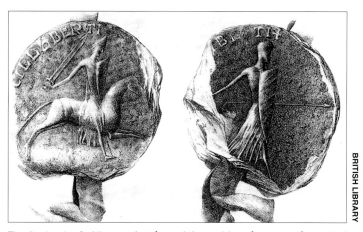

BRITISH LIBRARY

Fig. 3 An Anglo-Norman knight and foot-soldier shown on the seal of Richard de Clare, earl of Pembroke (Strongbow), leader of the first invaders, who landed at Passage in Waterford Harbour in 1170.

leading citizens of Waterford were captured and executed by breaking their legs and throwing them off the cliffs. A woman named Alice of Abervenny, whose lover had been killed in the battle, helped with the executions. When the Anglo-Norman leader, Richard de Clare (known as Strongbow), landed shortly afterwards at Passage, he was joined by le Gros and together they took the town of Waterford, whose men had been decimated at Baginbun. The battle at Baginbun came to be regarded as a decisive episode in Irish history and was remembered in later years by the rhyme: 'at the creeke of Baginbun, Ireland was lost and won.'[5]

Parishes were generally created in areas of Anglo-Norman settlement by the tithe-paying tenantry on the manors, following the introduction of a parochial tithing system at the Synod of Cashel in 1172. This makes it possible to identify the extent of medieval manors by examining the layout of medieval parishes (later called civil parishes). Montmorency organised his new estates according to the laws of the feudal system. He established his headquarters on what is now Great Island, in the river Barrow, probably because of its strategic location and existing infrastructure associated with the monastic enclosure of Kilmokea. The island subsequently became known as Hervey's Island, and his lands were referred to as the manor of the Island. A ringwork and a large

Fig. 4 The ships in which the Anglo-Normans made the crossing from Pembroke to south Wexford in 1169 were similar to those depicted one hundred years earlier on the Bayeux Tapestry.

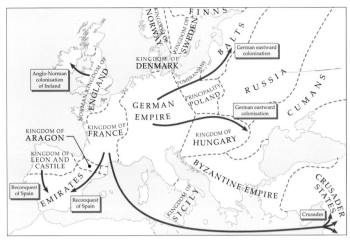

Fig. 5 The establishment of an Anglo-Norman base in Ireland, and the introduction of settlers, was part of a much wider movement of people that was taking place across Europe during the twelfth century.

moated site on the island may represent the period of Hervey's occupation.[6]

Hervey's principal contribution to the settlement of the area was the granting of a large estate for the foundation of a Cistercian abbey at Dunbrody.[7] A series of factors led to the granting of most of the land in southwest Wexford to ecclesiastical interests. The bishop of Ferns already had two manors here, at Fethard and at Kinnagh, where the circular enclosure around the church site indicates a pre-Norman origin. During his visit to Ireland in 1172, King Henry II granted the Hook peninsula, south of a line from Duncannon to Carnivan, to the Knights Templars as a security measure to protect the strategically significant Waterford Harbour. As a result of a vow made at sea when in danger of shipwreck, William Marshal, earl of Pembroke, Strongbow's heir, founded another Cistercian monastery, in unusual proximity to Dunbrody, on the shore of Bannow Bay.

Fig. 6 Most of the banks of this large moated site at Great Island (c. 125m by 165m) have been levelled but the outline can still be identified as a field boundary. The site was presumably constructed during Hervey de Montmorency's occupation of the Island in the late twelfth century.

B. COLFER

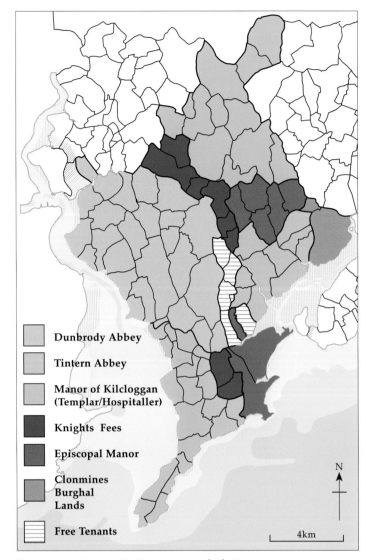

Dunbrody Abbey

Tintern Abbey

Manor of Kilcloggan (Templar/Hospitaller)

Knights Fees

Episcopal Manor

Clonmines Burghal Lands

Free Tenants

4km

N

Fig. 7 Anglo-Norman land grants in south Shelburne.

Here monks from Tintern Abbey in his manor of Chepstow in Shropshire established a monastery which became known as Tintern de Voto (of the Vow).

Part of de Montmorency's land in Shelburne was distributed to lay tenants, some of them located in a narrow corridor between the lands of the abbeys of Dunbrody and Tintern. These particular grants may have been made in conjunction with William Marshal's grant for the foundation of Tintern Abbey, with the intention of creating a 'buffer zone' between the two Cistercian estates. Small military tenancies were created, each held by the service of a quarter of a knight's fee.[8] To the north, the manor of Killesk (consisting of the townlands of Killesk, Knockea, Drillistown and Carrowanree) was initially granted to Auger de Ponte Chardun (Punchardun); it passed in the second half of the thirteenth century to a branch of the FitzGeralds, who held it until the mid-seventeenth century. The manor of Killesk (with three townlands belonging to

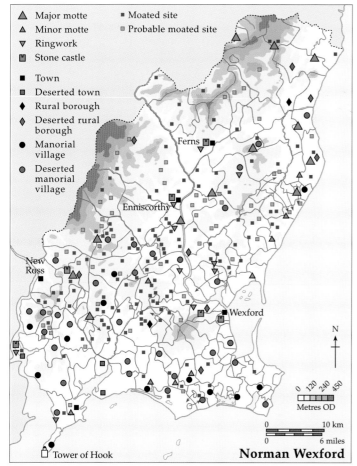

Fig. 8 The distribution of Anglo-Norman settlement features in Wexford reflect the success of the colony in the county. Sites are scarce in the north, which the Irish had recovered by the end of the thirteenth century. Defensive earthworks are concentrated across the centre of the county which was the interface between Irish north and English south. Manorial villages are concentrated in Forth and Bargy, which became known as 'the English baronies.' The parochial structure evolved from the land-holding system introduced by the Anglo-Normans as the payment of tithes to the manorial church ensured that manor and parish became synonymous.

Dunbrody Abbey) formed the parish of Killesk. Gilbert Drul, who was recorded in the area in the second half of the thirteenth century, may have held the townland of Drillistown as a sub-tenant on the manor. The neighbouring manor of Tullostown (modern Tullerstown) was held by John de Tullos (from Toulouse) in 1247 but later passed to the Keating family. The manor (the townlands of Tullerstown, Burkestown, Ballygowney, Baylestown and Milltown) formed part of the episcopal manor of Kinnagh. A moated site (now removed) in Tullerstown, the typical settler farmstead of the late thirteenth century, probably represented the manorial centre. The names of the townlands of Burkestown and Baylestown suggest that they were held by sub-tenants. South of the manor of Tullerstown, the townlands of Balliniry, Ballyveroge, Winningtown, Dungulph and Gorteens completed the corridor of lay grants between the two Cistercian estates.

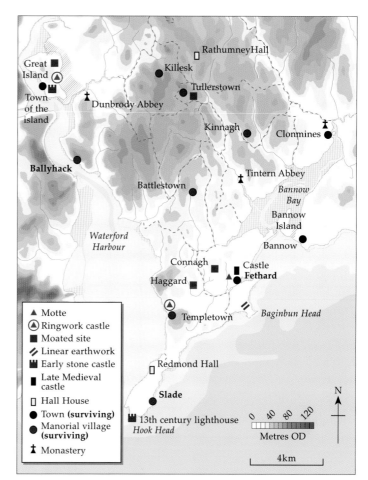

Fig. 9 Settlement features in Shelburne from the medieval period.

These townlands, held by rent-paying tenants, formed part of the episcopal parish of Fethard. The townland of Connagh, possibly with Ralph (Rath), both in the parish of Fethard, may have been held as a quarter knight's fee, initially by William Maunsell but later by the Furlongs. This would explain the presence of a moated site at Connagh, recorded as a rectangular earthwork on the first edition of the Ordnance Survey in 1841.

Towns and villages

Manorial organisation was accompanied by nucleated settlement including chartered boroughs and manorial villages.[9] The boroughs of Clonmines, Fethard and the town of the Island were established in the Hook region. The town of the Island, whose exact site is not known, was associated with the monastic centre of Kilmokea, on Great Island, identified only from its archaeological remains. The island, located in the river Barrow where it enters Waterford Harbour, was ideally positioned as a trading centre. It also straddled the road from Wexford to Waterford, which crossed the river by ferry at this point. The town must have been founded by Hervey de Montmorency, who established his *caput*, or headquarters, on the island. Initially, it was obviously intended to develop it as a town, but, from a practical perspective, it is doubtful if this was feasible following the foundation of New Ross by William Marshal. During the thirteenth century, a bitter dispute between the Marshal ports of Ross and the Island and the king's port of Waterford resulted in a royal embargo on foreign shipping trading with the ports in county Wexford. This may have caused more damage to the town of the Island than to New Ross, which was better placed to attract trade from manors throughout Leinster. Nevertheless, during the thirteenth century, some development took place, as by 1231 a stone castle had been constructed at the Island.[10] By the late thirteenth century, however, signs of decay were becoming apparent. A 1286 account records that: 'scarcely any tenant remained in the town' and 'scarcely anyone came to the oven [corn-drying kiln] because of the impoverishment of the community.' In the same year, the mill was 'flooded by the sea' and had to be rebuilt.

Three years later the situation had not improved, as the 'town remained waste.' In spite of the unfavourable economic outlook, and perhaps in an effort to reverse it, considerable money was spent on repairing and re-roofing the castle in 1286. The meticulous accounts relating to the repair work provide a detailed insight into the period. The expenditure of £9 4s 9d, mostly on the roof of the castle, represented a considerable investment. However, its effectiveness was short-lived, as by 1307 the castle was unroofed and valued at nothing. It is unlikely that the town of the Island, overshadowed by the burgeoning economic power of New Ross, survived as a port for much longer.[11]

Located on a small inlet at the entrance to Bannow Bay, the borough of Fethard provided a private port for the

Fig. 10 This detail from Francis Jobson's map of Waterford Harbour in 1591 shows a substantial castle on 'The Great Island'. The island, still surrounded by water at that time and wooded, was strategically placed at the junction of the Barrow and Suir.

Repairs to the castle of the Island 1286

For one wagon and ten stone of lead bought for the castle of the Island to be newly roofed, together with the carriage of the same from Wales, 60s.

Paid a certain plumber for melting and applying the said lead, 7s 4d.

For breaking slates for newly roofing the said castle.

For 16 quarters of lime for the castle, together with the carriage, 4s 10d.

For roofing anew the castle by taskwork, 26s 8d.

For mortar made beside the lead, as by agreement, 2s.

For timber bought for the repairs to the said castle, and for turf and combustible materials obtained for melting the lead, 11s 10d.

For 200 boards bought for the same castle with their carriage, 7s 6d.

For sundry nails bought for the same, 11s 11d.

For 250 laths bought, 1s ½ d.

For tin bought, for tallow for the waggon fetching stones, for digging the land and for porterage, as appears by particular items, 11s 8d.

For crest tiles bought for the same, 2s.

For a certain carpenter hired by the day, 27s 6d.

For a certain man employed in repairing the slates on the castle of the Island, at taskwork, 18d.

For the moat, for lime, and for nails bought for the castle of the Island, 8s 11d.

bishop's manors. The castle, constructed in the late fourteenth century, became an episcopal residence when Ferns was abandoned due to the state of war in the north of the county. Fethard's survival, when ports around it failed, must have been due to its role as the port for the diocesan manors. The construction of a castle in the late fourteenth century demonstrated the bishops' commitment to the town.

It is difficult to reconcile the establishment of Clonmines at the head of Bannow Bay by William Marshal[12] with the development of New Ross as the port of Leinster. Clonmines, located on a torturous channel and with a limited hinterland, would inevitably be at a disadvantage. Indeed, this proved to be the case, leading ultimately to its abandonment. However, other factors influenced the decision, at least in the short term. One of these is related to Marshal's narrow escape from shipwreck on the occasion of his first visit to Leinster and the subsequent construction of the Tower of Hook as a navigation aid. In bad weather, it is notoriously difficult

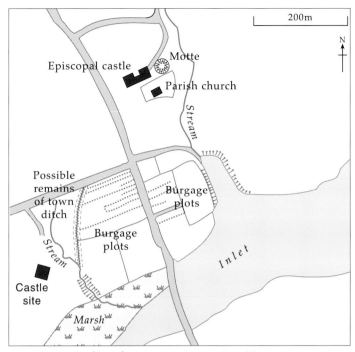

Fig. 11 Plan of Fethard showing surviving medieval features.

for boats and smaller ships coming from the east to round the point of Hook and gain entrance to Waterford Harbour. In quite recent times mail-boats from Liverpool sometimes dropped the mail at Fethard rather than attempting to reach Waterford Harbour in hazardous weather conditions. By avoiding the dangers off the Hook, a port at Clonmines gave Marshal a sheltered alternative to New Ross during the winter months. The land journey of fifteen miles between the two ports was relatively straightforward, so that goods could be transported between them for import or export. In 1233, a reference to the 'main road' between Clonmines and Wexford shows that attention was given to developing a road network.[13] The port of Bannow could have been used as an alternative, but the harbour was exposed to winter storms, while the longer land journey to New Ross was made difficult by the wide marshy valleys of the Owenduff and Corock rivers. There may also have been a political factor in Marshal's decision to establish Clonmines. From the early thirteenth century, continuous

Fig. 12 After successfully contesting the granting of the manor of Fethard to Christ Church, Canterbury, the bishop of Ferns founded the town of Fethard, probably to provide a seaport for the produce of the six episcopal manors. The parish church, Early Christian in origin and dedicated to St Mogue (still in use), a small motte which marks the site of an early castle and the fourteenth-century castle represent the core of the medieval town. In 1200, Christ Church, Canterbury allocated a site for a 'court' to the north of the church, presumably associated with the surviving motte. The early twentieth-century ball-alley, built against the west wall of the castle, was removed as part of a conservation programme initiated in the early 1990s and still on-going.

GILLIAN BARRETT

Fig. 13 This aerial perspective of Clonmines, taken from the north at low tide, illustrates the difficult nature of the torturous channel which shipping had to negotiate in order to reach the port at the head of Bannow Bay. The town was originally surrounded by water and marsh on three sides, but this has been changed to some extent by land reclamation in the foreground along the Owenduff.

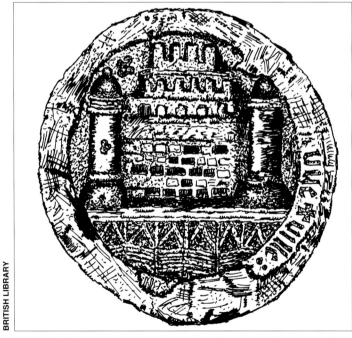

BRITISH LIBRARY

Fig. 14   A drawing of an impression of the seal of Clonmines which depicts a fortified building with what appears to be a wharf with wattle matting in the foreground, perhaps used to cover the muddy foreshore.

directives were issued to shipping entering Waterford Harbour to land at the king's port of Waterford instead of Marshal's ports of Ross and the Island. Marshal provided shipping with an alternative by establishing the port of Clonmines, which was well placed to take advantage of the trade generated by the monastic estates of Tintern, Dunbrody and Kilcloggan.

Documentation for Clonmines is scarce, possibly because it was economically detached from the rest of the county at the partition of Leinster between Marshal's daughters in 1247, following the death of his sons without male heir.[14] It was functioning as a town in the fourteenth century; in 1356, the provost, bailiff and community were fined for having the pillory broken and in 1364 a sheriff for the county was elected there. In the early fifteenth century, it was the venue for inquisitions and in the late sixteenth century Clonmines was still referred to as a town.[15] In the seventeenth century, the town had a portreeve and burgage lands 'within and without' the town. The mining operation which was carried on briefly on the opposite shore of the estuary during the sixteenth century may

B. COLFER

Fig. 15 Clonmines is the most impressive example in Ireland of a deserted medieval town where only the stone elements survive (three small castles and three churches); there are no visible remains of the ordinary houses of wood and clay. The town of Clonmines was founded, probably by William Marshal senior, in the early thirteenth century. At the partition of Leinster in 1247, Clonmines, with Taghmon, as part of Agatha Mortimer's share, became detached manors of the Liberty of Kildare. This separated Clonmines economically from the rest of the county and may have contributed to its eventual decline.

have given the town an economic boost. In 1684, however, it was described as:

> a place of great trade in times passed, and a harbour for shipping of indifferent bulk until the sand filled up the ancient passage near the town of Bannow, which was the destruction of both these towns, so that there is now only a narrow passage for boats on the west side of the island, between it and the lands of Fethard; for on the east side towards the town of Bannow, where the ancient passage was, and ships used to come in, it is now a perfect dry strand and may be walked over from the island to the town.[16]

The surviving remains include an Augustinian priory, two tower houses, a fortified church, the parish church of St Nicholas and the ruins of a Jacobean house.[17] An 1826 account which described 'the foundations of numerous

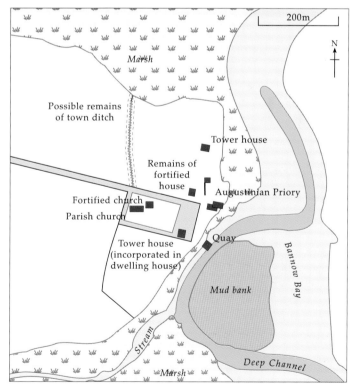

Fig. 16 An interpretive map of Clonmines showing surviving features and its location beside the deep-water channel that meandered through the treacherous mud flats of Bannow Bay before finally reaching the open sea.

B. COLFER

Fig. 17 Templetown is a fine example of a deserted medieval village. The mound at bottom left may have been the site of the original Templar castle. This aerial view reveals a complex system of cultivation ridges and possible house plots. The field above the church was cultivated after the photograph was taken in the late 1980s and yielded finds of medieval pottery shards. In 1837, the village had a population of fifty, some of them living in a row of thatched houses to the left of the church. The name of the Templar's Inn, on the cross-roads, is an example of the adaptation of a heritage reference to modern usage.

R.S.A.I.

Fig. 18 This pencil sketch by G. Du Noyer, c. 1850, shows the ruins of the medieval Templar church still standing to the right of the tower at Templetown. The early nineteenth-century church is to the left of the tower. The drawing also depicts a considerable settlement in the vicinity of the church. The row of thatched houses to the left of the church no longer exists. The graveyard is shown without a boundary wall, which was not built until the 1880s.

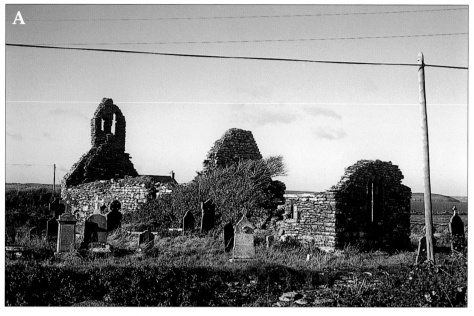

B. COLFER

Fig. 19 As the parish system developed in the thirteenth century, the medieval parish church became a ubiquitous feature in the landscape. Most of these churches were abandoned and became ruinous following the sixteenth-century Reformation. The parish church of Hook, shown here (A), of which there are extensive remains, is a good example of this type of building. Like many others, it was based on an Early Christian church, of which some elements remain. An extension (G) built to the west with round-headed doorways (D) had a double bell-cote and a loft supported on corbels. A later chancel has a three-light ogee headed east window (B) and lancet windows (H) with dundry (a yellow sandstone imported from Bristol) cut-stone. Other features include a broken stoup (C) a piscina where the sacred vessels were washed (E) and a recess to the north of the altar (F) which is thought to be an Easter Sepulchre. The church's graveyard is still used by a number of families in the Hook.

other buildings throughout an extent of at least twenty acres' has been backed up by a limited resistivity survey carried out in the early 1990s which identified underground features.[18] The town defences, described as a 'vallum and fosse' in 1837, may be represented by a large bank and fosse running northwards from the parish church, which protected the landward side of the headland on which the town was situated.[19] The extensive remains of stone buildings indicate the substantial nature of the town until its demise, probably in the sixteenth century.

By the sixteenth century, the town of the Island and Clonmines had ceased to function, presumably due to the accelerating economic superiority of New Ross. The port of Fethard also suffered, because of silting at the harbour mouth. Its survival as a settlement was due to its reincorporation in 1613 and development as an estate village on the Loftus estate in the eighteenth century. The exact site of the Town of the Island is not known, but it may have been associated with the enclosure of Kilmokea, as many Anglo-Norman towns occupied existing monastic sites.

Manorial villages, based on a church, a castle and sometimes a mill, developed on some manors and also on the granges of the monastic estates. These villages were the social, economic and administrative centres of the manor. Although most of these villages did not endure as settlements in the landscape, their locations can be identified by the remains of a church and adjacent castle.[20] At seven sites in the Hook, a church and castle are found in close proximity. Three of these, Ballyhack, Templetown and Churchtown, can be identified as parish centres, which strengthens the case for identifying them as manorial villages. Ballyhack, Ramsgrange, Churchtown and Slade survive as villages in the present-day landscape; Templetown retains some signs of former village status while Nook and Battlestown are deserted. There were tower houses in six of the villages and three survive at Ballyhack, Slade and Templetown. In two cases the castle was built at a distance from the church: Kilcloggan Castle was associated with Templetown and Redmond Hall with Churchtown. Ballyhack and Slade could be described as industrial villages, as their origins were related to their advantageous locations as fishing ports.

THE CISTERCIANS

The Cistercians took their name from the monastery of Cîteaux in France where they were founded in 1098 for the purpose of pursuing monastic reform. The Order quickly spread and the monastery of Clairvaux, established in 1115, became its principal foundation. In pursuit of their

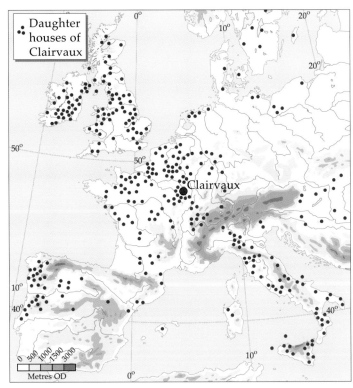

Fig. 20   The European distribution of Cistercian abbeys affiliated to Clairvaux. All Irish Cistercian houses were part of this group. The arrival of the Cistercians at Dunbrody and Tintern brought the south-west Wexford region into the mainstream of thirteenth-century European ecclesiastical and agricultural development and had a fundamental impact on the development of landscape and settlement.

aims, the Cistercians sought to escape from the distractions of the world and pursued lives of asceticism and self-denial, based on an exacting interpretation of the Benedictine Rule. The simplicity of their rule was reflected in a new ascetic approach to the architecture of their monasteries. Self-sufficiency was an essential part of the rule and estates were sub-divided into granges (out-farms) worked, initially at least, by lay brothers. The Cistercians were brought to Ireland by Bishop Malachy of Armagh, who visited St Bernard of Clairvaux in 1140. Two years later the Cistercian monastery of Mellifont was established in county Louth. The order spread rapidly and by the arrival of the Anglo-Normans in 1170 there were thirteen foundations in Ireland; twenty-three more were established in the following century.[21]

Dunbrody Abbey

Hervey de Montmorency's determination to endow an ecclesiastical foundation on his fief in south Wexford illustrated the priority given to the establishment of religious houses within feudal society. Having failed in his attempt to attract monks to Bannow, he offered a large estate in the manor of the Island to the monastery of Buildwas in Shropshire in 1172, for the foundation of the

SALEM ABBEY

Fig. 21 A medieval illustration from the Cistercian abbey of Salem in Germany showing monks and lay brothers at work building an abbey. The 750 Cistercian abbeys throughout Europe were built to a typical plan with the intention of reflecting the asceticism of the Order in the architecture and simplicity of the buildings. The ban on sculptures was not always observed, as at Tintern for example, where a series of stone carvings can be seen.

first Anglo-Norman Cistercian house in Ireland. Hervey may have regarded the grant to the Cistercians as the best way of organising part of his extensive fief. The location of the grant along the eastern shore of Waterford Harbour may also have been a deliberate tactic, in conjunction with Henry II's grant to the Templars, to pacify the area and provide security for the vital waterway. His reasons for selecting Buildwas as a mother house are not known but may have been related to the presence of the abbot, Ranulf, at the Synod of Cashel in 1172. A report prepared by a Brother Alan, who was sent by Buildwas to investigate the proposed grant, provides a description of the area in the late twelfth century that is perhaps somewhat prejudiced, as the writer had to live in a hollow oak tree. The monks of Buildwas:

> were careful to appoint one of our converts, a laybrother, Alan by name, circumspect and discreet, to these parts. Who when he came thither and found the place a solitary waste, took up his dwelling in a certain hollow oak and there made his abode during the time of his sojourn, and led a life of penury and toil; finally the

bounds of the aforesaid lands and tenements being limited and assigned, he returned to us with speed, informing us to the full concerning the waste of the place, the sterility of the lands, and the wildness and ferocity of the neighbouring barbarians … We might incur no small damage or loss, if we should attempt to send any to those parts in order to inhabit and dwell.

As a result of this most unfavourable report, Buildwas declined the grant, offering it instead to St Mary's Cistercian abbey in Dublin.[22] The offer was accepted in 1182 and in 1201 the new monastery, called the Port of St Mary of Dunbrody, was consecrated by Herlewyn, bishop of Leighlin, a nephew of the founder.[23]

In the early thirteenth century, disputes over land as well as some small grants from individuals resulted in variations in the amount of land held by the abbey. In 1227, the general chapter increased the Dunbrody estate by a grant of the impoverished abbey of Ghinewadam in county Waterford.[24] The use by the Anglo-Normans of existing Gaelic territorial divisions in the process of sub-infeudation and the close link between manorial and

DÚCHAS

Fig. 22 Dunbrody Abbey is regarded as one of the most impressive Cistercian monuments in Ireland. The large early Gothic church, built c. 1210–40, has three rib-vaulted chapels in each transept. The central tower was added in the fifteenth century. Around the cloister garth, there are partial remains of the monastic buildings including the sacristy, chapter house, slype (passageway) and dorter undercroft (a room under the dormitory). On the south side, the walls of the rectory stand almost to full height. The cloister contains what may have been a small lavabo and fragments of a cloister arcade.

parochial development in medieval Ireland, combined with evidence from charters and monastic extents, makes it possible to map the extensive medieval church lands in the Hook area. Of twenty place-names listed in the charter to Dunbrody, eight can be identified with modern townlands; another name, used to describe a small river, survives in the name of Campile village (cam pill: a winding inlet).[25] When these are used in conjunction with the possessions of the abbey at dissolution in 1537, an accurate estimate of the lands of the monastery can be ascertained.[26] The monastic estate consisted of approximately 40 carucates or ploughlands; as a ploughland was equal to about 300 statute acres (121 ha), this was the equivalent of 13,000 acres (5,260 ha) in modern terms. The Dunbrody lands corresponded to the medieval parish of St James and Dunbrody and part of Killesk, with the townland of Kilmannock in the parish of Kilmokea.

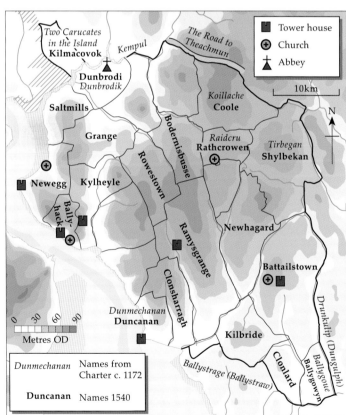

Fig. 23 Dunbrody Abbey lands; principal granges were located at Nook, Ballyhack, Ramsgrange and Battlestown.

Tintern Abbey

Tintern Abbey was founded as a result of a vow made by William Marshal when in danger of shipwreck on his first voyage to Ireland in 1200, the year given in the Irish annals for the foundation of the monastery.[27] On reaching land safely, Marshal fulfilled his vow by granting land for the foundation of a monastery on the shores of Bannow Bay, possibly near the spot where his ship made a safe landfall. It was colonised with Cistercian monks from

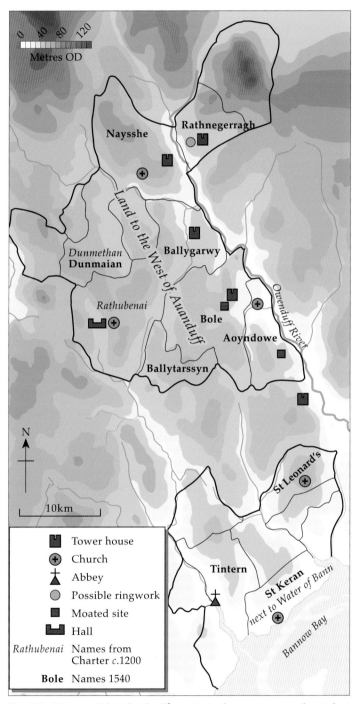

Fig. 24 Tintern Abbey lands. The principal granges were located at Rathumney, Rathnageeragh, Nash and Boley. The abbey lands were divided in two by the episcopal manor of Kinnagh.

Map labels:
Metres OD
0 40 80 120
Naysshe
Rathnegerragh
Dunmethan Dunmaian
Land to the West of Auanduff
Ballygarwy
Rathubenai
Bole
Aoyndowe
Owenduff River
Ballytarssyn
N
10km
St Leonard's
Tintern
St Keran next to Water of Bann
Bannow Bay

Legend:
Tower house
Church
Abbey
Possible ringwork
Moated site
Hall
Rathubenai Names from Charter c.1200
Bole Names 1540

Fig. 25 The seal of Tintern Abbey. The figure of an abbot, holding a crozier, was a standard thirteenth-century form. The inscription reads *Sigillum abbatt … de Voto* (the seal of the abbot of [Tintern] of the vow).

Tintern Abbey in Marshal's manor of Chepstow and named Tintern Minor or de Voto (of the vow). King John's confirmation of a grant by Marshal of thirty ploughlands for the foundation of the abbey was made in 1200, but Marshal's actual charter can be dated to 1207–13 from the names of the witnesses.[28] The land granted to the Cistercians was part of Hervey de Montmorency's fief, but it reverted to Marshal after Hervey's death in 1205. This may have delayed the conferring of a charter of foundation following the initial grant of land in 1200. Of nine place-names mentioned in the charter to Tintern, four can be identified in the modern landscape.[29] The land was described as 'next the water of Bann[ow]' and to the 'west of Auanduff,' a reference to the Owenduff river, which formed the eastern boundary of the estate. The townlands of Rathumney and Dunmain, also mentioned in the charter, were the sites of granges on the monastic estate. By using this information in conjunction with the extent of the foundation's possessions in 1539, it is possible to estimate the extent of the lands granted by

DÚCHAS

Fig. 26 Tintern Abbey was founded c. 1200, by monks from Tintern Major in Wales on lands granted by William Marshal. The abbey complex, dating to c. 1300, was typically Cistercian in layout but only the chancel, the crossing tower, the central aisle of the nave and the Lady Chapel of the south transept survive. Archaeological excavations indicate that the north transept, north aisle and possibly the south aisle were demolished by the Cistercians during a major reorganisation of the church in the 1440s. The domestic buildings, apart from the arched gateway, did not survive post-Dissolution destruction but excavations have revealed the layout of the cloister walkway. The two bridges spanning the inlet are post-Cistercian. Following conservation work by Dúchas The Heritage Service, of Cistercian and some later elements, the abbey, with an extensive Colclough museum, is open to the public.

Marshal.[30] The monastic estate, equivalent to the civil parishes of Tintern and Owenduff, contained almost 15,000 statute acres (6,070 ha), or approximately fifty ploughlands. This is considerably more than the thirty mentioned in the charter, suggesting that the ploughlands of the charter contained a larger acreage, possibly comprising wasteland and forest; as at Dunbrody, the original grant may also have been augmented by grants of land from other sources. According to the charter, a considerable part of the land had formerly been held by other individuals, presumably tenants-at-will, who were removed to make way for the Cistercians. It was not possible to remove established tenants from all of the land, as the grant to the Cistercians was divided in two by the parish of Kinnagh. The fact that this parish was

PRIVATE COLLECTION

Fig. 27 A late eighteenth-century moonlight view of Tintern Major on the river Wye in Wales, made famous by William Wordsworth's celebrated poem. The 'vagrant dwellers in the houseless woods' mentioned in the poem (dated 13 July 1798) were possibly refugees from Wexford escaping the horrors of the Rebellion which took place in that year.

based on an episcopal manor must have made it impossible to alienate it to the Cistercians.

Hervey's decision to become a monk in Christ Church, Canterbury, to which he granted church livings and lands in south Wexford, had implications for Tintern de Voto.[31] The bishop of Ferns contested Hervey's grant to Canterbury. By an agreement of c. 1230, Canterbury retained the lands and church livings of Kilmore, Kilturk, Tomhaggard, Kilcowan, Bannow, Killag, Carrick and the Saltee Islands, all in the cantred of Bargy, leaving the lands and church of Fethard in the hands of the bishop. Canterbury found the grant, which resulted in 'more vexation than profit,' to be a liability and in 1245 it was conveyed to Tintern for a payment of 625 marks (1 mark = 13s 4d) and an annual rent of 10 marks. The payment was to be made at the cathedral of Bath every year, but a clause in the agreement allowed for delays caused by stormy seas. This arrangement was to prove a continuous bone of contention between the two monasteries, as Canterbury was perpetually demanding arrears of rent.

Early in the thirteenth century there was much dissension between the Cistercians of the Irish Mellifont affiliation and the foundations established after the arrival of the Anglo-Normans.[32] In 1227 Stephen of Lexington was sent by the general chapter to investigate the 'Mellifont conspiracy' and, despite initial resistance, succeeded in restoring a certain level of discipline. He received strong support from Dunbrody and Tintern, which were not part of the Mellifont group and supported the general chapter. During his visitation of the Irish houses, he was accompanied by a monk from Dunbrody and he completed his work by holding an assembly of Irish abbots at Tintern.[33] During the fourteenth century, the temporal power of the Cistercian foundations assumed a greater importance and the monasteries were frequently in disagreement with one another. In 1341, the abbot of Dunbrody, Philip de Chirchull, was deposed for refusing admission to the abbot of the parent house, St Mary's, Dublin. However, when the dispute was brought before the general chapter in 1342, Dunbrody was made independent of St Mary's.

THE MILITARY ORDERS

The great military orders of Knights Templars and Knights Hospitallers, described as 'the most distinctive institution to arise from the crusading movement; a fusion of opposites, monks who were fighters,' were founded in Jerusalem at the beginning of the twelfth century to protect and care for pilgrims to the Holy Land.[34] The orders quickly expanded throughout Europe, becoming

N.L.I.

Fig. 28 Henry II. During his visit to Ireland in 1172, he granted lands to the Templars that included Clontarf in county Dublin, Crook in county Waterford and the manor of Kilcloggan in county Wexford, which consisted of the Hook Peninsula south of a line from Duncannon to Carnivan.

rich and powerful in the process. Both orders were involved in various battles in the Holy Land, suffering many fatalities. The intense rivalry between the two groups escalated into outright enmity and was seen by the Pope as contributing to military losses. The Templars were regarded as being particularly culpable, and after failed attempts at reconciliation the order was eventually suppressed in 1307. Templar property subsequently passed to the Hospitallers.[35]

The military orders were introduced into county Wexford in the early days of the Anglo-Norman occupation.[36] Although their original mandate was of a dual military/religious nature, the military aspect took precedence in Ireland, as the orders' primary role was maintaining law and order. The Templars were introduced into Ireland by Henry II, who had vowed to provide for the support of two hundred Templars as part of his reparation for the murder of Thomas Becket. Henry's charter, dated 1172, granted to the Templars 'the vill of Clontarf, mills in Waterford, mills in Wexford, Crook and

Fig. 29 A crusader knight from a *Book of Hours*. The grant by Henry II of the manor of Kilcloggan to the Knights Templars created a direct link between the Hook and the crusading movement.

Fig. 30 A fourteenth-century illustration of the assault on Jerusalem during the first crusade in 1099. Over the next two centuries, further crusades were organised to recover the Holy Land and Jerusalem, sacred to Jews, Muslims and Christians, for the forces of European Christianity.

Kilbarry in Waterford and the church of St Aloch near Wexford with the lands belonging thereto.'[37] The exact location of the church of St Aloch with its lands has been a source of contention but is identified by the subsequent history of the Templars in the county. The words 'near Wexford' have been the source of the confusion, but in later charters of confirmation dated 1199, 1226 and 1280 these words are omitted. In 1290 the original grant from Henry II was described as referring to the lands of Crook and Kilbarry in county Waterford and Kilcloggan in county Wexford, identifying the church of St Aloch of the charter as Kilcloggan (pronounced Kilogcan) on the Hook peninsula, the site of an early Christian monastery founded by Alloc.[38]

The Templars occupied their lands at Kilcloggan probably before the end of the twelfth century, as the grants to the military orders in Ireland were confirmed in 1183,[39] establishing their headquarters at Templetown, which still bears their name. Two other areas associated with Templar foundations, Temple House in county Sligo

and Templetown in county Louth, were similarly named. They located their church at the head of a small valley overlooking a landing beach, now called Templetown Bay. In the field to the north of the church, the degraded remains of an earthwork, located at the top of a steep slope, may represent the initial ringwork castle fortification erected by the Templars. The military orders were deployed to provide security at strategic locations throughout Europe and they were presumably installed on the eastern shore of Waterford Harbour for the same purpose, especially as they were also installed at Crook and Kilbarry on the opposite shore. The manor of Kilcloggan consisted of the combined medieval parishes of Hook and Templetown, comprising approximately 5,162 statute acres (2,090 ha).[40]

Fig. 31 A Templar knight from a twelfth-century mural in a Templar chapel in France. Following its foundation in the Holy Land, the Order became very powerful, expanding rapidly throughout Europe.

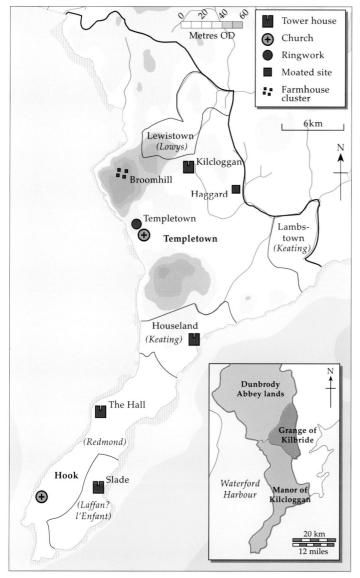

Fig. 32 The Templar/Hospitaller manor of Kilcloggan. Much of the manor was held by hereditary free tenants; principally Redmond of the Hall, Laffan of Slade, Keating of Houseland and Lambstown and Lewis of Lewistown.

The Templars initiated aggressive lawsuits against their neighbours, the Cistercians of Dunbrody Abbey.[41] A lawsuit over ownership of five ploughlands (about 1,500 statute acres: 607 ha) at Crook in county Waterford dragged on for twelve years, forcing the abbot to complain that 'he could not keep hospitality or rule his convent if he was to further prosecute this plea against such powerful adversaries.' In 1290 the abbot surrendered his right to the land in return for a payment of 100 marks. The most significant of these lawsuits concerned the grange of Kilbride, located to the north of Kilcloggan and bordering on the lands of Dunbrody. Although it would appear to have been part of the original grant to Dunbrody, Kilbride became a Templar grange where, on occasion, recruits were admitted into the order. In 1279

the master of the Templars in Ireland claimed seven ploughlands (about 2,100 statute acres: 850 ha) in Kilbride from the monks of Dunbrody; after a prolonged lawsuit, judgment was given in favour of the Templars. The dispute continued, however, and was not finally resolved until 1334, when the Hospitallers, who had by then succeeded to Kilcloggan, handed over the grange of Kilbride to Dunbrody.[42] The medieval grange of Kilbride was much bigger than the modern townland and perhaps included the adjoining townlands of Battlestown, Clonlard and Ballygow. The combined acreage corresponds to the seven ploughlands mentioned in 1280. The name Battlestown would appear to be of later origin, as John Battaile was a tenant of Dunbrody Abbey in 1390. In Battlestown, a church site known as Templeboy, and an adjacent castle site, may indicate the manorial centre of the disputed grange.[43]

The attitude of the Templars towards the Cistercians of Dunbrody is an illustration of the cavalier way in which they used their influence to further their own ends. Their power and privilege won them many enemies: when Philip of France, anxious to acquire their possessions, ordered their arrest in 1307, he received the backing of the Pope and Edward II of England. The justiciar, John Wogan, was instructed that all brothers of the Military Order of the Temple should be 'attached by their bodies for certain causes,' their lands seized and an inventory made of their possessions.[44] After the arrest of the

BRITISH LIBRARY

Fig. 33 A depiction of the burning of the Templars in a fourteenth-century French manuscript. On the continent, the Templars were handled with great severity; the Order was treated more leniently in Ireland.

B. COLFER

Fig. 34 Kilcloggan tower house was built in the fifteenth century by the Knights Hospitallers as their manorial headquarters. Projections at the north and south corners accommodate a stairs and garderobe. Fragments of the bawn wall and gateway survive at the north angle.

Templars the preceptory of Kilcloggan was placed in charge of the sovereign and bailiffs of New Ross. The Templars were imprisoned in Dublin Castle and the issues of the manors of Kilcloggan (in county Wexford) and Crook and Kilbarry (in county Waterford) were allocated for their upkeep.[45] The king lost no time in putting the possessions of the Templars to his own use. In 1307, the justiciar was ordered to provide 'victuals for the war in Scotland against Robert de Brus, 1000 qrs. of wheat, 1000 qrs. of oats, 200 qrs. of beans and peas, 300 tuns of wine, 3 tons of honey, 200 qrs. of salt, 10,000 hard fish, to be levied from the Templars goods in Ireland in the king's hand.'[46]

Following the dissolution of the Templars by the Pope in 1312, their manors were handed over to their great rivals, the Knights Hospitallers, who were ordered to continue paying the 2d per day which had been allowed for the support of each Templar. The Hospitallers had been introduced into county Wexford by Strongbow c. 1175, granting them ten ploughlands and one burgage at Ferns and the church of St Michael in Wexford town. In about 1210 William Marshal added to their possessions in

Wexford town, granting them the churches of Sts John, Patrick, Brigid and Mary Magdalene. Marshal also granted the manor of Ballyschauc to the Hospitallers, which became their principal thirteenth-century preceptory in the county.[47] The association of Ballyschauc (variously written Ballyscaok, Balicaoc, etc.) with Ballyhack on the east shore of Waterford Harbour was made in the seventeenth century and has been accepted by numerous commentators since then, despite various difficulties presented by this identification. For example, Ballyhack was included among the possessions of Dunbrody Abbey and the church was dedicated to St James, not St John as at Ballyschauc. A careful analysis of documentary sources shows that Ballyhack and Ballyschauc were, in fact, two different places, but all references to either one have been assumed to refer to Ballyhack.[48] This inevitably raises the issue of the location of Ballyschauc. This can be ascertained, not from contemporary Hospitaller sources, but from an examination of the distribution of Hospitaller lands following sixteenth-century dissolution. In 1618, a grant to Adam Loftus of the Hospitaller lands listed the townlands of Forest, Kereight, Galbally, Ballymorris and Garranstackle as part of Ballykeok.[49] These townlands made up the medieval parish of Ballykeoge, situated on the right bank of the Slaney just south of Enniscorthy. Written 'Ballykeoge' on John Rocque's 1760 map of Ireland, the area is now known as Ballyhoge. The Hospitallers were unable to take possession of Kilcloggan until 1326, as it was one of the manors which had been retained to provide support for the Templars. The two Hospitaller manors were subsequently administered as one preceptory: in 1327, John FitzDavid was commendator of both Ballyhoge and Kilcloggan.[50]

EPISCOPAL MANORS

Because of the significance of his ecclesiastical status within the feudal system, the bishop was the only landowner in county Wexford able to protect his rights during the Anglo-Norman settlement. Bishop Ailbe Ua Maolmhuidhe was at least partially successful in challenging grants of land which he considered rightfully belonged to the diocese. Hervey de Montmorency's gift of churches and lands in Bargy and Shelburne to Christ Church, Canterbury, was contested by the bishop, who claimed that some of them belonged to the diocese of Ferns. Following a long dispute, Canterbury quit-claimed the church and manor of Fethard to Ferns in return for land and churches in Bargy.[51] This agreement was arrived at before the year 1245, as in that year Canterbury leased the churches to the Cistercians of Tintern de Voto.[52] The dedication to St Aidan suggests that there was an Early Christian foundation at Fethard, where the small motte may date to c. 1200, when Canterbury reserved a site to the north of the church as a 'fit place to hold a court.'[53] At the end of the thirteenth century, the six episcopal manors of Fethard, Kinnagh, Ballingly, Mayglass, Polregan and Ferns with Clone had a combined acreage of about 40 ploughlands and an income of £240, making the bishop one of the principal landowners in the county. Two of the manors, Fethard and Kinnagh, where the circular church enclosure is also a strong indication of an Early Christian origin, were located in Shelburne.[54]

B. COLFER

Fig. 36 The decorated medieval font is still in use in Fethard church.

there were also a significant number of farm labourers. At Fethard a burgess rent of £6 indicates that it may have been planned as the principal episcopal borough, perhaps because of its maritime location. As 1s was the usual burgage rent, the figure of £6 shows that Fethard had a maximum of 120 burgesses. Allowing five persons to each family, this suggests a burgess population of about six hundred.[55] However, this figure may be too high, as some individuals may have rented multiple plots. This was not the total population, as there was also a considerable amount of rent from tenants who were not burgesses. Income from the mills was significant, indicating that corn

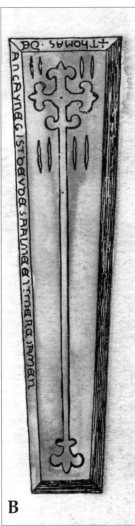

A **B**

Fig. 35 (A) Thirteenth-century episcopal effigy in Ferns Cathedral. For at least five centuries, the manor of Fethard was held as part of the bishop's possessions in the diocese of Ferns; (B) Graveslab at Fethard Church of Bishop Thomas Denne who died c. 1400.

The accounts for the two manors provide some information about economic and social organisation on the episcopal lands. Rent contributed by free tenants was the main item of income on the manor of Kinnagh, where

B. COLFER

Fig. 37 The circular enclosure at the church site on the former episcopal manor of Kinnagh indicates an Early Christian origin.

Accounts for the manors of Fethard and Kinnagh in 1282

Fetherd (Fethard)

Meadow and pasture	£0 4s 6d.
Rents of cottages	£0 1s 2d.
Rents of free tenements	£4 17s 9d.
Rents of burgages	£6 0s 0d.
Mill rents	£2 13s 4d.
Rabbit warrens and dovecots	£0 3s 0d.
Gardens	£0 0s 4d.
Prisage (tax) of beer	£0 10s 0d.
Perquisites (profit) of court	£0 2s 6d.
Manor of Fethard	£1 6s 8d.
Total	**£15 19s 3d.**

Kynheth (Kinnagh)

Rents of lordships, pasture and woods	£2 5s 0d.
Meadow	£0 2s 6d.
Cottagers	£0 0s 9d.
Farms and farm labourers	£4 6s 6d.
Rents of free tenements	£9 9s 0d.
The mill	£2 0s 0d.
Perquisites of court	£0 2s 6d.
Total	**£18 6s 3d.**

was a principal crop on both manors; in contrast, revenue from meadow and pasture was relatively small. The rabbit warrens mentioned at Fethard may have been located in the two areas of sand-dune still known as 'the Big Burrow' and 'the Little Burrow.'

SETTLEMENT ON THE MONASTIC ESTATES

Dunbrody Abbey, situated where the Campile river enters Waterford Harbour, and Tintern de Voto, at the mouth of a small river flowing into Bannow Bay, were similarly located: the rivers provided the essential water supply and the estuaries afforded access to the world of trade and commerce. The founding of Tintern Abbey at a distance of only five miles from Dunbrody was contrary to the statutes of the order, which stated that new monasteries should not be founded within twelve leagues (60km) of another house. The location of Tintern was dictated by Marshal's vow when in danger of shipwreck, and his request to establish a monastery, following an investigation by the abbots of Mellifont and St Mary's, was allowed.[56]

The granting of vast estates to the Cistercians represented a drastic intervention in the development of settlement and society in the Hook. According to the rule of the order, no lay tenants were allowed on monastic lands: the estate was divided into granges or out-farms worked by numerous laybrothers. Because of the difficulties experienced in recruiting lay brothers, a decree was passed in 1220 permitting the leasing of land. During the thirteenth century the practice of renting the monastic granges to lay tenants increased.[57] In 1302 a papal bull allowed Cistercian lands to continue free of tithes even though worked by serfs or tenants. Allied to political strife

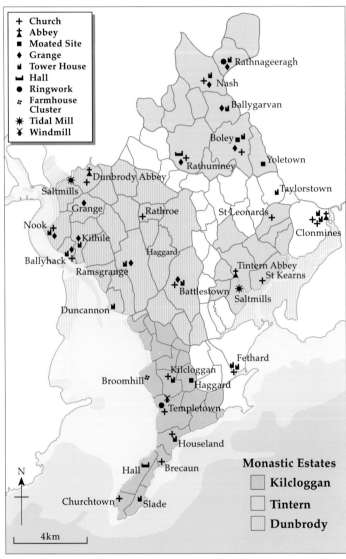

Fig. 38 Due to varying circumstances, settlement on the three monastic estates developed individual characteristics. The Templars did not use a grange system, instead dividing up their lands into manors which were mostly let to free tenants. The development of the Dunbrody estate was influenced by its association with Waterford Harbour, beside which several granges were located. Settlement on the Tintern estate was somewhat different due to the divided nature of the lands and the vulnerability of the detached northern section, which required protection along the line of the Owenduff river.

Fig. 39 A medieval illustration from Salem Abbey in Germany showing lay brothers at prayer during a break from work on a monastic grange.

and the effects of the Black Death of 1348–9, this led to the introduction of numerous lay tenants on Cistercian lands during the fourteenth century when there was little to distinguish the abbot from a secular landlord. The granting of lands to lay tenants was accompanied by the imposition of feudal rights and privileges, although these were also banned by the statutes of the order.[58]

The location of some of the monastic granges can be identified. On the lands of Dunbrody, out-farms were located in the townlands of Grange, Ramsgrange, Kilhile. Haggard and probably Shielbaggan. Settlements at Ballyhack and Nook, located on Waterford Harbour to take advantage of the economic opportunities offered by the estuary, were commercial rather than agricultural granges. The building of a church, and later a tower house, at each place represented a considerable investment by the monks. Tower houses were also erected, probably by lay tenants, on the granges of Battlestown (Battaile's town), Kilhile and Ramsgrange.[59]

The principal granges on the Tintern Abbey estate were located at Rathumney, Dunmain, Nash, Rathnageeragh, Ballygarvan, Boley and Yoletown on the detached northern portion of the lands. Rathumney, mentioned in the foundation charter, where the remains of an early

Fig. 40 A grange site at Booley, on the Tintern estate, is marked by a circular earthwork thirty metres in diameter with a fosse about five metres wide with an external bank. The grange was close to the defensive line of the Owenduff River and was protected by a fifteenth-century tower house which has been completely removed.

Fig. 41 At Rathnageeragh (the rath of the sheep) on the Tintern lands, a ringfort may have been occupied by Irish tenants involved in raising sheep on the Cistercian grange. The circular site, about forty metres in diameter, has an external fosse, c. seven metres wide, fed by a stream. As at Boley, a tower house was later built on or near the earthwork.

B. COLFER

Fig. 42 Rathumney was one of the place-names mentioned in Marshal's charter to Tintern and the village originated as a grange on the lands of the Abbey. Based on a medieval church and hall, the grange may have served as the headquarters for the detached, northern portion of the estate.

thirteenth-century hall-house and a church site survive, may have been developed as the headquarters of the detached portion of the estate.[60] Moated sites at Boley and Yoletown, significantly located along the defensive line of the Owenduff river, indicate that these lands were more vulnerable than the rest of the Cistercian estate. Higher up on the river, the circular earthwork at Rathnageeragh may have been an early ringwork castle, possibly based on a pre-existing ringfort, as the name suggests. The site, about forty metres in diameter, is surrounded by a stream-fed fosse about seven metres in width. The masonry rubble on the site possibly represents the remains of a later tower house.[61]

The high level of taxes generated at New Ross by the new custom imposed on wool and hides in 1275 indicates that Dunbrody and Tintern became involved in sheep farming during the thirteenth century, in common with other Cistercian houses.[62] The produce of the Cistercian abbeys of Jerpoint on the Nore and Duiske on the Barrow would also have been exported through Ross. A considerable part of the Duiske estate was located in county Wexford, on the eastern slopes of the Blackstairs mountains.[63] In 1233, the deforestation charter of the manor of Ross referred to 'the bridge of the sheep of the

monks' in the vicinity of Rathnageeragh on the Tintern estate.[64] The Irish place-name of Rathnageeragh (Rath of the sheep) suggests that the monks depended on Irish tenants to look after the sheep on the northern part of the estate. The English townland names of Ramsgrange, on

B. COLFER

Fig. 43 Rathumney Hall is an unusual example of an early thirteenth-century hall-house. The rectangular structure had a central ground floor hall which rose to the full height of the building. At each end, the hall had two storeys with a complex of small rooms including two garderobes.

Fig. 44 Reconstruction drawing of a moated site, based on the description of an example built on the manor of Old Ross c. 1280.

B. COLFER

the Dunbrody estate, and Lambstown, on the Templar lands, also originated in sheep-raising activities. The townland names on the northern portion of the Tintern estate were almost exclusively Irish, unlike Dunbrody, where there was a core of townlands with English names, indicating that the monks of Tintern may have depended to a greater extent on Irish-speaking tenants. The names of tenants listed at Dissolution support this contention: of twenty named tenants on the Tintern estate, ten (50%) had Irish names; on the Dunbrody lands, only six (16%) of thirty-six tenants had Irish names; on the manor of Kilcloggan, five (12%) tenants out of forty had Irish names.

The detailed inventory of the Templars' possessions in 1307 provides an insight into activity on the demesne lands of the manor of Kilcloggan early in the fourteenth century.[65] It paints a picture of a highly organised, self-sufficient community, involved principally in agricultural production. Scores of household and farmyard items are listed as well as church fittings and furniture. The military aspect of the Templars is not reflected in the inventory, as the only weaponry mentioned consisted of a balista, a bow, two tunics and two belts, but the individual knights may have been allowed to bring their personal arms with them. There was intensive mixed agriculture on the

manor, perhaps dominated by cereal growing. Manorial production of cereals peaked at this period to feed English armies fighting in France and Scotland. The presence of 65 oxen and 12 heifers for ploughing indicated the extent of the arable production, which produced 220 crannocks of wheat (the most important crop), 190 of oats, 26 of barley and 14 of beans and peas (the crannock varied from quarter to half a hundredweight). Perhaps influenced by

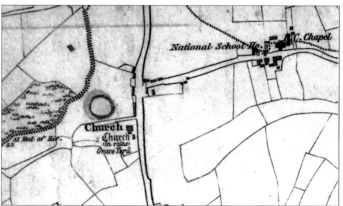

ORDNANCE SURVEY

Fig. 45 The Ordnance Survey map of 1841 shows a concentration of houses in the vicinity of Templetown cross. The mound shown immediately to the north of the church (known as 'the hill o' the moat'; now largely removed) may have been associated with the early earthwork castle erected by the Templars. It could also have been used as a site for a windmill.

Inventory of the Templars' goods and chattels 1307

At Kilcloggan
In the Haggard:
60 crannocks of wheat, 4s each
80 crannocks of oats, 40d each
12 cows and 1 bull, 5s each
24 oxen and 8 heifers for ploughing, 5s each
8 horses for 3 wagons, each horse 6s 8d
3 wagons, each 3s 6d
500 two-year-old sheep, each 8d
60 pigs, 8d each
Brass vessels in the hall and kitchen, 40s
Vestments, jewels and books
Preceptor's horse, £3 6s 8d
1 horse as a hackney, £1 13s 4d
4 colts and fillies, 13s 4d each

At Templeston [Templetown]
In the Haggard:
20 crannocks of wheat, 4s each
26 crannocks of oats, 40d each
10 crannocks of beans and peas, 4s each
12 oxen and 4 heifers for two ploughs, 5s each
3 horses for 1 wagon, 5s each
1 plough, 40d
60 sheep, 8d each

In the grange of Kilcloggan
In sheaves and threshed corn, 60 crannocks of wheat, 5s 6d each
For tithes, 20 crannocks of wheat, in sheaves and threshed corn, 5s 6d each
40 crannocks of oats, 4s 6d each
24 crannocks of oats for tithes, 4s 6d each
4 crannocks of beans in the granary, 5s 6d each
12 crannocks of peas, 4s 6d each
5 crannocks of best barley, 5s 6d each
21 crannocks of ordinary barley, 4s 6d each
4 tables, 2s each
2 forms or chairs, 6d each
1 helmet, 12d
The bed of the preceptor, Peter de Malvern, 1 mark
2 leather jackets, 1 mark
3 small books, 3s
2 horns, 2s
1 basket, 12d
6lbs of wax, 9d
Wax candles, 1s 6d
1 balista [an implement for throwing missiles] and 2 belts, 3s
1 bow, 1d
1 bed belonging to brother Walter de Joneby, 1 mark
do. to brother Adam de Langport, 6s 8d
do. to brother Wm. le Chapeleyn, 10s

36s 6d in money
2 casks, 7 pipes, 11 tuns [a large cask for wine, ale or beer], 3 trendells [a measure for liquor], 1 great tun, 18s
120 bands of new wood for repairing the casks, 6s
Two great furnaces, old and broken, 5s
3 brass jars, 5s each
2 smaller jars, 20d
2 other jars, 5s each
Another jar, 12d
1 small vase, 2s
1 lock for the kitchen door, 8d
2 tripods, 2s
1 wicker basket, 6d
2½ carcasses of beef, 4s each
10 of bacon, 20d each
1 of mutton, 4d
lard, 1s 6d
80 squared boards, 2s
9 preserved hides, 15s
68 cocks and hens, 1½d each
7 ducks, 2d each
23 geese, 2½d each
2 horses, 1 mark each
1 horse, 10s
1 mare, 10s
2 'pullani' [?], 5s each
5 heifers, 6s 8d each
29 oxen, 6s each
20 cows, 5s each
2 bulls, 3s each
6 mares, 3s each
11 two-year-old-steers, 2s each
53 pigs, 9d each
2 pigs in the stye, 2s each
360 ewes, 8d each
195 wether sheep, 6d each
11 hives of bees, 16d each
Half a stone of wool, 15d
40 yds of canvas, 3d per yd.
8 bundles of hides, 10d each
5 sacks of wool and 2 winnowing/winding sheets, 8d each
74 acres of land sown with wheat, 4s 6d per acre
6 acres sown with winter wheat, 4s 6d per acre
3 acres sown with peas, 3s per acre
5 acres sown with oats, 3s per acre

Instruments for the smith and the forge
An anvil, 2s
2 large 'malholi' [?] and 2 'folles' [?files], 2s
2 large augers, 8d; 4 smaller ones, 8d
4 locks, 1s

2 pick axes and 3 saws, 1s
A fork, 1d
Bands of iron for the plough, a pair of pincers, a lock and 20 plates of iron, 15d
1 piece of iron, 1s
1 saw, 1d
44 bars of iron, 4d each
700 nails, 21d
1 large lock, 3s
Various tools: 1 'twybil' [?], 2s; 1 'adis' [?adze], 1s
2 saws, 6d
1 'schwyre' (?screw) and 2 'nangeres' [?augers] 8d
Iron for the repair of the broken sail of the windmill, 2s 6d
Divers other small iron instruments, 1s
1 hawser and other pieces of rope, 4s 6d

In the chapel
1 missal, 40s
2 portifors [?breviary], 10s each
2 psalterias, each 2s
1 gradual [mass-book], 12s
1 epistolar, 5d
1 antiphonar [hymn book], 5s
1 martyrology [book on the martyrs], 6s 8d
1 chalice, 13s 4d
Vestments for the altar (1 alb, 1 amice, 1 chasuble, 1 tunic, 1 damassin, all of silk), £5
Ordinary vestments, with other apparatus for the chapel, 6s
3 napkins and 2 hand towels, 6s
10 silver spoons, 10d each
A silver dish, 1s 8d
7 silver spoons, 9d each
2 silver cups, 6s 8d each
4 'mazer' cups, 18s
1 tin pitcher to hold wine, 8d

In the church
1 missal, 20s
1 goblet, 22s
1 antiphonar [hymn book], 5s
1 'logend', 5s
2 gradals [mass book], 2s
1 psalter, 1s
Other small books, 4s
1 alb and 2 chasubles, 6s 8d

Total value of goods and chattels: £140 4s 6d

Taken into the hands of the king, with the free tenants, by Adam de Rupe, seneschal of the liberty of Wexford.

T.C.D.

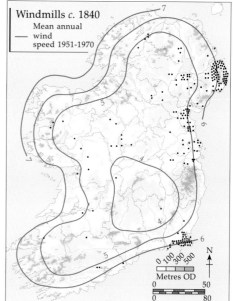

Windmills *c.* 1840
Mean annual
— wind
speed 1951-1970

N

Metres OD

B

B.L.

C

Fig. 46 As the map illustrates, the tradition of using windmills was strong in south Wexford, particularly in Forth and Bargy. The use of windmills in the Hook goes back at least to the fourteenth century and continued until the nineteenth century, probably because of suitable wind conditions and the lack of streams to provide water-power. A windmill (A) was shown at Templetown on a 1591 map of Waterford Harbour; a windmill (B) was recorded on the high ground over Duncannon in the mid-seventeenth century. A 1794 survey of Waterford Harbour showed a windmill at Carnivan (C). Windmills were also located at Clonmines and Ingard Point. The ruins of the last stone windmill to be used in the Hook (D) still survive at Houseland. A pre-fabricated mill designed by a local tradesman and imported from the US, was erected at Slade c. 1890 (E).

D

B.COLFER

E

KING MILNE

Tenants-at-will on the manor of Kilcloggan 1541

Tenant	Acres	Rent/Services	Location	Townland
Demesne lands	125	42s	Kilcloggan ?Haggard	
1. John Caddell	3	1s 2 capons 1 hookday	in vill of Templeton	Templetown
2. Richard Talon	3	1s 2 capons 1 hookday	in vill of Templeton	Templetown
3. Robert Ketyng [Keating]	3	1s 2 capons 1 hookday	in vill of Templeton	Templetown
4. John Manglere	8	2s 2 capons 1 hookday	lands called Scorlock in Ballyer	not known
5. Nicholas Waddyn [Wadding]	15	5s 2 capons 1 hookday	Lyes	not known
6. Alicia Dongyn	1 tenement & garden	6d 1 capon 1 hookday		not known
7. Laurence Wylmot	5	1s 4d 1 capon 1 hookday		not known
8. James Conynk [Connick]	16	4s 2 capons	Cook's land	not known
9. John Maygill	18	4s 6d 2 capons 1 hookday	Wyken	not known
10. Nicholas Ketyng [Keating]	18	4s 6d 2 capons 1 hookday	Johan Hore's land	not known
11. Matthew Lovell	7	2s 1 capon 1 hookday	Hore's land	not known
12. Patrick Valle [Walle]	6	1s 6d 1 capon 1 hookday	Kelly's ground	not known
13. Patrick Mason	8	2s 2 capons 1 hookday	Scorlock	not known
14. Edward Gregory	18	4s 6d 2 capons 1 hookday	Whytmay	not known
15. Johanna Tege	9	2s 4d 2 capons 1 hookday		not known
16. James Woode	16	4s 2 capons 1 hookday		not known
17. Robert Gybbon	9	2s 3d 2 capons 1 hookday	Dolyon's land	not known
18. James Wyke	18	2s 2 capons 1 hookday	Dolyon's lands	not known
	8	2s 2 capons 1 hookday	Santery's land	not known

Average rent for tenants-at-will almost 3d an acre plus services.

capon: a castrated domestic cock fattened for eating
hookday: a day's work with the reaping hook at harvest time

Free tenants on the manor of Kilcloggan 1541

Tenant	Acres	Rent	Location	Townland
Alexander Redmond	360	20s	in vill of Hook	Loftus Hall Churchtown, Portersgate
Nicholas Laffan	120	6s 8d	in vill of Hook	Slade
James Lowys	?	10s	Lowystowne	Lewistown
	20	2s 6d	part of Lamystowne	Lambstown
— Hatton	60	6s	part of Lamystowne	Lambstown
Robert Keating	?	2s 6d	part of Lamystowne	Lambstown
James Wyken	60	5s	Palmerstown	?
John Oge	20	5s	village of Templeton	Templetown
James Woode	1 messuage and 6 acres	1s 6d	village of Templeton	Templetown
James Marnell	20	5s	Slyne ys ground	?
Richard Walsh	40	10s	Hoore (in Templetown)	Templetown
John More	30	8s	Stanter (in Templetown)	Templetown
Henry Ketyng	30	3s 4d	castle of Homisland	Houseland

Average rent for free tenants 1d an acre

Names of tenants and farmers on the manor who carried out the survey (inquisitors)

Matthew Lovell*, Philip Raymond, Nicholas Laffan*, James Wyken, Richard Lowes, Richard Power, John Chepman, Laurence Gangeogh, John McGyll*, James Connyk*, Nicholas Waddyng*, Patrick Wall*, Richard Walsh*, John Colle, John Devereux, Henry Ketyng*, Nicholas Ketyng*, Robert Ketyng*, Richard Calgay, John O'Murrey, John Cosger [Cosgrave].

Tenants already named are marked with an asterix

the neighbouring Cistercians, livestock raising was confined mostly to sheep, of which there were 1,055 on the manor. Numbers of other farm animals were quite small, with 115 pigs, 51 cattle and 20 horses. There were also some poultry, with 68 hens, 23 geese and 7 ducks. There were eleven hives of bees, indicating that Wexford's reputation as a honey-producing county is of long standing. The grange of Kilcloggan mentioned in the survey could be represented by the adjacent townland of Haggard (hay garth; a rickyard), where a moated site, since removed, was recorded on the first edition of the Ordnance Survey. This site could represent the haggard mentioned in the inventory, as moated sites were typically the defended farmsteads of the late thirteenth century.[66]

The inventory indicates that there was a manorial brewery, with coopers to make the tuns, or casks, needed to hold the beer. The smith was also a crucial craftsman, needed to keep the ploughs and tools in working order. Milling was a substantial source of income for the

B. COLFER

Fig. 47 The origins of this farm in the townland of Houseland can be traced to medieval times when it was held by the Keatings as tenants of the Templar and Hospitaller manor of Kilcloggan. A tower house site (A) is marked by a pile of stones and rubble. The ruins of a windmill (B) are located in the adjacent field. There was a chapel and well dedicated to St Helen in the townland, just outside the picture to the right.

Templars: their charter granted them mills in Waterford and Wexford. Perhaps unusually, they used windpower at Templetown, as the inventory lists 'iron for the broken sail of the windmill,' in spite of the existence of a stream suitable for a watermill. This tradition of using windmills persisted at Templetown down to the nineteenth century. The lands, whose rents were valued at £45 11s 11d, were surrendered with the free tenants, so it seems likely that the land-holding structure which can be identified under the Hospitallers had been initiated by the Templars. The final source of income was £12 17s 4d, from the tithes of the churches of Kilcloggan, Meelnagh and Killurin. The survey details the contents of a church and a chapel, probably referring to the churches of Kilcloggan and Templetown, including a set of silk mass vestments valued at £5, the most expensive item on the manor. A thirteenth-century graveslab, with floriated cross and Agnus Dei, on the medieval church site is the only known Templar artefact to survive at Templetown.

The Hospitallers were probably responsible for the fortification of the church at Templetown by adding the surviving square tower, which was restored and altered in the early nineteenth century as a belfry and sacristy for a new church. Old field patterns and possible house plots revealed by aerial photography in the fields adjacent to Templetown church, together with stray finds of thirteenth-century pottery, provide evidence for an associated village. The former existence of a rectangular moated site at Haggard suggests that settlement was being expanded at Kilcloggan in the late thirteenth century. The tower house at Kilcloggan, which originally had an accompanying enclosure or bawn, is substantially intact. The lands of Ballyhoge were not listed among the Hospitallers' possessions in 1541, which could indicate abandonment of manor and tower house. Kilcloggan, on the other hand, was valued at £19 7s 11d, with a 'castle or fortilage in good repair, very necessary for the defence of the country in time of war of the Kavanaghs and other Irish, near whose countries the castle lies.'[67]

The surveys carried out at dissolution provides considerable information on the organisation of land-holding on the three monastic estates, concentrating on the

R.S.A.I.

Fig. 48 The original Templar church at Templetown, dedicated to St Mary, was located to the south of the tower (shown above in a detail from a drawing by Du Noyer c. 1850). The fortified tower was probably added by the Hospitallers during the turbulent fourteenth century. When a new Protestant church (to the left) was built north of the tower in the early nineteenth century, the medieval tower was renovated and used as a sacristy and belfry. A thirteenth-century graveslab in the graveyard, with floriated cross and an *Agnus Dei* (Lamb of God) in relief, provides a direct connection with the Knights Templars.

land held by various tenants, where the land was located, and the rents and services which were due (Appendix 1).[68] The manor of Kilcloggan, where surname evidence indicates that twelve per cent of the tenants were native Irish, was the only one of the estates where land was held by free tenants. As the Hospitallers had inherited the land-holding system, and as these tenants held their lands in perpetuity, their holdings had originally been granted by the Templars in the thirteenth century. The lands held by the principal free tenants can be identified: Alexander Redmond of the Hall (now Loftus Hall) held most of the parish of Hook; Nicholas Laffan held the townland of Slade in the Hook; Henry Keating held the townland of Houseland; James Lowys held the townland of Lewistown with part of Lambstown; and Robert Keating held part of Lambstown. The name of an early tenant survives in the place-name Galgystown, a small townland on the Hook peninsula. Richard Calgay, one of the tenants who carried out the survey in 1541, may have been a member of the same family. The other free tenants held smaller farms, whose locations cannot be precisely identified. Twenty-nine tenants, probably tenants-at-will, held plots of between three and eighteen acres in the parish of Templetown, paying a small amount of rent in money as

well as rendering customary services: typically, two capons (chickens) and one hookday (presumably a day's work with the reaping-hook). The areas occupied by tenants-at-will cannot be precisely identified.

The status and permanence of free tenants is reflected in the names of the districts where they held their lands, as fifty-five per cent of these can be identified with modern townlands. None of the lands held by tenants of lower status can be equated with townlands, indicating smaller holdings and less secure tenure. This insecurity of tenure is also indicated by the fact that a tenant's land was often defined by using the name of a former tenant: James Connyck held Cook's land and Patrick Valle held Kelly's ground. The lands described as 'mountain common and other lands,' which were waste and vacant, must refer to the high ground of Templetown Hill and Broomhill and perhaps the poorer land to the north of the manor. Farmhouse clusters at Broomhill, Lewistown and Herrylock, where much of the land is still held in dispersed plots, could represent the Irish quarter on the manor, as many of these clusters are considered to be medieval in origin.[69] Despite the change in ownership, however, surname evidence suggests that many of the original tenants continued to occupy the lands as they

B. COLFER

Fig. 49 Ballyhack was developed as a grange on the Dunbrody estate to exploit the economic potential of the estuary. The castle was well placed to regulate the lucrative ferry crossing and fishing activities. The approach road (bottom right) by the water's edge was built in the nineteenth century.

had done under the monastic regime. The principal free tenants on the manor of Kilcloggan retained possession of their lands until the Cromwellian confiscations in 1650. The impact of the settlement pattern established by the military orders on the manor of Kilcloggan, and outlined in the survey of 1541, can still be traced in the modern landscape.

The classification of land on the Cistercian estates as arable, pasture, meadow and moor indicates that the tenants were engaged in mixed agriculture. Tenants paid a money rent as well as services, usually a number of hookdays and weeding days at harvest time on lands farmed by the abbey, and one sheep. Four tenants on the demesne lands of Dunbrody were also expected to contribute sixty gallons of beer! Of thirty-six tenants named on the Dunbrody lands, six (16%) had Irish surnames in comparison to ten (50%) out of twenty on the Tintern lands. Perhaps not surprisingly, the principal tenants, the Devereuxes on the Dunbrody lands and the Powers at Tintern, were related to the last abbots before dissolution.

The frequent allocation of land in ploughlands (120 acres), half ploughlands and quarter ploughlands indicates that the measurement of holdings may not have been very precise. The description of the different farms shows that

N.L.I.

Fig. 50 This detail from a 1685 drawing by Thomas Phillips shows Ballyhack with a well-developed pier. The castle is surrounded by several substantial houses and some cabins. The parish church of St James on the cliff-top is roofless, presumably as a result of post-Reformation pressures in the area. The village was close to the deep shipping channel.

Fig. 51 The fortified church of St Catherine, built on the Dunbrody estate near Buttermilk Castle on the grange of Nook overlooking Waterford Harbour. A niche beside the doorway may have held a light to guide shipping. The drawing c. 1850 by Du Noyer shows the east window of the church.

the lands of Dunbrody Abbey (where there were fourteen references to arable land, fourteen to pasture, twelve to meadow, one to moor and one to wood) were more settled and productive. By comparison, there were twelve areas of arable, eleven of pasture, three of meadow, four of moor and twelve of wood on the Tintern estate. This can be partly explained by better quality land on the Dunbrody estate, but Tintern's location adjacent to 'the land of war' must have been a factor: seven farms were described as waste or partly waste because of 'wars with the Irish.' Place-name identification also indicates a difference in stability between the two estates: on the Tintern lands, of sixteen place-names mentioned in the survey, eleven (69%) can be identified with modern townlands, but this rises to 85 per cent on the Dunbrody lands where eighteen out of twenty-one place-names can be identified.

Apart from land, the surveys also identify a number of economic activities, mostly on the Dunbrody estate. The tidal waters of the inlets near the abbeys were harnessed to operate mills, referred to as salt mills, located in what became the two townlands of Saltmills. Another mill at Tintern, referred to as 'le overshot mill,' was probably located on the stream near the abbey, on the site of the later Colclough mill. A rental of 48s 4d from three fishing weirs, equivalent to the income from about half a ploughland, underlined the economic value of the estuary to Dunbrody Abbey. At Ballyhack, nine fishermen lived in nine tenements belonging to the abbey and, as well as rent, contributed a custom in fish valued at 13s 4d.

During the turbulent fifteenth and sixteenth centuries, an attempt was made to protect southern Shelburne by constructing seven tower houses along the line of the

Fig. 52 A reconstruction drawing by G. Du Noyer suggests the original appearance of St Catherine's church. The turbulent fourteenth and fifteenth centuries led to the fortification of a number of churches, including Dunbrody Abbey itself, Templetown, Clonmines and Killesk.

Fig. 53 An illustration from a medieval manuscript in Salem Abbey, Germany, of monks fishing with a seine net. Fishing contributed a significant part to the economic life of Dunbrody Abbey.

SALEM ABBEY

A

B

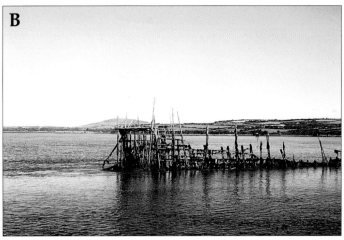

N.L.I.

B. COLFER

Fig. 54 (A) A mid nineteenth-century drawing of Buttermilk Castle showing it with a thatched roof. The castle was built by the monks of Dunbrody on the grange of Nook as a base from which lucrative fishing activities on the Barrow could be controlled. The origin of the adjacent fishing weir with attendant fishermen can be traced to monastic times. (B) A modern (1970s) fishing weir on the site of the monastic weir at Buttermilk Castle. The method of construction and fish-catching technique probably varied little over the centuries.

Owenduff river, which formed the eastern boundary of the barony. These were located at Taylorstown and Clonmines (2), with four on the lands of Tintern Abbey at Rathnageeragh, Nash, Ballygarvey and Boley, probably built by lay tenants who had occupied the granges.[70] Tower houses were also built, again possibly by lay tenants, on the lands of Dunbrody Abbey at Battlestown, Ramsgrange and Kilhile. The castles of Ballyhack and Buttermilk were built by the monks themselves as bases from which to exploit the economic opportunities presented by Waterford Harbour. The fortified church of St Catherine's, located at Nook near Buttermilk castle (called Skeroirke castle in the *Civil Survey*), and a chapel on the second floor of Ballyhack castle indicate an ecclesiastical connection.[71] A castle at Duncannon, strategically placed on a promontory projecting into

Waterford Harbour, may have been built by John Talbot, earl of Shrewsbury, who received a temporary grant of Duncannon early in the fifteenth century.[72] All of the other tower houses in the area were built on the Hospitaller manor of Kilcloggan. The surviving tower at Kilcloggan must have been constructed by the Hospitallers themselves. Three others were built by tenants on the lands of the manor: Redmond Hall (replaced by Loftus Hall) was built by the Redmond family, Houseland Castle by the Keatings and Slade Castle by the Laffans (? L'Enfant). No trace of Houseland Castle survives, but Slade Castle, with an adjoining stone house, is in an excellent state of preservation and is maintained as a National Monument.[73] The Laffan holding was quite modest, so it is surprising that they could afford to build such an impressive residence. They were obviously able to

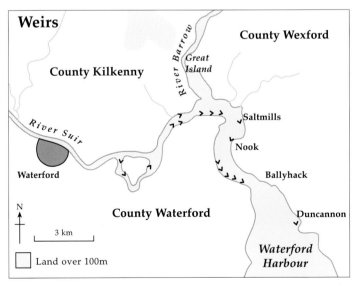

Fig. 55 Fishing weirs (including the one at Nook) still in operation in the Waterford estuary in the mid twentieth century.

B. COLFER

Fig. 56 A traditional fishing boat on the Campile river near Dunbrody Abbey. The rounded design of the boat allowed it to be easily pulled through shallow water over mud-flats in the river and estuary. A rudimentary jetty gives access to the deep channel.

Fig. 57 In this c. 1850 view of Dunbrody Abbey by G. Du Noyer, the dam and sluice-gate of the millpond used to drive the tidal mill at Saltmills are shown on the right of the inlet in the foreground. The millpond is now silted up but can be traced in the modern landscape.

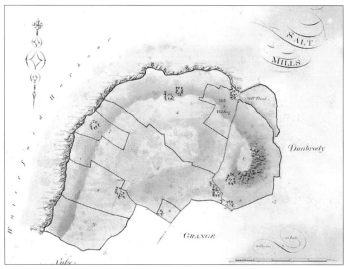

Fig. 58 A map of Saltmills townland from the 1803 Dunbrody estate maps showing the tidal mill and millpond on an inlet of Waterford Harbour. When the incoming tide had filled the millpond, the sluice gate was closed; at low tide, the water was released to operate the mill-wheel. The site of the mill is shown beside the dam to the left of the pond. The inclusion of the mill on the map suggests that it was still in use.

Fig. 59 At Tintern and Dunbrody, in the townlands of Saltmills, the monks used tidal power to operate corn mills. The use of these mills continued for centuries. This sketch, based on a detail from a 1796 engraving of Dunbrody by T. S. Roberts, shows a small tidal mill in Saltmills on the inlet south of the abbey. The dam and millpond (now silted up) can still be identified.

Fig. 60 English place-names as an indicator of settlement. Townlands with English names form a pattern related to Anglo-Norman settlement. The lands of Dunbrody Abbey and the Knights Templars contain a core of English names, while the names in the knight's fee of Tullerstown were almost completely anglicised. Place-names on the lands of Tintern Abbey remained Irish to a greater degree, particularly in the northern detached part of the estate, perhaps an indication that the monks relied on Irish tenants to farm this more remote district. Eight townland names contain a personal name followed by the suffix 'town', a place-name element diagnostic of Anglo-Norman settlement. Five (Lewistown, Battlestown, Drillistown, Tullerstown and Templetown) can be related through documentary sources to the original Anglo-Norman landholders. Other names refer to activity associated with a particular townland. These include two Granges, two Haggards, two Saltmills, a Ramsgrange, a Lambstown, a Haytown and a Milltown. Four names, Loftus (formerly Redmond) Hall, Houseland, Porter's Gate and Stonehouse, indicate the former existence of specific settlement features. Three names (Broomhill, Castleworkhouse and Ramstown) are of later origin.

generate an income from the sea; perhaps, as was the custom elsewhere, they exacted a levy from continental fishermen who needed to process their catch on dry land before returning home. There is also the possibility that the legend of 'the pirate Laffan from Slade' may have had some basis in reality.[74]

The confiscation of the monastic estates had the added political significance of providing the crown with the opportunity to install a new category of loyal landowner to act as a bulwark against the 'rebel Irish.' The process introduced another layer to the social mix, as the Elizabethan adventurers who acquired the lands were committed to the new, official Protestant religion. The dynasties which they established would dominate all aspects of life in the region for more than three centuries. The development of the estates had profound implications for society and landscape.

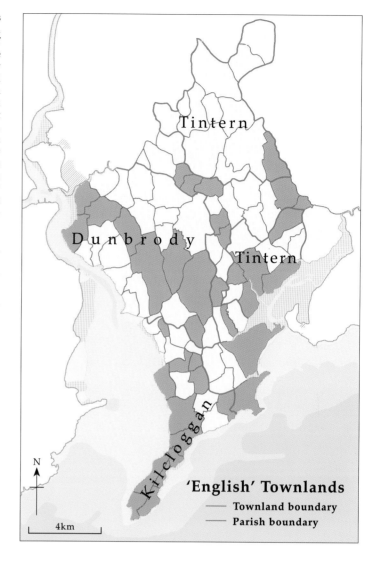

'English' Townlands
—— Townland boundary
—— Parish boundary

Fig. 1 Dunbrody Abbey from the east. Left of the tower can be seen the Tudor windows and chimneys of the house built by the Etchinghams. The tower was added in the fifteenth century.

Fig. 4 The east entrance to the cloister complex. A dormitory window can be seen at top right.

Fig. 2 Rib-vaulting in a north transept chapel.

DUNBRODY ABBEY

Situated beside an inlet on the east shore of Waterford Harbour about fifteen kilometres down-river from the Anglo-Norman town of New Ross, the ruins of Dunbrody Abbey form one of the most impressive Cistercian monuments in Ireland.[1] The

Fig. 3 Original tiles *in situ* in the north transept.

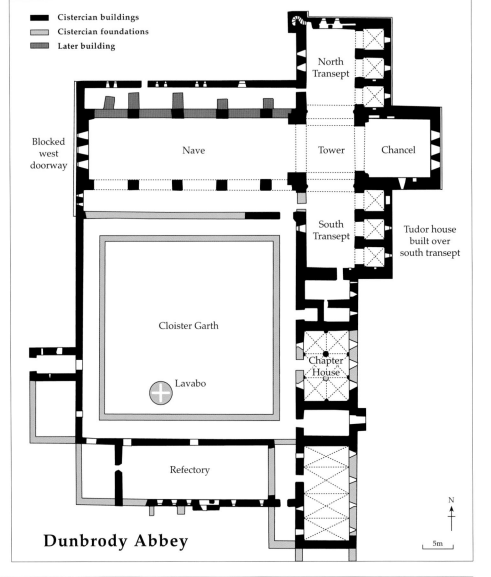

- ■ Cistercian buildings
- ▨ Cistercian foundations
- ▨ Later building

North Transept

Blocked west doorway

Nave

Tower

Chancel

South Transept

Tudor house built over south transept

Cloister Garth

Chapter House

Lavabo

Refectory

Dunbrody Abbey

N

5m

N.L.I.

Fig. 5 An early nineteenth-century etching of Dunbrody Abbey showing the west door and window. The window was subsequently destroyed when most of the west gable collapsed.

B. COLFER

Fig. 7 A decorated corbel on a pier in the arcade of the nave at Dunbrody Abbey.

estate of about 10,000 acres (4,000 ha), on which it was built was given to the abbey of Buildwas in 1171–75, by Hervey de Montmorency, the uncle of Strongbow. After the English abbey received an unfavourable report from one of its lay brothers on the location, the land was transferred to St Mary's Abbey, Dublin, which sent a community to the site in 1182.

The ruins are dominated by the large early Gothic church (c. 1210–40) with three rib-vaulted chapels in each transept. The whole well-proportioned design is severely simple. Three tall lancet windows light the east wall of the presbytery and three small lights, with rounded heads, are situated above these in the gable. The nave, somewhat later in date than the

chancel and transepts, lost its south arcade and aisle in 1852, but the north elevation is well preserved. It has five pointed arches carried on square piers chamfered at the angles. Each arch had soffit-ribs, some chamfered, some fully moulded, and were carried by moulded capitals as corbels, tapering downwards to finish in a bent, floral tail. The four clerestory windows have two trefoil-pointed lights and are sited over the piers. In the west wall there were originally three lancet windows below multifoiled circles above a doorway which is now built up. A massive central tower was erected in the fifteenth century, supported on

WEXFORD COUNTY LIBRARY

Fig. 6 Dunbrody Abbey from Grose's *Antiquities*, 1791. This view shows the west window (left of picture) and the south wall of the nave, both of which fell in the mid-nineteenth century.

B. COLFER

Fig. 8 A two-light clerestory window in the north wall of the nave of Dunbrody Abbey.

Fig. 9 A study of the nave and tower of Dunbrody Abbey in Grose's *Antiquities* (1791), before the collapse of the south arcade. The crossing tower was added in the fifteenth century.

Fig. 10 A mason's mark from a north transept chapel in Dunbrody Abbey.

Fig. 11 Side chapels with Dundry stone moulding in the south transept of Dunbrody Abbey.

additional arches and buttress piers inserted into the crossing.

To the south of the church, some of the buildings are still partially intact around the large cloister space. On the east side, beyond the sacristy and book repository, is the chapter room, in which two pillars supported a groined vault of six bays. Next is the slype or parlour and dorter undercroft (a room under the dormitory). In the south range, the walls of the refectory and kitchen stand almost to full height; it is possible that the buildings on the west range were never built. The cloister contains what may have been a small circular lavabo and fragments of a fifteenth-century cloister arcade. In the field to the south are the remains of a gatehouse and possibly a chapel.

Due to raids by the Irish, some of the estate was waste when the monastery was dissolved. The abbey, with its lands, was taken over by the crown in 1536 and granted to Sir Osborne Etchingham. His family adapted the abbey as a dwelling, constructing a house with mullioned windows and large chimney stacks over the south transept. With the construction of nearby Dunbrody Castle in the early seventeenth century, the abbey was abandoned to become a picturesque ruin on the estate. The family later moved to Dunbrody Park in their estate village of Arthurstown.

The abbey is now a National Monument and the key can be obtained at the visitor centre and tearooms which have been developed at nearby Dunbrody Castle. No significant work has been carried out on the abbey and a conservation programme needs to be put in place.

B. COLFER

Fig. 12 A 1970s view of Tintern Abbey from the south before conservation work began. The leaning tower in the foreground, built by the Colcloughs, possibly as an ornamental feature, was removed in the late twentieth-century. The gables and windows of the Colclough house can be seen on the nave.

B. COLFER

Fig. 13 Rib-vaulting with decorated bosses in the south transept chapels at Tintern Abbey.

TINTERN

The surviving buildings at Tintern are later than Dunbrody Abbey, dating to c. 1300, when the buildings belonging to the early thirteenth century were largely replaced.[2] Although smaller in scale, the design of Tintern de Voto has comparisons with Tintern Major in Wales. Of the church, originally cruciform in plan, the only standing remains are the chancel, the crossing tower, the centre aisle of the nave and the rib-vaulted Lady Chapel of the south transept. A large east window, probably with elaborate tracery like that at Tintern Major, was removed in the fifteenth century, when the moulded jamb stones were incorrectly re-used in a much narrower window that replaced it. The outside walls of the chancel are strengthened by shallow buttresses, linked by a corbel table. The crossing tower at Tintern is one of the few surviving examples of the early phase of Cistercian tower building in the late thirteenth to early fourteenth centuries. Archaeological excavations indicate that the north transept, north aisle and possibly the south aisle were demolished during a major reorganisation of the church which took place during the 1440s.

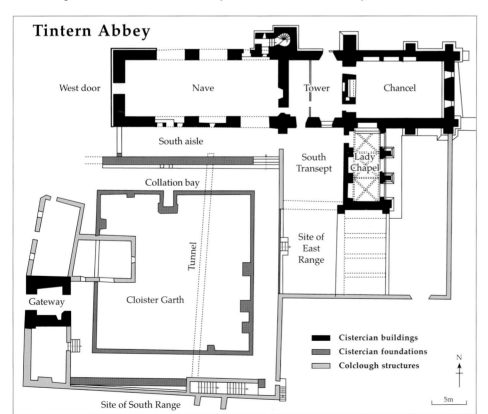

Tintern Abbey

West door — Nave — Tower — Chancel
South aisle
Collation bay
South Transept — Lady Chapel
Tunnel
Site of East Range
Gateway — Cloister Garth
Site of South Range

■ Cistercian buildings
■ Cistercian foundations
☐ Colclough structures

N

5m

B. COLFER

Fig. 14 Plain square arches with Old Red Sandstone quoins divided the nave at Tintern into three bays. Apart from some of the neo-Gothic windows inserted into the arches, the residence which the Colcloughs created in the nave has been largely removed.

Fig. 15 Tintern Abbey from Grose's *Antiquities* (1791). The artist showed the church as a Cistercian ruin, with part of the south transept and the monastic buildings removed but without alterations added by the Colclough family. The small tower on the left was built by the Colcloughs.

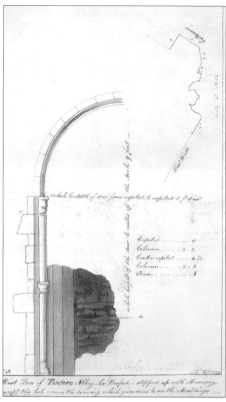

Fig. 16 A c. 1780 study of the west doorway of Tintern Abbey, blocked up by the Colcloughs, showing details of decorative stonework.

The tower was also heightened, in response to the volatile political climate of the time. The stair turret to the north of the tower may have been erected at the same time. The only surviving feature of the domestic buildings is the arched gateway, the main entrance to the cloister, now incorporated in later outbuildings. Excavations have revealed the layout of the cloister walkways, which provided easy access to the church and the other rooms of the abbey as well as providing a sheltered area for spiritual readings and meditation. Of particular interest is the collation bay on the north side, with the remains of the abbot's seat on the church wall opposite. Each evening, the monks assembled here to partake of a collation and listen to a reading. At the time of the Dissolution, some of the walls in this part of the cloister were painted in hues of orange, brown and grey/black.[3] Original floor tiles have been found at the abbeys of Tintern and Dunbrody and also at Clonmines Priory.[4]

By the end of the fourteenth century, the use of sculpture had increased in Cistercian churches. At Tintern, three small carvings of ecclesiastics survive, none in its original position. More secular in nature are a series of grotesque heads carved on the corbel table, high up on the exterior of the north and south walls of the chancel. The eighteen heads at Tintern, both human and monstrous, with some hybrids, are the best example of this type of carving in Ireland.[5]

Tintern Abbey, with its lands, was taken over by the crown in 1536. The estate was granted to Sir Anthony Colclough, who adapted the abbey as a dwelling house, destroying many Cistercian buildings in the process.[6] The tower was initially converted into a five-storey tower house by blocking up arches and inserting floors and fireplaces. Surviving oak floor joists were cut from trees felled between the autumn of 1569 and the spring of 1570.[7] The chancel was later similarly adapted, with Tudor mullioned

windows inserted into blocked-up Gothic windows. At the end of the eighteenth century, the abbey was surrounded by 'walls and battlements

Fig. 17 The recently exposed west doorway of Tintern has a moulded surround of local Old Red Sandstone. The external ground level was lowered during the Colclough period.

DÚCHAS

Fig. 18 At Tintern, a series of eighteen grotesque heads adorn the corbel table, high up on the exterior of the north and south walls of the chancel.

B. COLFER

Fig. 19 Although sculptures were forbidden by Cistercian rule, some stone carvings do exist at Tintern. This one portrays an ecclesiastical figure with a large rounded head in robes cut in strong tubular folds. He is holding a book in his right hand and a crozier in his left. The figure was moved by the Colcloughs from its original position to its present location in the chancel at the side of the east window.

DÚCHAS

Fig. 20 A reconstruction drawing of the arcade which originally supported the roof of the cloister walkways at Tintern, based on recovered fragments of cut and dressed stone.

in the ancient style, so well executed that a few years will give them the appearance of being part of the original building'.[8] These battlemented walls, with a circular tower, survive to the south of the abbey; a similar tower which had become unstable was removed in the early 1990s. In the nineteenth century, the nave was transformed into a Georgian Gothic house, the windows filled with thin wooden tracery. Much of this survived until the late twentieth century, when it was controversially removed in order to reinstate the Cistercian ruin.

B. COLFER

Fig. 21 Tintern Abbey viewed from the fortified bridge built by the Colcloughs over the estuary.

B. COLFER

Fig. 22 As part of the conversion of Tintern Abbey to a dwelling house, the lancet windows of the chancel were blocked up and mullioned Tudor windows inserted. On the right, part of the infill has been removed to reveal the remains of the original decorative tracery.

B. COLFER

Fig. 23 A perimeter tower constructed by the Colcloughs in the eighteenth century, using recycled cut-stone from the abbey.

B. COLFER

Fig. 24 A number of fireplaces and corbels for upper floors were inserted by the Colcloughs in the blocked-up windows of the chancel.

Fig. 25 Archaeological excavations at Tintern have revealed the layout of the cloister walkways. Of special interest is a collation bay on the north side of the cloister, with the remains of the abbot's seat and collation bench on the church wall opposite. Each evening the monks assembled here for collation and listened to a reader who read from a lectern in the bay.

Fig. 26 At Tintern, the blocked-up original west entrance to the cloister complex, with quoins of local Old Red Sandstone, is the only standing remains of the conventual buildings.

DÚCHAS

Fig. 28 A chancel window at Tintern, with tracery reconstructed as part of the conservation programme. The sloping sill followed the roof line of the removed north transept.

B. COLFER

Fig. 29 An example of decorated Cistercian stonework, removed from its original position and re-located in the perimeter wall.

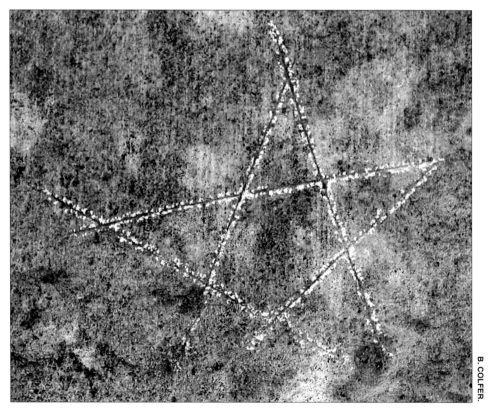

B. COLFER.

Fig. 27 A recently discovered mason's mark on the collation bay at Tintern Abbey.

Fig. 30 The fashion of covering floors with decorated, lead-glazed, earthenware tiles was introduced into Ireland in the mid-thirteenth century and remained in vogue until the mid sixteenth century. The distribution pattern of known examples indicates that these tiles were largely confined to areas of Anglo-Norman influence. Initally imported, they were also made in local kilns. The examples of medieval floor tiles shown here (coloured for this publication) were found in the Cistercian abbeys of Dunbrody and Tintern and in the Augustinian priory of Clonmines.

B.COLFER

Fig. 31 Morning sun on Clonmines. The Augustinian Priory with enclosure is on the left; the tower house known as the 'Black Castle in the centre foreground. On the right, the parish church of St Nicholas and the fortified church are partly hidden by trees.

CLONMINES

The town of Clonmines was founded at the head of Bannow Bay by William Marshal early in the thirteenth century. It would appear that the land for the town was reserved when the grant was made for the founding of Tintern de Voto in 1200. The tortur-ous, barred approach to Clonmines placed the port at a disadvantage and was ultimately given as the reason for its abandon-ment. The demise of the town must also have been related to its failure to compete economically with the more successful ports of New Ross and Wexford. By the end of the seventeenth century, Clonmines was no longer functioning as a port. The population of merchants and artisans who depended on trade and com-merce for their existence had no reason to stay and, inevitably, Clonmines became a ghost town. Over time, the abandoned houses of the townspeople, built of clay and wood, disappeared. Only the high-status stone residences and institutional buildings survived to mark the site of what had been a bustling medieval centre. The quality and quantity of these buildings testify to the town's former importance. The surviving remains include an Augustinian priory, two tower houses, a fortified church, the parish church of St Nicholas and the ruins of a seventeenth-century house.[9]

WEXFORD COUNTY LIBRARY

Fig. 32 Clonmines priory from Grose's *Antiquities* (1791), showing the tracery of the west window of the nave before its collapse. Part of the enclosure can be seen in the left foreground.

Fig. 33 Nineteenth-century views of (A) Clonmines Priory made after the collapse of the west window of the nave, and (B) a window in the chancel.

Fig. 34 The fortified church at Clonmines by G. Du Noyer c. 1850. The ground floor had two entrances, on the north and south walls. The top was accessed by a spiral stairway in the north-west corner. The west door is defended by an overhead machicolation; the battlemented look-out platforms can be seen on the summit.

Fig. 35 An 1899 sketch of Clonmines depicting the 'Black Castle' and the Augustinian Priory.

Parish church

On entering the gate, the fortified parish church of St Nicholas is the first building on the right. The structure consists of a nave and chancel, with a tower with a vaulted ground floor attached to the west of the nave. Gaps in the nave walls probably mark the sites of doors. The chancel has good quoins, a blocked window, an aumbry of dressed stone and a piscina (basin). There is a round-headed doorway on the north wall and a destroyed window on the east gable.

Fortified church

An unusual building resembling a small tower house is located within the precincts of the parish church. This rectangular structure, referred to as a fortified church, is complete to stepped battlements. A doorway on the north is pointed and a rounded one on the west is protected by a machicolation and had a stoup (now removed) inside. The ground floor has a barrel vault with a gallery at the west end and is open to a groin vault at the east. The interior is lit by two-light windows in the east and south

Fig. 36 A drawing of the interior of the fortified church by G. Du Noyer c. 1850, showing the ground floor divided into two sections, one covered by a barrel vault and the other by a more decorative rib-vault. A stoup (now removed) can be seen beside the far door.

Fig. 37 Three consecration crosses incised on the plaster of the fortified church at Clonmines were recorded by G. Du Noyer in the mid-nineteenth century. Only traces of the crosses survive at present.

Fig. 38 Clonmines from the townland of Maudlintown (presumably the location of the town's medieval hospital) on the east side of the estuary. Only the 'Black Castle' (right) and the Augustinian priory and tower are visible; the parish church and the fortified church are hidden in the trees.

B. COLFER

walls and single-light windows in the north and south walls. The south wall, from which a piscina has been removed, contains an aumbry. Three consecration crosses incised in the wall plaster are now almost undetectable. A spiral stairway leads to the gallery and continues on to the roof. There are look-out turrets over the north-west and north-east corners.

Augustinian priory

The Augustinian priory was founded in 1307 and enlarged in 1385, when fortifications may have been added. The remains consist of a nave and chancel with south aisle. Most of the west wall, which had a large window, has been removed. The chancel had a large east window and three surviving but damaged three-light ogee-headed windows in the south wall and a destroyed window in the north wall. An aumbry and sedila (now destroyed) were located in the south wall of the chancel and a possible tomb niche in the north wall. A later tower was inserted at the east end of the nave; a spiral stairway leads to the wall-walk of the nave and chancel and to the first storey above the vault of the tower, continuing on to the belfry. The top of the tower has a stepped parapet with look-out platforms at two corners.

North of the church, the remains of a rectangular enclosure has a slender tower at the north-west corner. The gatehouse to the enclosure, attached to the west end of the church, had a pointed entrance passage and inner portcullis.

Tower houses

North of the priory, a rectangular tower house known as the 'Black Castle,' originally with four floors, with a loft under the stone vault over the ground floor, survives to wall-walk level. A pointed doorway on the west side is protected by an exterior machicolation and murder-hole over the entrance lobby. The stairway ascends through the wall to the upper floors. The first floor has windows with seats in the north and south walls, a destroyed fireplace and mural chambers, one a garderobe. The second floor had similar arrangements. The stairway continues on to a third floor and destroyed battlements, with the remains of a look-out platform at the north-east corner.

Another tower house is now part of the modern farmhouse. The rectangular tower with base batter survives to first-floor level but is modified as a modern dwelling.

Fortified house

Fragments of a fortified house, possibly of seventeenth-century origin, can be seen just west of the priory. The remains consist of the south gable, with an attic light and parts of a bartizan at the south-west corner. The house was probably one-storeyed with an attic.

At Clonmines, the finest example in Ireland of a deserted medieval borough,[10] surviving remains combine with a spectacular location to evoke a sense of the atmosphere, colour and intimacy of the medieval town. Clonmines is located on private land and, at time of publication, is not accessible to the public.

B. COLFER

Fig. 39 The ruins of the parish church of St Nicholas in Clonmines. The church had a fortified tower at the west end. The interior of the church is still used as a graveyard by some local families.

TURMOIL AND CHANGE: THE IRISH RECOVERY

During the first half of the thirteenth century, the area under Anglo-Norman control in Ireland was expanded and consolidated.[1] From 1250, the settlers experienced a reversal, due, in part, to more efficient opposition from a new generation of Irish leaders. The Irish recovery was aided by a complicated partition of the lordship of Leinster in 1247, with an ensuing long-term damaging effect on the stability of the colony.[2] The partition resulted in the fragmentation of authority and ownership in county Wexford, with a consequent decrease in political and financial control. Factional conflict amongst the settlers accelerated a gradual decline in the colony and an increase in lawlessness. By the end of the century, the Leinster Irish, led by the Mac Murchada, were in general revolt. During the fourteenth century, the Bruce invasion of Ireland (1315–18) was followed by the Black Death, which appeared in 1348 and continued to devastate the population, particularly the colonists in the towns, for the remainder of the century.[3] The Irish recovery had a dramatic impact on the English colony in county Wexford, and by the end of the fourteenth century the north of the county was controlled by the Irish. The settlers of English extraction were largely restricted to the southern 'English' baronies of Forth, Bargy and Shelburne, protected by the natural defences of Forth Mountain and the Corock and Owenduff rivers. The concentration of moated sites (the typical defended farmstead of the settlers) across the centre of the county testifies to the efforts that were made to survive in the hybrid frontier zone. The Mac Murchada, successfully operating in both cultures, succeeded in regaining the kingship of Leinster and effectively destroyed much of the English colony. The difference between the Irish north and English south of the county is reflected in the contrast between the cultural and settlement landscape of both regions.[4]

Fig. 1 The meeting of Art Mac Murchada and the earl of Gloucester. In this illustration, Jean Creton, a Frenchman who accompanied Richard II's expedition to Ireland in 1399, used contrasting landscapes, dress and military techniques to create a stereotypical image of the two cultures.

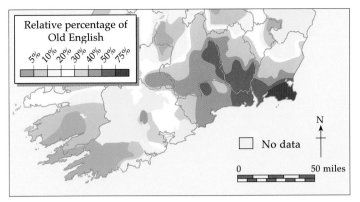

Fig. 2 The relative distribution of Old English as returned in 1660 poll-tax returns. This map shows that high concentrations of Old English names corresponded to the original areas of dense Anglo-Norman colonisation in the south-east lowlands. The baronies of Forth and Bargy in south Wexford had the highest concentration of Anglo-Norman names in the country. The Hook was in the second highest category. The map highlights the division of county Wexford into an Irish north and an English south, with a hybrid area in between.

THE COLONY UNDER PRESSURE

In 1429, a subsidy was granted to build towers or castles within the Dublin Pale and this policy was extended to county Wexford in 1441, when an act was passed for the building of towers along the Corock river.[5] During the next century and a half, at least 170 of these small castles, now called tower houses, were built in the county, mostly concentrated in the southern baronies. Over sixty survive in various states of preservation and provide the most dramatic visual evidence for the survival of the colony in the south of the county.[6] The need for security also led to the addition of towers to the churches of Templetown, Nook and Clonmines; a tower was added to Dunbrody Abbey and an existing one at Tintern was extended. Early in the sixteenth century, the need for security was emphasised when the countryside between Ross and Clonmines was devastated by the Kavanaghs and their followers.[7]

Because of the volatile political situation, the bishop transferred his headquarters from Ferns to his southern manor of Fethard during the last quarter of the fourteenth century. The castle at Fethard dates to c. 1375, at which time Bishop Denne was acting as custodian of the peace in county Wexford with powers to administer both civil and martial law, and his status is reflected in the architectural quality of the surviving castle.[8] Denne's connection with Fethard is also suggested by a graveslab, now in the churchyard but originally in the church, which, almost certainly, bears an inscription to Denne in Anglo-Norman French, a language which he is known to have used.[9]

There were at least two castles in Fethard, but only the one built by the bishop survives. The site of the castle was first mentioned c. 1200 as 'a site fit for a court to the north

of the church,' possibly a reference to a structure associated with the small surviving motte.[10] The later building incorporated elements of the first structure, including a gate-tower, which gave access via a drawbridge to an enclosed courtyard. Apart from its location close to the church, the episcopal association is suggested by the quality of the L-shaped building, which, for example, had three garderobes (toilets) and a large hall on the first floor. As one of the largest landowners in the county, the bishop had the resources to construct such a high-status building. A slender round tower, in which the rib-vaulting may be modelled on the Tower of Hook, served as a belfry, emphasising the ecclesiastical function.[11] In the fifteenth century, the other castle, on glebe land to the west of the town, was referred to as the parsonage, an indication that it was occupied by the vicar rather than the bishop. The site is still occupied by the Old Rectory. The unique design of the castle at Fethard probably influenced the layout of Dungulph Castle, built by the Whitty family three kilometres to the north. This

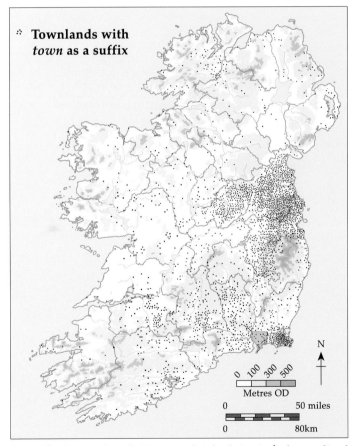

Fig. 3 The density of Anglo-Norman sub-infeudation in the late medieval period is manifested in the distribution of townland names containing the suffix 'town.' The heavily settled baronies of Forth and Bargy in south Wexford contain the highest concentration of these names. The lower frequency of 'town' names in the southern part of the barony of Shelburne, where most of the land was held as monastic granges, reflects the impact of the Cistercian estates on the development of place-names.

N.L.I.

Fig. 4 A nineteenth-century representation of Art MacMurrough Kavanagh. Art emerged as leader of the Leinster Irish in the 1370s, laying claim to the kingship of Leinster and exacting a Black Rent throughout the province. His success led to the arrival of Richard II, who landed at Waterford with the largest army to be sent to Ireland in the Middle Ages. Art burned New Ross and withdrew into the woods of the Blackstairs. The Irish leaders submitted but the government failed to honour the agreement made with Art and he resumed his role as king of Leinster. A second expedition led by Richard II ended in failure. Art, the 'most dreaded enemy of the English in Leinster,' continued to dominate Leinster until his death under suspicious circumstances at New Ross in 1418.

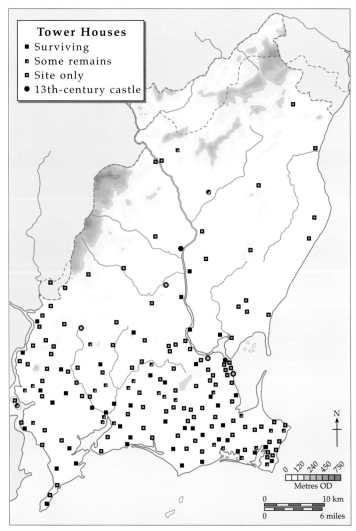

Tower Houses
- ■ Surviving
- ▣ Some remains
- ◻ Site only
- ● 13th-century castle

Fig. 5 The distribution of tower houses in county Wexford is concentrated in the south of the county, particularly in the baronies of Forth and Bargy.

was also a defended residence rather than a tower house, with a circular tower at one corner.[12]

An incident in 1532 illustrates the disturbed state of the country and how the situation could be exploited to solve personal disputes – even by the bishop! In that year, Bishop John Purcell had a disagreement with the townspeople of Fethard, perhaps over unpaid rent, and used a most unclerical way of resolving it. He enlisted the aid of Cahir Mac Art, chief of the Mac Murchada, and at three o'clock in the morning, led by the bishop, they attacked the town and robbed and burned the houses. Three years later, the bishop again called on the 'wild Irish' to attack Fethard. This time they drove away 115 cattle and a great number of sheep and swine. The bishop arranged to have his own cattle stolen with the rest and shortly afterwards sent his servant to retrieve them. The same bishop was in dispute with his clergy in 1569, when he imprisoned Thomas Hay, dean of Ferns, in a dungeon called 'Gadd's black pit' in Fethard Castle. Apparently the bishop wanted the deanery for his own brother. This

reference to a 'black pit' in the castle shows that the surviving castle at Fethard, which has a bottle dungeon in the base of the tower, was the episcopal castle.[13]

PRIVATE COLLECTION

Fig. 6 Dungulph Castle in the early eighteenth century. The layout, including the corner tower, may have been influenced by Fethard Castle. Restored by the Cloney family in the early twentieth century, Dungulph is one of the few late medieval castles still in use as a private residence.

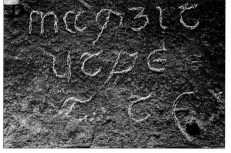

Fig. 7 Fethard Castle (A) is an L-shaped structure consisting of a main hall with a circular corner tower, with an independent wing to the north. Elements of an earlier building, particularly the gatetower with drawbridge recess, are incorporated into the building. The tower was used as a belfry and had a bottle dungeon at its base (C). The first floor of the hall (B) has a large fireplace and a stone stairway to a higher level. A stone with a mysterious inscription, originally associated with the castle, is now in a nearby farmyard (D).

DISSOLUTION OF THE MONASTERIES

The sixteenth century was one of political and social turmoil in Ireland. The Gaelic Irish were encroaching everywhere and English control was confined to an area around Dublin known as the Pale. The southern part of county Wexford, where the baronies of Forth and Bargy, and to a lesser extent Shelburne, formed a Wexford Pale, was under constant threat from the Leinster Irish, led by the Mac Murchada. In spite of the protection afforded by the building of tower houses, the colony in the south of the county came under increasing pressure from the resurgent Irish. By 1530, when Cahir Mac Art was ravaging the county, the countryside from New Ross to Clonmines was described as 'a vast wilderness.'[14] The advent of the Reformation, with the proclamation of Henry VIII as head of the Irish church in 1536, precipitated profound changes in social and political life.[15] The monastic estates were targeted by the new regime, mainly to gain access to their extensive lands, partly because of a decline in religious life but also because they were regarded as places of refuge for the rebel Irish. The authorities decided to suppress the monasteries and grant their properties to men who would protect the land and attract new tenants from England. This decision had profound implications for the Hook,

Fig. 8 Boley castle, drawn c. 1850 by G. Du Noyer, was originally located on a grange of Tintern Abbey beside an earlier defensive earthwork which still exists. This was one of the tower houses constructed along the defensive line of the Owenduff river. Part of the bawn wall and doorway are shown. Although the structure seems to have been relatively sound in the mid-nineteenth century, no trace of it survives at the present time.

where most of the land was held by the church. During the fifteenth century, the growing secularisation of the Cistercians contributed to the political impetus which eventually led to their downfall. In the case of Dunbrody, the right of sanctuary written into its charter must have been an added incentive for its closure. In 1533, a report advised that Dunbrody and Tintern, with other abbeys, should be suppressed because they were 'adjoining the Irish and giving more support to those Irishmen than to the king or his subjects.'[16] Tintern may also no longer have been economically viable, as in 1511 a directive from Rome ordered that, if the annual value of the monastery did not exceed 38 marks (£25 6s 8d), it should devolve to the apostolic see.[17] The abbeys of Tintern and Dunbrody were suppressed on the same day, 6 May 1536. Both abbots, Alexander Devereux of Dunbrody, and John Power of Tintern, had rented monastic lands to family members. The abbots received annual pensions of £15; Devereux became the first post-Reformation bishop of the diocese in 1539 and was buried at Fethard in 1566. The preceptory of Kilcloggan and the Augustinian priory of Clonmines were

also dissolved. The last commander of Kilcloggan, William Keating, was given a pension of £18.[18]

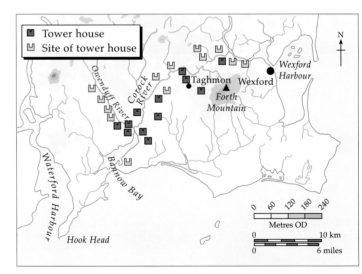

Fig. 9 During the fifteenth and sixteenth centuries, about 170 defended residences, known as tower houses, were built for security reasons in county Wexford by the descendants of the Anglo-Norman colonists. Twenty of these towers were built along the line of the Corock river to protect the English Pale in the south-east of the county.

SLADE CASTLE

Slade Castle is one of the best preserved of its type and is maintained as a National Monument. Some towers had attached houses or halls, usually of timber and mud construction. The castles at Slade, Bargy and Coolhull had adjoining stone halls and are regarded as forming a distinctive group. The tower house has four floors with stone vaults over a ground-floor loft and third storey. A half-storey on top, with a look-out platform overhead providing access to the machicolation. A mural stairway in the south wall leads to the loft under the vault; a well-preserved spiral stairway continues to the top, where almost complete stepped battlements survive. The principal chamber on the first floor has a fireplace, garderobe and windows with seats. The somewhat later fortified house connected with the corner of the tower but no provision was made for internal communication. A link was later provided by building a structure in the angle and knocking out two rough openings at first-floor level. The vaulted ground floor has loops in embrasures and a mural chamber high on the south wall. Two internal walls were later inserted as well as a large fireplace and chimney on the west wall. From an entrance lobby, protected by a murder-hole, a stairway ascends in the south wall to the first floor. Now divided by a later wall, this floor, with a loft, was originally a large room with a garderobe (now destroyed), free-standing fireplace and chimney. Some ogee-headed windows had double lights and window seats. Stairs in the south wall continued to mezzanine level at the east end. Access to the wall-walk and surviving stepped battlements was presumably from this level. An external stairway on the east wall was part of eighteenth-century alterations.

Fig. 10 Slade Castle is thought to have been the prototype for tower houses with attached stone halls as, at Slade, the tower was built first, probably in the second half of the fifteenth century, followed by the fortified house or hall in the early sixteenth century.

Fig 11 Surviving wicker-work centering in the mortar over a first-floor window alcove.

Fig 13 The fireplace, with storage alcove, on the first floor of the fortified house.

Fig. 12 A window embrasure with seats on the first floor of the fortified house of Slade Castle. Hinges for shutters survive in some windows.

Fig. 14 One of a number of embrasures with loops on the ground floor of the fortified house, which also has a mural chamber at loft level.

THE TOWER OF HOOK

The Tower of Hook, located on the tip of the headland as a navigation aid, was built in the early thirteenth century as part of the development of the lordship of Leinster. Realising the importance of Waterford Harbour and its river system for trade and shipping, Marshal established the port of New Ross on the river Barrow, 30 kilometres from the open sea. Other towns in his lordship were also located on the Barrow and Nore rivers, principally Carlow and Kilkenny. Perhaps influenced by his own narrow escape from shipwreck, Marshal knew that shipping needed to be guided safely into Waterford Harbour through the dangerous waters off the point of Rinn Dubháin if his new port of Ross was to be successful. As a navigation aid, he had a thirty-six metre high circular tower constructed at the tip of the peninsula to act as a landmark by day and a fire-tower by night. The monks from the monastery of Rinn Dubháin were involved in the construction of the tower and acted as lightkeepers; in 1247, the custodian and chaplains of St Saviour's of Rinn Dubháin 'who there built a tower as a beacon for

Fig. 2   Marshal may have seen the Pharos lighthouse in Alexandria when on crusade to the Holy Land. Built by the Greeks in 279 BC, the Pharos was visible twenty-five miles out to sea until it fell during an earthquake in 1307. This illustration, taken from a thirteenth-century mosaic in St Mark's basilica, Venice, shows the saint with his companions arriving at Alexandria.

ships' were granted maintenance in 'money and otherwise' from the Pembroke estate, with 'all arrears due to them.'[1] The payment of arrears indicates that the tower had been in operation for some time. As the construction would have taken some years, it was presumably started in the early decades of the century. The use of the monks as custodians was not unusual: in medieval times, religious establishments were often associated with the display of warning lights.[2]

Marshal's idea for a light-tower may have been inspired by Mediterranean examples, such as the crusader lighthouse at Acre or the Pharos lighthouse in Alexandria, which he presumably saw when on crusade to the Holy Land.[3] The Tower of Hook was based on the cylindrical castles (known as keeps) which were popular in France, where Marshal spent many years. Marshal castles at Chepstow, Pembroke, Ferns, Carlow and Kilkenny also had circular towers.[4] The

monks lived in the tower, which served as a monastery as well as a lighthouse. For four centuries after its construction, the Tower of Hook remained in the control of Marshal's town of Ross. In 1411, the sovereign and community of the town of Ross held the Tower of Hook, with twelve acres of adjoining land.[5] An account from 1586 also referred to the Ross connection:

> At the very mouth of the harbour there runneth out a narrow neck of land which presented unto the sailors a high turret erected by the citizens of Ross when they were in a flourishing state that they might the more safely enter into the river's mouth.[6]

On a 1591 map of Waterford Harbour, the tower is shown with crenellations and seven years later the Tower of Hook was included in a list of the principal castles in the county.[7]

It is not known how long the monks continued to act as custodians:

Fig. 1   Effigy of William Marshal in Temple Church, London, where he was buried.

Fig. 3   The Tower of Hook was built in the early thirteenth century as a navigation aid for Marshal's new port of Ross. The lower tier has three rib-vaulted chambers with a stairway ascending through the thickness of the wall. The narrower upper section carried the warning beacon. Still in use as a lighthouse, the substantially intact tower may be the only secular medieval building in Ireland still serving its original function. Guided tours of the tower are provided by Hook Heritage Ltd.

Fig. 4   The marks left by the plank centering which was erected to support the stonework during construction can be seen on the rib-vaulting over the three chambers. A small piece of the original timber was discovered *in situ* during a recent survey. As the building was designed to have a beacon fire on its summit, the stone vaulting would have acted as a barrier to prevent fire speading in case of accident.

Fig. 5   The mural stairway of one hundred and fifteen steps ascends through the thickness of the wall, making one and a half circuits of the medieval tower on its way to the summit.

Fig. 6   A projection at the base of the tower was part of a feature that no longer exists; it possibly contained a chapel for the use of the monks.

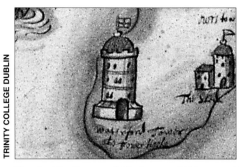

Fig. 7 The Tower of Hook on a 1591 map of Waterford Harbour, drawn by Francis Jobson in the aftermath of the Spanish Armada.

it is unlikely that their role survived the dissolution of the monasteries in 1540. The work may have been continued by lay people after the departure of the monks, as the depiction of the tower on sixteenth-century maps of Ireland is an indication of its continuing importance as an aid to shipping.

By the middle of the seventeenth century, the light, described as 'a gallant sea-marke, formerly a lighthouse to conduct shipps into the harbour,' was no longer in operation.[8] After the devastation of the 1640s, Ireland's economy recovered quickly as new owners began to develop trade and commerce. In 1657 a petition to have the beacon restored stated:

> There is a tower called the tower of Hook, standing upon the mouth of the river of Waterford, on a cape of land running into the sea, which had formerly been maintained

as a lighthouse, and used to be white limed for a land mark by day, and to have a great fire kept on the top thereof for a mark by night. For want of maintenance of which, several ship wrecks have lately been

on these coasts, to the discouragement of merchants, seamen and others.[9]

In spite of this and other petitions, nothing was done until 1671, when Robert Readinge was granted £500 a year to build and repair six light-

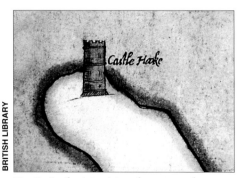

Fig. 8 In the late sixteenth century, the tower was included in a list of castles in county Wexford. On this early seventeenth-century map of Waterford Harbour, it is shown with battlements and is described as Castle Hooke.

Hook Tower at the Entrance of Waterford.

Fig. 9 This detail from an aerial perspective of the Hook c. 1685 shows the tower complete with battlements. The annex at the base, which has been partly removed, may have been a chapel. The first glass lantern, erected in the 1670s, is clearly visible. The domestic buildings and hay stack indicate that the keepers were also engaged in farming activities on the adjacent 'tower lands.'

COMMISSIONERS OF IRISH LIGHTS

Fig. 10   Three Waterford schooners off the Hook Light (on right) in the early nineteenth century.

houses, one of these being the Tower of Hook.[10] Readinge erected the first glass lantern on the tower to protect the coal-burning beacon from the elements. A 1684 report referred to the Tower of Hook as being 'made use of now as a lighthouse' to direct ships into the harbour.[11] The significance of the newly installed light was acknowledged by the mayor and corporation of New Ross in 1687, who claimed their authority over the tower by travelling to the point of Hook, where they shot an arrow into the sea and 'went up to the new lamp on top of the tower.' In order to establish title to the tower, the corporation decided that 'money be raised of the revenue to pay for getting the clause in the charter about the tower of Hooke.'[12] In 1704, the responsibility for Irish lighthouses was given to the Revenue Commissioners; further work was carried out at that time, as a *Report on the state of Irish Lighthouses* in the same year contained an estimate for repairs and the following detailed description of the tower and the lantern erected by Readinge:

> For the repair and alteration of the lanthorn at Hook Light-house, lyme for pointing and ruffcasting the outside of the tower, and other mason's work about the lanthorn and battlements, also 140 foott of glass for the lanthorn, iron for the great bricks for the breast of the lanthorn.[13]

In the late seventeenth century the ownership of the tower passed to Henry Loftus, who had acquired the lands of the Hook subsequent to Cromwell's campaign in Ireland. In 1706, he leased the tower to the authorities for twenty-one years at

CUSTOM-HOUSE, DUBLIN,
16th August, 1791.
TO ALL MARINERS.
Light-house of Hook Tower,
at the entrance of
THE HARBOUR OF
WATERFORD.

For the greater advantage and security of vessels trading to and from the ports of Waterford, Ross, etc. a new lantern has been erected on the Tower of Hook which is to be lighted with oil lamps, reflectors and lenses, instead of coals.

The Commissioners of His Majesty's Revenue have ordered the said lantern to be lighted on the night of the 29th of September next, and so to continue thereafter, from sun-set to sun-rise throughout the year.

This light will be much larger and more brilliant, and therefore seen at a greater distance than the present; it will be steady, always appearing the same in storm and in calm, and not flash and disappear as that of fire when stirred or affected by the wind.

WEXFORD COUNTY LIBRARY

Fig. 11   In Grose's *Antiquities* (1791), the tower is shown with depleted battlements, still with a lantern similar to the one shown in 1685. In 1791, the installation of a lamp burning whale oil provided a more reliable light and represented a major technological improvement.

Anglo Norman Tower. Hook point.
now the present lighthouse.

R.I.A.

Fig. 12   A watercolour of the tower by Du Noyer (c. 1850) shows the lantern that had been installed at the beginning of the nineteenth century. At that time the tower was still 'white-limed as a landmark,' as it had traditionally been for centuries. The distinctive bands were probably added in the 1860s, when major improvements were carried out. Initially, there were three red bands but in the early twentieth century they were replaced by two black bands. The unique colour coding, combined with an individual three-second flash, makes the tower easily identifiable from the sea.

£11 a year. The lease included 'a place where the stock of coal is kept and also a convenient passage for carrying up coals at all times to supply the said lighthouse'; in other words, the ground floor was used for storing coal and the mural stairway for carrying coal to the lantern. The

JIMMY CULLEN

Fig. 13   A 1794 chart by Laurie and Whittle of Fleet Street shows the Tower of Hook with its plume of smoke still rising from a coal fire, although an oil lamp had been installed in 1791. Other coastal features include Doornogue Point, the Race, Conigear, Nurd Point and Slade Pier.

first and second floors of the tower were not included in the lease, being rented to another individual. In 1728, Nicholas Loftus threatened to close the lighthouse in an attempt to have the rent increased to £200 per annum. He apparently carried out his threat, as he was subsequently known as 'the extinguisher'; his successful tactic secured him a rent of £120 a year. The outcome to his demand for an even higher rent in 1749 is not on record.[14] During the eighteenth century, Loftus continued to generate income by leasing the tower; in 1780 the massively built base of the building was used as a magazine, presumably by the military from Duncannon Fort.[15]

During the 1780s, the poor condition of the light led to repeated requests from mariners for the installation of a more efficient

system.[16] Following negotiations in 1791, between Loftus Tottenham and the New Ross authorities, the coal-fired light was finally abandoned and replaced by a whale-oil lantern, twelve feet in diameter with twelve lamps.[17] This change-over from coal, which had been used for five centuries, must have caused considerable excitement; in 1790, a lightkeeper proudly told a visiting journalist about the proposed new technology:

N.L.I.

Fig. 14   The Tower of Hook before the construction of the keepers' houses in the 1860s.

Fig. 15 The gasometers in the gas-yard are shown in this photograph taken in 1906. The fog gun was kept in the small building on the extreme right, known as the gun-house. The whitewashed stones along the edge of the road were typical of the traditional neatness associated with lighthouses.

My next visit was to the Tower of Hook, the lighthouse to Waterford Harbour, which is said to be one of the most useful lights in the kingdom. The man who attends it told me it was speedily to undergo an entire alteration, by erecting a new lantern, to be lighted with oil-lamps, reflectors etc. instead of coals, which it is now lighted with.[18]

Following the handing over of the tower to The Corporation for Preserving and Improving the Port of Dublin (Ballast Office) in 1810, £4,280 was expended on new apparatus. Early in the nineteenth century the lighthouse was described as follows:

> This is perhaps the oldest lighthouse in these kingdoms. The lower part is divided into three great vaults. The lower vault is a coal store and in it can be seen the beds used by the military when the tower was garrisoned in 1798. The second vault is occupied by the assistant keeper and the upper vault contained the principal's rooms which are now being altered for the gunner of the fog-gun.[19]

Further improvements were carried out in 1864 during which the

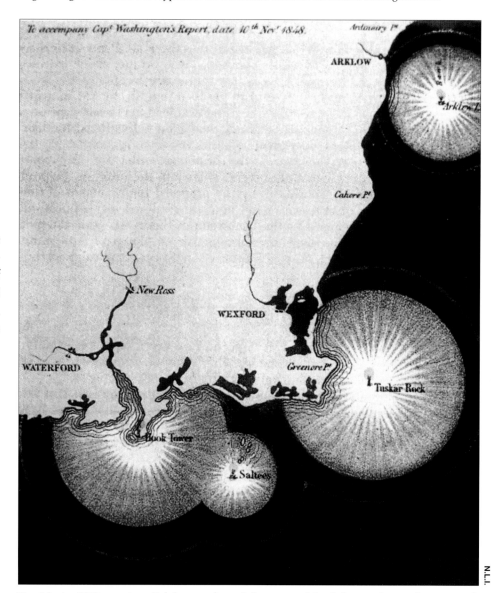

Fig. 16 An 1848 report on lighthouses showed the range of the lights on the treacherous south Wexford coast. A lightship had been installed at the Coningbeg Rock, south of the Saltees, in 1822; attempts to construct a lighthouse on the rock during the nineteenth century were abandoned. A report suggesting the building of two lighthouses on the Saltees was not implemented.

KAVANAGH COLLECTION; JIMMY FITZGIBBON

Fig. 17. This late nineteenth-century photograph shows the lantern that was installed in the 1860s. The distinctive bands, initially three in number and red in colour, were added at the same time. The keepers' houses presumably date from the same period. They are now used as a cafe and craft shop.

lantern was given its present shape. During the work a large bed of cinders was uncovered, the residue of the coal fires which had been used for centuries. In 1867 the body in charge of lighthouse services became known as the Commissioners of Irish Lights. The Commissioners, who are still responsible for the provision and maintenance of lighthouses and other aids to navigation for the island of Ireland, are funded from light dues charged on commercial shipping in Irish and British ports, supplemented by an annual contribution from the Irish government.

During the 1860s, three dwellings were built for the light-keepers and their families. New gas lights were installed in 1871, lit by gas manufactured in the enclosure still known as the gas-yard. Paraffin oil subsequently became the source of power and in 1911 a clockwork mechanism was installed to change the beacon from a fixed to a flashing light. The mechanism, which had to be wound up every twenty-five minutes, rotated a platform on which three huge lenses were mounted. Finally, in 1972 electricity became the power source and light-sensitive switches were installed to control the lantern. A fog signal is operated from the lighthouse as a warning to seafarers during the dense menacing fogs which can suddenly descend on the peninsula. The signal was essential in the days before radar and radio. At one time, a fog gun on the edge of the cliff was fired every ten minutes (the modern foghorn is

B. COLFER

Fig. 18. In 1911, a clockwork system was installed to change the beacon from a stationary to a flashing light. The mechanism had to be wound up by hand every twenty-five minutes.

B. COLFER

Fig. 19 The light is magnified by a system of lenses which rotates on a bed of mercury.

B. COLFER

Fig. 20 The Tower of Hook in the 1980s. Little change has taken place in the profile of the complex for more than a century. The building at the base of the tower on the right, added in the late 1970s, contains modern technology and served as an observation post before automation.

locally referred to as 'the gun'). This was replaced by a hooter, which in turn was replaced by detonators or rockets, exploded on metal arms extending from the top of the lighthouse. In 1972 a foghorn worked by compressed air was installed and during foggy weather its melancholy sound reverberates over land and sea.

In March 1996, the Hook lighthouse was converted to automatic operation and the last of the light-keepers who had climbed the stairs and tended the light for almost eight hundred years was permanently withdrawn from the station. The lighthouse is now remotely controlled and monitored from the control centre at the Lighthouse Depot in Dún Laoghaire.

The Tower of Hook, one of the oldest operational lighthouses in the world, has an intrinsic attraction as a distinctive landmark and as a unique example of intact medieval architecture. Following automation, on the initiative of the Commissioners of Irish Lights and Wexford County Council, a trust known as Hook Heritage was set up to make the medieval tower accessible to the public. Following a comprehensive archaeological and architectural survey of the tower and the conversion of the keepers' houses to a visitors' centre, the complex was opened in 2000 by Mary McAleese, President of Ireland and receives up to sixty thousand visitors each year.

CONFLICT AND CONFISCATION: THE SEVENTEENTH-CENTURY LANDSCAPE

In 1595, Gaelic Ireland, led by Sir Phelim O'Neill of Ulster, rose in rebellion, appealing to Catholic Spain for assistance. Led in Leinster by Fiach Mac Aodh Ó Broin, the Irish enjoyed considerable success and in 1601, 4,000 Spanish, led by Don Juan del Aquila, landed at Kinsale in county Cork. The Spanish were surrounded by an English army and, when O'Neill marched south to join them, he was comprehensively defeated; the Spanish surrendered and returned home. The battle of Kinsale completed the Tudor conquest and is regarded as marking the end of Gaelic Ireland. The crucial events during the following century of political and social upheaval impacted directly on the Hook. In the early seventeenth century a policy of plantation was revived to attract colonists and settlers from Britain as the population of Ireland, as low as 750,000 in 1600, was reduced even further by an incipient emigration to continental Europe and America. Apart from the planned plantations, individual landlords promoted a movement of British tenants and artisans to Irish estates. Hopes for a relaxion of anti-Catholic legislation on the accession of James I in 1603 were not realised and political tensions in Ireland increased. The Catholics were mostly of old stock, either Gaelic or Anglo-Irish. To distinguish themselves from the native Irish and the newly arrived Protestant English, and in order to show their loyalty to the crown, the Anglo-Irish increasingly called themselves Old English, even though by that time they had assimilated much of Gaelic culture. Following the accession of Charles I to the throne in 1625, the political situation in England deteriorated rapidly and the king offered concessions, known as 'graces,' to Irish Catholics in return for £40,000. The resentment generated by the failure to implement the promised reforms further alienated the Catholic community.[1] The failure of the Confederate rebellion of the 1640s copperfastened the control of the New English and provided a secure space for the developing estate system.

Fig. 1   As the principal stronghold of the parliamentary forces in county Wexford, Duncannon Fort was the focus of considerable activity during the Confederate War of the 1640s. The fort fell to the Confederates in 1645 and was held by them until 1650, when it was taken by the Cromwellian forces.

Fig. 2 Ballyhack Castle, c. 1850, by G. Du Noyer. At the outbreak of rebellion, the castle was occupied by Confederate forces. After the bombarding of the castle by Parliamentarian ships, a raiding party was sent ashore to burn the village. The castle was occupied by the Cromwellians in 1650.

THE REBELLION OF 1641

Against a background of political, economic and religious friction in Britain and Ireland, the native Irish and Old English, forced into an uneasy alliance, contemplated armed rebellion. During the middle decades of the seventeenth century, political upheaval was widespread across Europe, where the Thirty Years War was raging. The situation was made more complex by the eruption of Civil War in England between king and parliament in August 1642, with the Scots entering the war on the side of parliament. In Ireland, the rising had started in Ulster in October 1641, the insurgents claiming not to be rebels but supporters of the king. Atrocities were committed by both sides, but those inflicted on Protestant settlers, particularly in Ulster, were deliberately exaggerated to create a massacre myth for propaganda purposes.[2] In 1642, a meeting of the Confederate Catholics at Kilkenny established an executive supreme council as well as a legislative general assembly.

The rebellion spread quickly to county Wexford, where 2,300 men were mustered and Wexford town became one of the principal ports of the Confederation.[3] The next ten

Fig. 3 Fethard (ffether) Castle on a 1591 map of the Hook region. The castle was used by the Confederates as a headquarters during the 1640s.

Fig. 14 Sixteen soldiers from Duncannon Fort were killed in a skirmish with Confederate forces near the Whitty castle of Dungulph. This nineteenth-century drawing shows the castle with a thatched roof.

years brought the most dramatic period of conflict and social upheaval in the history of the Hook. Duncannon Fort, controlling access to the ports of Waterford and New Ross, and the only government stronghold in the county, was soon targeted by the Confederate forces, led by William Browne of Mulrankin and Thomas Rossiter of Rathmacknee.[4] The governor, Lord Esmonde, initially had only one hundred men under his command, but, early in 1642, they were augmented by two hundred more from Bristol, commanded by Captains Thomas Ashton and Anthony Weldon. A ship arrived from Youghal with badly needed supplies, as the fort, a haven for Protestant

Fig. 5 During the 1640s, Dunkirk frigates, like this one, were issued letters of marque by the Confederates allowing them to attack English shpping. From their base in Wexford, and to a lesser extent Waterford, the privateers roamed the seas, inflicting considerable damage on English shipping and trade.

refugees, suffered from recurring food shortages. The beleaguered fort was not under continuous siege and during the next few years there were sporadic confrontations and skirmishes with the 1,300-strong Confederate force in the area. Military depredations, combined with constant raids by both sides to procure provisions, devastated the surrounding countryside for almost a decade. The general state of confusion and fear facilitated indiscriminate looting. For example, Michael Laffan of the Hook was later accused of being part of a group stealing cows in county Waterford and bringing them across on the ferry from Passage to Ballyhack as well as removing goods and corn from Kilcloggan.

The seizure of hostile Protestant estates was among the initial Confederate objectives. Fethard Castle (whose owner, Nicholas Loftus, had fled to England) was taken by

Fig. 6 (A) Seal of the Catholic Confederation of Kilkenny combining the symbols of harp and crown. (B) Part of a Confederate flag.

a group of rebels led by Dermot McDowlin Kavanagh and held by a garrison commanded by Captain James Downes of Adamstown. Among the Confederates involved were local men Thomas Redmond and James Sutton. Fethard was subsequently used by the Confederates as a rendezvous and recruiting centre. The Confederates established their headquarters at Shielbaggan, on the Dunbrody estate, with another camp at nearby Burkestown. Ballyhack Castle, another Confederate strongpoint just up-river from the fort, was pounded by cannon fire from a parliament ship in the river and the village was burned by a raiding party. In early 1642, a detachment of soldiers from Duncannon captured twenty-three Confederate troops in Ramsgrange Castle: the castle and village were burned and eighteen of the prisoners were hanged. Shortly afterwards, another company of soldiers from the fort attacked the Whitty castle at Dungulph and sixteen of them were killed by a group led by Captain Thomas Rossiter. Tintern Abbey, the fortified Colclough residence (referred to as Tintern Castle) garrisoned by thirty soldiers from Duncannon Fort under the command of Major Edward Ashton, was used as a

DÚCHAS

Fig. 7 Following the outbreak of hostilities, Tintern Abbey was used as a place of refuge by local Protestants. It was attacked by the Confederates and after a siege lasting a fortnight was forced to surrender. This photograph shows the abbey as it was c. 1950, in the final days of Colclough occupation.

refuge by two hundred local Protestants. In the summer of 1642, Tintern was attacked by a group of Confederates led by Colonel John Devereux and, after a siege lasting a fortnight, was obliged to surrender.[5] Ashton, with others, was sent to Munster by ship from Fethard. The Colclough owners of Tintern had previously fled to England. Their Catholic relations, Dudley, John and Anthony Colclough, from the Duffry branch of the family, participated in the attack on Tintern and seized possession of the castle and estate. Among those later accused of taking part in the attack were prominent local men James Lewis of Graigue, Walter Whitty of Dungulph, Hugh Rochford of Taylorstown, Richard Sutton of Clonmines and William Sutton of Ballykeerogemore. Skirmishes also took place at Kilbride and Shielbaggan, and at Battlestown where the castle was burned. A contingent from Duncannon Fort went by sea to burn Dunmore on the Waterford side of the harbour because it was being used by the Confederates to land supplies. Like their Colclough neighbours, the

Etchinghams presumably fled from Dunbrody at the outbreak of the rebellion. Later claims for compensation made by the family indicate that their estate, on which Duncannon Fort was located, suffered extensively.

The bloodiest skirmish took place in July 1642, when Captain Ashton brought ninety men by sea to attack Redmond Hall on the Hook Peninsula. The hall was clearly visible from the fort and its owner Alexander Redmond was a known Confederate. The attacking party landed near the hall but many of the soldiers immediately scattered throughout the district to pillage for provisions. The rest brought two cannon ashore from the ship and proceeded to batter the hall, but the Redmonds, with only nine supporters, put up a stiff resistance. When the weather deteriorated, the ships' captains wanted to withdraw, but Ashton refused, as his men were still dispersed around the peninsula. This delay proved fatal, as a heavy fog descended which rendered the muskets of the soldiers unfit for use. The gunfire had been heard by a party of two hundred Confederates, led by Captains Rossiter and Roche, and the fog allowed them to approach the hall unseen by the attackers. Only thirty of the soldiers escaped, seventeen were taken prisoner and the rest, including Captain Ashton, were either killed or drowned while trying to escape. The prisoners were later hanged, some at Ballyhack, probably in retaliation for the execution of the Confederates captured at Ramsgrange, while Ashton's head was taken to Wexford and displayed as a trophy.

During the next two years, there were fewer direct clashes between the two sides. Lord Esmonde made repeated appeals to the authorities for food and supplies; there was so much distress in the fort that the garrison was constantly on the verge of mutiny and some actually absconded to Waterford and Wexford. The condition of the fort also caused concern and, in 1643, parliament sent money for essential repairs. Political divisions festered within the garrison and the strongly Royalist Esmonde removed some officers because of their pro-parliament sympathies. In 1644, everyone in the fort, except the governor, declared for parliament, resulting in a dramatic improvement in the flow of supplies and personnel. Ironically, this ultimately led to the fort's undoing, as the damage which improved conditions allowed the soldiers to inflict on the surrounding district forced the Confederates to take decisive action. On 20 January 1645, General Thomas Preston arrived in front of the fort with a force of 1,200 infantry and eighty cavalry. Cannon were positioned on the high ground to bombard the fort and extensive siege works were constructed. The Confederate guns damaged Parliamentarian ships in the harbour and the flag-ship, named the *Great Lewis,* foundered, reducing the chances of supplies being delivered by sea. Following fierce exchanges during the next two months, the fort was forced to capitulate on 20 March, just before a number of ships arrived in the harbour with much-needed supplies. Twenty-seven soldiers had been killed in the fort during the siege. The garrison was allowed to leave for various destinations; Lord Esmonde died at Adamstown on his way home to Limerick, near Gorey.

Fig. 8 An imagined reconstruction by an unknown artist of the attack on Redmond Hall from Hore's *History of Wexford.* In the foreground, the soldiers laying siege to the hall are in turn coming under attack from a Confederate force which came to support the Redmonds, alerted by the sound of gunfire. The Redmonds remained in the hall but surrendered to Cromwellian forces in 1649. The hall with its lands were subsequently confiscated.

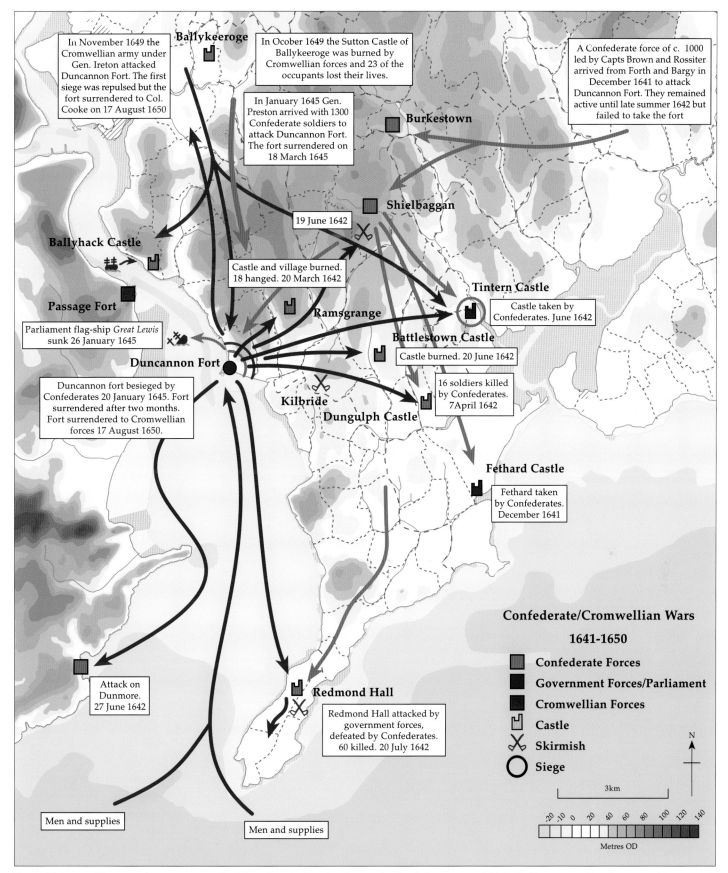

In November 1649 the Cromwellian army under Gen. Ireton attacked Duncannon Fort. The first siege was repulsed but the fort surrendered to Col. Cooke on 17 August 1650

In Ocober 1649 the Sutton Castle of Ballykeeroge was burned by Cromwellian forces and 23 of the occupants lost their lives.

In January 1645 Gen. Preston arrived with 1300 Confederate soldiers to attack Duncannon Fort. The fort surrendered on 18 March 1645

A Confederate force of c. 1000 led by Capts Brown and Rossiter arrived from Forth and Bargy in December 1641 to attack Duncannon Fort. They remained active until late summer 1642 but failed to take the fort

Ballykeeroge

Burkestown

Shielbaggan

19 June 1642

Ballyhack Castle

Castle and village burned. 18 hanged. 20 March 1642

Passage Fort

Parliament flag-ship *Great Lewis* sunk 26 January 1645

Ramsgrange

Tintern Castle

Castle taken by Confederates. June 1642

Battlestown Castle

Castle burned. 20 June 1642

Duncannon Fort

Duncannon fort besieged by Confederates 20 January 1645. Fort surrendered after two months. Fort surrendered to Cromwellian forces 17 August 1650.

Kilbride

Dungulph Castle

16 soldiers killed by Confederates. 7 April 1642

Fethard Castle

Fethard taken by Confederates. December 1641

Confederate/Cromwellian Wars

1641-1650

▨ **Confederate Forces**

■ **Government Forces/Parliament**

▦ **Cromwellian Forces**

⌂ **Castle**

✗ **Skirmish**

○ **Siege**

N

3km

-20 -10 0 20 40 60 80 100 120 140

Metres OD

Attack on Dunmore. 27 June 1642

Redmond Hall

Redmond Hall attacked by government forces, defeated by Confederates. 60 killed. 20 July 1642

Men and supplies

Men and supplies

Fig. 9 This map illustrates the movement of soldiers from both sides during the Confederate war of 1641–50. Duncannon Fort, because of its strategic location on Waterford Harbour, was the hub of all military activity in the area. The tower houses of an earlier era also assumed a strategic importance, perhaps for the last time. Local Catholic landowners who were involved with the Confederates subsequently lost their lands.

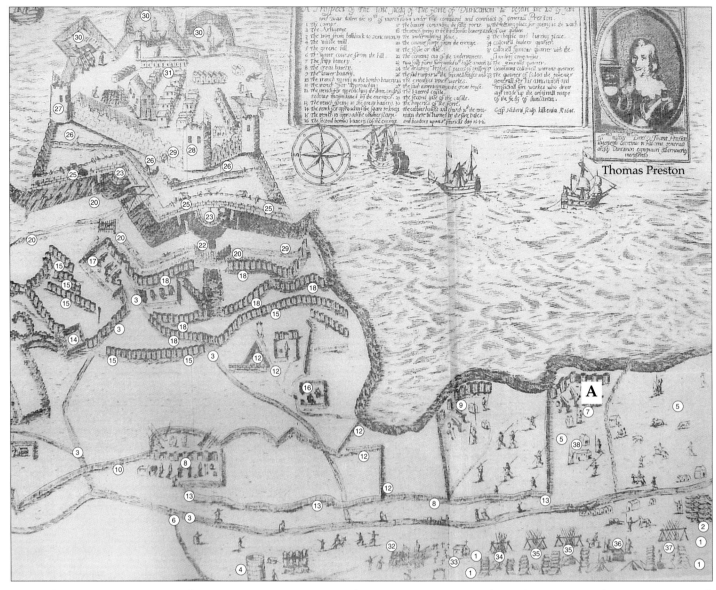

Thomas Preston

Fig. 10 The most significant record of the 1645 siege of Duncannon Fort is this unique pictorial map (north at right) drawn by Nicholas La Loue, a French 'ingenier' working for the Confederates. The map conveys an impression of the complexity of the siegeworks, bearing in mind that it shows several phases occuring simultaneously. The map shows the small fleet of parliamentary shipping that supplied the fort. A shipwreck, found recently on the edge of the deep channel about 1.5 kilometres south of Duncannon and currently under investigation by Dúchas, may be the parliament flagship, the *Great Lewis*, which was sunk during the siege by Confederate cannon located at (A) for the purpose of bombarding the ships supporting the fort.

1. The camp
2. The artillery
3. The way from Ballyhack to Duncannon
4. The windmill
5. The green hill
6. The water course from the hill
7. The ship battery
8. The great battery
9. The lower battery
10. The trench going to the bomb battery
11. The trench for approaching
12. The trench for approaching the three angle redoubts maintained by the enemy
13. The trench going to the great battery
14. The trench for approaching the square redoubt
15. The trench to approach the counter scarp
16. The second bomb battery (of the enemy)
17. The battery commanding the sally ports
18. The trench going to the third bomb battery
19. The undermining place
20. The counter scarp from the enemy
21. The fosse or dyke
22. The coming out of the underminers
23. The sally ports surrounded with half a moon
24. The drawing bridge
25. The said rampart with the sentinel houses and pieces of artillery
26. The enemy's inner works
27. The south turret joining (?) to the great house
28. The battered castle
29. The second gate of the castle
30. The batteries of the fort
31. The cabins, houses and church with the ammunition therein burned by the fire bales and bombs upon St Patrick's Day 1644
32. The meeting place for going to the watch
33. The chapel and burying place
34. Colonel Butler's quarter
35. Colonel Sinnott's quarter
36. The general's quarter
37. Lieutenant Colonel Warren's quarter
38. The quarter of La Loo the engineer general for his ammunition and artificial fire works who drew and made up the original map of the siege of Duncannon

Fig. 11 In 1646, the Papal Delegate, Archbishop Giovanni Rinuccini, visited Duncannon Fort to show his support for the Confederate garrison.

Fig. 12 Oliver Cromwell paid a brief visit to Duncannon before the surrender of the fort to his troops in 1650.

The Confederates, commanded by Captain Thomas Roche, occupied the fort. In 1646, the significance of the fort to the Confederate cause was demonstrated by the arrival of the Papal Delegate, Archbishop Rinuccini, to show his support and to encourage the garrison. The revenues from the Etchingham, Colclough and Loftus lands were requisitioned for the support of the fort for the next four years.

Following the parliament's victory in England, Oliver Cromwell arrived in Ireland in August 1649 to deal with the Confederate challenge. Fear escalated following his

dramatically ruthless massacres at Drogheda and Wexford. The garrison at Duncannon was an obvious Cromwellian target and, in an effort to strengthen it, Colonel Edward Wogan was put in joint command with Roche. Confederate fears were justified. After the fall of

Men from the Hook region involved with the Confederates in the 1641 rebellion

Francis Wise, Clonsharragh	Francis Redmond, Fethard
Stephen Devereux, Drillistown	Richard Sutton, Clonmines
James Duffe, Stonehouse	Alexander Redmond, the Hall
Walter Whitty, Dungulph	Jasper Prendergast, Gurchins
Michael Laffan, Alriske	Martin FitzHarris, Kinnagh
James Lewis, Graigue	Adam Whitty, Dungulph
Philip Lewis, Graigue	John Lewis, Lambstown
James Rochford, Taylorstown	Arthur Itchingham, Dunbrody
William FitzJames, St Leonards	Charles Itchingham, Ballyvelig
Marcus Stafford, Rathnageeragh	Edward Walsh, Coole
Matthew Devereux, Coolroe	Edward Sutton, Tinnock
Nicholas Meyler, Shielbaggan	William Devereux, Haggard
John Laffan, Fethard	James Devereux, Haggard
James Laffan, Fethard	Walter Devereux, Ballyhack

Fig. 13 A recently discovered seventeenth-century shipwreck on the edge of the deep channel just south of Duncannon is currently being examined by the Underwater Archaeology Unit. It may prove to be the remains of the *Great Lewis*, sunk by the Confederates in 1645. The picture shows one of six cannon discovered during the survey of the wreck.

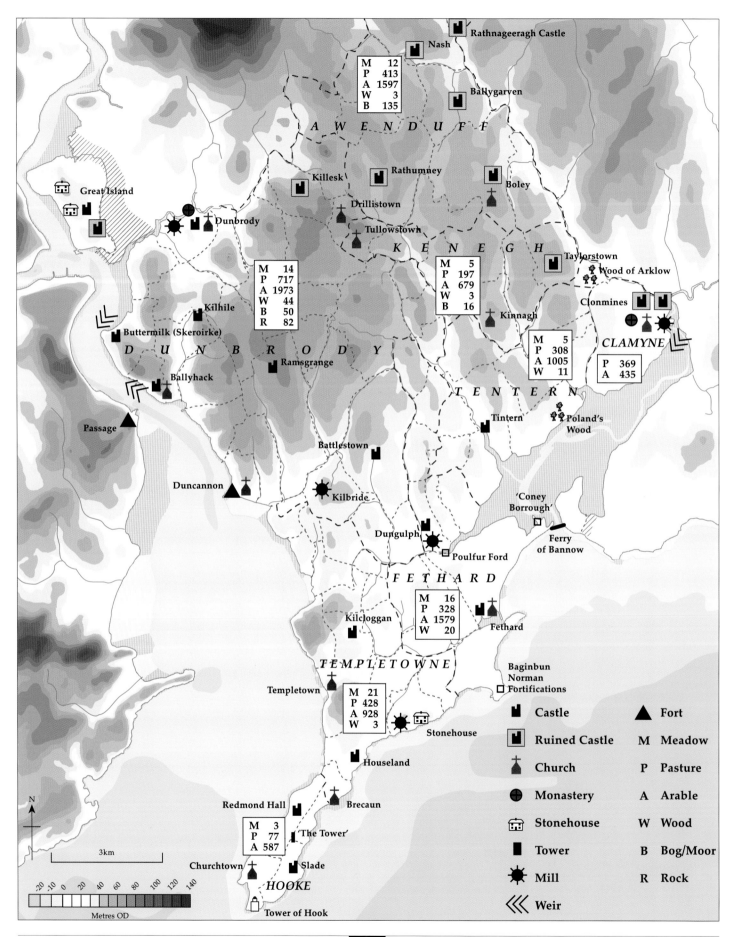

Rathnageeragh Castle

Nash

M	12
P	413
A	1597
W	3
B	135

Ballygarven

A W E N D U F F

Killesk

Rathumney

Boley

Drillistown

Great Island

Tullowstown

Dunbrody

K E N E G H

Taylorstown

Wood of Arklow

M	14
P	717
A	1973
W	44
B	50
R	82

M	5
P	197
A	679
W	3
B	16

Clonmines

CLAMYNE

Kilhile

Buttermilk (Skeroirke)

D U N B R O D Y

Ramsgrange

Kinnagh

M	5
P	308
A	1005
W	11

Ballyhack

T E N T E R N

P	369
A	435

Passage

Tintern

Poland's Wood

Battlestown

Duncannon

'Coney Borrough'

Kilbride

Ferry of Bannow

Dungulph

Poulfur Ford

F E T H A R D

Kilcloggan

M	16
P	328
A	1579
W	20

Fethard

T E M P L E T O W N E

Baginbun Norman Fortifications

Templetown

M	21
P	428
A	928
W	3

Stonehouse

Houseland

Redmond Hall

Brecaun

M	3
P	77
A	587

'The Tower'

Churchtown

Slade

HOOKE

Tower of Hook

N

3km

-20 -10 0 20 40 60 80 100 120 140

Metres OD

	Castle			Fort
	Ruined Castle		M	Meadow
	Church		P	Pasture
	Monastery		A	Arable
	Stonehouse		W	Wood
	Tower		B	Bog/Moor
	Mill		R	Rock
	Weir			

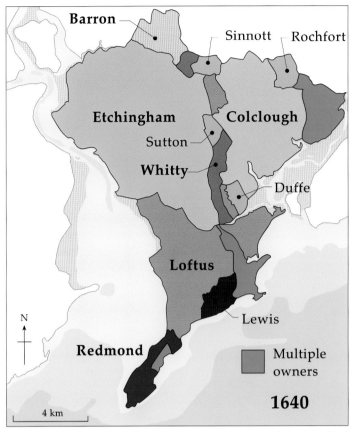

Fig. 15 Land-holding in the Hook in 1640. Seventeenth-century land divisions were based on Anglo-Norman land grants. In the Hook, some grants had been held by the same family for four centuries.

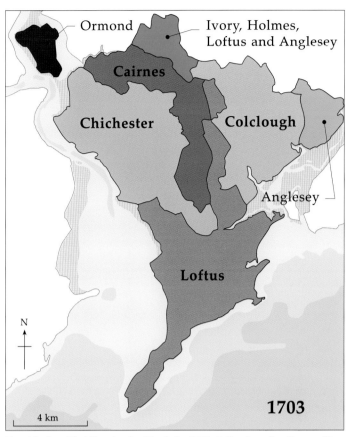

Fig. 16 Land-holding in the Hook in 1703. Following the Cromwellian confiscations, the smaller holdings in the south of the region (the parishes of Hook, Templetown and Fethard) had been swallowed by the Loftus estate.

Ross, the fort was besieged by 2,000 troops accompanied briefly by Cromwell himself and initially under the command of General Michael Jones. The Cromwellian forces occupied Tintern Abbey and other small castles in the vicinity and controlled the river from Ballyhack Castle and the fort at Passage. The besieging army, now led by General Ireton, was attacked by the Confederates and retreated. Ballyhack Castle was re-taken and Wogan was taken prisoner during an attack on the fort at Passage, although he managed to escape and return to Duncannon. At this stage, following the arrival of reinforcements, there were 640 Confederates in the fort and provisions were constantly a problem. In 1650, the overcrowded and insanitary conditions led to an outbreak of plague in the fort; many deaths followed, including that of Captain Roche. Later the same year, the Cromwellians attacked again and, as Waterford had already been taken, the fort was surrendered by Colonel Wogan on 17 August 1650.

The importance placed by both sides on the control of Duncannon Fort during the period of the war, when it had been held for five years by the Confederates, emphasised

its strategic significance as the key to the ports of Waterford and New Ross. As the fort had been constructed to combat a naval threat, it was ironic that the only period of military activity in its history was land-based. After the war, Duncannon was reserved for the defence and protection of the kingdom. The *Civil Survey* of the mid-1650s described it as 'the famous and impregnable fort of Duncannon commanding and securing the harbour as one of the master keys of this land.'[6]

SEVENTEENTH-CENTURY SURVEYS

The aftermath of the Confederate rebellion revolutionised subsequent political and social development. The Cromwellians who had helped parliament to defeat the Confederates, either as investors (known as 'adventurers') or soldiers, were to be paid in land. In 1652, the Act of Settlement decreed that all landowners who had fought as Confederates were to lose their estates and receive lands in Connacht in exchange. Ballyhack was used as a disembarkation point for transplantees and the phrase 'to go to Ballyhack' assumed ominous connotations. Two

Fig. 14 Landscape features in the Hook mentioned in the *Civil Survey* of 1654–56. The settlement elements, principally churches and tower houses, some already in ruins, belonged to an earlier era and most of them would soon be abandoned in the changing social, economic and religious climate which followed the Cromwellian confiscations. Tintern Abbey, Redmond Hall and Fethard Castle continued to be used as residences until the twentieth century.

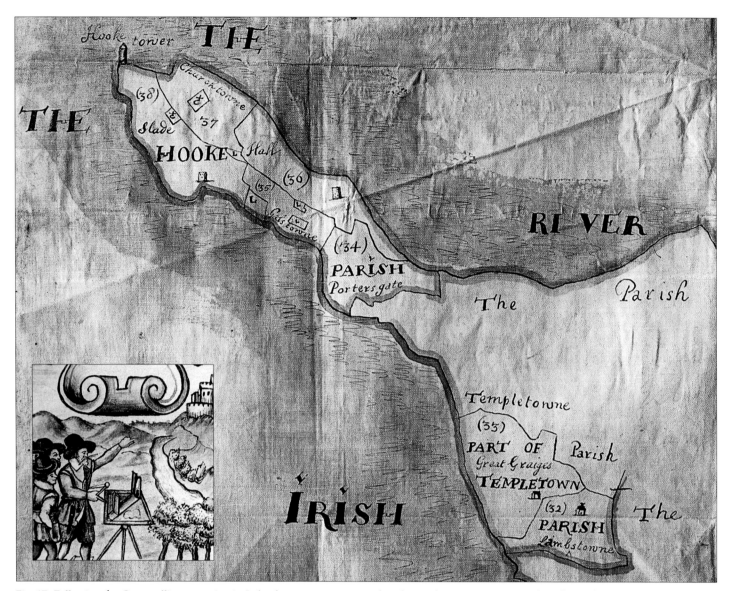

Fig. 17 Following the Cromwellian campaign in Ireland, surveyors were employed to make accurate surveys of confiscated estates (inset). A certified copy of the *Down Survey* map for the Hook earmarks the lands that would be confiscated. These were added to the aggressively expanding Loftus estate.

surveys were carried out to facilitate the confiscation of land: the *Civil Survey* (1654–56) established land ownership and value in 1640, while the *Down Survey* of 1654 mapped the lands that were to be forfeited.[7] Details of the many changes in land ownership during the second half of the seventeenth century were later recorded in the *Books of Survey and Distribution*. Nearly half of Ireland was confiscated by the English parliament and transferred from Catholic to Protestant ownership; Catholic owners were to vacate their estates and migrate across the Shannon. The possibility of removing all Catholics to the west was considered, but in practice only landowners were transplanted, as the new owners petitioned that labourers and tradesmen should be allowed to remain to work on the land. Many soldiers and adventurers who received grants of land made a quick profit by selling

them on; others married Irish women and their children were raised as Catholics. As much of south-west Wexford was already held by Protestant landlords prior to 1641, the confiscation of land in the Hook, following the Act of Settlement, was confined to a small number of Catholic landowners who had been active with the Confederates.[8] The confiscated lands, mostly located in the parishes of Fethard, Templetown and Hook, were acquired by the Loftus family, whose estate already extended over most of the three parishes.

As well as providing details about land ownership, the *Civil Survey* and, to a lesser extent, the *Down Survey* contain information on man-made landscape features. Some of these, in particular castles and churches, are survivals of settlement activity during the previous centuries. The formerly important centres of Clonmines and Great Island are indicated by a number of relict features. Almost all of the castles which are described as being in ruins are located along the line of the Owenduff river, perhaps indicating a building date in the first half of the fifteenth century and early abandonment, as, at the dissolution of Tintern Abbey in 1541, this district was described as 'waste because of the Irish wars.' Some economic features are also mentioned, particularly mills, weirs, the ferry at the entrance to Bannow Bay and the coney (rabbit) burrow of Fethard (still referred to as 'The Burrow'). The only historical reference was to the promontory of Baginbun, 'where the English first landed' and where 'part of the fortifications built by them' still survived.

The 'Census' of 1659

The 'census' of 1659 (an abstract of the poll-tax returns for 1660) provides a partial listing of adults over fifteen years of age. Single adult females and most single adult males who were not servants or otherwise gainfully employed were excluded and a multiplier of 2.5 has been proposed to estimate the overall population. Although the 'census' has limitations, it provides an insight into the complex society of seventeenth-century Ireland. The 'census' grouped townlands into units referred to as 'quarters.' In the Hook region, the quarters equated to the three large estates of Dunbrody, Tintern and Loftus Hall (Hook). Townland populations, divided into English and Irish, are given for each barony and the principal surnames and their numbers are also listed. The categories have religious and political implications, as in this context 'English' refers

to recently arrived Protestants and 'Irish' includes Old English Catholics.[9] The information contained in the 'census' allows some tentative comments on the mid-seventeenth-century population in the region. Hook quarter, with an estimated population of 998, had the lowest number of people, with an estimated 1,285 in Tintern and 1,370 in Dunbrody. However, the highest number of English were recorded on the Loftus estate, where 25 (6%) out of 399 were placed in this category. This

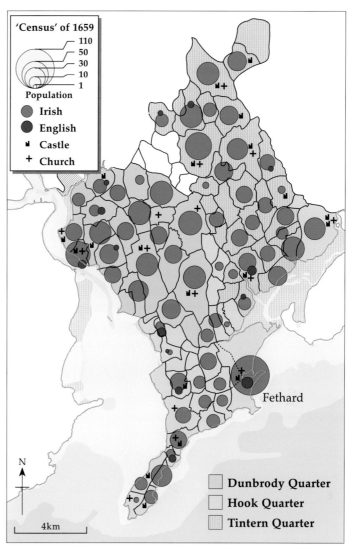

Fig. 18 The 'census' of 1659 shows that Fethard on the Loftus estate, with its hinterland, was the principal centre of population in the region, reflecting its status as a medieval town. The rest of the Loftus estate was thinly populated, especially the less fertile lands to the north. It is noticeable that the heaviest concentrations on the Tintern estate were on the former Cistercian granges to the north, principally Rathumney, Dunmain, Nash and Boley. Similarly, on the Dunbrody lands, population was greatest on the grange sites of Ballyhack, Shielbaggan, Boderan, Coole, Ramsgrange and Battlestown. It is likely that a nucleated settlement clustered around the tower house or church, and sometimes both, existed at most of these grange sites. In general, newly arrived English settlers tended to remain close to estate cores. This may have been for security reasons or the lack of land on the more heavily populated periphery. Perhaps for convenience, Clonmines was included with the Hook.

Principal names recorded in the 'census' of 1659 for the barony of Shelburne (and their numbers)			
Old English			
Walsh	(27)	Browne	(10)
Sutton	(25)	Colfer	(9)
Power	(25)	FitzJames	(9)
Roche	(18)	Synnott	(8)
Cullen	(14)	Chapman	(8)
Keating	(13)	Furlong	(8)
Forrestal	(12)	Redmond	(7)
Kent	(11)	Barron	(5)
Devereux	(11)		
Native Irish			
Murphy	(33)	Bane	(9)
Doyle	(19)	Kavanagh	(9)
Kelly	(16)	Bryan	(8)
McEdmund	(14)	Loughlan	(8)
Brannagh	(13)	McTeige	(8)
Whelan	(12)	Laoye [?Leary]	(7)
O Boe	(10)	McDonnagh	(7)
McShane	(10)	McRichard	(7)
Byrne	(9)	Ogan	(7)

Fig. 19 Duncannon Fort by Thomas Phillips in 1685. As no pier had been constructed, boats used the sheltered landing beach to the north of the fort. The large fishing weir under the fort, which probably originated in the Cistercian period, was presumably used to supply the garrison with fish.

compared with fifteen (3%) out of 531 at Tintern and thirteen (2%) out of 548 at Dunbrody.

The 'census' indicates a total estimated population of c. 998 for the combined parishes of Templetown, Hook and Fethard, with 298 of these concentrated in and around the town of Fethard. Of these, an estimated fifty-eight were English Protestants, an indication that the post-Cromwellian influx had not yet impacted to any great extent. Protestant newcomers were concentrated to the north of the manor of Kilcloggan, owned by the Loftuses since the late sixteenth century, and in Fethard, occupied by them since 1634. No Protestants were recorded in the townland of Hall, indicating that Henry Loftus had not yet occupied Redmond Hall as his residence. Speculative comments can be made about the settlement structure of some townlands. The relatively high estimated populations in Kilcloggan (65), Houseland (53), Dungulph (35) and Slade (32) could be attributed to the presence of nucleated settlements associated with the tower houses in those townlands. At Templetown (45) aerial photography indicates the former existence of a hamlet adjacent to the medieval church. In 1837, there were still 50 people living in the now deserted village.[10] The high population of Galgystown (83) is particularly significant, as it can be attributed to the cluster of cabins shown there on a 1591 map of the peninsula. Similarly the estimated population of Connagh (50) can be linked to a farmhouse cluster in that townland. The unusually low number shown for Churchtown (2) may indicate that the farmhouse cluster which was later occupied by the labourers on the Loftus estate had not yet developed but it is more likely that the under-tenants and cottiers who occupied the townland were not recorded. The principal surnames listed for Shelburne show that the ethnicity of the barony was evenly shared between Irish and Old English. Of the named individuals, 218 shared Irish surnames, principally Murphy and Doyle, and 209 had Old English surnames, principally Walsh, Sutton and Power.

Fig. 20 A perspective from up-river by Thomas Phillips, 1685, shows Ballyhack on the left, the village of Passage with its Waterford merchants' substantial houses on the right, with Duncannon Fort in the background. The fort at Passage was well placed to control the shipping channel.

EUROPEAN INFLUENCES

At the end of the seventeenth century, the internal struggle that was taking place in England had a peripheral connection with the Hook. The conflict between James II and his adversary William of Orange was played out on Irish soil. In 1690, after the decisive Battle of the Boyne, the defeated James fled south and took ship from Duncannon. Shortly afterwards, the fort fell into Williamite hands and was also used by William as a port of departure. In the early eighteenth century, the political and religious conflict that was engulfing Europe again impacted briefly on the Hook, providing a local illustration of the international nature of Irish affairs in the early eighteenth century. On 3 May 1707, a French privateer landed eighty men to strip and plunder the town of Fethard. The ship, carrying six or eight guns with a crew of one hundred, mostly Irish and Scottish, anchored off-shore, probably at Baginbun, as the cliffs were described as 'very high.' Eighty well-armed men were sent ashore in the ship's boat to 'surprise' the inhabitants of Fethard. The French were aided by local Catholic Jacobite sympathisers. They were said to be guided by a local man named Thady Doyle, who showed the privateers which houses they should plunder. Members of the Protestant community were reportedly singled out for attack. The property of Captain Kent, the surveyor at Passage who lived in Fethard, was plundered and Mrs Kent was 'stripped to her smock.' Two cartloads of goods were taken from Captain Mildway, because it

was reported that he 'had been fighting King Philip at the last siege of Barcelona.' He lost everything except 'his plate and church plate,' which were saved by throwing them into a 'tub of wort' (unfermented beer). The French did no harm to the houses of the 'Romans' (Catholics) and said that they would not burn the town for their sake. A messenger was dispatched to Duncannon Fort seeking urgent assistance. An officer and forty men left the fort in an attempt to get between the French and their ship but they arrived ten minutes too late; the French, accompanied by some of the Irish (i.e. Catholics), were safely on board. An advance party of horsemen reached the cliffs in time to exchange fire with the enemy, but no damage was done on either side.[11]

The turbulent political and social events of the seventeenth century in Ireland had profound consequences for the subsequent development of society. The dramatic change was epitomised by the widespread transfer of land from Catholic to Protestant ownership. In 1610, most of the land was owned by 2,000 Catholic gentry; in 1641, 59 per cent of the land of Ireland was owned by Catholics; by 1660, this had collapsed to 22 per cent and by 1703 only 14 per cent of the land was in Catholic hands.[12] Although Ireland still had a majority Catholic population, the land and political institutions were now controlled by a Protestant minority. This led to the emergence of an Anglican ascendancy which would dominate Ireland for more than two centuries, resulting in the implementation of far-reaching societal and landscape changes.

BRITISH LIBRARY

Fig. 21 An aerial perspective of the Hook attributed to Thomas Phillips, 1685. The Tower of Hook is the centre of interest, but the peninsula and estuary are shown faintly in the background. The promontories of Duncannon and Baginbun can be seen in the distance and Loftus Hall and Slade Castle are also depicted. In the left foreground, a small fishing boat with its crew can be seen close to the rocks, near to a cove where, until recently, small fishing boats were kept during the summer season. The medieval lighthouse is shown complete with crenellations, with the lantern newly erected in the 1670s.

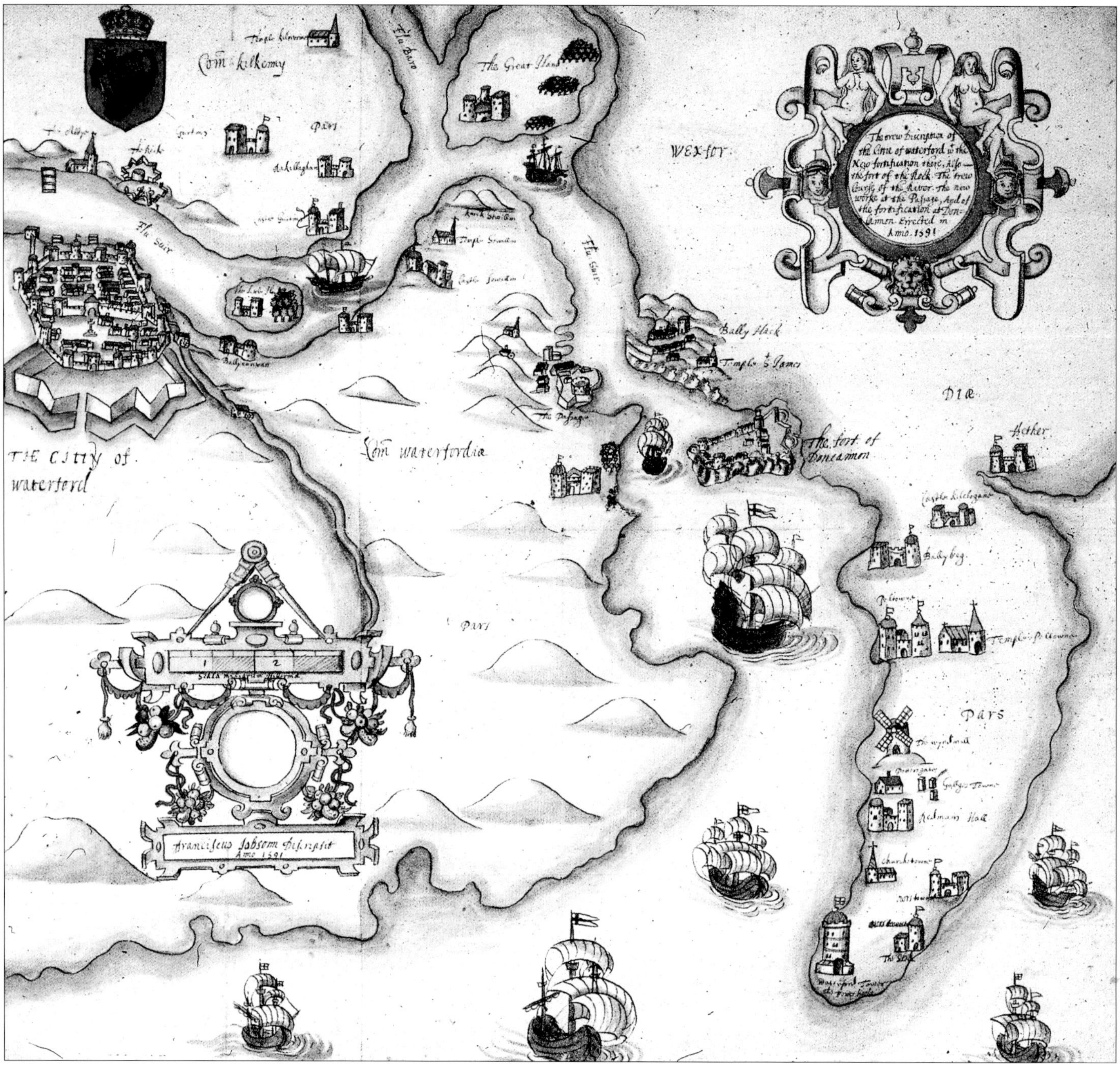

Fig. 1 A 1591 chart of Waterford Harbour prepared by Frances Jobson in the aftermath of the Spanish Armada. The purpose of the map was to show the defences at Duncannon, Passage and the city of Waterford. The depiction of Duncannon is speculative, as it is shown with a water-filled moat, which it never had. Prominent landscape features are shown, particularly on the flat promontory of Hook, as landmarks and navigational aids for shipping.

In post-Reformation Europe, political differences and alliances between states assumed a religious dimension. The Irish, by their refusal to adopt the new reformed religion, were propelled into mainstream European politics, where they naturally allied with Catholic France and Spain rather than with Protestant England. The prospect of Catholic Ireland being used as a 'back door' for invasion by England's continental enemies became a real possibility and forced a review of strategic thinking about the 'Irish problem.' As the best natural harbour in the south-east of Ireland, Waterford Harbour presented an obvious target for unfriendly naval forces. From the mid sixteenth century, concerns were expressed about its security, as it controlled

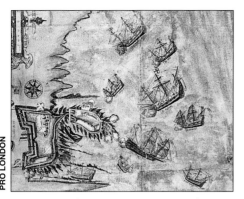

Fig. 2 Spanish landing at Smerwick. The need for a fort at Duncannon was emphasised by the landing of a small group of Spanish and Italians at Smerwick in county Kerry in 1580.

Fig. 3 The threat posed by the Spanish Armada of 1588 led to a decision by the authorities to complete the work on Duncannon Fort.

access into the heartlands of Leinster and Munster. This had direct implications for the Hook, as the measures taken to secure the harbour introduced another layer to the social, economic and political life of the area.

The rocky promontory of Duncannon, ideally situated to control the deep channel, was identified as the most suitable location for the

construction of a fort. A proposal was made in 1551 that it should be acquired from Etchingham for that purpose.[1] Duncannon was described as 'a place very meet and fit indeed for the purpose, for it is a rock and little castle adjoining to the river where the channel doth so cast as no shipping can pass without coming within a stone's cast thereunto.' The castle on the promontory was probably built during the fifteenth century when Duncannon was temporarily in the possession of the crown due to non-payment of debts by Dunbrody Abbey. The building of the fort, prompted by rumours of a Spanish invasion, was given further impetus by the landing of a small force of Spanish and Italians at Smerwick in county Kerry in 1580. Another consideration was the protection of shipping against pirates, who infested the harbour and with whom Edward Etchingham, then occupying Duncannon Castle, was said to be involved. According to tradition, the cave on Creadan Head was a pirate haunt; steps hewn into the rock beside the cave gave access to a path leading to Waterford. The Irish name of the path, 'Bóthar na mná gorm' (the road of the black women) could indicate that slave traders were using this route to bring African slaves to Waterford, presumably for re-export to the New World.

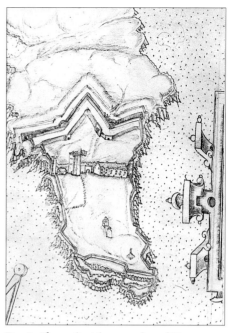

Fig. 5 The earliest known plan of Duncannon Fort, possibly late sixteenth or early seventeenth century. The fort is depicted with moat and drawbridge with defensive walls around the perimeter of the promontory. The original castle is shown, as well as the ruins of a church.

The safety of the fishing fleet was also a major concern: in 1590, it was claimed that 450 fishing boats in the harbour could be destroyed by five enemy ships. The importance of the harbour as a fishing ground was remarked on in 1684, when it was reported that it had an abundance of cod, gurnard and whiting, as well as lobster, crab, prawns, shrimp and oysters.[2] Work finally began on the fort in 1587, when two small fortifications were constructed.[3] Although doubts were expressed about the suitability of the site, which 'could not prevent the landing of troops either behind it on the side of Wexford, or over against it on the side of Waterford,' a decision was taken by the Privy Council to complete the work in 1590, following the threat of the ill-fated Spanish Armada of 1588.

Fortifications were erected at Waterford and Passage at the same time, the work being carried out by 400 'pioneers' from the surrounding counties. Ten cannons were installed

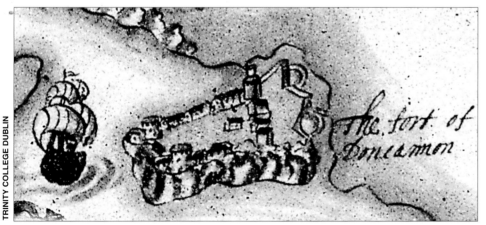

Fig 4 A detail from Jobson's map of 1591 showing the fort of Duncannon.

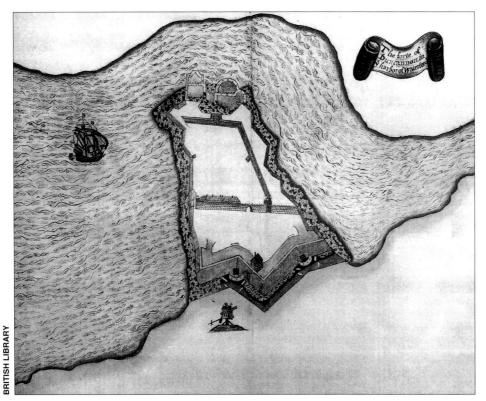

Fig. 8 A sentry post overlooking the pier on the northern rampart of Duncannon Fort.

Fig. 6 An early seventeenth-century plan of Duncannon Fort, showing the improvements carried out in 1604–6. A windmill was located on the high ground overlooking the fort to the east.

Fig. 9 Gun emplacements on the western point of the fort, overlooking the deep channel.

in Duncannon Fort with a permanent garrison of twenty-five men under the command of the first governor, Sir John Dowdall. Warnings of attacks by the Spanish persisted and there was general dissatisfaction with the unfinished nature of the work and the small garrison. Although £500 was allocated in 1591 for the completion of the fortifications and the complement of soldiers was increased to 100, there were continuous complaints about meagre resources and the inadequate nature of the fort. In 1601, the governor, Sir John Brockett, again complained about the deficiencies of the defences. The defeat of the Spanish at Kinsale may have lessened fears of an attack on the fort, as the new governor had time for other activities. There was a general shortage of silver coin at the time and the governor capitalised on this by making his own coins in the fort. He also leased the Tower of Hook, where coining tools could be

disposed of in deep water in case of emergency. His precautions were unsuccessful, however, as in 1603 he was arrested while on a visit to

London, on suspicion of coining, and never returned to Ireland. In 1604, Sir Josias Bodley was appointed governor of the fort and initiated

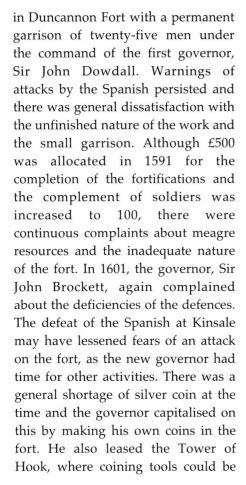

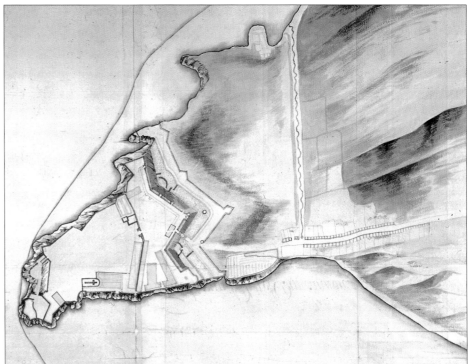

Fig. 7 A 1685 plan of Duncannon Fort by Thomas Phillips. The village houses are also shown.

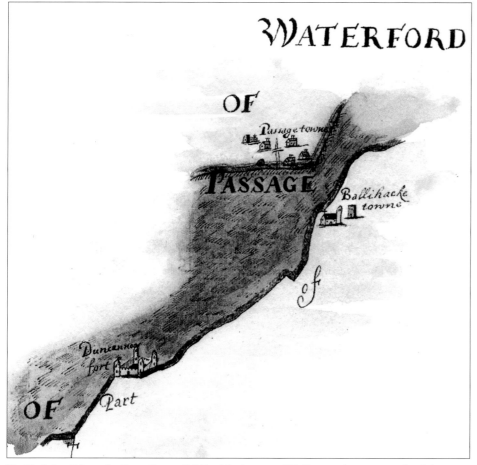

Fig 10 A detail from the *Down Survey* (1655) of the barony of Shelburne, showing a stylised depiction of the forts of Duncannon and Passage and the castle and village of Ballyhack.

complaints about its neglected condition, some repairs were carried out. It had considerable fire-power by 1684, when it was equipped with thirty-two cannon of various makes. In the same year, Robert Leigh of nearby Rosegarland wrote the following description:[5]

> About a mile from Ballihack to the south-east nearer the mouth of the river of Waterford lies the fort of Duncannon, account-ed of considerable strength and well manned with a sufficient number of great guns and other armour, and commands the mouth of the river, so that no ship can go in or out but shall be called to account by those in the fort. The fort itself belongs to the king who has settled about £300 per annum land of inheritance for main-taining the same in repair and defraying other charges there, but none of these lands lie near the fort, all the lands thereabouts to the

further improvements. These in-cluded strengthening the landward rampart, enlarging the ditch and installing a new drawbridge, gate and gatehouse; he also surrounded the fort with a stone wall backed by an earthen rampart. At the same time, gun platforms were improved and the barracks was repaired.[4] In 1606, Sir Laurence Esmonde, a member of a well-known north Wexford Old English family, was appointed governor and remained in charge until the Confederate war of the 1640s, the most turbulent period in the fort's history.

Duncannon Fort benefited from the land confiscations following the Cromwellian campaign, as £300 a year was granted out of forfeited lands in county Waterford for its upkeep. Although there were frequent

Fig. 11 A nineteenth-century depiction of King James II taking ship from Duncannon after the Battle of the Boyne in 1690. His opponent, William of Orange, chose the same port of departure.

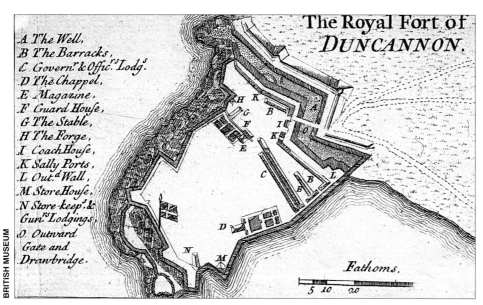

A The Well,
B The Barracks,
C Govern.r & Offic.rs Lodg.s
D The Chappel,
E Magazine,
F Guard House,
G The Stable,
H The Forge,
I Coach House,
K Sally Ports,
L Out.d Wall,
M Store House,
N Store-keep.rs &
Gun.rs Lodgings,
O Outward
Gate and
Drawbridge.

Fathoms.
5 10   20

BRITISH MUSEUM

Fig. 12 Vallancey's 1770 plan of Duncannon Fort. His report emphasised the inadequate nature of the defence which the fort could provide for the harbour and again pointed out that the fort was vulnerable to attack by enemy forces from the higher ground overlooking it to the east.

B. COLFER

Fig. 14 The construction of a lighthouse in Duncannon Fort in 1791 coincided with the installation of the first oil-fired light in the Tower of Hook at the mouth of the harbour.

B. COLFER

Fig. 15 Blackhill lighthouse, built on the cliff just north of the fort in 1838, was used, in conjunction with the fort lighthouse, to guide shipping up the deep channel in the harbour.

very wall belonging to the Earl of Donegal.

However, not everyone agreed with Leigh's assessment. A 1686 report by Thomas Phillips on the defences of Munster and Leinster emphasised the inadequacies of the fort, pointing out that it was not sufficient to protect:[6]

one of the most noble rivers in all the three kingdoms, having a very large and spacious road coming in, above which, about five or six miles up, three rivers spread themselves into the heart of all the south part

of this kingdom, being navigable for thirty and forty miles each of them, and passes by several of the most considerable towns for trade in the whole kingdom.

His proposal that it should be replaced by a fort on the rock of Passage at a cost of £42,000 was not implemented.[7]

Further repair and development work was carried out on the fort during the eighteenth century, principally in 1724 and 1753. A report by Major Charles Vallencey in 1770 again drew attention to the fort's

weaknesses, particularly its vulnerability to attack from the adjacent high ground. In general, the condition of the fort was given priority only when there was a threat of foreign invasion, initially by the Spanish and later by the French. In 1783, the first record of the village of Duncannon described it as 'a mean street mostly consisting of poor cabins.' The *Hibernian Magazine* of 1790, possibly reacting to renewed fears of invasion after the French Revolution of 1789, described the fort as follows:

WEXFORD COUNTY LIBRARY

Fig. 13 Duncannon Fort viewed from the beach, from Grose's *Antiquities* (1791). The lighthouse built in that year, is not shown, indicating that the drawing had been made some time previously.

B. COLFER

Fig. 16 One of two Martello towers built c. 1812 on high ground overlooking Duncannon Fort.

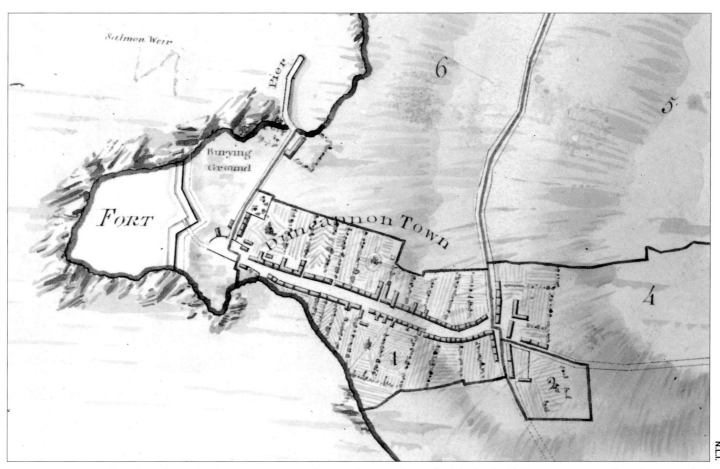

Fig. 17 Duncannon village from the Dunbrody estate map 1803. The weir shown to the north of the fort by Phillips in 1685 was still in place; a pier had been constructed during the eighteenth century. The houses are shown along the present main street but the road along the beach had not yet been built.

Fig. 18 Duncannon Fort from the south. The complex is now in the care of a trust which operates it as a tourist attraction and local amenity. The buildings contain an art centre, museum and café. In 1999, it was used as one of the settings for a film version of the *Count of Monte Cristo*.

B. COLFER

Fig. 19 Duncannon Fort and village from the harbour. The Martello Tower built on the high ground behind the fort can be seen at right centre. The lighthouse was erected in 1791. The mid nineteenth-century Catholic Church dominates the skyline.

Duncannon Fort, which commands the harbour of Waterford, is all surrounded by a strong wall, and you enter it over a draw-bridge. It is built on the flat of a rock, that overlooks the sea, as we may now call it; and a perpetuity of land was granted by Queen Elizabeth, to keep this fortress in repair. It mounts upwards of thirty guns, all in good order. Cromwell made an attack on this fort in the winter of 1649, but the garrison defended itself with spirit against his ravages. Duncannon town is despicable to a degree.

During the Rebellion of 1798, Duncannon Fort was a government stronghold and place of refuge for members of the loyalist community. Soldiers from the fort marching to the relief of Wexford town were routed by the rebels at Three Rocks on Forth Mountain. After the rebellion, the New Line road, with Nelson's Bridge over the Owenduff and Wellington Bridge over the Corock, was constructed by the military to improve communications between the fort and the town of Wexford.[8] During the Napoleonic Wars, the authorities, motivated by fears of a French landing, finally addressed the problem of the high ground overlooking the fort. Of thirty small forts, known as Martello Towers, built around the coast of Ireland early in the nineteenth century, three were located in the Hook region: one at Baginbun and two on the hill above the fort at Duncannon. These towers added

greatly to the fort's capacity but were never called upon to prove their worth.[9] The fort was not involved in any further military action during the nineteenth century. In 1860, considerable additions and alterations were carried out. Provisions were made for mounting 68-pounder Armstrong guns on transversing platforms, capable of throwing shot and shell six miles to the entrance of the harbour. Two extra magazines and five shell rooms for the storage of ammunition for these guns were also built, as well as four banquettes for riflemen (a raised step running along the inside of a rampart).[10]

By the late nineteenth century the fort had been downgraded and was only used for the training of local militia. Following the War of Independence, the fort suffered some

Fig. 20 Duncannon village from the gate of the fort c. 1890. Most of the houses shown are still occupied. Note the two cannon guns placed at the entrance.

damage during the Civil War and subsequently lay abandoned. At the outbreak of World War II, the Irish Army occupied the fort and some work was carried out on military installations. Subsequently, the army continued to use the fort, mostly as a training centre, until 1986, when the Department of Defence decided that it was surplus to their needs. Following the withdrawal of the military, a committee made up of local and statutory interests was formed to develop the fort as a local amenity.[11] It is currently operating as a visitor attraction and has a maritime museum, an art gallery and a restaurant.

A NEW REGIME: THE DEVELOPMENT OF THE ESTATE SYSTEM

By the end of the seventeenth century, Britain's involvement in America had moved Ireland, long an offshore island on the European periphery, to centre-stage in the Atlantic world. This shift in Ireland's strategic importance led to rapid economic growth, with planned settlement and demographic expansion resulting in considerable landscape changes. This transformation was accompanied by intense social and cultural trauma as the native elite was swept aside and society was dominated by a new, Protestant and British landed class which would dominate the economic, political and social life of Ireland for two centuries. From the end of the seventeenth century, restructuring the rural landscape revolved around initiatives prompted by the owners of the new estates. These included a phase of house, demesne and village building, agricultural and infrastructural development, the exploitation of natural resources, and settlement reorganisation. Due to local variables, and the ambition, ability and assets of landlords, there was obvious diversity in estate development. This was especially true of south-west Wexford where long-established monastic estates had been acquired by new owners in the second half of the sixteenth century. The grantees were members of an English Elizabethan class of soldiers and officials who were prepared to operate in a hostile environment in the hope of advancing their social and economic status.

The prospect of acquiring the rich acres of the recently vacated monastic estates in the relatively secure south Wexford, seen as a 'great and opulent county,'[1] attracted the interest of some highly-placed Englishmen who were already actively involved in Ireland.

N.G.I.

Fig. 1 Dunbrody Abbey by Henry Brocas (1766–1838). The ruins of the Cistercian abbey symbolise the two superimposed estate systems, ecclesiastical and secular, that dominated landscape development in the Hook region for eight centuries. The grange of Nook is shown in the middle distance.

Fig. 2 The tomb of Anthony Colclough, with an inscription in Latin and English, is in Tintern church, believed to have been the Cistercian *capella ante portas*, beside the original roadway leading to the abbey. The building was renovated by the Colcloughs for use as a parish church.

Here lieth the body Syr Anthony Colcloughe Knight, eldest sune of Richard Colcloughe of Wolstanton in Stafordshire Esquire who came first into this land the 34 yere of Henry the 8 and then was Captayn of the Pensioners in which place and others of great charge he continued a most fayhtful serviter during the life of Edward the VI and Queen Mary and until the XXVI yer of our most noble Queen Elizabeth and then died the IX day of December 1584. He left his wife, Clare Agare, daughter of Thomas Agare Esquier 7 sonns, Frances, Ratlife, Anthony, Syr Thomas Colclough, Knight, John, Mathew, Lenard and 5 doghters, Jaqnet who married to Nicholas Walshe Esquier of the Priveie Counsayle and one of the Justice of the Kings Bench in Ireland; Fraunc married to William Smethwike of Smethwik in Cheshier; Clare married to William Snead of Brodwal in Stafordshire Esquier; Elinor died iunge.

THE COLCLOUGH FAMILY

The lands of Tintern Abbey were granted in 1543 to Anthony Colclough (pronounced 'Cokely') from Staffordshire. As Colclough was on active duty with the king's army in Ireland, he did not take possession of his new estate until 1562. In 1566, he applied to the authorities for money to fortify the abbey, as it was 'on the borders,' and

undertook to defend the surrounding countryside from the queen's enemies. Colclough's title to Tintern was confirmed and he was directed to build 'a sufficient fortress' within three years and to maintain three English horsemen and four archers or arquebusiers (soldiers carrying an early type of portable firearm).[2] Two years before his death in 1584, he was knighted by Elizabeth I.

Fig. 3 Sir Thomas Colclough, Anthony's son, married into the Loftus family. He acquired the Duffry lands in the north-west of the county that later passed to the Catholic family of his second wife, Eleanor Bagenal.

Fig. 4 Margaret Colclough married Robert Leigh of Rosegarland. Following her death without heir in 1723, the Tintern estate passed to the Catholic branch of the Colcloughs of Duffry Hall.

His monument survives in the little church near the abbey where successive generations of the family were interred.

Anthony Colclough's son, Thomas, inherited Tintern and also acquired an estate in the Duffry, in the wooded north-west of the county.[3] Thomas married twice: the Tintern estate passed to Adam, son of his first wife, Martha Loftus; the Duffry estate passed to the Catholic family of his second wife. Apart from the Tintern and Duffry Colcloughs, other minor branches of the family proliferated in the county and elsewhere, creating an intricate network of relationships and connections; the frequent repetition of 'Caesar' as a Christian name added to the complexity. The title expired in 1687 with the death of Sir Thomas's great-grandson, Caesar, and when his daughter died childless in 1723 the Tintern estate passed to 'The Great' Caesar of the Duffry. On his death in 1766, Tintern passed to his grandson, Vesey, who died in 1794. Vesey's heir, another Caesar, had been in France during the revolution and was unable to return for political

Fig. 6 The Colcloughs were patrons of Irish sport, music and culture. This portrait, known as 'the Colclough Piper', by Joseph Patrick Haverty (1794–1854), hung in Tintern Abbey until the estate was handed over to the nation in 1959.

Fig. 5 'Sir' Vesey Colclough (1745–94) inherited the Tintern estate from his famous grandfather, 'The Great' Caesar, in 1766. He married Catherine Grogan of Johnstown Castle and had two surviving sons, Caesar and John. He reputedly had numerous children with other partners. He was responsible for founding the first group of the militia known as the Volunteers and is shown here wearing their uniform.

reasons. Another son, John, looked after the estate until his controversial death in a celebrated duel in 1807.

During the twenty years following Caesar's death without heir in 1842, a bitter internecine legal wrangle over succession burdened the estate with crippling legal costs from which it never recovered. The courts eventually found in favour of Mary Colclough, a great-grand-daughter of 'The Great' Caesar of Duffry Hall and daughter of another Caesar who had been Chief Justice of Prince Edward Island and Newfoundland. Mary married Thomas Rossborough, who took the Colclough name. Their daughter Louisa, who succeeded, married Captain Frank Biddulph; their daughter, Lucy Marie Biddulph Colclough, lived in the abbey until 1959, when, at an advanced age, she moved to a house in Saltmills. With no family to succeed her, the last of the Colcloughs offered the abbey to the state and, in 1963, it was vested in the Board of Works.

The Colcloughs were, for the most part, benevolent landlords and were held in high regard by their tenants. Politically, they were liberal in outlook and were opposed to the conservative faction in the county with which the Loftus family was associated. The Duffry family was involved with the Confederate Catholic cause during the 1640s and subsequently lost part of their estate. Caesar, of Tintern, was in France during the French Revolution and was suspected of harbouring republican sympathies; his popular brother, John, was arrested after the 1798 Rebellion but was released without charge.[4] Their distant cousin, John Henry Colclough of Ballyteigue Castle, actively involved in the rebellion, was arrested and executed. In 1807, John Colclough was killed at Ardcandrisk by William Alcock of Wilton Castle, in a politically motivated duel. In the eighteenth century, when the Penal Laws were still on the statute books, the Colcloughs donated a site for a Catholic church at Ballycullane and established schools for their tenants; a school built at Saltmills in 1839 has been recently restored as the Colclough Memorial Hall. The family was mostly resident in earlier years and involved themselves in the cultural and social lives of their tenants. 'The Great' Caesar, a noted sportsman, is credited with promoting hurling and earning the soubriquet by which Wexford natives are known. The description 'yellow-bellies,' now applied to anyone from the county, was bestowed on members of his hurling team, because of their distinctive yellow sashes, when he took them to play a match in Cornwall in the eighteenth century.

THE ETCHINGHAM FAMILY

Sir Osborne Etchingham from Suffolk, fourth cousin of Queen Anne Boleyn and a high official in the court of Henry VIII, was marshal of the English army in Ireland and a member of the Privy Council.[5] In 1545, he successfully petitioned for a grant of the Dunbrody Abbey estate in exchange for lands which he held in England; it is doubtful if he ever occupied his new property, as he died

Fig. 8 The Tudor house built by the Etchinghams over the south transept of Dunbrody Abbey. It is likely that they also used other parts of the building for various domestic and defensive purposes.

in the following year. He was succeeded by his son Edward, whose title was confirmed in 1565. Described as 'of dissolute character,' Edward compromised the estate by taking out various mortgages and issuing disadvantageous long leases to different people, principally Sir William Drury and Sir Nicholas White. He was arrested at Duncannon Castle for being involved with pirates but managed to escape to England, where he allegedly died in the Tower of London. The uncertainty about ownership may explain why the lands of Dunbrody were raided in 1572 by a group led by Brian Mac Cathair Ó Caomhánach, Fiach Mac Aoidh O Broin and renegade Furlongs. The raiders, as well as burning and plundering, killed some tenants, including members of the Devereux family, who were tenants on the estate.

Edward Etchingham died in 1582 and was succeeded by his brother's son, John. Ownership continued to be disputed between the Drury and White families, but, when Sir Nicholas White, who was accused of treason in 1593, died in the Tower of London, the lands of Dunbrody were finally confirmed to John Etchingham in 1602. Following his death at Ballyhack Castle in 1616, the lands passed first to his son and then to his grandson, John. On John's death without male heir in 1650, most of the estate passed to his daughter, Jane, who married Sir Arthur Chichester, earl of Donegal. Jane's uncle, Arthur Etchingham (who held the townlands of Coole, Drillistown, Boderan, Killesk, Tinnock and Carrowanree), disputed the succession and a bitter physical and legal struggle ensued until 1665, when the estate was restored to Chichester by parliament. Since then, ownership of the estate has passed in a direct line through twelve generations. Jane's great-grandson, Arthur, became first marquess of Donegal and his son, also Arthur, became Lord Templemore in 1831.

Fig. 7 Ballyhack Castle and village by G. Du Noyer, 1862, showing a row of houses, now removed, along the water's edge. The castle was occupied as a residence by the Etchingham family in the late sixteenth century. Shipping on the estuary included a steam-driven paddle-boat at the pier.

THE LOFTUS FAMILY

Following dissolution, the manor of Kilcloggan was granted to Sir Henry Radcliff for twenty-one years in 1560. By 1596 the manor had been transferred to Sir Dudley Loftus, a member of an important English family established in Ireland as part of an Elizabethan strategy for the subjugation of Ireland.[6] The Loftus dynasty in Ireland was founded by Dudley's father, Adam Loftus from Yorkshire, who was made Protestant archbishop of Dublin in 1567. He later became Lord Chancellor of Ireland and first provost of Trinity College, which he helped to establish in 1592. He built Rathfarnham Castle, where he raised a large family; his numerous descendants occupied influential positions in the realms of politics and administration.[7] They were also involved in military affairs, two of his sons being killed in action against the Irish: Adam, a captain of horse, was killed fighting the

PRIVATE COLLECTION

Fig. 10 An early plan of Trinity College Dublin, of which Adam Loftus became first provost following its foundation in 1592.

Irish of the Wicklow Mountains while Edward died at the siege of Kinsale in 1601. A great-grandson, Adam, a commander in the Williamite army, was killed by a cannon-ball at the siege of Limerick in 1691.[8] The family's Viscount of Ely title, came from Robert, brother of the archbishop, who acquired lands in Ely O'Carroll (modern county Offaly).[9] In the Hook the title was always pronounced Elee, as it would have been in Irish.

Dudley Loftus took up residence in Kilcloggan Castle, where he died in 1616. At that time, the family also held 400 acres in the former Hospitaller manor of Ballyhoge, on the right bank of the Slaney below Enniscorthy, as well as the castle of Bannow with its lands.[10] Dudley was succeeded by his son, Nicholas who was made sheriff of Wexford in 1620. Nicholas Loftus added to his estates in 1634, acquiring the manor of Fethard from the bishop of Ferns in exchange for other lands, giving £300 to the bishop for the construction of a new episcopal residence in Ferns.[11] The name of Bishop Ram, the last episcopal occupier, survives in the place-name Ramstown, a townland just south of Fethard. At the same time, the former Devereux manors of Ballymagir in the barony of Bargy, and Adamstown in Shelmalier, were added to the Loftus estate.[12] Further lands were acquired by Loftus following the Confederate war and the Cromwellian campaign. As most of the Hook was already held by Protestant proprietors, confiscations were confined to a small number of hereditary Catholic tenants with relatively small holdings who had been active with the Confederates.[13] The principal confiscations took place on

TRINITY COLLEGE DUBLIN

Fig. 9 Adam Loftus, the founder of the Loftus dynasty in Ireland, was made Protestant archbishop of Dublin in 1567. This is one of six portraits in Trinity College Dublin, of which he was co-founder and first provost.

Fig. 11 A late eighteenth-century painting of Rathfarnham Castle, county Dublin. Built by Archbishop Adam Loftus at the end of the sixteenth century, the castle became the principal family home. His brother, Robert, acquired lands in Ely O'Carrol (modern county Offaly) from which the title Viscount Loftus of Ely was taken.

the manor of Kilcloggan, where Alexander Redmond lost the townlands of Hall, Porters Gate and Churchtown; Thomas Laffan lost Slade, Robert Redmond, Thomas Chapman, Michael Laffan and Michael Keating lost Galgystown and James Lewis lost Lambstown and Great Graigue, all of the lands being added to the Loftus estate. Nicholas Loftus also acquired the Whitty holding of Dungulph, Winningtown and Ballyvaroge, the Sutton townland of Balliniry and the Barron holding of Killesk. In Fethard, he acquired the lands lost by Thomas Redmond, James Lewis, Richard Keating, James Sutton, Peter Whitty and John Laffan.[14] According to the Loftus Papers, the lands were initially granted to 'several soldiers and adventurers' and purchased from them by Nicholas Loftus.[15]

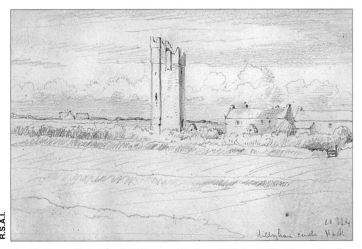

Fig. 12 A pencil sketch of Kilcloggan Castle, c. 1850, by G. Du Noyer. Dudley Loftus (d. 1616) took up residence here at the end of the sixteenth century.

The Colclough and Etchingham families obviously lacked the political connections and economic resources of the Loftuses, as they did not acquire any of the confiscated lands. In 1601, Thomas Colclough had leased the episcopal manor of Kinnagh, which divided the Tintern lands in two, and, after several unsuccessful attempts by the bishop to retrieve the lands, Kinnagh became part of the Colclough estate.[16] However, even in this case the Loftus influence was evident, as they acquired the townlands of Baylestown and Ballygowny in the parish of Kinnagh.

Nicholas Loftus took up residence in Fethard Castle, where he died in 1666 and was buried in Fethard church. Henry Loftus, brother of Nicholas, occupied Dungulph

Fig. 13 Henry Loftus (d. 1716) of Loftus Hall: a portrait by the well-known Irish artist Garrett Morphy, painted early in the eighteenth century.

Castle and succeeded to the manor of Kilcloggan when his brother's sons died without male issue. Henry moved to Redmond Hall on the Hook peninsula, which, renamed Loftus Hall, became the principal family residence. When Henry died at an advanced age in 1716, he was succeeded by his son, another Nicholas, who served as member of parliament for county Wexford. In 1756, Nicholas was raised to the peerage as Baron Loftus of Loftus Hall and Viscount Loftus of Ely. His son, also Nicholas, earl of Ely, member of parliament for Fethard and Bannow, held the estate for a short time until his death in 1766. His son, another Nicholas, died unmarried three years later and the

Fig. 14 Henry, earl of Ely and 4th Viscount Loftus of Ely (1709–83), painted by Robert Hunter. The title was first conferred on Robert, brother of Adam the archbishop, who was made Viscount Loftus of Ely (modern county Offaly) in 1622 and later passed to other branches of the family.

estate reverted to his father's brother, Henry, earl of Ely, and member of parliament for Bannow. On Henry's death in 1783, the titles became extinct and the estate passed to his nephew, Charles, son of his sister, Elizabeth, who had married John Tottenham of Tottenham Green near Taghmon, south county Wexford. Charles, who served as member of parliament for Clonmines, assumed the Loftus surname and in 1785 was given the title Lord Baron Loftus of Loftus Hall, with the estates of Loftus Hall, Rathfarnham Castle in Dublin and Castlehume in county Fermanagh. Throughout the nineteenth century, the title and estates were held by four of his successors, including the fifth marquess of Ely, the last of the family to own Loftus Hall.

For most of the eighteenth century, the Loftus family dominated Wexford politics; at the end of the century the first marquess of Ely was referred to as 'the great leviathan of the county.' The Colcloughs, who controlled the town of Enniscorthy, were also prominent, but on the more liberal side of the political divide. A dependence on a loyal electorate for political control encouraged the introduction of Protestant tenants on the better farms, as throughout most of the eighteenth century the franchise was restricted to Protestant forty-shilling freeholders.[17] Through a system of political patronage, Loftus controlled the appointment, and the loyalty, of many minor officials in the county, such as Alexander Fenner, a revenue officer who died at Slade in 1763.[18] Of the eighteen representatives returned for Wexford, the Loftuses controlled at least nine: two each for the 'rotten boroughs' of Bannow and Clonmines, two for Fethard, one each for New Ross and Wexford town and one for the county. Their power-base in Wexford town was maintained by appointing tenants of the Loftus Hall estate (known as 'the Fethard freemen') as freemen of the borough.[19] Subsequent to the Act of Union of 1800, Loftus was granted £15,000 for each of the abolished boroughs of Bannow, Clonmines and Fethard,[20] but the political power of the family ebbed inexorably in the wake of that event.

MANOR HOUSES

As the new owners of the monastic estates inherited a variety of residences, there was no immediate house-building activity and no construction of the characteristic eighteenth-century Georgian houses typically built on other estates; the new owners simply occupied existing structures. The Colcloughs adapted the Cistercian church at Tintern as a residence, which they were to occupy for four centuries; the crossing tower was converted into a five-storey tower house; fireplaces were inserted in blocked-up arches, Gothic windows were built up and mullioned Tudor windows inserted. Stone from the dismantled monastic buildings was used to build defensive walls and a battlemented bridge. In the late eighteenth century, visitors who stayed at Tintern commented on the neglected condition of the house and

Fig. 15 Fethard Castle from Grose's *Antiquities* (1791). Following the acquisition by the Loftuses of the manor of Fethard in 1634, the episcopal castle became one of the family residences.

Fig. 16 A late eighteenth-century water-colour by Gabriel Beranger depicting Tintern Abbey converted to a manor house. This seems to be a somewhat fanciful representation: the windows which were inserted in the chancel are Gothic instead of Tudor and the roof on the nave does not correspond to the one shown in late nineteenth-century photographs. Apart from the doorway and window, the tower and stairway turret are accurately shown.

estate. In 1780, the artist Gabriel Beranger recorded that the tower was used as a dwelling and that the rest of the abbey was uncovered and waste; even the tower was not very comfortable, as rats, mice and rain all had free access.[21] Perhaps not surprisingly, Grose's *Antiquities* recorded that further conversion of the abbey had taken place by 1791:

> The tower and its beautiful arch have long been stopped up, the ancient windows are contracted, and the western door and its mouldings can scarcely be seen. The present owner has surrounded the abbey with walls and battlements in the ancient style, and so well executed that a few years will give them the appearance of being part of the original building. Many of the dependent chapels and outer buildings were removed at different times, the stone being used in erecting the parish church and a neat bridge thrown over a meandering river that waters the demesne. The present mansion is chiefly formed from the chancel of the ancient church, and is not well adapted to the purposes of a liberal domestic establishment.[22]

Considerable improvements were planned at the end of the eighteenth century, including the roofing of the abbey, so it is likely that the final stages of the residence were completed in the early nineteenth century. Perhaps because of the natural advantages of the location, the demesne at Tintern was never organised along formal lines, but some landscape planning did take place. The existing tree cover is the result of extensive tree planting, the construction of a new winding avenue opened up a panoramic aspect of the abbey and the view to the south of the abbey was enhanced by the fortified bridge. One of the principal undertakings was the building of a fine, presumably eighteenth-century, walled garden across the stream at a distance from the house. The tower which existed until recently between the abbey and the bridge was intended as a decorative, rather than a defensive, feature.

The Etchinghams lived in a Tudor house built over the south transept of Dunbrody Abbey by Edward Etchingham after 1565 and the family also occupied the castles at Duncannon and Ballyhack. The construction of a large defended residence known as Dunbrody Castle was initiated in the early seventeenth century but never

Fig. 17 A late eighteenth-century study of Dunbrody Abbey by Gabriel Beranger illustrating its proximity to an inlet of Waterford Harbour. The title to the picture is given as Dunbrawdy Abbey, indicating that the current local pronunciation of the place-name is historically correct.

completed. Dunbrody Park at Arthurstown, surrounded by a walled demesne, was completed by Arthur Chichester, who became Lord Templemore in 1831. Dunbrody Park was the residence of the family until the late twentieth century.[23]

Kilcloggan Castle was occupied by Dudley Loftus at the end of the sixteenth century and, following the acquisition of the manor of Fethard from the bishop of Ferns, the family occupied the castles of Fethard and Dungulph. In the late seventeenth century, Redmond Hall was taken over by Henry Loftus and, as Loftus Hall, it became the family's principal residence for more than two centuries.

Fig. 18 The construction of Dunbrody Castle, a short distance east of the abbey (visible on the left), was initiated by the Etchinghams in the early part of the seventeenth century. The structure was evidently never completed but the ground floor was converted for use as a residence.

Fig. 19 Redmond Hall on Jobson's 1591 map of Waterford Harbour. Following the acquisition of the Redmond lands, Henry Loftus took up residence in the hall, which he renamed Loftus Hall. Parts of the old hall were incorporated into the present building.

Fig. 20 Dunbrody Park, and the estate village of Arthurstown, was completed by Arthur Chichester in the early nineteenth century and was occupied by the family until it was sold in the late twentieth century. It is now operated as an exclusive hotel known as Dunbrody Country House.

ESTATE DEVELOPMENT

The new proprietors' first priority was to modernise their estates. They introduced advanced farming methods including fertilising, draining, reclamation and field enclosure. The creation of personal demesnes in the immediate vicinity of the manor house involved moulding the landscape as a status symbol.[24] As well as being an exercise in image building, demesnes served as an example to tenants: the financial return to landlords came from better management of individual farms. Inevitably, there was considerable diversity in estate evolution due to location, previous settlement, land quality, financial resources and personal ability and ambition. This is clearly demonstrated in south-west Wexford, where each of the three estates acquired a distinctive landscape character.

Landlords were aware of the importance of exploiting natural resources and expanding trade and commerce. In 1684, Robert Leigh, who had acquired the Rosegarland estate to the east of the Tintern lands following the Cromwellian confiscations, wrote an account of south county Wexford which contained some information on settlement features but concentrated more on economic potential.[25] He described south-west Wexford as being divided into three 'peeces' or quarters, Dunbrody, Tintern and Hook, each one corresponding to an estate. Being one of the new breed of landlords, he was concerned with estate improvement and fiscal possibilities. He specified

the quality of land in each district and the variety of crops grown, principally wheat, barley, peas, beans and oats. The absence of any mention of potato-growing indicates

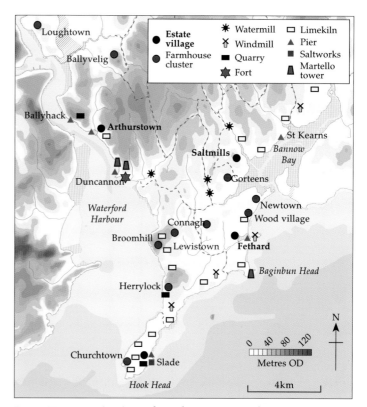

Fig. 21 Features related to eighteenth- and nineteenth-century settlement and industrial development on the three estates in the Hook region.

that a medieval diet was still being consumed in the region at the end of the seventeenth century. He commented on the fishing grounds in Waterford Harbour and Bannow Bay and noted that Loftus was building a quay for fishing boats at Slade. His reference to the English landing at Baginbun (quoting the rhyme 'At the creek of Baginbun, Ireland was lost and won') is an indication of how this crucial event had impacted on local memory and perhaps was used to put English ownership of the land into perspective. A comparison of Leigh's account with the *Civil Survey* of 1654–6 indicates a

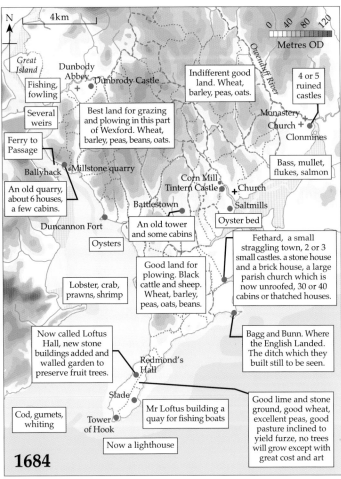

Fig. 22 Information about the Hook contained in Leigh's account of 1684, presented in map form. As well as providing an assessment of the economic potential of farming and fishing, Leigh commented on a variety of landscape features, including dwellings, towns and villages.

significant shift in perspective. The *Civil Survey* was essentially backward looking, describing a landscape that had evolved over several centuries. Leigh's account, on the other hand, is more concerned with present and future possibilities and with business opportunities offered by the management of land and sea, signalling an era of landscape development that would intensify during the following century.

Fig. 23 Robert Leigh of Rosegarland, who wrote an informative description of south Wexford in 1684, including an assessment of the economic potential of the Dunbrody, Tintern and Loftus estates.

A cartographic survey of the Loftus lands carried out in 1771 identified the economic strengths and weaknesses on the estate.[26] Each farm was rated according to land quality, enhancements, dwelling house and crops grown. Comments about land varied from 'very rich and profitable, finely improved and laid down and fit for any purpose' to 'in a state of nature.' The

Fig. 24 The retaining wall and pier built by the Colcloughs at St Kearns on Bannow Bay. The pier has recently been damaged by rough seas.

B. COLFER

Fig. 25 The old pier at Duncannon, constructed during the eighteenth century. Piers were built on the Dunbrody estate at Duncannon, Arthurstown and Ballyhack to facilitate trade and to encourage tenants to become involved in the fishing industry. Blackhill lighthouse is in the background.

benefits to land from the application of 'sea manure' (sea weed or woar) and lime were emphasised. Some limestone was already being burned; a field on the demesne of Loftus Hall was called Limekiln Park. The survey recognised the crucial lime resource of the area: a comment that 'lime might be burned very cheap' at Slade indicates that this survey initiated the expansion of lime-burning and the construction of the many limekilns which still dot the landscape. Only thirteen slated houses, one 'good cabin' and one castle are identified, so it is clear that the majority of people, and in particular under-tenants and cottiers, lived in single-storey, thatched, mud-walled cabins. Industrial activity

included a salthouse at Slade, a millstone quarry at Templetown, a quay and pier at Ingard (now Innyard)[27] and a mill at Winningtown. The estate was held by sixty-five named tenants, many of whom were middlemen who sub-let to under-tenants. Churchtown, for example, was rented to Alexander Neale and partners but was occupied by 'his lordship's labourers.' The townland of Booley was held by Thomas Broaders but was in the hands of his cottiers; he also held the townlands of Aldridge, Knockanduff, Ballinphile and Connagh (which he held as a sub-tenant of Philip Devereux). This was the famous Rev. Thomas Broaders (1700–73) who had been involved in the well-known 'ghost' incident in Loftus

Extracts from the Loftus Estate Maps 1771 for the parishes of Hook, Templetown and Fethard

Townland	Tenant	Buildings/remarks	Townland	Tenant	Buildings/remarks
Loftus Hall (with Galgystown)			**Ballinphile**	Thos. Broaders	Same remark as above
Part of demesne	Mr. Breen	Whitehall house	**Ballystraw**	Allen	The tenant intends building a house
Churchtown	Alex. Neale & partners	in the hands of his lordship's labourers	**Aldridge**	Thos. Broaders	This farm is in a state of nature
Portersgate			**Ballinruan**	Richard Frizell	
Part of demesne	Widow Prendergast	Brecaun church	**Knockanduff**	Thomas Broaders	Priest Broaders lives on this farm
Slade	Henry Mansell	Good slated dwelling			
Including tower lands		house and offices Salthouse, pier, quay	**Haytown** (part of)	Caulfield	
			Part of	George Tegart	Cold and barren ground
Houseland					
Castle qr.	John Lumsden	Houseland Castle	**Connagh**	Philip Devereux Sub-tenant Priest Broaders	An old slated house
Part called Murrice	John Lumsden Wm. Dunn John Tweedy				
Part called Heuclus	Laurence Barry	A good house	**Rath** [Ralph]		
Templetown	Widow Lewis	Good house	Part of	Widow Furlong	
Part called Cors [Corse]			Part of	George Duffin	
Upper quarter	John Lynn	Millstone quarry	Part of	Philip Jacob	
Church quarter	Mr Sutton Frizell	ruined mill, orchard	Part of	John Mason	
Great Graigue	Thomas Chapman	Good slated house	Part of	John Nagle	Good cabin
Little Graigue (part of)	Executors of Patk. Furlong	Good farm house	Part of	Thos. Winskill	
Part of	Laurence Devereux		Pillfarm	Exec. of Pat Donoghoe	Houses and improvements decayed
Haggard (part of)	Phelix Neale	Farm house	**Lambstown**		
Part of	Richard Frizell		Part of	Exec. of Pat Donoghoe	Good dairy farm; good farm house
Kilcloggan	Reps. Of Doct. Fogarty	Old slated house 10 acres of wood and scrub	Part called Carnivan	Grace & partners	adjoins the sea, very improveable by seaweed
Broomhill	Henry Houghton	Very rich profitable farm, finely improved	**Ramstown**		
The sheep walk		and laid down and fit	Part of	Exec. of Pat Donoghoe	
Dairy quarter		for any purpose	Part of	Thomas Duffin	
The Firzyhill			Part of	— Rossiter	
Mountpleasant			Part called Ingard [Innyard]		Adjoins the quay of Fethard where there is a good pier for shipping and is a very convenient situation for fishermen. .
Lewistown	Laurence Barry				
Booley	Thos. (Priest) Broaders	This farm is in the hands of Priest Broaders' cottiers and is much abused			

Hall (see p. 183), which may explain the highly unusual situation of a Catholic priest being rented five townlands on the staunchly Protestant Loftus estate.[28] The episode provides an unusual example of the impact of the supernatural on landscape development. As well as Churchtown, two other areas were held in common as both Gurtins (Gorteens) and the Wood of Grange were held by 'sundry tenants' and part of Grange was held by Simon Brien and Partners and Foley and Partners.

There was a marked contrast between the land-holding pattern on the former Cistercian estates, noted for being agriculturally progressive, and the manors of Kilcloggan and Fethard, where there were numerous small dispersed holdings and fields held in common, probably a relic survival of the medieval three-field system. During the eighteenth century, settlers had been attracted from England to become tenants and middlemen on the estate: of the sixty-five tenants named in the survey, only twenty had surnames that could be identified as Irish or Old English. Some continuity is indicated by the presence of six surnames – Lewis, Chapman, Devereux, Duffin, Brown and Mason – that were recorded in the region at the dissolution of the monasteries in 1541. Surnames indicating a more recent arrival in the area included Mansell, Lumsden, Lynn, Frizell, Hurdis and Boyce.

Leigh's account of 1684 highlighted the potential of the fishing industry. Thomas Colclough was credited with introducing oysters into Bannow Bay early in the seventeenth century, at a place still known as Oyster Point. The development of harbours for fishing and trade was of primary significance on the three estates. Shortly after Henry Loftus acquired the Hook peninsula, he had 'a quay for fishing boats' built at Slade in 1684. In the same year there was 'a convenient creek for fishermen at Fethard, but no quay; yet they make good use of it, and take good seafish thereabouts.' By 1771, there was a 'good pier and quay for shipping and a very convenient situation for fishermen' at Fethard, where early in the following century 'a considerable fishery of herrings, lobsters, and other fish of superior quality, especially plaice' was

Extracts from the Loftus Estate Maps 1771 for the parishes of Hook, Templetown and Fethard (cont.)

Townland	Tenant	Buildings/remarks
Part called Ingard [Innyard] (cont.)		
(Ingard divided into)		
Green field		
Holding	Martin Walshe	
Stubble field		
Field	Widow Clancey	
Hill of sea meadow		
Tate's garden	Tate	
Flaxfield		
Holding	Mr Clancey	
House and Garden	Widow Clancey	
Field	Mr Loftus Lynn	
Grange		
Part called Booley Hill	John Lynn	Convenient to manure
	as it adjoins the pill	
Part of	John Hurdis	
Part of	Richard Lewis	
Part of	Wm. Boyce	
Part of	Exec. of Pat Donoghoe	Held by poor cottiers
Grange wood	Sundry tenants	Noble farm convenient
		to sea manure
Rabbit burrow & marsh	John Lynn	House and garden;
		rabbits are a great part
	of the profits	
Strand to the burrow		
Part called the middle qr.		
Part of	Simon Brien & partners	
Part of	Foley & partners	
Dungulph	Philip Savage	This farm has always
		been the residence of a
		Gent., is in good order,
		has a good house, orchard
		and improvements on it
Pill to ditto		
Stonehouse	Philip Savage	Very convenient to
		manure

Townland	Tenant	Buildings/remarks
Pill to ditto		
Gurtins [Gorteens]	Sundry tenants	Very convenient to
		manure
Pill to ditto		
Winningtown	Execs. of Sam Butterton	New mill lately built
Ballyvaroge	Wm. Shehee	Much out of order
Balliniry		
Part of	Wm. Sheehee	Much out of order
Part of	Murphy, Bearney &	These poor people have
	partners	manured part of their
		grounds
Balistown [Baylestown]		
Part of	Robert Shaw	Good thatched house
Part of	Widow Clerk	Same remark
Burkestown		
Part of	Thomas Duffin	New slated house,
		orchard
Part of	Michael Downes	Good farm house
Drillistown	Mr Orphier	Remains of a good
		slated house
Bog		Could be kept for the
		use of the estate
Killesk		Much out of order; an
		old castle
Coarse farm of **Fethard**	George Houghton	The last eight farms are
	James Murphy	in a state of nature,
	William Roe	many of the old
	Oliver Powell	freeholders are dead
	Wm. Clerk	and should be replaced.
	John Wheatly	
	(now Wm. Clerk)	
	Adam Wiley	
	(now Wm. Clerk)	
	George Duffin	
	Nathaniel Smith	
	Michael Barron	

carried on. The only naval action during the Rebellion of 1798 occurred at Fethard Harbour, which was bombarded by two ships.[29] Restoration work was carried out immediately by the government, presumably at the

B. COLFER

Fig. 26 The quarrying of rock for burning in limekilns is remembered in the name Carraigahoy (Carraig an Aith: limekiln rock) a former quarry on the coast south of Slade. The name indicates that quarrying was taking place in the eighteenth century when Irish was still commonly spoken.

insistence of the well-connected Loftus family. Quays were also constructed at St Kearn's on the Colclough estate and at Arthurstown, Duncannon and Ballyhack on the Dunbrody estate. The discovery in Ballyhack Castle of fine mid seventeenth-century decorated pottery of French, Portuguese, Dutch and English origin, as well as a Spanish olive-jar, indicates that the Etchingham family had extensive continental trading connections.[30]

Local stone was exploited extensively on the Loftus estate. At Herrylock on the cliffs at Templetown, millstones, water troughs, land rollers, grinding stones, ridge tiles and other objects were cut from the Old Red Sandstone. The first known reference to this quarry was in 1736, when 'Templetown mill and a part of Houseland with the millstone quarry' formed part of a marriage agreement between Nicholas Loftus and Mary Hume of Fermanagh.[31] It was referred to again in the estate maps of 1771. The method used to quarry the millstones at Herrylock was described in 1772: 'They poole or cleave the rocks with wedges and bring them to the form of millstones with picks and pickhammers (for no chizzel

B. COLFER

Fig. 27 Limestone rock from the Hook was brought by boat to this limekiln beside the bridge at Tintern Abbey. The top of the limekiln was battlemented to match the architecture of the bridge and abbey.

will cut them) and they are very sound and grind corn clean and well: and I have known good walls to have been built of this stone: for they dress tolerably well with the hammer and bind hard in their mortar.'[32] The presence of Herrylock millstones in numerous mills throughout the south-east is an indication of the commercial significance of the quarry.

Because of its scarcity elsewhere in county Wexford, there was a constant demand for Hook limestone during the nineteenth century. The limestone, reduced to powder by burning in kilns, was used to improve the quality of land and was mixed with sand to make lime mortar for building purposes. In a survey carried out in 1807, when lime was being brought by cart from county Carlow, no mention is made of limestone-burning at the Hook.[33] However, some small-scale production of lime for local use must have been taking place in 1771, as one of the fields was then called Limekiln Park. The same survey noted that 'lime might be burned here very cheap for use of the estate.' Some quarrying was going on throughout the eighteenth century, as in 1746 the Colcloughs paid one and a half guineas to Walter Breen of the Hook for 60 tons of limestone for the use of the tenants on the estate, probably delivered by boat to the double limekiln beside the quay at St Kearns.[34] The long tradition of lime-burning

is also suggested by a place-name on the cliffs at Slade where a former quarry is still referred to as Carraigahoy, from the Irish 'Carraig an Aith' (Limekiln Rock). The commercial potential of lime was obviously appreciated, as by 1837 Lewis noted that there was extensive quarrying of limestone on the Hook. Not only was the rock burned locally but it was also transported by boat to other parts of the county; fifteen boats were employed in conveying limestone from the Hook to Fethard, 'whence it is sent up the river Scar (Corock) into the interior of the county.'[35] This is indicated by the survival of limekilns at St Kearn's and at Tintern Abbey, where limestone and coal were brought by lighters as far as the bridge. Hook limestone was sent even further afield, to Pembrokeshire; schooners carrying a cargo of coal from south Wales to Slade returned with a load of limestone rock as ballast. This may have been the destination of the 'boats of large tonnage' which took on stone at the pier of Slade as late as 1864.[36]

B. COLFER

Fig. 28 During the nineteenth century, limestone rock was quarried extensively at Slade. A roadway, cut through the rock to give access to the quarry and the seashore, is still referred to as 'Johnny's Road.'

FARMHOUSE CLUSTERS

In spite of the efforts made by landlords to modernise their estates, some land continued to be held and worked in a more traditional fashion, showing that improving landlordism and time-honoured farming practices were not mutually exclusive. Although the Loftus estate was one of the biggest in the county, it contained some of the finest examples of archaic agrarian landscapes to be found in south Leinster. These were the farmhouse clusters, usually without a church or other institutional buildings, associated with unconsolidated holdings sometimes consisting of scattered parcels of land in 'open-fields.' The allocation of strips, originally dispersed to ensure a fair distribution of different land types and periodically re-assigned, gradually came to be permanently occupied by the same family. Unlike the majority of Gaelic clusters in the west and north, the south-eastern examples, located on good land, are believed to have originated on the manors of the medieval period. The south-west Wexford examples can be seen as an extension of the south Kilkenny grouping, which is regarded as the heartland of this type

Fig. 30 The farmhouse cluster of Herrylock in Templetown, where, as well as holding dispersed plots of land, some residents also worked as stone-masons in the millstone quarry on the adjacent Old Red Sandstone cliffs.

of farm village.[37] The clusters located in Old English baronies appear to be deep-rooted, containing communities where traditional values and practices thrived. Far from being primitive, the farmhouse cluster, with occupants frequently bonded by kinship ties, facilitated

Fig. 29 The farmhouse cluster of Broomhill in the mid-1980s. The occupants, with others who lived in a smaller cluster called The Spring, held dispersed plots scattered throughout the townland. The cluster has disintegrated to a large extent, with new houses being built along the road at the top of the picture.

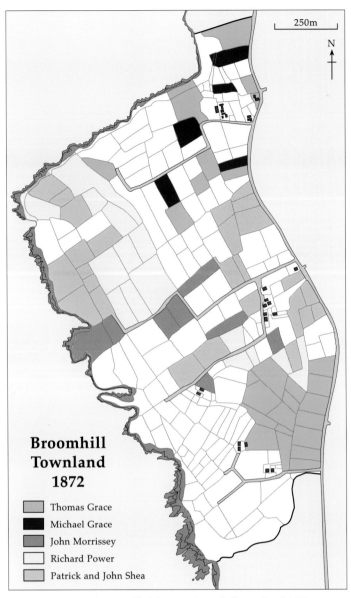

Fig. 31 Pattern of dispersed holdings in Broomhill townland, 1872.

families of Gaelic origin. Some of the farmhouse groups were of significant size; for example, the townland of Broomhill had 143 occupants in 1841 living in twenty-one houses, mostly in a farmhouse cluster.[40] Today only one house remains occupied and the cluster has disintegrated. The isolated nature of the peninsula may have contributed to the survival of these clusters, as they were concentrated on the Loftus lands in the more remote part of the area, suggesting that they originated on the Templar/Hospitaller manor of Kilcloggan and the episcopal manor of Fethard.

ESTATE VILLAGES

The encouragement of villages was an essential component of estate development.[41] As well as providing accommodation for estate workers, these villages facilitated economic and administrative activity as well as providing religious, educational and social services. During the first quarter of the 1800s, Arthur Chichester built the estate village of Arthurstown on the Dunbrody estate, which became a focal point for the surrounding area. Services included a hospital, a coastguard station, a police barracks and a courthouse; revenue was earned by the estate through tolls on markets for agricultural produce. The building of a pier at Arthurstown in 1829 provided extra revenue, as tolls were levied on all transactions, particularly coal and culm imported from Wales.[42] The existing villages of Duncannon – where a new pier was constructed in 1851 – and Ballyhack were also improved for the tenants on the estate. At Ballyhack, the centre of the salmon fishery, the ferry contributed to estate income, as did rents from fishing weirs inherited from the Cistercians; in 1853, ten salmon weirs in the estuary

co-operation and the pooling of labour and equipment.[38] Unconsolidated holdings with associated farmhouse villages were dominant features on the 1841 Ordnance Survey maps in the townlands of: Churchtown (where the farmhouses were clustered at the parish centre) and Slade in the parish of Hook; Broomhill, Herrylock and Lewistown in Templetown parish; and at Connagh, Wood Village, Newtown and Gorteens in the parish of Fethard. One possible example existed at Ballyvelig on the Dunbrody estate. In the townland of Grange on the Loftus estate, which contained the farm villages of Wood Village and Newtown, eight families with the south Munster name of Foley worked forty hectares of land in forty-five separate parcels.[39] The presence of other names at Grange (Barden, Power, Devereux, Grace and Hurdus) indicated that traditional farming practices were not confined to

Fig. 32 The chapel village of Ramsgrange from an 1803 Dunbrody estate map. (North to the left of picture.) Originally a Cistercian grange, the village developed around a tower house and a triangular fair green with a characteristic concentration of cottier cabins. The location of the chapel suggests that the green was a public commons. The chapel, burned in the aftermath of 1798, may have been rebuilt with compensation money.

Fig. 33 A school in Saltmills, built by the Colcloughs for their tenants as part of the development of the estate village, has been restored by the local community as the Colclough Memorial Hall.

Fig. 34 The estate village of Saltmills, with a new bridge and church, was built down the inlet from the abbey early in the nineteenth century, replacing the old village of Tintern which was located close to the abbey.

generated £250.[43] As the owners were, for the most part, absentee landlords, the 12,000-acre estate was let to tenant farmers, apart from demesne lands around Dunbrody Park and other lands in the vicinity of the abbey. The individual farm units were inherited from the Cistercian system of sub-division. Some farmers were presumably descendants of former monastic tenants, although the Chichesters did bring in a handful of Scottish tenants in the second half of the nineteenth century.[44]

The seventeenth-century *Down Survey* maps contain illustrations of tower houses surrounded by groups of cabins, an expression of a society where the different social classes shared the same settlement site, probably a

Fig. 35 The village of Arthurstown, built by Arthur Chichester at King's Bay on the shore of Waterford Harbour in the early nineteenth century.

Samuel Lewis's description of the Tintern estate in 1837

The soil is fertile, and the system of agriculture is much improved, green crops for winter feeding having been introduced with success; and the cottages of the farmers and peasantry exhibit a considerable degree of neatness and comfort. An inlet from Bannow Bay is navigable to the old bridge near the abbey for lighters bringing limestone and coal and there is a small fishery. Tintern, the property of Caesar Colclough, and now the residence of his agent, J. W. Goff, is beautifully situated in a sequestered spot near the margin of the bay, and in the midst of a richly wooded demesne; the family mansion has been formed principally from the chancel of the ancient conventual church, of which the tower and parts of the wall form a picturesque feature in the grounds; but from the frequent alterations which the abbey has undergone, these ruins have lost much of their original character. Subsequently to the formation of the present mansion, the ancient domestic buildings were removed and the materials were used in the erection of the chapel of ease and the bridge near the abbey. The church [at Saltmills], a

neat edifice in the later English style, with a square tower crowned with pinnacles, was erected in 1818, at an expense of £1,000. The [Catholic] chapel at Ballycullane is an ancient and spacious building near which a residence for the priest has recently been erected; and at Gusserane is a handsome modern chapel, adjoining which also is a residence for the priest. ... A school at Saltmills is supported by Mr. Colclough and a school house has lately been erected at Ballycullane; in these and in the private schools of the parish about 160 children are educated. The village of Tintern which was contiguous to the abbey of that name, was taken down within the last twenty years and rebuilt upon the townland of Saltmills, by which name it is now more generally known. In 1831, [the village] contained 29 houses and cottages, all neatly painted and ornamented in front with small gardens. The female inhabitants are mostly employed in straw-platting and bonnet making, which are carried on to some extent; and some of the males are employed in fishing. A school for boys and a dispensary are entirely supported by Mr. Colclough.

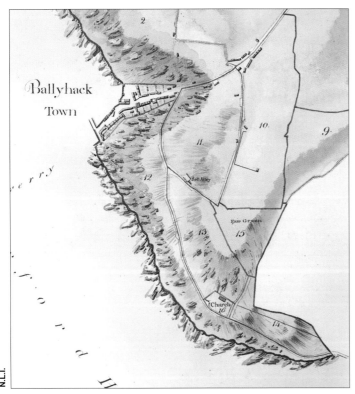

Fig. 36 The 1803 Dunbrody estate map shows the village of Ballyhack with an upper and lower section, as at present, and with a row of houses, which no longer exist, along the water's edge. The church and triangular fair green were located on the high ground to the south of the village. The early ball-alley near the fair green is of particular interest.

survival of the medieval manorial villages where houses were clustered around the castle and church. In the eighteenth century, however, economic and social forces accelerated the abandonment of this settlement form and the movement of farmers and labourers away from the 'big house.' The old village of Tintern was located just to the south of the abbey and in 1812 a visitor observed signs of decay in the village, which the proprietor did not desire to be so near his mansion.[45] Following Caesar Colclough's return from France, the old village of Tintern was abandoned and a new village was constructed further down the estuary in the townland of Saltmills, a mile distant from the abbey. The village of Saltmills included a new parish church and a new bridge across the estuary.[46]

Fethard

In 1613, while it was still in the hands of the bishop, Fethard had received a new charter constituting it as a free borough. The corporation, consisting of a provost (or portreeve), twelve burgessess and a commonalty, was dominated by members of the Old English community, principally the Suttons and Keatings. The first corporation members were James Keating (provost), with William King, James Sutton, William Woodes, Richard Farrell,

David Rowrie (?Rowe), William Keating, Nicholas Sutton, Alexander Keating, Peter Sutton, Robert Sutton, John O'Neill and Richard Devereux. The corporation was empowered to have a guild market, to send two members to parliament, to hold a court on Thursdays, to have a free market on Wednesdays and a fair on the 5th of August and the day following.[47] After the acquisition of the manor of Fethard by the Loftus Hall estate in 1634, the borough was developed as its economic and administrative centre. Following the Cromwellian confiscations, lands in Fethard that had remained in the hands of the principal Catholic families in the area (Redmond, Keating, Laffan, Sutton, Lewis) had been transferred to new, presumably Protestant, tenants. Thomas Redmond, a member of the Redmond Hall family, suffered the biggest loss, but Elinor Redmond, possibly his widow, managed to retain a small amount of land. A survey made at that time shows the town in ruins, with only eight thatched cabins in the two streets, High Street and Church Street. Most of the gardens or 'strips' were described as having house plots only.[48]

Fig. 37 The original artwork for a coat of arms granted to Fethard by the Principal Herald, following the town's reincorporation in 1613. The depiction of a warrior on the crest was based on the false assumption that the name Fethard originated as Fighthard, because of the association with nearby Baginbun where the English invaders first landed and fought.

B. COLFER

Fig. 38 This 1980s aerial view of Fethard shows the wide street of the estate village which was developed during the eighteenth century. Some medieval elements can be identified, particularly the complex of church, motte and castle to the north of the street and relic burgage strips at the rear of the houses. An incipient tourist development can be seen at top left. During the 1990s, much of the green space shown around the village in this picture has been covered by holiday home developments. The Old Rectory, standing on glebe land at bottom right, replaced an earlier castle on the same site. The rectory was home to the Fethard Observatory (1908–18), established by Rev. W. F. A. Ellison (1864–1936), who installed a 7.3 inch (185mm) reflector in a dome of his own making. When Ellison was appointed director of Armagh Observatory in 1918, he brought the Fethard telescope with him. His son, Mervyn Archdall (1909–63), born in Fethard, also a well-known astronomer, held a number of high-profile positions, including director of Dunsink Observatory.

In 1684, Fethard comprised two or three small castles, about forty cabins and thatched houses, and a roofless church.[49] At that stage fishermen and sailors had to make do with a sheltered cove, as no harbour had been built. This description of a dilapidated medieval town indicates that no real development had taken place at that stage. During the following century, the village was given its present shape. A 1771 survey described the 'two rows of handsome brick houses' which lined both sides of the present street.[50] One of the castles, presumably the one that still survives, was in good repair. A pier and quay had been built and the town had a 'king's barge, a surveyor and a boatman.' The Loftus family intended to use Fethard as a port, but this was made difficult by the increase of the sandbar at the mouth of the bay, probably the same bar that contributed to the desertion of the town of Bannow. A 1770 report observed that Fethard had been a seaport of some consequence in former days, but that the harbour and town had 'dwindled into insignificance' because of the increase of the bar. The surnames of tenants recorded in the 1771 estate suvey in and around Fethard indicate

that the majority of them had arrived from Britain during the previous century, creating, as the surviving records of St Mogue's church show, a substantial Protestant community. The extent of the social transformation is

B. COLFER

Fig. 39 The pre-Norman origin of Fethard church is indicated by the base-batter on the walls and its dedication to St Mogue (Aidan), the first bishop of Ferns. As the parish church on the medieval episcopal manor and the present-day place of worship for the Church of Ireland community, it has been in almost continuous use for a millennium.

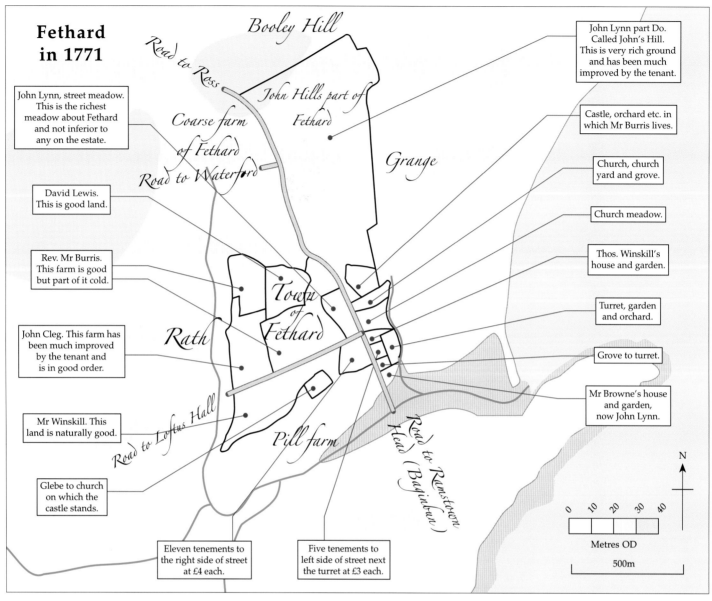

Fethard in 1771

Booley Hill

Road to Ross

John Hills part of Fethard

Coarse farm of Fethard

Road to Waterford

Grange

Town of Fethard

Rath

Road to Loftus Hall

Pill farm

Road to Ramstown Head (Baginbun)

John Lynn, street meadow. This is the richest meadow about Fethard and not inferior to any on the estate.

John Lynn part Do. Called John's Hill. This is very rich ground and has been much improved by the tenant.

Castle, orchard etc. in which Mr Burris lives.

David Lewis. This is good land.

Church, church yard and grove.

Church meadow.

Rev. Mr Burris. This farm is good but part of it cold.

Thos. Winskill's house and garden.

John Cleg. This farm has been much improved by the tenant and is in good order.

Turret, garden and orchard.

Grove to turret.

Mr Winskill. This land is naturally good.

Mr Browne's house and garden, now John Lynn.

Glebe to church on which the castle stands.

Eleven tenements to the right side of street at £4 each.

Five tenements to left side of street next the turret at £3 each.

N

0 10 20 30 40

Metres OD

500m

Fig. 40 A map of Fethard from the 1771 Loftus estate maps superimposed on a modern base. The part of Fethard to the right of the road was included in the townland of Grange by the Ordnance Survey in 1841. The land held by John Lynn is still known as John's Hill.

indicated by the inclusion of only one surname of the 1613 corporation members among a subsequent list of tenants. One of the 1771 tenants, John Lynn, is remembered in the area known as John's Hill just north of the village. No effort was made to modernise the land-holding system around Fethard, particularly in the townland of Grange. The 1872 estate maps show a complex agrarian pattern of small fields and dispersed fragmented holdings in Grange, possibly a relic of the burgess lands on the medieval episcopal manor. Extensive remains of this land-holding system survive to the present time. In 1837, the parish of Fethard had 2,153 inhabitants; 320 of these were in the town, where some of the houses were occupied by members of the coastguard. The harbour had been built, or rebuilt, by the government since 1798 and, as well as

considerable fishing activity, there was some trade in coal, timber, iron, slates, cattle and pigs.[51]

Linen production

The rapid population growth during the eighteenth century was accompanied by a sustained rise in agricultural trade. Progressive landlords stimulated improvements in agricultural techniques and supported the linen industry as a means of boosting the income of smaller landholders. Linen production rose dramatically in Ireland, principally in the north-eastern Ulster counties.[52] The Colclough estate strove to establish a 'cottage' weaving enterprise, which resulted in an influx of skilled workers from outside the region. In 1755, for example, land in Saltmills was let to Joseph and John Rea,

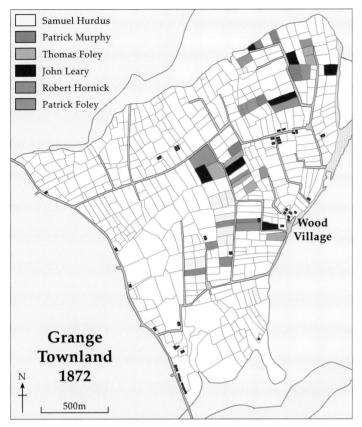

Samuel Hurdus
Patrick Murphy
Thomas Foley
John Leary
Robert Hornick
Patrick Foley

Wood Village

Grange Townland 1872

N

500m

Fig. 41 The pattern of dispersed land-holding in Grange in 1872 is shown by plotting the land occupied by six individuals. This type of fragmented holding presumably originated on the burgage lands of the medieval episcopal town of Fethard and continues to influence land ownership and the pattern of settlement and new house building in the townland.

two linen weavers from Waterford.[53] In 1761, Tintern was one of the centres of linen production in the county. In that year, a society formed to promote the linen industry in the county and to increase the number of weavers sold flax seed to cottiers and gave a spinning-wheel to each person who sowed flax.[54] John Bernard Trotter, who stayed at Tintern, for a month in 1812, observed that the Colcloughs had greatly encouraged manufacture in the village of Tintern to which skilled workmen were brought from all parts to weave linen, diaper, check, jane and woollens on thirty-six looms in the district.[55] The extent of the industry required the setting up of a yarn market and market house. The widespread involvement of the tenants is evident from the numerous references to weavers in the eighteenth-century church records. In 1812, there were still some looms on the Tintern estate, operated by a family of Palatines descended from those brought over from Germany, and in 1819 two bleach yards supported the manufacture of linen. In 1837, there was still a bleach field in use beside the Owenduff river at Yoletown on the northern part of the Tintern lands. As the linen industry was based on the growing of flax, weaving had a strong agricultural basis. The crop required considerable processing and field-name evidence suggests that many farmers grew a small amount to meet the requirements of the industry; for example, there is a 'flaxfield' at Ballygarret near Saltmills. Flax was also cultivated on the

B. COLFER

Fig. 42 A number of mills, including this example at Dungulph, one of several on the Dungulph stream, were used as flaxmills when required.

Fig. 43 The Tintern craft tradition continues in the work of basket-makers Barbara Kelly and Irene Stafford of Ballyvaroge, whose ancestors were involved in the spinning and weaving industry on the Colclough estate.

other two estates, which supported, and in a sense exploited, this initiative. On the Loftus estate there was a

flaxfield at Ingard in 1771 and a flaxpark at Loftus Hall: a small field at Churchtown is still known as the 'flax garden.' Two derelict mills on the Dungulph river were originally flaxmills and a former mill, still known as Flaxmill, was located in the townland of Ramsgrange on the Dunbrody estate.

PENAL LANDSCAPE

In the aftermath of the Reformation, religion and politics became inextricably linked and by the 1570s it was clear that a choice had to be made about religious affiliation. The great majority of Irish and Wexford people opted to remain Catholic, despite the severe political and social difficulties which accompanied this option. The decision to adhere to a religion other than the official state religion was unusual and would ultimately lead to dispossession and social upheaval.[56] Although Catholic practice survived until the mid-seventeenth century, the political climate in

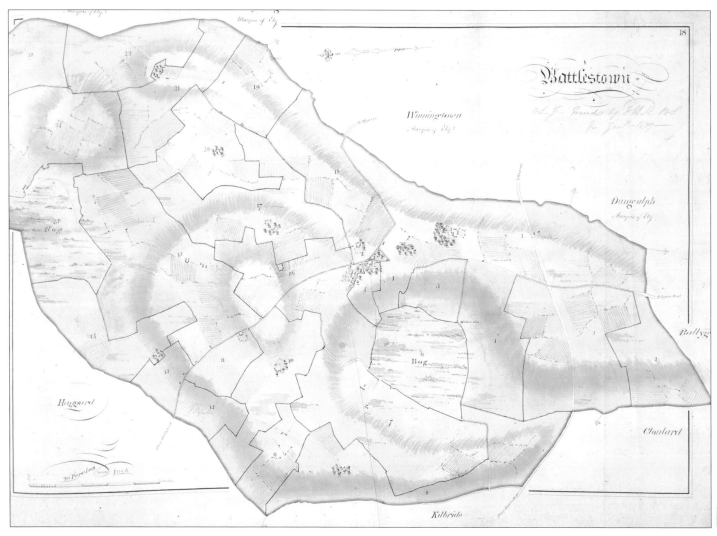

Fig. 44 The townland of Battlestown from the Dunbrody estate maps, 1803 (north is at left of map). The townland was divided into a system of tenant farms which formed the basis for the modern agricultural units. The bog in the south of the townland (an unusual feature in the Wexford landscape) is drained by the Poulfur stream. The townland got its name from the Bataille family, who were tenants on the Cistercian estate of Dunbrody.

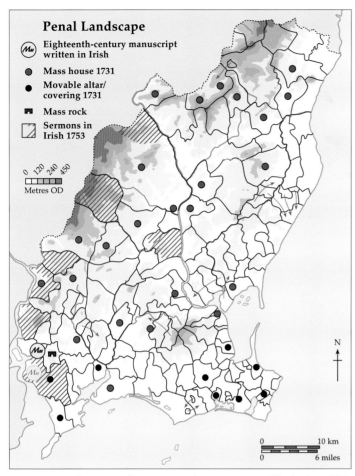

Fig. 45 Mass-houses and temporary altars in county Wexford in 1731. Concentrations in the Hook and the barony of Forth indicate that the landlords in those areas were active supporters of the Penal Code. The medieval parish layout shown here (now referred to as civil parishes) was abandoned after the Reformation and the Catholic and Protestant churches organised dual parochial systems which bore no relation to the obsolete medieval divisions. The survival of Irish manuscripts and the delivering of sermons in Irish provide evidence for the use of the language in the south-west of the county in the eighteenth century.

the aftermath of the Confederate and Williamite wars saw the enactment of anti-Catholic legislation. The Anglican Church of Ireland was established by law, entitling it to be maintained by tithes from the entire population. The Penal Code was aimed not so much at the elimination of Catholicism as the maintenance of social and economic control by the minority Anglican ascendancy over the majority Catholic population.[57] However, the Penal Laws were not universally implemented and by 1730 there was a rudimentary Catholic parochial system in county Wexford. In 1731, a report on the state of 'Popery' in Ireland recorded thirty mass-houses, ten recently built, and ten temporary altars (presumably including mass-rocks) in the county.[58] The temporary altars were concentrated in two districts: the barony of Forth, which had many small Cromwellian landlords, and the Loftus and Dunbrody estates in Shelburne. As the implement-

ation of the Penal Laws depended to a large extent on the attitude of the local magnate, this is a strong indication that the construction of mass-houses was not permitted by the landlords in these areas. Significantly, there was a mass-rock in Killesk, an outlying townland on the Loftus estate. This hard-line attitude of the Loftus family is contradicted by the holding, in 1771, of five townlands on the estate, as a middleman tenant, by Thomas Broaders, the local Catholic priest.[59] This gives credence to the supposed supernatural incident, known as the 'Ghost of Loftus Hall,' which Broaders is credited with having exorcised some time previously.

In the period 1745–86, the Catholic diocese of Ferns was organised by Bishop Sweetman.[60] When Confirmation was administered in thirty-four parishes in 1753, there was a church and priest's house in each place.[61] The sermon in Ramsgrange church was given in Irish, indicating that the native language was widely understood in the district; thirteen per cent of the population of Shelburne was Irish-speaking in 1781, the highest figure for the county.[62] Two eighteenth-century manuscripts in Irish containing assorted material were compiled in the region. The

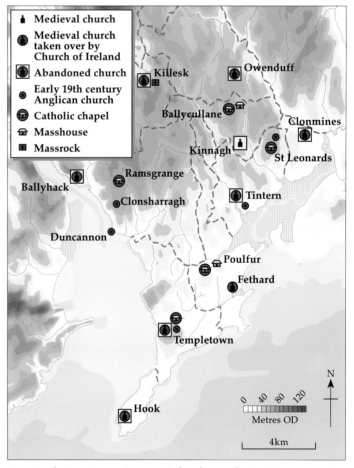

Fig. 46 The location and status of churches in the Hook region during penal times. Fethard and Clonsharragh (Killesk) church are still in use.

Fig. 47 The surviving mass-house at Tomhaggard in the barony of Bargy, drawn by Mai McElroy in the 1950s, provides an example of the archaic structures used by the Catholic community during penal times. It was located on the Devereux farmstead, the old landlords of the area.

Fig. 49 A mass-rock with incised cross (inset) in the Loftus townland of Killesk. Originally located beside a small stream at the bottom of a sloping field which formed a natural amphitheatre, the rock was recently moved to its present position on a stone outcrop in the centre of the field.

earliest, by Pilib Ó Giobúin of Kilhile, mentioned the famine which followed the heavy frost and snow of 1740; the second was written by Séamus Ó Murchú of Campile in the 1770s.[63] As late as 1812, Trotter commented on the widespread use of Irish in the vicinity of Dunbrody and made special mention of the Irish-speaking boatmen on the Barrow.[64]

By the 1780s, the dismantling of the Penal Laws had begun and continued, despite political difficulties, until Catholic Emancipation was finally achieved in 1829. The existence of registers for the parish of Hook (including Templetown, Fethard, Duncannon and Ramsgrange) from the 1790s is a strong indication of an efficient pre-Emancipation parish organisation. Statistics recorded by the Commission of Public Instruction in the 1830s provide

information on the relative numbers in the two church communities. In 1831, there were 521 Protestants and 3,508 Catholics in the parishes of Fethard, Templetown and Hook.[65]

The post-Reformation religious divide had significant landscape implications, as many of the old parish centres were eventually abandoned, except for burials, and the churches gradually fell into desolate ruin. No church-building subsequently took place for almost two hundred years. In 1615, three Protestant pastors were ministering in the area: Richard Thompson in Fethard, Thomas Fleming in the Hook and Templetown and Richard Allen in Tintern (where the church had been restored by Thomas Colclough). The churches of Clonmines and Ballyhack were vacant.[66] All of these churches (with the exception of Fethard, although it too was described as unroofed in the late seventeenth century) were eventually abandoned. On the Loftus estate, Templetown church continued to be used by the Protestant community for two centuries. Early

Fig. 48 The remains of a cruciform chapel built in 1795 at Boratray in Templetown. It continued in use until the present parish church was built a century later. During the Land War, the doors of this church were barricaded as a public protest against the transfer of a popular priest.

Fig. 50 The church at Poulfur was built c. 1820 in a secluded hollow (poll: a hole; fothar: a wooded hollow), probably on the site of an earlier chapel, to the same cruciform plan as the church in Templetown. The church was renovated in the early 1980s.

Fig. 51 The medieval parochial centre of Templetown continued in use as a centre of worship until the middle of the nineteenth century. This chalice, donated in 1639 to St Mary's church in Templetown by Nicholas Loftus of Kilcloggan, is one of the earliest surviving examples of Irish church silver.

in the nineteenth century, a new church was built at Templetown incorporating the medieval tower as a sacristy and belfry. As the Church of Ireland community was concentrated in and around Fethard, Templetown church was closed later in the century and St Mogue's church in Fethard became the only Protestant church on the Loftus estate. In the early nineteenth century, new Protestant churches were built at Tintern (Saltmills) and St Leonards on the Tintern estate and at Clonsharragh on the Dunbrody estate. The church at Saltmills is a typical example of the Board of First Fruit churches, which were built throughout Ireland at this time.

Catholic chapels were built in the region before the Penal Laws had been removed from the statute books. A chapel existed at Ramsgrange in 1753 and another cruciform chapel was erected at Templetown in 1795.[67] A small eighteenth-century chapel at Ballycullane was replaced by a cruciform church early in the nineteenth century.[68] According to local tradition, a mud-walled thatched penal chapel was built in the eighteenth century in a secluded location at Poulfur (poll fothar: a wooded hollow) on the Loftus estate. In about 1820, this was

Fig. 53 The Protestant church at Tintern, a typical First Fruits building, was erected in 1818 as a replacement for the old medieval church near the abbey. The Board of First Fruits raised funds by collecting contributions of 'first fruit' products from parishioners. The church is no longer in use.

Fig. 52 The Anglican church of All Saints (Killesk church) was built at Clonsharragh on the Dunbrody estate in the early nineteenth century.

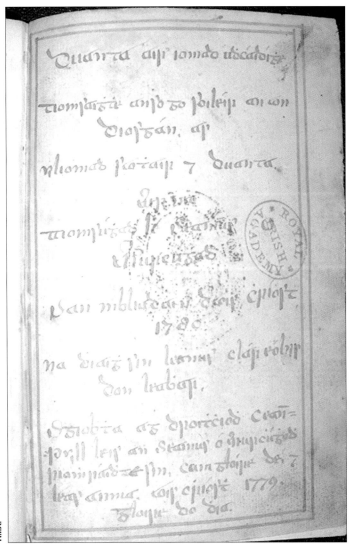

R.I.A.

Fig. 54 The title page from an Irish manuscript, written at Campile in 1779. This title page mimics the conventions of a contemporary printed volume, both in layout and phraseology. That influence can also be seen in the neat index, the use of explanatory footnotes, and the modelling of the collection on popular English-language miscellanies. The writer is clearly modifying the older Gaelic tradition of the Duanaire (manuscript volume of poems) to suit contempory taste. Murphy was an active scribe in the 1780s, indicating the continuing presence of a vibrant Gaelic culture in the Hook area. In this, as in many other ways, the Hook belongs to Munster. If one looks at Irish-language transcription in the eighteenth century, Campile was the point furthest east of the most active region, stretching from Clare to south Kilkenny.

replaced by the present cruciform chapel, which is similar to the one at Templetown. A 1798 gravestone inscription in the graveyard suggests that the new church was built on the site of its penal predecessor.[69]

EMIGRATION FROM SOUTH-WEST WEXFORD TO NEWFOUNDLAND
By improving agricultural techniques and exploiting natural resources, the estate system brought economic benefits to the area and provided considerable employment, helping to make south Wexford one of the most advanced agricultural regions in Ireland. However, the the rising tide of the

Title page from an Irish manuscript, Campile 1779

Duanta air iomaid udhcáidíghe timsiaghte anso go suiléir an aon diosgán as uliomad sathair & duanta arna tiomsaighadh le Seamus Ó Murchughadh san mbliadain daois Criost 1780 Na dhiagh sin leannus clar eolas don liubhar

Sgriobhtha ag droithchiod Cean-pull leis an Seamus Ó Murchughadh raimraidte sin cuin gloire De & lei'anmna aois Criost 1779 gloire do Dhia

(Poems for every occasion readily collected in one volume from many works and poems collected by James Murphy in 1780, followed by an index to the volume. Transcribed at the bridge of Campile by James Murphy for the glory of God and his own soul.)

eighteenth-century economic boom did not lift all boats. The poorest families, even on the most advanced estates, were the labourers and 'cottiers,' often occupying areas where archaic agrarian practices continued.[70] As population levels rose, a combination of economic and social pressures forced these often landless labourers to avail of the opportunities offered by the Newfoundland fishery. The connection between Waterford Harbour and its river system with Newfoundland is well established. Because of the unifying nature of the harbour, there has been a historical affinity between south-west Wexford and Waterford, typified by a distinctive estuarine accent, the centuries-old ferry from Ballyhack to Passage, and the frequent occurrence of Munster surnames in the Hook region.

From the end of the seventeenth century to 1830, the Waterford Harbour catchment area was a major source of supplies and labour for the English fishery in Newfoundland, known in Irish as Talamh an Éisc, or the fishing ground.[71] Early in the eighteenth century, fishing ships from the west country ports in England began to call to Waterford to collect cheap provisions and labour for the cod fishery. For more than a century, the vast majority of migrants were young unmarried men, with a small number of women who worked as servants. Throughout the eighteenth century, the Irish were mainly seasonal migrants and there were probably no more than 500 settled Irish in Newfoundland in the 1730s, rising to 4,000 by 1770. Immigration increased in the late eighteenth century, with a big influx after 1800. By 1836 there were approximately 35,000 Irish living in Newfoundland, representing 50 per cent of the population. Because of the sophisticated supply system established in Waterford, and to a lesser extent New Ross, the estuary of Waterford Harbour, with the three 'sister rivers,' the Barrow, Nore and Suir, was the source of most of this movement of people. Ninety per cent of all emigrants came from within forty miles of Waterford with a quarter of the total coming

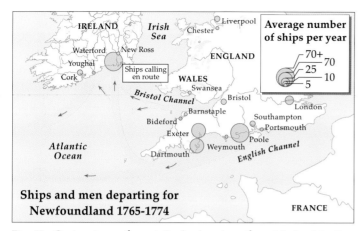

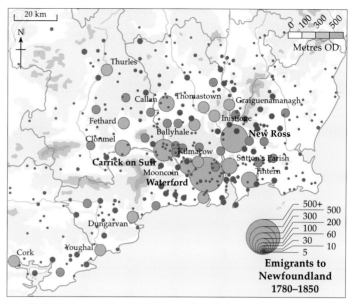

Fig. 55 Centres in south-west England and south-east Ireland trading with Newfoundland in the late eighteenth century. Many ships from the English ports called to Waterford Harbour for men and provisions.

Fig. 56 The known origins of emigrants from Ireland to Newfoundland.

from county Wexford. In Newfoundland, the Irish community was concentrated south of St John's on the Avalon peninsula. Companies in the south-east became actively involved in supplying both provisions and workers to the Newfoundland fisheries, principally the Penroses, Rivers, Jacobs, Watsons, Nevins and Strangmans of Waterford, the Koughs of Ross (originally Koch, a Palatine family) and the Sweetmans of Newbawn.

The decision to go to the fishery in Newfoundland was taken for complex reasons. In the mid-seventeenth century, the Shelburne area was in the middle range of population density; a lack of suitable tenants is suggested by the introduction of Protestant immigrants. Although numbers were rising in the eighteenth century, it is unlikely that high population levels was a factor, at least until after 1780, when there was a massive surge in numbers. In 1841, for example, the Hook had a population of over 500, four times the present figure. The chance to avail of seasonal work in exchange for ready cash, with the added convenience of boarding ship at Ballyhack or New Ross, presented an attractive proposition, and the injection of money into the economy of the Shelburne area must have been significant. A story recounted by the nineteenth-century folklorist, Patrick Kennedy, in which he describes a visit to a house just outside Ross, highlighted the financial incentives for young men who signed on for the fishery:

> I was never in their house for five minutes without hearing of the young man who was in Newfoundland, and would be sending home quintals of dried fish, and goodness knows what besides, next fall; and come home himself some day with a load of money; and keep the old couple snug and comfortable; and give his sister a pretty little fortune when her turn came to be married.[72]

The return of people with money and stories created a snowball effect which could be compared to the situation in the 1950s and 1960s, when the affluence of those coming back from England encouraged others to return with them. Newfoundland also offered an opportunity for adventure and a different, if demanding, lifestyle. The attractions of the voyage are hinted at in a description of the Shelburne area in 1816:

> The men in general are dressed like sailors and frequently migrate to Newfoundland, whither both young men and women repair in crowds 'on a venture' every spring, and in like numbers return every autumn; and from habit they think

Fig. 57 An eighteenth-century illustration of cod processing in Newfoundland on a platform, referred to as a stage, on the seashore. The requisite skills would have been widely practised in the Hook.

Seventeenth-century surnames from Shelburne later recorded in Newfoundland

Shelburne		Newfoundland	
Byrne	9	Byrne	3
Bryan	8	Brien	2
Colfer	9	Colford	4
Cullen	14	Cullen	1
Chapman	8	Chapman	1
Doyle	10	Doyle	6
Furlong	8	Furlong	1
Kavanagh	9	Kavanagh	2
Keating	13	Keating	1
Kelly	15	Kelly	1
Lacey	7	Lacey	1
Power	16	Power	6
Redmond	7	Redmond	2
Sutton	25	Sutton	1
Sinnott	8	Sinnott	1
Walsh	27	Walsh	3
Whelan	12	Whelan	1

Other Shelburne families recorded in Newfoundland

Breen, Burke, Connor, Cowman, Donoghue, Duggan, Dwyer, Fardy, Finn, Fortune, Grace, Gleeson, Howlett, Kehoe, Kennedy, Kent, Lawlor, Molloy, Moran, Rossiter, Ryan, Wallace, White, Whitty, Hanton

as little of the voyage as they do of passing over the river Barrow.

Apart from the town of New Ross, the largest volume of recorded emigration in the south-west Wexford area came from Tintern and Suttons parishes. The relatively low numbers from the Dunbrody and Loftus estates suggest a higher level of security and employment. The high numbers from Suttons parish may have been because it was outside the large estate system and its location adjacent to the river. There is no indication that emigration was politically motivated, although Tintern parish, from which there was a high level of emigration, was riven by sectarian tensions during the 1798 Rebellion. However, the probability that the Tintern estate was the least developed

economically could also account for the higher emigration rate. By contrast, Fethard, on the Loftus estate, where there was a considerable number of Protestant tenants, had a very low level of emigration.

Seafaring experience was an obvious advantage for those going to the Newfoundland fishery, as men with a certain level of skill in seamanship and fishing were in demand. Different categories of workers were sought, presumably with different rates of pay; in 1776, an advertisement seeking 'a number of good fishermen, boatmasters, midshipmen and foreshipmen, and a few good salmon fishermen' was placed in a Waterford newspaper. In an area so closely related to sea and river, with a long tradition of maritime activity, the men from the south-west Wexford region must have read (or heard) the advertisement with interest. The maritime experience and skills of many men in south-west Wexford, particularly from coastal communities, made them very suitable candidates for the cod fishery in Talamh an Éisc and was probably one of the reasons why many decided to go. The extent of movement of people from the area to Newfoundland is vividly illustrated by a comparison of family names in the two regions. The 'census' of 1659 lists thirty-five principal surnames in Shelburne, and of these eighteen (just over 50%) are recorded in Newfoundland as having originated in south-west Wexford. Twenty-five other surnames recorded in Shelburne between the sixteenth and nineteenth centuries, many of them still very prominent in the surname profile of the area, are also present in Newfoundland with documented south-west Wexford origins.[73] People did not emigrate empty-handed: they brought with them their customs, sport, language (including expressions such as 'Ballyhack dirty butter'!), place-names, religion and loyalties.[74] Hurling matches were played between Wexford 'yellow-bellies,' Waterford

Individuals from the Hook region recorded in Newfoundland; date when recorded and place of origin, if known.

John Breen	1816		Michael Fardy	1863		— Molloy	1823	
Mary Breen	1831		John Fortune	1841	Churchtown	Bridget Murphy		
James Brien	1810		Patrick Fortune		Slade	Links Murphy	1824	
Thomas Brien		Booley	Anne Gleeson	1817		Richard Phelan	1848	
Peter Brian	1819		Mary Gleeson	1850		Bridget Power		
John Browne	1814	St James's Parish	Patrick Gleeson	1808		James Power		
Walter Burke	1811	St James's Parish	Margaret Grandy	1830	Duncannon	Mary Power	1851	
Patrick Byrne	1821		John Hanton			Margaret Reid	1829	
James Campbell	1836	Duncannon	Matthew Hearn	1827	The Hook	John Rossiter	1824	
Patrick Chapman			John Hearn	1803	Ballyhack	Thomas Ryan		Slade
John Coady	1816		Bridget Hearn	1819	Saltmills	Mary Ryan	1820	Ballyhack
Brigid Conway		Duncannon	Pat Jackman	1819	Duncannon	John Sinnott	1830	Duncannon
Margaret Cowman	1827		Catherine Keating			Michael Walsh	1855	
Catherine Donoghue	1829		Thomas Keating	1842		Richard Walsh	1852	
Ambrose Doyle		Slade	Mary Kent	1829		Ann Wallace	1826	
Mary Duggan	1830	Ballyhack	Michael Kent	1815	Tintern	John White		Slade
Pat Dwyer	1844		Joanna Kent	1848		James Whelan	1826	
James Eagan	1839		Patrick Lacy	1841		John Whitty	1849	

B. COLFER

Fig. 58 Petty Harbour on the Avalon peninsula south of St John's, is a typical example of the coastal settlements founded by the emigrants who sailed from Waterford Harbour to Newfoundland. The remains of fishing 'stages,' on which the cod was processed, can be seen in the foreground.

'whey-bellies' and Kilkenny 'cats'; there is a still a 'yellow-belly corner' in St John's! Apart from family names, the close relationship between the two regions is manifested by the stubborn survival in Newfoundland of many aspects of cultural expression, including the distinctive accent, personality, furniture, music, song and dance which the emigrants brought with them on ships from Waterford, Ross, Passage and Ballyhack.[75]

Fig. 59 A plaque erected at Porters Gate by Henry Loftus in 1680.

LOFTUS HALL DEMESNE

A demesne consisted of the land kept for the personal use of the landlord in the immediate vicinity of a manor house; it contained buildings, gardens, farmland and woods. On early demesnes the deerpark was the most distinctive feature, stocked mostly with fallow deer introduced into Ireland by the Anglo-Normans. Rabbits were also raised, in colonies known as conigears. From the late seventeenth century, it became the fashion to design the demesne landscape on a large scale: fields were organised into regular grid-like patterns, trees were planted and long vistas were created to reflect the owner's wealth and status. From 1720 onwards, a simpler approach evolved and it became customary to adorn the

B. COLFER

Fig. 60 The reason for the erection of this plaque in 1703, at the entrance to the demesne, is not known. It is still at Porter's Gate but re-located.

Fig. 61 The Loftus family occupied the medieval Redmond Hall and developed it as a residence, changing the name to Loftus Hall. This drawing from Hore's *History of Wexford*, shows the hall as it appeared in 1835. The piers with cylindrical tops were replicated throughout the demesne.

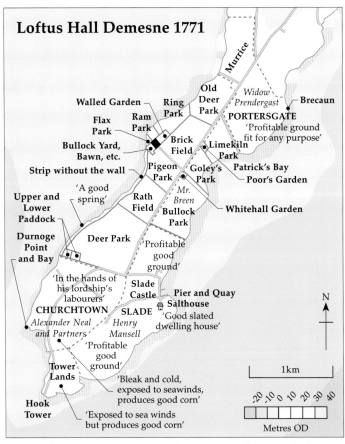

Fig. 62 The 1771 Loftus estate maps have been used to compile this map of late eighteenth-century landscape features in the Hook.

grounds by building 'temples' and other structures. After 1750, the emphasis was on creating natural-looking landscapes: walled gardens were built at a distance from the dwelling, sunken fences (ha-has) gave unrestricted views of the house, while walks and drives were provided so that the demesne landscape could be enjoyed. This period also saw the building of estate cottages, gate lodges and farm buildings. All of this work was facilitated by rising rents, an abundance of cheap labour and the need to provide employment. Subsequent to the trauma of the Great Famine, social and economic conditions changed and estates declined.[76]

Following the Confederate war, the Loftus family took over the confiscated lands of the Redmonds and Laffans on the Hook and made Redmond Hall their principal residence. This property consisted of the parish of Hook, containing the townlands of Hall, Churchtown, Slade, Galgystown and Porter's Gate. Townland boundaries varied in two instances compared to the present time, probably because of adjustments made by the Ordnance Survey in 1841. An area known as Murrice, now in Porter's Gate, was part of Houseland in 1771 and the 'Tower Lands' were included in Slade, not Churchtown as at present.[77] The Redmonds had previously made some efforts to create a demesne environment. On the 1771 estate maps, an old deerpark is shown as well as the new one developed by

Loftus, and a rabbit warren must have been constructed in an area on the cliffs near the lighthouse still known as Conigear ('coney' was the Middle-English word for a rabbit; rabbits were introduced into Ireland by the Anglo-Normans and farmed in coneygers, or warrens, for their flesh and fur). The place-name Porter's Gate pre-dates the Loftus takeover; it may have been the formal entrance to the Redmond estate. A house shown at Porter's Gate on a 1591 map of the Hook could have been an entrance lodge. A cluster of cabins at Galgystown is shown on the same map.[78] This is presumably the B. [G]auley shown on sixteenth-century maps, as cartographers sometimes substituted 'bally' for 'town.'

Loftus lost no time in modernising his newly acquired property. To establish the public identity of the manor house and demesne, 'Henry Loftus of Loftus Hall Esq. 1680' was inscribed on the entrance piers at Porter's Gate. Although they were removed in the 1930s, the spot where they stood, and where part of the inscription survives, is still referred to locally as 'the piers.' (The granite spheres on the gateway of the adjacent house came from the piers.) An account by Robert Leigh in 1684 gives an insight into the changes initiated by the new landlord in the Hook:

> The parish belongs at present to Henry Loftus Esq. who has repaired the old Mancon [mansion] House there, and added other considerable buildings of lime and stone thereunto, and enclosed his gardens with high stone walls to preserve some fruit trees newly planted there, and dwells in that house now. It was formerly called 'Redmond Hall' from ye old proprietor, it is now called Loftus Hall. Mr. Loftus is now building a key [quay] for fishing boats, on the east side of the peninsula neere a place called ye Slade.[79]

B. COLFER

Fig. 63 The high stone wall around the deerpark had a series of openings at eye level which must have been used to observe (?or shoot) the deer.

Demesne developments in the Hook were located for the most part in the townland of Hall, later Loftus Hall. The walls and gardens built by Loftus, including a large deerpark with impressive late seventeenth-century piers, still survive, along with an estate landscape of large regular

B. COLFER

Fig. 64 The piers to the deerpark established on the Loftus demesne in the late seventeenth or early eighteenth century. Similar piers were erected at Porter's Gate and around the hall, including in the walled garden.

fields surrounded by walls of local limestone. Similar piers were constructed at the gates of the manor house and at Porter's Gate. The priority given to the building of a walled garden was a response to the difficulty experienced in growing plants on the wind-lashed and salt-swept peninsula. The road from Porter's Gate to the deerpark piers was straightened and enclosed with substantial stone walls; the use of readily available stone was a response to the absence of trees on the peninsula. The presence of a labour force with an expertise in stonework must also have been a factor. The network of stone walls which still survives on the peninsula, although in a dilapidated state,

Fig. 65 The entrance to the demesne at Porter's Gate had piers and a gateway. Part of a plaque erected on the piers is still *in situ*. The three kilometre road from the demesne entrance to the deerpark piers was widened and lined by stone walls with a footpath on the west side.

was encouraged by Loftus, who allowed a rent reduction on land enclosed by walls built by tenants. Along the shoreline from Loftus Hall to the deerpark, the stone wall (about one and a half kilometres long) which formed the field boundary was built about ten metres back from the cliff edge. This 'strip outside the wall,' probably with a cobbled surface, was developed as a cliff walk for the occupants of the hall. For safety and aesthetic reasons, a winding retaining wall was skilfully constructed to ground level along the cliff edge. Sections of this wall survive, but much of it has been swept away by coastal erosion. A substantial 'storm wall' was built to ground level along the cliff edge in the vicinity of Loftus Hall itself to protect the building from encroachment by the sea. The walk to the deerpark, which was difficult to reach because of the strong wind, was described by Gabriel Beranger, a visitor to the hall in 1790; his concise description of the peninsula, 'iron coast, nothing but rocks and sea,' was quite apt.[80]

Maps drawn of the Loftus estate in 1771 by Richard and Charles Frizell (possibly members of the Frizell family who held land on the estate) presents a detailed account of the demesne as it was late in the eighteenth century.[81] The description is so effusive that it could well have been aimed at prospective buyers, but it was doubtless intended to please the owners!

This demesne is beautifully situated on an isthmus at the entrance of Waterford Harbour commanding a most pleasing prospect of the adjoining parts of the counties of Wexford and Waterford, the Fort of Duncannon, the towns of Ballyhack and Passage, and the ships at anchor in the harbour as well as all that sail in and out also of St George's Channel and all the ships that sail coastways. The dignity and grandeur of the situation, the richness and fertility of the land

Fig. 66 In 1771, the Galgystown part of the demesne was occupied by a Mr Breen, whose dwelling was, and still is, called Whitehall.

B. COLFER

Fig. 67 A winding stone retaining wall was built along the cliff edge to create a cliff walk, possibly cobbled, for the occupants of Loftus Hall. Most of the wall, as well as the field boundary wall, has been removed by coastal erosion. The piers on the right provided access from the deerpark to the seashore.

being all enclosed with lime and stone walls, the great plenty of fish, wild fowl, pigeons and rabbits at all seasons, also it being the seat of the ancient and noble family of the Loftus's whose characters were always conspicuous not only for their hospitality but for their warm support of the Protestant interest, makes this a most desirable situation.

The demesne consisted of the townlands of Loftus Hall, Churchtown, Galgystown and part of Porter's Gate. The townland of Slade was never part of the demesne and was occupied by the son of William Mansell, who had received a lease of the townland in 1685. By 1771 the extent of the planned demesne had contracted, as only the deerpark and some small fields around the Hall were held directly, the rest being let to tenants. Breen, the principal tenant, who lived in Whitehall, held the townland of Galgystown and most of Loftus Hall townland, apart from the deerpark. Porter's Gate townland was occupied by Widow Prendergast, while Churchtown was held by middle-men Alexander Neal and partners but was occupied by 'his lordship's labourers.'

Field-names recorded on the maps are of particular interest, as four of them are still in use, an indication of the tenacious endurance of these minor place-names: Deerpark is now the Park; Pigeon Park is Pigeon Meadow; Rathfield (Rawfield) and Bullock Park have not changed. The name of Goley's Park in Galgystown could perhaps be attributed to the medieval tenant who gave his name to the townland. The names of Brecaun church, Patrick's Bay and Durnoge Point also remain unchanged. The pier and quay mentioned at Slade must be the 'key for fishing boats' built there by Henry Loftus in the 1680s.

The first detailed description of landscape development in the Hook is provided in the six-inch Ordnance Survey maps of 1841.[82] These maps show that the land held directly in demesne had contracted even further. Houses had been built for tenant farmers in the townlands of Porters Gate (Sea Lodge) and Loftus Hall (the Dairy House); a house had also been built for a tenant in the Deerpark, which had been sub-divided into a number of fields. The presence of seven limekilns on the peninsula indicates that the quarrying and burning of limestone was of considerable significance at that time. The field system recorded in these maps serves as a social commentary, as it vividly portrays the contrast between the large regular fields on the demesne farms, occupied by tenant farmers, and the small fragmented fields in the districts, particularly the townland of Churchtown, occupied by under-tenants and labourers.

The names of the tenants in the Hook were recorded in Griffith's Valuation of 1853 and the Loftus estate maps of 1872. The surnames in both instances remain substantially the same, suggesting a large degree of continuity in occupancy. As the land held by each tenant can be identified from the estate maps, an analysis of the land-holding in the areas occupied by labourers and under-tenants can be undertaken. Slade and Churchtown, the two southernmost townlands on the peninsula, both contain remnants of dispersed holdings, some in large open-fields, with associated villages. The open-field strips, known as 'quarters,' are separated by narrow lengths of uncultivated ground called 'bones' (presumably from the middle English 'boun/bound': a boundary line). In Slade two open-fields were held by a number of tenants. 'The Waste' contained nine acres and was held in unenclosed strips by eight tenants; 'the Lord's Gardens' contained eighteen acres and was held by fifteen tenants. These fields are still divided in substantially the same manner. The townland of

B. COLFER

Fig. 68 Cylindrical piers with conical caps were a feature of the walls built on the Loftus demesne. Many have been removed to facilitate modern machinery. The ones shown here retain their original forge-made gate.

Fig. 69 The surviving field pattern in the Hook provides remarkable landscape evidence for the the social structure which developed under the Loftus regime. The large regular fields of the Loftus demesne with its substantial tenant farms are in marked contrast to the miniscule plots and strips held by labourers and fishermen in the townland of Churchtown (bottom left). In Slade townland (bottom right), held by a tenant, a similar pattern evolved.

B. COLFER

Fig. 70 The farmhouse cluster of Churchtown grouped around the medieval church. The long narrow sub-divided fields contrast strongly with the large stone-walled estate field at top right of the picture. The lane to the seashore led to a number of wells from which the residents drew their water supply.

Churchtown contained 221 acres shared by twenty-eight tenants, some of them holding less than an acre. The

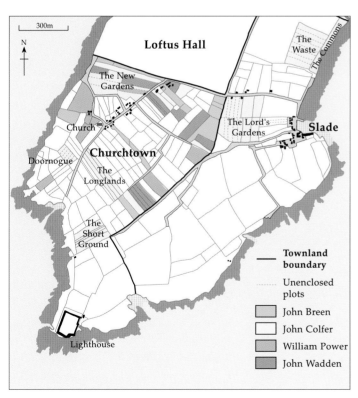

creation of increasingly smaller fields must have been caused by repeated sub-division, due to the demands of an expanding community. Churchtown's 1841 population of 158 people, living in 29 houses, is now reduced to 40, living in 14 houses.[83] The lands of four of the principal tenants are shown in the accompanying map, illustrating the dispersed nature of the holdings. The medieval system of land tenure survived into the nineteenth century in parts of county Dublin.[84] Similarly at Slade and Churchtown the modern pattern of land-holding, with long narrow strips, dispersed holdings and open-fields, may have originated in the manorial three-field system of land tenure. This was well illustrated in the 1872 estate maps and remains relatively unchanged at the present time.

Fig. 71 The Loftus estate maps of 1872 provide a detailed account of land-holding in Churchtown. The townland contained 88 hectares which was shared by twenty-eight tenants, some holding as little as .4 hectares. The lands of four of the principal tenants serve to illustrate the dispersed nature of the holdings. John Breen held 6.5 hectares in seven lots, John Colfer held 3.7 hectares in six lots; John Wadden held 5.2 hectares in eight lots and William Power held 6.8 hectares in seven lots. A field called 'The New Gardens' was held in ten unenclosed lots by nine tenants and other holdings in open-fields were unenclosed also. 'The Short Ground' had five strips and five owners and 'Doornogue' had seven 'quarters' and two owners. This system of land-holding, with long narrow strips, dispersed holdings and open-fields, may have originated in the manorial three-field system of land tenure.

SÉAMUS AND MARY KENNEDY

Fig. 1 In Grose's *Antiquities* (1791), a well-preserved Slade castle is shown perched on the cliff edge directly overlooking the harbour, as the present road between castle and dock was not constructed until the Famine relief works of 1847. The quay on the left was built by Loftus in 1684; the other one by Mansell in the early eighteenth century. The scene portrays a busy harbour with several vessels of considerable size as well as smaller fishing boats.

The village of Slade, located on a sheltered bay into which a small stream flows through a shallow depression (Old English 'slade,' a valley), is advantageously situated at the only natural landing-place on the peninsula. Originally held by the Laffan family as tenants on the manor of Kilcloggan, Loftus leased the castle and lands in 1685 to his wife's brother-in-law, William Mansell, a political refugee from the Gower peninsula in south Wales.[1] Mansell had supported the Duke of Monmouth in his unsuccessful rebellion against James II and, in 1685, following Monmouth's defeat at the Battle of Sedgemoor and subsequent

execution, Mansell fled to Ireland. He settled at Slade which he subsequently set about developing as a miniature estate village. The old village was to the south, in what had been the bawn of the castle, now known as 'the square.' Mansell, who was regarded as an eccentric entrepreneur, built a row of slated houses to the north of the inlet for his tenants. He also constructed a new pier and beside it he established a saltworks, in a range of buildings with remarkable roofs of corbelled stone which still survive in a ruinous state (the use of stone reflecting the scarcity of timber and the availability of stone on the headland). He may have built the

saltworks with the intention of supplying the flourishing Newfoundland fishery which depended for much of its supplies on the hinterland of Waterford Harbour. In Britain, salt was subjected to continually escalating taxes and duties until their abolition in 1825, but, from 1722 onwards, salt enjoyed a favourable tax regime in Ireland. At Slade, salt was manufactured by boiling rock salt, imported from Cheshire, where there was a plentiful supply; in 1777, for example, the *Peggy* of Wexford arrived at Slade with a cargo of rock salt from Liverpool.[2] Mansell also imported coal to Slade, presumably from his native Wales, and invented a

B. COLFER

Fig. 2 Fishermen repairing nets at Slade in the 1970s. The quay on which they are working, known as 'the Old Quay', is probably the 'key for fishing boats' built by Henry Loftus in 1684. Lobster pots, like the ones shown here, were traditionally made by the fishermen during the slack winter months.

machine, driven by sails, for carrying the coal to the saltworks. A 1746 account indicates that the pier was decayed by then and that the saltworks were no longer in use:

> About a mile to the N.E. of the tower, is a place called Slade Bay, which is foul ground. The best anchoring place in it is found by bringing the pier head and castle in one, opposite to a stone wall extended to the sea-shore, then there is about 5 fathom water clear sandy ground. An E. by N. and W. by S. moon makes high water on full and change days, and in the pier it then ordinarily flows 13 feet. This pier is of great use to distressed mariners and others, and was founded at the private charge of the late ingenious Mr. Mansfield [Mansell], who carried on a salt-work here; but the pier is at present in a state of decay, though worthy of improvement and repair.[3]

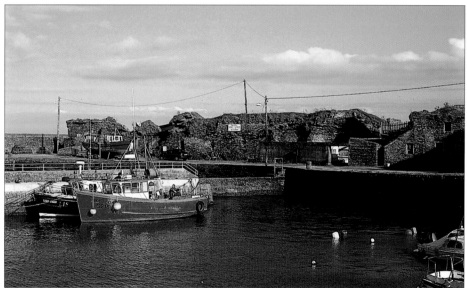

B. COLFER

Fig. 3 The ruins of the salthouse beside Slade dock. A portion of the corbelled roof, originally circular, can be seen in the partly destroyed building at right centre. The corbelling survives in the roof of the long, narrow building which, in the days of sail, was used for storing long boat masts.

Fig. 4 A drawing of Slade made in 1850 by Du Noyer showing the remains of the corbelled salthouse on the left. The artist recorded a typical scene of two men repairing a boat watched by several 'advisers.' Wandering asses were common in the area until the mid-twentieth century. The external stairway on the castle was constructed to allow independent access to the first floor of the hall.

The saltworks, unleased in 1771 but described as potentially profitable, were mentioned as an economic asset in 1772, in a lease of Slade to John Breen of Taghmon.[4] No further attempts were made to revive the industry, as by 1826 part of the complex was being used as a hedge school.[5] Mansell built a large comfortable dwelling house and the castle was later converted into a 'tenement' by dividing it into several 'apartments.' This involved the building up of doors, the insertion of extra doors and windows and the construction of external steps to the first floor on the east wall of the fortified house. Because of this, the castle continued to be occupied and maintained until early in the twentieth century. Slade Castle was taken over by the Office of Public Works as a National Monument in the 1940s and much of the damage inflicted by the conversion was subsequently repaired. In 1847 a new road was built behind the castle to give access to the pier, which was built at the same time. Because of this intervention the castle at Slade is usually seen from the

back, as the view of the south-facing front – where the entrances are located – is obscured by high stone walls and nineteenth-century houses.

By the end of the eighteenth century, Slade was being used as a seaside resort. In 1790, a visitor observed that he went 'to a sorry village called Slade, passing near Loftus Hall, the seat of Captain Tottenham. This village is much frequented by company, who retire here from various parts for the benefit of seabathing.'[6] In 1837, the village was described as follows:

Slade, a village in the parish of Hook, barony of Shelburne; contains 164 inhabitants. The place is situated on the bay and small harbour to which it gives its name. It contains thirty houses, and is chiefly inhabited by fishermen; the scenery derives some interest from the remains of Slade castle. The harbour is situated about a mile to the eastward of Hook lighthouse, and is fit only for small vessels, being dry at low water. Between the

quay heads are eleven feet of water at high spring tides, and from eight to nine feet at neap tides; but the pier is in a very dilapidated state. In the bay to the north-east of the Light-house, vessels may anchor in good ground, under shelter from northern and western wind.[7]

The building of Slade pier

The passing of a new act in 1846 to encourage the development of fishing facilities led to an application by the people of the Hook to have a new pier built at Slade.[8] This was seen as a practical undertaking, providing much-needed employment in the short term, and enabling fishermen to provide food for the community. Slade, traditionally an important port for boats and small ships, had always been a landing-place of some description. The first recorded pier, the one still known as the 'Old Quay,'

Fig. 5 A corbelling technique, using slabs of local limestone, was utilised in the construction of late seventeenth- and early eighteenth-century houses at Slade. Some of these houses survive, including part of the salthouse shown above, where, after two centuries, the corbelled roof (with swallow's nest) is still waterproof.

Fig. 6 An early photograph (c. 1890) of Slade Castle showing it as a tenement with the roof still in place on the hall. The diamond-paned windows were presumably meant to match the antiquity of the building. The exterior of one ground 'apartment' had been white-washed by the occupant. The Loftus estate maps of 1872 record three families living in the castle at a rent of five shillings a year. The clay-pipe-smoking fisherman was probably one of the occupants. Until the castle was taken over by the O.P.W., the rooms were known locally by the names of the last people who lived in them.

was built by Henry Loftus in 1684, shortly after his arrival in the Hall. Soon afterwards, William Mansell, from south Wales, acquired the townland of Slade on a long lease from Loftus, his wife's brother-in-law. Mansell established a saltworks in the village and built a second pier to the east, forming a safer, enclosed, harbour with a narrow entrance to the north-east. By the end of the eighteenth century, Mansell's pier had been swept away, leaving the harbour exposed to storms. In 1822 Mansell's successor, John Breen, was attempting to organise the construction of a new

pier, stressing the urgency of the situation as 'boats were forced to seek shelter elsewhere.' Two years later George Brownrigg of the Ballast Office, Waterford, again made the case for a new pier at Slade, in a letter to the Commissioners of the Irish Fisheries. He drew attention to the excellent situation of Slade for the establishment of a harbour, for fishing and other boats of moderate tonnage, adding that, prior to the 'dilapidation' of the pier, it had been much in use with double the number of vessels. The locals were prepared to contribute and the Marquis of Ely and the

Ballast Board of Dublin were expected to co-operate.

Fig. 7 The two houses on the left, in Slade 'Square', have vaulted stone roofs covered by slates, presumably constructed by Mansell in the late seventeenth- early eighteenth-century at the same time as the salthouse. They have recently been restored as a dwelling house with minor modification of the original features.

Fig. 10 A sketch by G. Du Noyer, c. 1850, of a typical mid nineteenth-century fishing yawl.

Fig. 8 This drawing of Slade by Wakeman, c. 1840, shows the castle perched on the cliff edge with a boat pulled up on a beach where the slipway is now located. In 1847, the cliff was skilfully faced with stone to create an approach road to the new pier. Part of the old village is shown around the castle. The houses on the right have been removed; some of the buildings on the left are still in use.

However, none of these efforts was successful and no progress was made until an act was passed in 1846, following the outbreak of the Famine in 1845, 'to encourage the sea fisheries of Ireland, by promoting and aiding with grants of public money, the construction of piers, harbours, and other works.' Obviously motivated by the distress in the parish, Rev. John Dunne, the curate in Templetown, organised an application to the Office of Public Works, in April 1846, to have a new pier built at Slade on the site of the old one. The application stated that since the fall of the old pier the people had been 'gradually approaching to want but were now on the point of destitution.' The application was signed by 131 men from Slade and Churchtown and Rev. Dunne said that, if necessary, he could supply three or four hundred more signatures. Out of a total of 131 names, 24 were classed as 'occupiers,' or landholders, the rest were fisher-men. Fifty-seven names were written beside

the owner's 'X', and others appear to have been written by the same hand, so it would seem that there was 50 per cent literacy (Appendix III).

Following the application, an O.P.W. engineer visited Slade and estimated that the pier would cost £1,200, of which £300 would have to be

raised locally. In July 1846, Rev. Dunne again wrote to the O.P.W., complaining that nothing was being done. He enclosed a list of people who had pledged money, including £100 from the Marquis of Ely and also a petition signed by captains of fishing boats from Dunmore. Although only £230 of the local contribution had been raised, the O.P.W. should 'act on the generous side, get on with the work and not be splitting hairs with a poor but industrious people,' especially as all the material, stone, sand and lime, could be obtained locally. Another letter from Rev. Dunne demanded a reply and stressed that 'employment must be found in the parish in quick time.' The Templetown curate's

Fig. 9 An 1850 drawing of Slade by Du Noyer, shortly after the completion of the pier. The newly constructed approach road can be seen in front of the castle and houses. The type of fishing boat in use at the time is also shown. The long corbelled house on the left was originally a bakery.

KAVANAGH COLLECTION: JIMMY FITZGIBBON

Fig. 11 This photograph of Slade dock in 1890 shows the pier built in 1847 in the background. The picture was taken before the creation of a sheltered inner harbour by the building of two internal cross walls at the turn of the century. The vulnerability of the harbour to storms from the east is shown by the mooring of the boats with heavy chains, away from the quays. A few of the well-designed, half-decked sailing boats (known as Baltimore boats) were in use until the second half of the twentieth century. Remains of the salthouse, including parts that have since collapsed, can be seen on the right.

persistence paid off, as in January 1847 a declaration was issued stating that all requirements had been complied with. In the following month two overseers with four men and one horse were clearing the site for the new pier with Patrick Maher in charge.

Patrick Maher, the superintendent at Slade, reported in October that the storm wall was levelled off by completing stonework 157 feet long by 2 foot 8 inches high in one week. The wall was to be coped the following week if suitable stones were turned out by the quarry. Thirty-six feet of Irish oak, at a cost of £7 4s 0d, would be needed for four mooring posts, but large stones, with ringbolts leaded in, would be only half the price. (The cheaper option was decided on, as the remains of the leaded-in ringbolts still survive.) By November the pavement was being laid, with 107 feet of the

pier completed and two months' work remaining. The work was being held up because the quarry could not be worked at all stages of the tide. (The

location of the quarry is not known, but limestone rock was probably quarried from the cliffs at locations close to Slade.) As coping stones could

B. COLFER

Fig. 12 The pier built in 1847 at Slade as a Famine relief scheme continues to be used by the present-day fishing fleet. The pier's aesthetic appearance, as well as the relatively good condition of the structure, is a tribute to the quality of the work carried out by mid nineteenth-century stonemasons.

B. COLFER

Fig. 13 This aerial perspective of Slade from the mid-1980s shows the Laffan tower house and hall with its enclosure or bawn, now called 'the Square.' In the eighteenth century, William Mansell, the tenant of the townland, built the substantial farmhouse at the bottom of the picture, with extensive outbuildings, which then replaced the castle as the dwelling of the landowner. He also built the row of houses at left centre for his tenants. The harbour is enclosed by two quays: 'the Old Quay' to the left, built in 1684, and 'the New Quay' on the the right, built in 1847 as a Famine Relief Scheme. The approach road along the cliff-top, with retaining wall, was built at the same time. The internal walls in the harbour were constructed in the early twentieth century.

only be quarried at low spring tides, the stone-cutters had been laid off until the next spring tides, which were expected to be lower. There was also the possibility of getting great red stones from a quarry at Duncormick.

By the end of January 1848, a year after the work started, Maher reported that the pier was almost completed. Some pointing needed to be done at spring tide on the lower part of the outside wall of the old pier. The road over the retaining wall was almost finished, as there was enough filling in it. The crane could now be taken down and he asked what he should do with it and the other implements. He did not wish to question the honesty of the locals but felt that the equipment

would not be safe in Slade! They should be stored in Duncannon Fort, from where they could be transported by water. By February 1848, Maher could report that the pier was finished; the crane had been dismantled and he had arranged with the Barrack Master at Duncannon to have it stored there. The official description of the completed work was: a stone pier, 200 feet in length (with parapet), and an approach road retained by a stone wall 500 feet in length, forming, with the old pier, a harbour 250 feet long by 200 feet wide, having 600 feet of wharfage. The final cost of the work was £1,388.

The relief scheme at Slade, instigated by the Famine, brought

about many changes and created the village and harbour as it is today. When it was built, the new pier contributed to a significant improvement in living standards, and it continues to be a vital element in the infrastructure of the area. The new structure would have been of far greater benefit if it had been constructed in deeper water. According to local tradition, this was not allowed by the local landlord who did not want his tenants to become full-time fishermen. The pier was not sufficient to exercise a stabilising effect on the population, as emigration continued, leaving Slade, which had a population of 164 in 1837, with about thirty-five inhabitants at the present time.

Slade: the development of a fishing village, 1450 to 1850

Fig. 14 The name Slade, an Old English word meaning a glen or valley, is of topographic origin. This is an accurate description of the locality, as the village is situated in a small valley through which the sole stream on the peninsula flows into an inlet. This bay is the only natural landing place on the headland, as it is sheltered from the prevailing south-westerly winds and has a sandy beach where boats could be brought ashore. The townland of Slade was held by the Laffans as tenants of the manor of Kilcloggan. Slade village, with its fifteenth-century tower house, was located just south of the inlet, possibly to take advantage of the protection it afforded and to utilise the natural harbour. Adjoining land to the south, which is still laid out in large regular fields, was retained by the principal tenant; the land north of the inlet, where there are unenclosed fields and small fields, was held by labourers and small tenants.

Fig. 15 Shortly after the construction of the tower house, probably in the late fifteenth century, a defended hall was added to the east. As the Laffans held only 81 hectares, other revenue, presumably from fishing and other maritime-related activities, must have been generated to construct such an elaborate dwelling. Although there was presumably an earlier pier, the first recorded quay was constructed by Henry Loftus in 1684. This was probably the still surviving 'Ould Quay' built to the north of the inlet. At the end of the seventeenth century, William Mansell, related by marriage to Henry Loftus, acquired the townland of Slade. Mansell developed Slade as a miniature estate village, building a substantial house for his family and comfortable dwellings for his tenants. He also set up a saltworks, housed in unusual corbelled stone buildings, some of which survive. As part of the development, he built a new pier to the east, forming a safer, enclosed harbour.

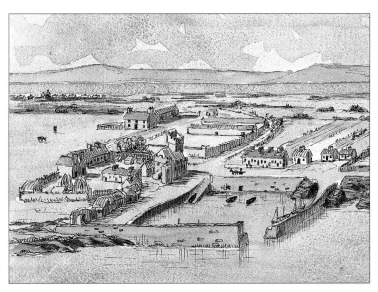

Fig. 16 By the end of the eighteenth century, Slade was leased to the Breens, a Catholic merchant family from Taghmon. The saltworks had been abandoned and the east pier was in a ruinous condition. The population of c. 200 was concentrated in 'the Square' to the south of the castle and in a row of houses to the west of the harbour. The castle, occupied by a number of families, had been developed as a 'tenement', with an outside stairway added to the east wall to give access to the first floor. At the onset of the Great Famine, a Famine relief scheme led to the construction of a new quay on the site of the east pier built by Mansell, which had been destroyed by winter storms. Later, two walls were built across the harbour, creating an inside dock to give greater protection to boats. At present, ten of the fourteen houses in Slade village are used as holiday homes. The harbour, which has the disadvantage of being dry at low tide, is used by local boats engaged in crab and lobster fishing, and by pleasure craft during the summer season.

B. COLFER

AN EVOLVING SOCIETY

The Catholic elite, dispossessed in the 1650s, continued as an 'underground' gentry, either as tenants on the lands which they had formerly owned, or in exile on the continent.[1] After the war of William and James, they were viewed with suspicion as Stuart sympathisers in league with England's Catholic enemies on the continent. This fear was sustained by incidents such as the Jacobite raid on Fethard in 1707. However, not all of the dispossesed Catholic gentry class left for the continent. Many remained as tenants and middlemen and the political leadership which they provided during the Jacobite phase was frequently carried through to the United Irishmen. When the dismantling of the Penal Laws began in 1778, the Jacobite claims to land ownership were abandoned by the upper ranks of Catholic society, backed by the Catholic Church because of fears of the 'French disease' which had decimated the Church in France.

The universal ideas of liberty, equality and justice ignited revolutions in America and France and were the inspiration behind the establishment of the United Irishmen in Belfast in 1791, with the principal aim of overthrowing a political system based on sectarian privilege and replacing it with a secular democracy.

These events, combined with the frustration and bitterness generated in the Catholic community during two centuries of social, economic and religious exclusion, generated intense upheaval during the crucial last decade of the eighteenth century. The merging of the United Irishmen with the more militant Defenders in 1795 was greeted with alarm and led to the foundation of the Orange Order to protect loyalist interests. A campaign of military terror initiated by the authorities led to a state of turmoil. At the end of May 1798, the country, and in particular county Wexford, rose in bloody rebellion. Although peripherally located, the Hook felt the shock waves of this climactic event.

While 1798 dominates historical events, landsacpe changes were mainly brought about by the ever-increasing population. On the eve of the Famine many people in the Hook region relied on the potato for survival. After the shock of the Famine, the population dropped as much as 30 per cent by 1901.

An unexpected result of this calamity was the rise in prominence of the middle-class tenant farmers. Ultimately, by the end of the century, they had acquired ownership of the land in the Hook and the status of the landed gentry was greatly diminished.

N.L.I.

Fig. 1 A fierce clash between the rebels and military in county Wexford during the 1798 Rebellion. The Hook was outside the main theatre of operations.

Testimonial to the Redmond family, 1732

I hereby certify to whom it may concern that Sr Peter Redmond Knt. of ye order of Christ is proprietor and chief of ye family of Redmond's Hall in the county of Wexford and diocese of Ferns and that he, as well as his lady Anne Parker, native of ye county Dublin, are of as good noble and gentle family as are in the Kingdom and esteemed to be such by the best gentry in the said countys who take it an honour to be related to the Knt. and his lady not only for their lineal descent, without blot or interruption from ancient and illustrious families ever since the first coming of the English into Ireland with Strongbow nearly 600 years ago. But for their ancestor's loyal adherence to their lawful kings and to the R.C. religion, without it ever being said or known that any of them ever deviated from either ye principles or policies of men of honour yet never undertook any mechanick or loose calling and yet ever since their being wrongfully devested by the usurper Cromwell of their sumptuous houses, patrimonys and estates they have lived in decency and respect and in good repute among ye best Catholic gentry of the kingdom who still claim them for their kin and relations. All of which I know to be true by the general tradition of the county and ye strict inquiry I have made to the unsuspected informations given by vertuous, learned and grave ecclesiasticks and also by faith worthy gentlemen … their hopeful children, 1 son and 4 daughters, now living in France with the lady their mother who all for ancient and noble birth cannot be doubted by any tribunal on earth.

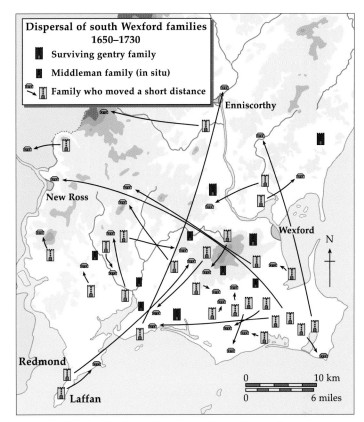

Fig. 2   The dispersal of south Wexford families, 1650–1730. The seventeenth-century land confiscations uprooted the Catholic gentry, many of them from lands held by their families for four centuries. Rather than going 'to Hell or to Connaught' most settled locally as middlemen and farmers, retaining their status as the political and cultural leaders of their communities. In the Hook, the Redmonds and Laffans were dispossessed and moved to Taghmon and Great Graigue respectively. Exercising greater influence than the new landlord class, these families saw themselves, and were seen, as an underground gentry, unjustly displaced by an iniquitous regime, sustaining the Jacobite agenda of redemption and restoration. Land ownership remained a live political issue in Irish society throughout the eighteenth century.

Fig. 2 The importance attached to maintaining gentry status is illustrated by an attestation of nobility written in 1732 by Ambrose O'Callaghan, Catholic bishop of Ferns, for Sir Peter Redmond, then living in France, whose family had formerly owned Redmond (Loftus) Hall.

THE REBELLION OF 1798

The Rebellion of 1798 has been described as 'the most ferocious civil war in Ireland and one of the most bitter in modern European history.'[2] It seemed anomalous that the Rebellion was most violent in Wexford, a region regarded as relatively quiet and prosperous, but some of the reasons can be found in the volatile political and social mix in the county. In Wicklow and north Wexford, where the most successful Protestant settlement outside of Ulster was located, there was rising tension as competition for property and status between Catholic and Protestant middlemen generated intense antagonism and bitterness. The division of the Protestant gentry in Wexford into the hard-line Loftus and more liberal Colclough factions increased political and social instability. The United Irish

organisation spread to the north of the county and began to recruit. Some members of the more radical Protestant group had links with the north of Wexford, which may explain their interest in, and subsequent involvement with, the United Irishmen: the Grogans held land in the north and both the Harveys and Colcloughs had links with the family of Miles Byrne of Monaseed, one of the United Irish leaders in the county. The Rebellion erupted on 26 May and spread quickly across north Wexford.[3]

While no part of Wexford escaped completely, destruction was relatively light in the south-west, which was outside the main area of confrontation.[4] It was, however, strategically important as a potential landing-place for expected French aid. Duncannon Fort was held by the military throughout the Rebellion and was a refuge for Protestant loyalists from the surrounding area. Soldiers from Duncannon garrisoned the Tower of Hook, which was used as a magazine, to prevent it falling into rebel

Fig. 3 An 1805 etching by Henry Brocas of Duncannon Fort. The fort was the only defended stong point in the county which could serve as a refuge for loyalists during the '98 Rebellion. Loftus Hall and the Tower of Hook are shown in the distance. The tower was garrisoned and used as a magazine.

hands. Correspondence between Caesar Colclough, a political detainee in France, and his brother John, in charge of Tintern in his absence, contains considerable insights into events in the south Shelburne region.[5] A reading of the letters must take into account that both brothers were suspected of being republican sympathisers: John referred to 'reasons that he didn't think proper to mention' and stated that 'letters were being stopped in Fethard,' located on the estate of Loftus, his political enemy. On 15 April, before the outbreak of the Rebellion, John Colclough reported that 'the tenants on the other estates were in a state of great disturbance,' but, because the Colcloughs were such good landlords, their tenants were 'perfectly tranquil.' Following the outbreak of the Rebellion, Colclough, with other Protestants, retreated into Duncannon Fort. He later wrote that he:

> was not afraid of his own people who feared that they would be forced to join the insurgents; that Lord Ely's estate and Lord Donegall's and all the surrounding countryside was rising, and as they must pass through Tintern, they would force every single male inhabitant along with them, or murder them and their families. The army could afford them no protection, for they were afraid to stir out of the fort, so that anything so distressing as their situation was cannot be conceived. For if they went to Duncannon they must starve and their families that they left behind would be murdered, and if they remained in their houses

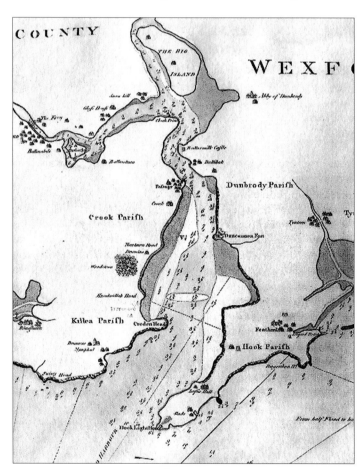

Fig. 4 Mackenzie's 1776 map of the Hook and Waterford Harbour depicts the late eighteenth-century landscape on the eve of the '98 Rebellion. Included are a representation of the old village of Tintern, a number of castles and churches, and the Hook lighthouse emitting a plume of smoke, as the coal-fired light was not replaced until 1791.

they would be carried off by the United men, so their destruction was and is inevitable.

The principal United Irish activity in the region was focused on the Dunbrody and Loftus estates under the leadership of Michael Devereux of Battlestown, assisted by Joshua Colfer and the Devereux brothers of Dungulph Castle, among others.[6] Rebel activities in the area included an ambush at Taylorstown on a column of troops fleeing from Wexford town, and the burning of houses in Duncannon. At the end of May, the rebels rounded up members of the Protestant community in Fethard and, on

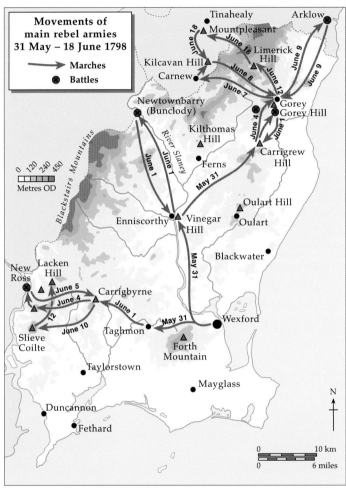

Fig. 5 The movement of the rebel armies in county Wexford and the location of the principal battles during the first half of June 1798.

4 June, a party of rebels seized suspected loyalists at Tintern. The captives were brought to the rebel camp at Carrigbyrne, where they were imprisoned in a barn at Scullabogue, evidently to be used as hostages if the need arose. After the defeat at the Battle of Ross on the following day, retreating rebels carried stories of army atrocities and in the panic and confusion the barn was set on fire and more than one hundred loyalists, including a small number of Catholics, were brutally murdered,

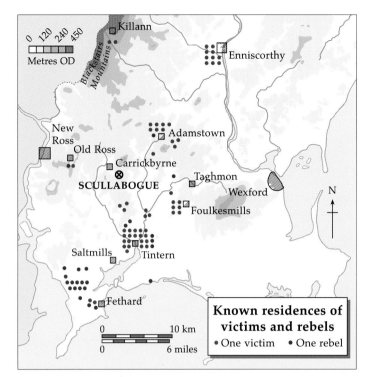

Fig. 6 The known residences of people who died in Scullabogue and the origins of rebels who brought the prisoners to the barn.

causing shock and revulsion among the United Irish leadership. The dead included twenty-five from Tintern and two from Fethard.[7] In a letter written after the Rebellion, John Colclough observed that 'most of the old Protestants of Tintern who were not able to go to Duncannon were burned at Scullabogue.'

Following the defeat at Ross, rebel activity in the Hook decreased. On 10 June, the naval gunboats *Louisa* and *Packenham* sailed from Duncannon to bombard the dock at

Fig. 7 A later, propagandistic, representation of the massacre of Scullabogue by George Cruikshank, the celebrated English illustrator of Charles Dickens. This sickening event was carried out in the panic and confusion after defeat at the Battle of Ross. The United Irish leadership were shocked at the atrocity and issued a proclamation threatening execution for anyone who 'killed, murdered, burned or plundered.'

Fig. 8 Innyard House near Fethard dock was occupied by the rebels during the '98 Rebellion, possibly in the hope that a French force would use the excellent anchorage and landing beach at nearby Baginbun.

Fethard, destroying a warehouse and a dozen fishing boats. The attack was in response to a group of rebels who occupied nearby Innyard House as their headquarters. After the defeat of the insurgents at Vinegar Hill on 21 June, the military from Duncannon Fort scoured the countryside for rebels. When a search for the Devereux brothers of Dungulph proved unsuccessful, the castle there was burned; their neighbours, Davy Walsh and his son Jackie, of Ballygow, were taken prisoner to Duncannon, where the father died. The Catholic chapel at Ramsgrange was burned, the only one in the area to be destroyed. Prisoners awaiting execution or transportation were held in Duncannon Fort as well as in Geneva Barracks at Crook, across the harbour in county Waterford; others were held in vessels moored offshore. Many escaped transportation by volunteering to serve with army regiments in the West Indies.[8]

Late in May, John Colclough departed by sea with his friend Tom McCord and remained in Fishguard for

Fig. 9 Fethard dock was the scene of the only naval action during the '98 rebellion. Twelve fishing boats and a warehouse were destroyed by a bombardment from two ships, the *Louisa* and *Packenham*.

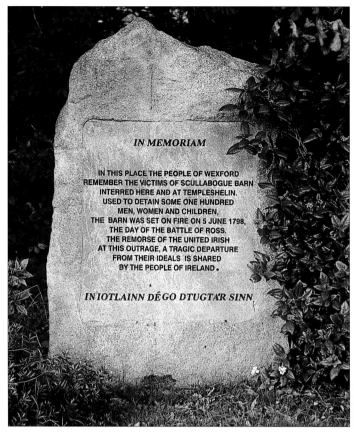

Fig. 10 This monument commemorating those who died in the barn at Scullabogue was erected in the graveyard at nearby Old Ross in 1998.

several months. On 30 July, he informed Caesar of the execution of their uncle, Cornelius Grogan, and their cousin, John Henry Colclough of Ballyteige – 'always suspected of being a United man.' He also described the devastated state of the countryside, although he thought that Tintern had not suffered too badly. He wrote again from Dublin on 22 August to tell his brother of his own

Fig. 11 After the Rebellion, the United Irish leaders, Bagenal Harvey and John Henry Colclough, took refuge in a cave on the Saltee Islands where they were arrested following the betrayal of their hiding place. Both men were brought to Wexford where they were court-martialled and executed.

Fig. 12 Members of the Village Players from Fethard-on-Sea who presented a pageant at Tintern Abbey, based on the activities of the Colclough family in the Rebellion, as part of the 1798 bicentenary commemorations, during which a plaque was erected at Tintern to the memory of John Colclough.

arrest as a suspected United Irishman, but this did not dampen his concern for the Tintern estate, which 'has not suffered very much, very few of the people have been killed [a rather surprising view considering the massacre at Scullabogue], the rest have all returned to peace and industry so that things are not so bad as I dreaded.' John Colclough was released without charge before Christmas and returned to manage affairs at Tintern. By March 1799, he reported that the tenants, fearing eviction, were paying their rents and that on the Loftus estate Lord Ely had evicted all his tenants. Colclough undertook to take care of 'all those poor Protestant women who lost their husbands' (presumably at Scullabogue) but added that very few of them were worthy of it. In view of the Colclough family's liberal and even republican attitude, it is difficult to understand why their Protestant tenants were deliberately targeted to such an extent. Colclough's success in keeping his tenants out of the Rebellion may have generated resentment. The presence of a Palatine community at Tintern, brought in initially to set up a

weaving industry, may also have been a factor: the houses and church of the Palatine community at Old Ross were burned during the uprising.

The Rebellion of 1798 was an exceptional event in modern Irish, and Wexford, history leading to the abolition of the Irish parliament under the Act of Union in

Fig. 13 This cartoon shows the 1807 duel at Ardcandrisk between John Colclough and William Alcock. The politically liberal Colclough was killed and his funeral was reputed to be the biggest ever seen in Wexford. Alcock was a member of the hard-line conservative group, in which Loftus was prominent, that lost support in the aftermath of the Rebellion.

B. COLFER

Fig. 14 In the early nineteenth century, fears of a French invasion led to the construction of small fortresses, known as Martello towers, at strategic locations around the coast of Ireland. The one at Baginbun, shown above, was among the first to be constructed in 1804. Massively built of regular granite blocks with battered (sloped) sides, it is unusual in having four defensive machicolations (projections open at the bottom) at parapet level. The door, accessed by ladder, was at first-floor level. The summit served as a platform on which a gun was traversed on an iron rail. Now used as a dwelling, the tower has been modified to some extent. Extra accommodation has been provided by the addition of two annexes.

1800. There was no political backlash in Wexford, as the county continued to return liberal candidates for much of the first half of the nineteenth century. John Colclough of Tintern, a prominent member of the liberal grouping and believed to have United Irish connections, was a victim of the political antagonism in the county as he was killed in a duel by William Alcock, a member of the hard-line conservative group in 1807.[9] In the aftermath of the Rebellion, continuing apprehensions regarding security led to precautionary developments in the Hook. Because of the continuous fear of invasion during the Napoleonic Wars, signal stations were erected at Baginbun and the Hook lighthouse as part of a coastal defence system.[10] Small forts known as Martello towers were erected on the

B. COLFER

Fig. 15 In the aftermath of the '98 Rebellion, the construction of Nelson's Bridge on the Owenduff river (above) and Wellington Bridge on the Corock river added greatly to the road infrastructure of the Hook region.

coast of Ireland during the early part of the nineteenth century; the international significance of the estuary and peninsula was emphasised by the construction of three of these in the Hook region, one on the headland of Baginbun overlooking the excellent anchorage and landing beach, historically a target for invading forces, and two on the high ground overlooking Duncannon Fort.[11] Early in the nineteenth century, a straight military road (still known as 'the new line') was constructed, connecting Duncannon Fort with Wexford town. This road improved access to the Hook quite considerably, as it involved the bridging, for the first time, of the Owenduff and Corock rivers at the head of Bannow Bay; the bridges were named after Nelson and Wellington, the British heroes of the Napoleonic Wars. Almost a century later, the construction of railway bridges over the rivers, and the building of a station, led to the emergence of the village of Wellington Bridge as a new focal point for the region.

ECCLESIASTICAL LANDSCAPE

From the early nineteenth century, and particularly after the granting of Catholic Emancipation in 1829, an increasingly confident Catholic Church began to establish new administrative structures, leading to widespread abandonment of old centres and divisions. There was little continuity between the new parochial system and the old medieval pre-Reformation parishes. In county Wexford, forty rural parishes replaced one hundred and forty medieval parishes and only twelve of these were named after the older divisions.[12] Most of the pre-Reformation church sites were abandoned: in the county only fifteen of eighty-three nineteenth-century Catholic churches occupied medieval parish centres, as the location of early nineteenth-century Catholic churches was frequently dependent on the patronage of a strong Catholic tenant farmer. Six Catholic chapels had been built in the Hook region before Catholic Emancipation, at Poulfur, Templetown, Ramsgrange, Duncannon, Bally-cullane and St Leonards; the medieval parish centres of Fethard and Templetown continued to be occupied, but eight others were deserted. Unusually, the medieval parish centre of Templetown was the location for both a Catholic and Protestant church for a period, but this was abandoned by the end of the century when the present Catholic parish church was built in 1896–98:[13] the Protestant church had been closed in mid-century in favour of the church at Fethard. The contrast between the locations of Poulfur church, built in an isolated wooded hollow at a time when the Penal Laws were still in force, and Templetown church, built high on a hill almost a

B. COLFER

Fig. 16 The annual 'pattern,' held every year in the graveyard of Hook church in Churchtown on the first Tuesday in July, represents a continuity of religious and community practice stretching back more than a millennium to the early Christian foundation of St Dubhán. Because of the isolation of the area, 'stations,' abandoned in the rest of the diocese, continued to be held at Hook church well into the twentieth century.

century later, makes an eloquent comment on intervening social and political changes. Of all the churches in the region, only St Mogue's Protestant church in Fethard, in both location and structure, provides a direct link with medieval times. At the other medieval church centres, however, the link is maintained by the continued use of the burial grounds and an annual 'pattern.' Four new churches replaced penal chapels in the post-Emancipation period: Ballycullane in 1840, Ramsgrange in 1843, Duncannon in 1896 and Templetown in 1899. Two of these, Ramsgrange and Templetown, were built in the style of the renowned

B. COLFER

Fig. 17 Duncannon church, built on the hill above the village in 1896.

B. COLFER

Fig. 18 Templetown church, built in the Pugin style in 1898.

Nineteenth-century schools in the Hook region

Location	Date	Type/Denomination	Pupils
Arthurstown	1837	Parochial school, Catholic	
Ballycullane	1837	School	
	18—	National School	
Ballyhack	18—	National School	
Duncannon	1837	2 schools, Catholic	
	18—	National School	
Loftus Hall	1837	Private school, Catholic	
	1885	National School, Catholic	
Fethard	1835	Day school, Catholic	50
	1835	Day school, Catholic	40
	1835	Female school, Protestant	40
	1835	Parochial school, Protestant	15
	1835	Sunday school, Protestant	33
	18—	National School, Protestant	
	18—	National School, Catholic (Poulfur)	
Parish of Owenduff	1837	3 private schools	100
Ramsgrange	1837	Parochial school, Catholic	
St Leonards	18—	National School, Catholic	
Saltmills	1837	Boys' school	
Parish of St James and Dunbrody	1837	9 schools, 2 attached to chapels	175
Slade	1826	Hedge school in old salthouse, Catholic	15
Templetown	1835	Day school, Catholic	50
	1835	Sunday school, Protestant	17
	1837	School, Catholic	100
	1841	National School	
	1931	National School	

architect Augustus Welby Pugin, who had designed impressive churches in the diocese.

During the eighteenth century, the provision of education for Catholics was mostly in the hands of hedge (meaning inferior) school masters, who were obliged to keep a low profile because of the restrictions imposed by

Fig. 19 Ramsgrange Catholic church, built in 1843, was the first post-Emancipation church to be constructed in the region. The new church did not occupy the site of the penal chapel (marked by the old graveyard), but was built in a new location just across the road.

Fig. 20 Loftus Hall school, built at Slade Cross in 1880, was one of a number of National Schools built in the Hook in the nineteenth century. The building has been adapted for use as a private residence.

the Penal Laws. Apart from a school in the salthouse in Slade, there are no records of hedge schools in the Hook.[14] However, by the 1830s twenty-six schools were in operation, with five of these located in Fethard.[15] The hedge school masters were viewed with suspicion by both church and state and new legislation introduced in 1831, which gave the clergy virtual control over education, resulted in the building of National Schools in close proximity to many churches, introducing a new element to the social structure of the area.[16] National Schools were built beside the Catholic churches of Templetown, Poulfur, Ballycullane, St Leonards, Ramsgrange and Duncannon, while a National School for Protestant children was built in Fethard. At Ramsgrange, two National Schools, a convent for St Louis nuns and a monastery for De La Salle brothers were established around the new church, providing a remarkable example of a characteristic new type of settlement referred to as a chapel village. A similar village, on a smaller scale, developed at Ballycullane.[17]

THE GREAT FAMINE

Between 1700 and 1845, the population of Ireland expanded dramatically from three million to eight and a half million, due in part to the increased use of the potato as an easily produced nutritious food. The growing population had profound implications for the landscape, as it generated intensive expansion onto marginal land, subdivision and reclamation. This in turn led to a demand for manure, including lime and seaweed, giving an added value to land which had access to the strand. The success of the versatile potato, particularly when it was efficiently grown using lazy-bed cultivation, meant that foods which had formerly formed part of the staple diet, particularly butter and oats, were sold to provide cash for rent and other necessities, creating a precarious over-dependence

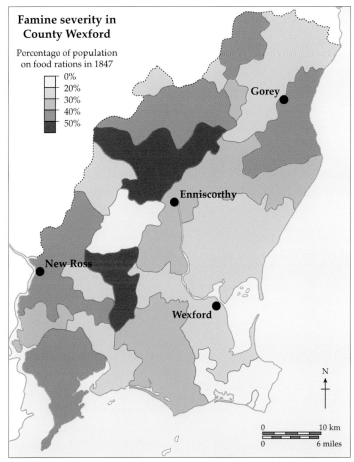

Famine severity in County Wexford

Percentage of population on food rations in 1847

- 0%
- 20%
- 30%
- 40%
- 50%

Gorey

Enniscorthy

New Ross

Wexford

N

0   10 km
0   6 miles

Fig. 21 Famine severity in county Wexford is indicated by the percentage of the population on food rations in 1847. In general, the west of the county suffered more than the east. The Hook region, where 40 to 50 per cent of the people received relief, was in the second highest category.

K. WHELAN

Fig. 22 An 1897 drawing of New Ross fish market. During the Famine the market was an important source of food for the neighbouring locality.

on a single crop, particularly among the labouring and cottier classes. By the 1830s one-third of the population (three million people) relied on the potato for over ninety per cent of their calorie intake. Following the end of the Napoleonic Wars in 1815, the demand for agricultural produce plummeted and the economy went into a sharp depression. This further increased dependence on the potato and when blight appeared in 1845 the effect was immediate and devastating.[18]

Although not the only famine experienced in Ireland during the eighteenth and nineteenth centuries, the trauma of the horrific Great Famine of 1845–48 led to permanent changes in all aspects of Irish life.[19] When blight struck the potato crop in 1845, the inability to provide an alternative food supply led to a major and ongoing disaster. The impact on the population was staggering. As well as the million people who died from hunger and related diseases, another million fled the country. Because of political ideology, the official response saw the Famine as an opportunity to replace the 'backward' potato with grain, regarded as a more

'civilised' crop. It was also seen as a chance to modernise estates by ridding them of a pauper tenantry. Official relief was limited mostly to public relief works, which, at their height, gave employment nationally to 700,000 men. The Famine inflicted devastating and permanent changes on Irish society. In the decade after 1841, the population fell from a high of over eight million to six and a half million, a loss of twenty per cent. Sustained emigration continued for the rest of the century and by 1901 the population had dropped to four and a half million, almost half the pre-Famine level.

The Famine impacted most severely on the densely populated regions along the western seaboard, but the more prosperous southeast did not escape unscathed. Shelburne barony in Wexford, although not one of the worst-hit areas, experienced considerable hardship.[20] For example, 1,000 people were given one pint of soup per

B. COLFER

Fig. 23 Between 1845 and 1870, a ship named the *Dunbrody* carried emigrants from New Ross to New York and Grosse Isle in Canada. As part of the Famine commemorations in 1997, a replica of the ship was built at New Ross, where it is moored at the quayside. Guided tours of the ship and emigration museum are available all year round.

Fig. 24 The many ruined houses in the Hook are a legacy of the high population levels which existed before the explosion of post-Famine emigration, driven by a combination of social and economic factors.

day in the New Ross Union in 1846 and in the following two years 7,222 and 6,531 people, respectively, received assistance, the highest numbers for any Union in the county.[21] In 1847, at a more local level, 1,744 people (42%) in the Fethard District Electoral Division were in receipt of relief, and 2,405 (45%) in Tintern D.E.D. These statistics show that the Famine caused considerable hardship in the Hook region, far more than is generally realised; the Famine resulted in a fall of over twenty per cent in the population of the civil parishes of Hook, Templetown and Fethard between 1841 and 1861.[22]

Applications for relief works in the barony of Shelburne related mostly to road improvements, including building bridges, levelling hills and filling hollows.[23] The Loftus estate took advantage of the situation to improve the road system: frequent references to repairs of roads from the limestone quarries of Hook and the roads from manure banks on the seashore are an indication of the importance attached to these resources. An application was also made for the restoration of the footpath beside the road from the deerpark piers of Loftus Hall to the piers at Porter's Gate. Lord Templemore

Fig. 25 Cultivation ridges high on the slope of Templetown Hill recall a pre-Famine era when the demand for potatoes created by an ever-increasing population forced cultivation on to marginal land.

borrowed £6,000 under the Land Improvement Act of 1847 to provide employment for workers on the Dunbrody estate; this was quite a significant sum out of a total of £40,000 borrowed by all Wexford landlords. In Tintern it was reported that 'the entire poor are employed, with the exception of those in Balistown and Burkestown, Lord Ely's property. We employ them in drainage, the women and girls and little boys throw stones into the drains, so that we have scarcely a family which is not able fully to support itself.'[24] In the Hook, a successful petition was made for a famine relief scheme to construct a new pier at Slade, which in addition to providing employment would allow the inhabitants to support themselves by fishing. The initiative was not led by the Marquis of Ely, but by John Breen, the tenant of Slade townland, and Rev. John Dunne, the curate of Templetown.

Documents relating to the application for the new pier throw some light on social conditions in the Hook during

Fig. 26 Patrick Kennedy, from Dunganstown, near the River Barrow south of New Ross, was among the many emigrants who sailed from Waterford Harbour in the post-Famine era. His great-grandson, J. F. Kennedy, visited his ancestral home in 1963 as president of the United States. The surviving part of the original dwelling house and outbuilding complex is now open to the public, having been developed as a Kennedy museum and heritage centre, in a restrained but effective manner, by Kennedy descendant Patrick Grennan.

the Famine.[25] It was pointed out that the outlook was very unpromising, as farmers were reluctant to employ the many labourers who were daily removed from the Public Works, not from an unwillingness to do so but because of a lack of work and the price of provisions. The importance of providing work as a means of warding off sickness and preserving the peace was emphasised, as the destitution of the locality was almost incredible. The potential use of fish as an alternative food supply was highlighted by a report on the unprecedented catches of sprat in the tideway of the Suir, Nore and Barrow. More than twenty tons per day were being sold at the quay of

Fig. 27   In 1851, one-roomed cabins inhabited by the cottier or labouring class, represented ten per cent of all houses in the barony of Shelburne. The one shown here was located in the south of the county near Bannow.

New Ross alone, where a few days previously nine large gabbards (a type of boat), filled to the gunwales with sprat, were surrounded by hundreds of people, each holding a sack in one hand and money in the other, all clamouring to be first served.

Although the gravity of the situation may have been exaggerated in making a case for the construction of the pier at Slade, and the word 'famine' was not mentioned, it is clear that there was real hardship experienced in the Hook during that period. The clearest proof of this is contained in the census figures, which show that the Famine had dramatic long-term demographic implications for the area. From a high in 1841, the population of the civil parish of Hook ('inside the piers') had dropped by 20 per cent in 1861, Templetown by 20 per cent and Fethard by 26 per cent. The barony of Shelburne lost 29 per cent of its population in the same period. This trend, exacerbated by famine-related emigration, was to continue.

Fig. 28   One of the few surviving thatched houses in the Hook region, located in Graigue Little townland. The dramatic fall in population following the Famine led to the abandonment of many houses of this type.

THE LAND LEAGUE AND THE HOOK 200

The Famine had a profound influence on political and landscape developments during the second half of the century.[26] Post-Famine evictions were actually encouraged by legislation: the £4 rating clause made landlords responsible for rates on all holdings valued at under £4 and the Gregory quarter-acre clause refused relief to anyone holding more than that amount. These regulations encouraged land clearances and led to the disappearance of the cottier class. In Ireland as a whole, one-roomed

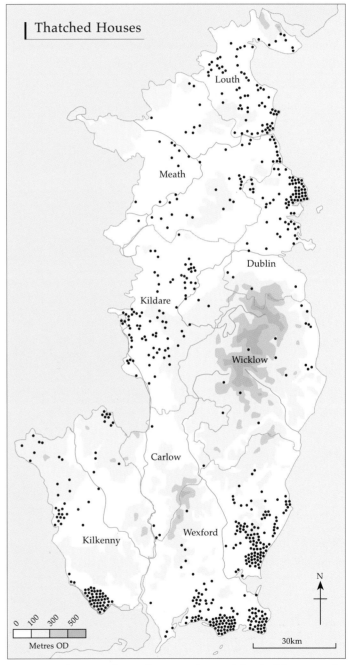

Fig. 29   As this map shows, the survival rate of thatched houses in the Hook is very low. This may be partly due to the influence of the landlords on the three estate. The Colclough Papers show that John Colclough was urging his tenants to build stone houses with slated roofs in the 1790s.

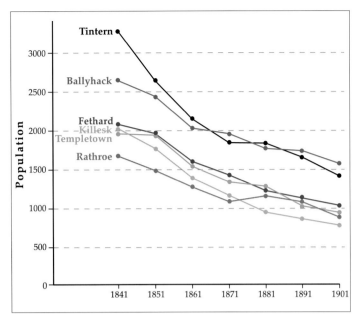

Fig. 30 Demographic changes in the six District Electoral Divisions in the Hook between 1841 and 1901. All showed a similar fall in population, with Tintern showing the most dramatic fall during the Famine decade. The population rose slightly in Templetown during the 1840s, possibly because of the availability of sustenance from the sea.

cabins fell from 30 per cent of all houses in 1841 to 10 per cent by 1861. These cabins were sometimes built by the 'wretched occupiers,' who held them at a 'moderate' rent but were also built by large farmers for their labourers whose work served as rent.[27] The corresponding figures for one-roomed cabins in county Wexford fell from 24 per cent to 7 per cent. In 1851, one-roomed cabins in Shelburne represented 10 per cent of all dwellings.[28] The post-Famine evictions brought security of tenure to the fore and made land reform an important part of the political agenda. The disappearance of the cottiers benefited the strong farmers but weakened the landlords, many of whom, already facing bankruptcy, were ruined by the added cost of famine relief, which was levied on them by the English government. The Famine and large-scale emigration cleared the way for a relatively smooth transition to tenant ownership. There were also considerable landscape implications, as new farming practices led to a dramatic increase in pasture and a halving of arable land between 1851 and 1911. As emigration increased, the retreat from marginal land left a legacy of overgrown cultivation ridges and ruined houses.

The relationship between landlord and tenant on the three estates in the Hook region varied considerably. On the Dunbrody and particularly the Tintern estate, there is no indication of significant social friction; on the Loftus estate, however, there was a history of sporadic agrarian conflict. This was evident in the aftermath of the 1798 Rebellion when (according to John Colclough of Tintern)

all the tenants on the Loftus estate were evicted.[29] In 1844, a commission into the occupation of land in Ireland was told, by a tenant whose family had held Great Graigue for three generations, that the Marquis of Ely did not recognise that his tenants had any rights.[30] The eviction of 121 people in 1865 by the agent Pat Hare created social unrest and in 1869 there were riotous scenes at a sports and race-meeting at Fethard when the same agent was abused for carrying out evictions at Killesk, an outlying townland on the estate. Rather incongruously, the agent was regarded as being solely responsible, as the crowd cheered and applauded the Marquis of Ely and his family when they appeared on the stage.[31]

As the Land War intensified, the general discontent felt by the tenants in the region, particularly on the Ely estate, was given a unity and structure by the arrival in the district of two priests who were also militant political activists. In 1862, Rev. Thomas Doyle (1816–1903) was

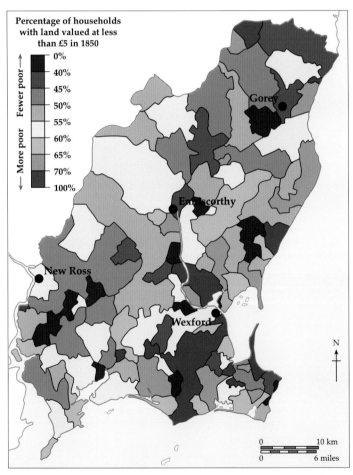

Fig. 31 The percentage of households in county Wexford c. 1850 with land valued at less than £5. The poverty-stricken element in the community is identified as the landless labourers and householders whose land was valued at less than £5. In Wexford, 57 per cent of dispersed rural households fell into this category, by far the largest single element in the population. In the Hook, the civil parishes of Fethard and the Hook, at 60 to 64 per cent, had the highest level of deprivation. This group were most at risk from the Famine and its after-effects.

PRIVATE COLLECTION

Fig. 32 An early photograph of Fethard c. 1870, taken from the top of the castle. The whitewashed cottages on the left may have been the scene of the evictions in 1882. The R.I.C. barracks is at bottom right. The high ground of Baginbun with the Martello tower can be seen at left centre of the picture.

appointed to Ramsgrange, then part of a parish which included Templetown, Fethard and the Hook, and in the following year he was made parish priest when Ramsgrange became a separate parish. He came from a politically active family, as his mother was a cousin of the 1798 leader John Kelly and, in 1831, his relations were involved in a Tithe War incident known as the 'Battle of the Pound' at Bunclody. He had previously been involved in the Tenant League and continued his political activities at Ramsgrange. When the Land League was founded by

B. COLFER

Fig. 33 This terrace of houses (now known as Tay Lane), built in Fethard by the Loftus estate in 1864, was named either Obstruction Row or Dynamite Row during the Land War. Some of the seventy people evicted from cottages in Fethard in 1882 may have been living here.

Michael Davitt in 1879, with the aim of protecting tenants from rack-rents and with the ultimate goal of tenant ownership, Doyle held mass meetings with the intention of establishing the League in the Hook.[32] In an attempt to discourage political involvement, nine tenants were arrested and gaoled in Kilkenny. Those arrested were: Breen and Dunne of Herrylock; Power of Sea Lodge; Grace and Egan of Broomhill; Breen of Templetown; Chapman of Carnivan; Walsh and Foley of Fethard.[33]

Rev. David Walsh (later known as O'Hanlon Walsh) had been politicised by the eviction of his family from their farm at Knocktartan in Ballymitty, county Wexford.[34] On his appointment to the Hook (Templetown) in 1881, he demonstrated his political allegiance by naming his residence Davitt Hall and declaring that two rows of cottages in Fethard would be known by the provocative names of Dynamite Row and Obstruction Row. He established a branch of the Land League for the tenants on the Ely estate, which became known for its unity and determination and was generally referred to as 'the Hook 200.'[35] It was supported by a branch of the Ladies' Land League, which had a membership of 130. A 'no rent' campaign was initiated to force a reduction in rents to what was considered an acceptable level and there were reports of antagonism against farmers who broke ranks.[36] In general, despite a request for an increase in the garrison of Duncannon Fort, there were no unlawful activities apart

MARY BYRNE

Fig. 34 A membership card for the Hook branch of the Irish National League issued to Richard Murphy of Airhill by secretary Maurice Breen of Templetown. Both men were stalwart members of the Hook 200.

B. COLFER

Fig. 36 One of the few violent incidents to occur in the Hook during the Land War was the breaking of windows in the gate-lodge of Loftus Hall.

dealings with the landlords. The refusal to pay rents led to the serving of sixty eviction notices on the Ely estate in early 1882, but no rents were paid in spite of the arrest and gaoling of nine tenants. The situation deteriorated further when seventy people were evicted from cottages in Fethard by the agent Godfrey Taylor.[38] Following the agreement of a compromise rent on the Dunbrody and Tintern estates, the Marquis of Ely's offer of a twenty per cent reduction was not accepted by his tenants and the agent decided to proceed with the evictions. This split the tenantry, with the two priests in opposite camps, as some paid their rents rather than face eviction.

Subsequent to this crisis point and the censure of O'Hanlon Walsh by the bishop, the land question in the Hook became less confrontational. After the disbanding of the Land League and the establishment of the Irish National League in the autumn of 1882, a branch of the new organisation was established in the Hook in mid-1883. In the following year, the depth of emotion generated by the Land War, and the esteem in which O'Hanlon Walsh was held, was demonstrated in a dramatic protest against

from the breaking of windows in the gate lodge of Loftus Hall.[37] As O'Hanlon Walsh's influence spread to the Dunbrody and Tintern estates, he was regarded as a threat by the authorities and efforts to have him removed were considered. Following a reprimand from the bishop, he became less active and his influence waned. He was also opposed by Rev. Doyle, who was more conciliatory in his

B. COLFER

Fig. 35 Templetown parochial house was named Davitt Hall by Fr. O'Hanlon Walsh, in honour of the founder of the Land League.

B. COLFER

Fig. 37 The building of labourers' cottages added a new feature to the landscape. By 1914, 50,000 had been built throughout the country.

The Battle of Coolroe

Up spoke Thomas Somers and said now my Wexford boys
To do a deed I'm willing which will your hearts rejoice.
If you will lend a hand with me and the bailiffs overthrow,
We'll prove the fire of '98's still burning in Coolroe.

Chorus
We are the boys of Wexford who fought with heart and hand
To guard the homes our fathers built and died for Ireland.
Then let us be united and triumphant we'll be seen
On the mountaintops of Ireland we'll plant the flag of green.

Then up spoke Bartle Rochford saying I am a smith by trade,
My father was a farmer, long in his grave he's laid.
The house that he was born in the bailiffs they laid low
With all my heart I'll give my hand to battle in Coolroe.

Into the forge then Bartle went and the anvil loud did ring,
And with his strong stout arm the heavy sledge did swing.
And as he shaped the iron the flying sparks did glow,
'Oh! I wish to God it was a pike', says Bartle of Coolroe.

They barred the doors and windows, they banked the house all round,
With banks of earth ten feet high from where it touched the ground,
'Twas sloped so neat and gentle that the least touch of a blow
Put all the peelers reeling back that morning in Coolroe.

The peelers scaled the ladders and the battering ram they tried,
Jim Ryan beleaguered to himself 'twas soon the ram he spied.
'The ram' says Jim, 'has got the fluke, some sheepdip on him throw,
'Twill deluge all the worms my boys this morning in Coolroe.'

The soldiers then fixed bayonets, bright flashing in the sun,
And tried the steep embankment 'til they thought the fort was won.
T'was then that they discovered no cowards were their foe,
For they put them reeling back again that morning in Coolroe.

Into the front our Canon steps and said now boys attend,
You know that I have been to you a counsellor and a friend,
You've done a deed for Ireland and while Slaney's waters flow,
We'll ne'er forget the fight you fought this morning in Coolroe.

Fig. 38 In 1888, Thomas Somers, a strong farmer of Coolroe on the Tintern estate, resisted eviction for a while by barricading and defending his house (subsequently called 'Somers' fort'). The constabulary removed the last of the defenders through the roof of the farmhouse.

the priest's transfer to Castlebridge near Wexford town. In an amazing display of defiance, the parishioners, normally conservative and subservient, nailed up the door of the church at Templetown in protest and refused access to his successor for three months.[39] O'Hanlon Walsh returned to the Hook on a few occasions to show his support for continuing agitation; in 1886, he attended an open-air demonstration at Templetown organised by the Hook 200 to demand a reduction in rent from Ely and to promote the building of labourers' cottages.[40] Following O'Hanlon Walsh's departure, Canon Doyle again became active and, when some initial attempts at reconciliation failed, he returned to the implementation of the 'no rent' campaign. The Marquis of Ely remained obdurate, however, and later in the year eleven families (fifty people) were again evicted at Fethard.[41] During the late 1880s there were high-profile evictions in south-west Wexford; the most notorious was in the townland of Coolroe, on the Tintern estate but in the hands of a middleman. In 1888, Thomas Somers was to be evicted from his farm at Coolroe, but the house was fortified (it later became known as Somers' fort) and occupied by twelve men.[42] A large force of police failed to gain admission to the house and, when they threatened to use their guns, Canon Doyle, who was present with a large

DÚCHAS

Fig. 39 Miss Lucie Marie Biddulph Colclough outside an ivy-covered Tintern Abbey with Louis Feeley of the Office of Public Works in 1963.

crowd of onlookers, eventually succeeded in getting the men to surrender.

The nationalist 'split' which followed the Parnell divorce case of 1890 led to the disruption of the land reform movement in the Hook. Canon Doyle became a vehement anti-Parnellite and withdrew from active politics, but he continued to air his opinions on many topics in contributions to various newspapers until his death in 1903.

THE END OF LANDLORDISM

The late nineteenth century witnessed the death-throes of the landlord system in Ireland. In the aftermath of the Famine, the landed class, generally regarded as having failed in their social and political responsibilities, lost the sympathy of the British establishment, encouraging an unusually broad programme of state intervention in private property. The move towards 'peasant proprietorship' was accelerated by subsequent agrarian and nationalist politics. A sequence of Land Acts (Gladstone 1881, Ashbourne 1885, Balfour 1891, Wyndham 1903, Birrel 1909) encouraged Irish landlords to part with their estates and four and a half million hectares were transferred to tenants, who purchased 316,000 holdings.[43] By the beginning of World War I, a remarkable social revolution had resulted in two-thirds of Irish tenants becoming owners of their land. As tenants purchased existing holdings, the transfer of ownership was carried out with minimal landscape changes. However, from 1883 onwards, the building of cottages for agricultural labourers made a considerable impact: by 1914, 50,000 of them had been built under the first public housing initiative in Britain and Ireland.[44]

The loss of lands inevitably had an influence on demesnes and big houses, many of which became economic liabilities and were abandoned or sold. In the Hook region, the destiny of the big houses followed diverse paths, reflecting the distinctive character of the three estates. At Tintern, the Colclough family continued to live in the crumbling abbey until 1959, when the last of the family, Marie Biddulph Colclough, moved into a house in Saltmills; in 1963, the abbey was handed over to the Board of Works. The Chichesters remained on in Dunbrody Park until the end of the twentieth century, when the house was sold. The family retained some of the former estate property, however, and are still resident in the area, a surviving remnant of an estate system that can be traced back to the late twelfth century. On the Loftus estate, in 1870, the old Hall had been levelled and a new mansion erected in its place, a rather enigmatic initiative given the economic and political atmosphere of the time, particularly as the family was mostly absentee. The doubtful nature of the decision was underlined by the sale of Loftus Hall in 1913, perhaps motivated in part by the turbulent history between tenants and landlord on the estate; the purchase of the hall by an order of Benedictine nuns and its subsequent use as a convent for sixty years, with an oratory for public mass, added a touch of irony to the transformation.

Fig. 1 The old Loftus Hall in the 1860s, shortly before demolition. This structure was the result of various developments since medieval times. The piers on the left are similar to the ones at the present entrance. The stone eagles on the gables are presumably the ones on the balustade of the modern building.

Loftus Hall originated as Redmond Hall, a late medieval residence erected by the Redmond family, who were tenants on the manor of Kilcloggan. In the late seventeenth century, this structure was occupied by Henry Loftus, who renovated and possibly enlarged the building and changed its name to Loftus Hall. In 1752, the house was described as follows:

> A late seventeenth-century house is gable-ended and of two storeys and nine bays, with a dormered roof and steep pedimented gable. It is fronted by a forecourt with tall piers surmounted by ball finials and has a haunted tapestry room.[1]

It is probable that further improvements were subsequently made, but, by the end of the nineteenth century, the hall was probably not in good repair. For some reason, a decision was taken in 1870 to level most of the old house and to erect the present structure on the same site, incorporating parts of the previous building.[2] Following demolition, the

Fig. 2 The new Hall c. 1890, about fifteen years after completion. Little attention had been given to landscaping and no work on that aspect of the development was subsequently undertaken.

Fig. 3 Loftus Hall is located on the eastern shore of Waterford Harbour, beside a beach known as the Hall Bay. Storm walls were erected along the cliff edge, probably when the new building was constructed, to protect against coastal erosion. A boat-house beside the Hall Bay has been eroded by the sea.

B. COLFER

PRIVATE COLLECTION

Fig. 4 A group on the entrance steps of the new Loftus Hall, shortly after its completion in 1872.

rubble was dumped along the cliff edge, where it can still be seen. This was part of a scheme to prevent coastal erosion which included the building of a storm wall along the cliff edge. The outbuildings, including the coach-house and walled garden, were left untouched and still survive in various stages of preservation.[3]

Built to a rather plain design, the new building is a rectangular Victorian pile of three storeys. The east-facing front façade has nine bays with hood mouldings over windows, pedimented on the first floor, and a projecting portico with glass panels; the south side has seven bays with a bow extension. Two stone eagles, probably taken from the old building, are perched on the decorative balustrade which hides the flat roof. The ground floor has several large reception rooms, some with panelled ceilings and elegant marble fireplaces. The main feature of the house, a splendid oak stairway in a central well lit by a cupola, ascends to a gallery around which the bedrooms are located. The stairway was imported from Italy and assembled by local craftsmen. The hall was fitted with hot-air central heating, gas lights with Waterford crystal chandeliers and running water, supplied from a reservoir built on higher ground at Herrylock two kilometres to the north.[4]

It is difficult to understand the reasons behind the major investment in

B. COLFER

Fig. 5 Some of the outbuildings and the walled garden pre-date the existing building. The surviving ruins of the coach-house, which lost its roof in the recent past, belong to a period earlier than the present hall.

B. COLFER

Fig. 6 The new hall was equipped with all modern conveniences. A piped water supply was brought underground from this purpose built reservoir on high ground at Herrylock, a distance of two kilometres.

JOHN SCANLON

Fig. 7 An ornate oak staircase, made in Italy, was installed in the new Loftus Hall by local craftsmen.

Fig. 8 Loftus Hall in the 1970s, when it was still a convent. The annex on the left gave access to the oratory in which local people attended mass.

B. COLFER

a new building, in view of the uncertain atmosphere of the time. The Land Acts of the following forty years resulted in the estate being reduced to a fraction of its former size.[5] In 1913, the hall with its remaining seventy acres (28 ha) was put up for sale and was purchased as a convent for Benedictine nuns. In 1936, the Benedictines left and the building was acquired by the Rosminian Order.[6] The first postulants, including some local girls, were accepted the following year. The Rosminians set up an oratory in one of the large ground-floor rooms so that local people could attend mass. They also opened the convent as a summer holiday venue for other orders of nuns, who had exclusive use of the private beach known as Hall Bay. In the 1980s, the nuns sold the property and it was subsequently run briefly as a hotel. At present, the building, still referred to locally as 'The Hall', is a private residence.

B. COLFER

Fig. 9 The piers at the entrance gate to Loftus Hall are much older than the present building and are similar to the deerpark piers and former piers around the old hall and at Porter's Gate. Piers at the entrance to the walled garden, erected in the 1680s, are similar but more decorative, so all were presumably erected in the late seventeenth century when Henry Loftus renovated the medieval hall.

TRADITIONAL LIFESTYLES

The geographically confined nature of the Hook peninsula created a close-knit community with strong kinship ties. This was particularly true of the point of Hook, where non-natives were habitually referred to as 'outsiders.' Although restrictive in some ways, this insularity inevitably led to a well-defined sense of local identity, with established practices linked to traditional occupations and seasonal activities on land and sea. An interdependence arising from the co-operative or *meitheal* approach, demanded by seasonal tasks that required manpower, had a profound integrating effect on the whole community. The division of the region into three major estates with distinctive characteristics added a touch of cultural variation, typified by the craftworkers of Tintern, the salmon fishermen of Dunbrody and the stoneworkers of Loftus Hall. People had to be adaptable to survive. Within every occupation there were subtle variations: as well as farmers and fishermen, there were farmers who did some fishing and fishermen who did a little farming. There were usually some locals who had experience of the outside world. Society was leavened by returning sailors who recounted experiences gleaned during voyages to ports around the world. However, on returning home they quickly settled into the rhythm of local life, although some expressed forthright views on matters of church and state. The landscape benefited from a conservative approach to time-honoured work practices and customs, while the use of indigenous materials and established layout resulted in a distinctive type of vernacular dwelling. The impact of the sea on the landscape was exemplified by the development or an elaborate coastal geography.

B. COLFER

Fig. 1 Tommy Murphy of Churchtown was the last builder of 'punts' in the Hook. Constructed of light timber and covered with tarred canvas, these small boats were rowed long distances by men who fished with hand-lines and set lobster pots. Tommy, a great story-teller with a wealth of knowledge on the lore of the Hook, liked to compare the attraction of lobster fishing to buying lucky-bags, because 'you never knew what might be in the next pot.'

STONEWORKING

The demise of the estate system precipitated a decline in the traditional skills and crafts that had survived because of landlord patronage. For well over a century, men skilled in stoneworking had been quarrying limestone around the cliffs and building stone walls and houses. At Herrylock, on the cliffs at Templetown, millstones and other objects were cut from the Old Red Sandstone. The place-name Herrylock (a sub-division of Templetown townland) is possibly of fairly recent origin. In 1578, part of the Redmond property was called Harrie's Hill, presumably the hill at Herrylock, as there are no hills on

Fig. 3 As well as making millstones, the stonemasons at Herrylock manufactured a range of other items from the Old Red Sandstone, including landrollers and feeding troughs like the ones shown here.

exposed on the cliff-face is ideal for millstones and many Herrylock stones are to be seen in mills around the county and further afield. The millstones were expensive items: in 1822, the construction of Brownscastle mill near Taghmon cost £147, of which £8 12s 10d was spent on two millstones and their carriage from Herrylock, where they had been made by millwright William Foley.[1] The arrival of the synthetic stone in the late nineteenth century signalled the end of the millstone industry at Herrylock and elsewhere in the Hook.

The method used to quarry a millstone was simple but ingenious: having selected a suitable section of red sandstone, a vertical cut was chiselled around the perimeter of the proposed stone and the surrounding rock was removed. Holes were then bored under the stone into which wooden pegs were inserted. The incoming tide wetted the pegs causing them to swell and the resultant pressure eventually split the millstone from the underlying bedrock. A number of shattered and

Fig. 2 At the site of the millstone quarry in the Old Red Sandstone cliff at Herrylock, circular depressions in the rock mark the spots from which millstones were extracted. A number of incomplete or broken millstones can be identified among the boulders at the base of the cliff.

the point of Hook. The group of houses known as Herrylock is at the foot of this hill, so it is possible that 'lock' comes from either the Irish *log* a hollow, or *loch* a pool, both of which would be relevant; in the 1880s, the name was written as Herrylock or Herrilough. At one time the farmhouse cluster at Herrylock was occupied by about ten families and many of the inhabitants were stone-cutters working in the quarry. The Old Red Sandstone

Fig. 4 A Herrylock millstone now used as a garden feature at Browne's mill in Old Ross. There has been a mill on this site since medieval times.

R.I.A.

Fig. 5 A detail from a painting of the Tower of Hook by Du Noyer, c. 1850, showing men at work quarrying stone from the nearby rocks.

abandoned millstones at Herrylock shows that this technique was not always successful. Because of the height of the surrounding cliff, the millstones were removed by water. The finished stones were manoeuvred at low tide to a ledge of rock known as 'the Old Quay,' and on the rising tide the millstone was lashed to the bottom of a small boat and in this manner transported to its destination. According to local tradition, one of the last millstones to be cut at Herrylock was being brought to Bannow in this way when the boat sprung a leak and was forced to put into Slade, where the millstone was abandoned and used for many years as a mooring for boats. Skilfully carved initials survive in a cave known as the Otter Hole, on the seashore just north of the quarry at Herrylock, indicating that it was used by the stoneworkers as a temporary base.

The masons at Herrylock did not confine their skills to millstones. The distinctive colour of the red sandstone is still to be seen around the district in such objects as landrollers, water troughs, hand querns and pier caps. A set of bollards on the quay at Duncannon and pier caps and a font in the old graveyard at Templetown, are all made from red sandstone. Its use for windows and other details in medieval buildings in the region, notably Tintern Abbey and Fethard Castle, suggests that there was a long-established local tradition of stone-cutting. Two types of sandstone, rough and smooth, occur in alternate layers at Herrylock. The rough type was used for millstones and most other objects; the smooth was used for making grinding stones, ridge-tiles and cut stone for house-building. The masons also worked on other parts of the coast where the rock was suitable, particularly at Ballyhack and Carnivan. Robert Leigh mentioned the manufacture of millstones at Ballyhack in 1684: 'Out of the rock that hangs over the village and quay is wrought a number of very good millstones, which with no small skill or less danger are rolled down a very high precipice to the aforesaid quay and so carried by water as occasion requires.'[2] Matthew Kelly, who died in about 1905, was the last of the stoneworkers at Herrylock. He left instructions that his last millstone, which he had cut at Carnivan, should not be sold for less than one pound.[3]

On the Loftus estate, the quarrying of limestone as a commercial activity provided employment for quarrymen and also for others who were skilled in 'firing a kiln.' The 1841 Ordnance Survey maps show fifteen limekilns on the promontory of Hook, six on the peninsula itself. Limestone was quarried at the Hook for well over a hundred years, not only for local use but also for export, and an enormous quantity of rock must have been removed from the cliffs during that time. A yearly rent of £40 paid for a quarry at Slade in 1872 (equivalent to the

B. COLFER

B. COLFER

Fig. 6 This limekiln (A), just north of the lighthouse, was the last one to be constructed on the headland, as it was the only one not shown on the 1841 Ordnance map. Unlike other kilns, which have stone arches over the 'eye,' this one has a wooden lintel, probably salvaged from a wrecked ship. The centre of the kiln (B) was lined with Old Red Sandstone, which could withstand the great heat necessary to reduce the limestone to powder.

B. COLFER

Fig. 7 A limekiln on the shore at Bullock Park in Galgystown townland.

rent of 50 acres of land) suggests the economic significance of quarrying in the Hook.[4] The importance of the industry is also indicated by frequent mentions in nineteenth-century Grand Jury Presentments of repairs to roads leading to the 'limestone quarries of the Hook.' It is said locally that the last limestone was burned in the 1920s to produce lime mortar for the building of labourers' cottages. 'Firing a kiln' required a certain amount of expertise if the operation was to be carried out successfully. The bottom of the kiln was filled with straw and dry furze bushes. Then the kiln was filled with alternate layers of limestone rock and culm (coal dust mixed with clay). The fire was started through the small opening called the 'eye' of the kiln. As the fire spread upwards, each layer of limestone was reduced to powder, which was eventually raked out through the 'eye.' Stones which did not burn were called 'scalders' and these half-burned stones can still be found in the fields. The abandoned kilns are now in a dilapidated state, with the ovens filled in and overgrown with bushes.

CUSTOMS AND FOLKLORE

The secluded cul-de-sac nature of the peninsula nurtured a close-knit society with an intricate web of inter-relationships, as most people married within the area. This was an advantage in a situation where many depended on the help of others in the operation of a *meitheal* (team) system as they eked out a subsistence living at farming and fishing. Entertainment was provided by frequent house-dances organised by the younger generation, sometimes in unoccupied houses that were commandeered for that purpose. There was usually a melodeon player available, but if all else failed someone could be relied on to provide 'gob music,' as lilting was called. Mumming was also popular throughout the region, with groups established at Porter's Gate, Fethard and Templetown.[5] Mumming involved step-dancing with rhythmical wooden sword-striking. Each team member, representing a historical figure, gave a long recitation. Some of the customs which were observed, such as the giving of a 'pleideóg' of eggs at Easter, may have been peculiar to the Hook. A more unusual custom was observed on New Year's Day when children searched for the first daisies of the year and distributed them to the houses. The expectation was that a penny would be given in return for the cheerful greeting

The ghost of Loftus Hall

The incident described as 'The ghost of Loftus Hall' is said to have occurred about 1760, when the hall was occupied by Charles Tottenham, who had married a Loftus heiress, and his daughter, Anne Tottenham Loftus. On a stormy winter's night, the family was startled by a loud rapping on the main door and were informed by a servant that a young man who had lost his way was seeking shelter for the night. The stranger was admitted and proved to be such a genial companion that he was asked to stay for a few days.

In the evenings the family played cards and the visitor, with Anne as his partner, won every game. One evening, Anne dropped a card and on bending down to pick it up she saw that, instead of a foot, the agreeable visitor had a cloven hoof. Anne's hysterical screams caused the 'devil' to exit in a ball of fire through the ceiling. According to tradition, the hole could not subsequently be repaired. Anne became deranged and was brought to the tapestry room where she was confined until her death some months later. The occupants of the hall continued to be disturbed by strange events and, at the suggestion of the servants, the Tottenhams sent for the Rev. Thomas Broaders, the local Catholic priest.

On his arrival, Rev. Broaders performed a long ritual of exorcism and commanded the malevolent presence to leave. The 'devil' departed in a clap of thunder leaving behind a pungent smell of brimstone. However, that was not the end of the story. For many years afterwards unsuspecting visitors who were assigned the tapestry room reported strange experiences, including the sighting of a lady in a flowered dress who crossed the room and disappeared into a closet in the corner.

The family's indebtedness to the priest is recorded in estate records. The Loftuses subsequently treated Rev. Broaders very well, leasing him several townlands which were occupied by his parishioners, an unusual situation in the circumstances of the late eighteenth century. According to tradition, Rev. Broaders was also allowed to erect penal chapels at Templetown and Poulfur. A rhyme relating to his burial place in the Tottenham cemetery at Horetown refers to the Loftus Hall episode:

Here lies the body of Thomas Broaders,
Who did good and prayed for all,
And banished the devil from Loftus Hall.

A Big Blaze in Slade Square

It being on a Sunday evening, in the merry month of May,
When the shags and murrs were singing, to Slade I took my way;
When going through the village it was filled with boys and chaps,
Sure I thought they were the Russians or otherwise the Japs.

Chorus
Courting in the kitchen, dancing on the flags,
No door nor window on the house, but a lot of phosphate bags.

It would remind you of a market, a race-course or a fair,
Jim Whitty the melodeon played as they marched up through the Square,
When they arrived at their shanty they began to sing and dance,
It was like a big theatre you would often see in France.

Now, all the boys and girls their names I will pen down,
They were from Slade and Portersgate and a place they call Churchtown;
They danced away like blazes, the night was calm and bright,
Pat Kennedy and A. Power, John Whitty and M. White.

Matt Colfer and Catherine White they done it in great style,
But Willie Breen and Polly Power would make a jackass smile;
The melodeon got out of order, but they didn't care a fig,
They were supplied with 'gob-music', Tommy Fortune he did jig.

James Colfer and Tommy Barry, they attended there as well,
And lots of other courting boys too numerous for to tell;
Mick Kennedy was also there, but not against his will;
He was diddling in the cupboard, with a girl from the Hill.

When the 'setting' was all over, their hearts were full of joy,
'Dublin Bay' and 'Blue Bell' was sung by a Churchtown boy;
He wears a little mouldy muss, his age is seventeen,
Now the way you all will know him, he is dobbin Willie Breen.

To please the company all around, Jim Whitty sang a song,
His voice was most melodious and it sounded like a gong;
When he was tired of singing, he got out to dance a reel,
But his head is too full of dancing to reach his toe and heel.

About two o'clock in the morning, I parted from the Square,
With all the information I could scrape up here and there;
There are other things that happened not so very long ago,
But I'll send a full report of them, in another week or so.

Now to conclude and finish, I will lay down my pen,
For it may be a long time till you see a dance again;
So all you shanty dancers, to you I do reveal,
That your names are sent to Kellystown for insertion in the 'Gale.

Published in the **Adamstown Nightingale**, *1906,*
under the pen-name Watty ould Phates.

'Happy New Year and here's your daisy!' Some stories were more generic in nature, particularly the well-known 'Ghost of Loftus Hall' and a tale about a mysterious coach that sometimes rolled through Slade at night. The most frightening story, possibly because it was related to local experience, concerned an all-night hooley that was held in a seaside cave known as Roomeen Glas, in the cliff near the lighthouse. Early in the night, a black hen with her chickens came out of the sea and walked into the cave. An old woman who was present warned that this was a sign of pending disaster and that everyone should leave. Naturally, she was ignored and before dawn a huge wave flooded the cave and all present were drowned.

Ballad writing was popular as a way of recording local happenings and there were always a few individuals who could make a ballad about any event, from wrecks to weddings. The social scene captured in a ballad called 'A big blaze in Slade Square,' describing an actual house dance which took place in the Hook in the early 1900s, probably remained unchanged for a century or more.[6]

The demographic profile of the Hook, composed of large interrelated families, ensured a warm and intimate experience at a social and community level. However, the limited resources were insufficient to meet the needs of so many and from the middle of the nineteenth century onwards there was continuous emigration. The high number of ruined and abandoned houses in the region bears testimony to those who had to go, sometimes in whole family units, to start new lives in Liverpool or London. People who come back, usually after many years, speak wistfully of their youth and the great times they had growing up in the Hook.

HOUSES

The vernacular Hook house, constructed of local stone, had two ground-floor rooms, lit by two front windows, with central fire and doorway, sometimes protected by a small porch. Two gable windows lit low loft bedrooms under a slated roof. Some houses had mud walls and thatched roofs but slate was preferred, particularly on the wind-swept peninsula. In the late nineteenth and early twentieth centuries, a new element was added to the landscape by the construction of 'Land League' cottages. These were of similar design to the traditional vernacular house but somewhat higher, giving more headroom on the first floor. Houses on larger farms were typically two-storeyed, slated, stone structures, lit by front windows on both floors. However, there were also smaller, single-storeyed farmhouses, occasionally thatched.

B. COLFER

Fig. 7 A house and outbuildings in the farmhouse cluster of Newtown in Grange townland. The small upper windows indicate that the house was probably originally thatched, with dormer-type windows on the first floor. Note the traditional cylindrical entrance piers with conical caps.

Fig. 9 A small single-storey farmhouse and outbuilding complex at Herrylock in the 1980s. The off-centre chimney suggests that the house was extended to the left at some stage. The alignment of the house gable with the road-side boundary is a feature of buildings in the Hook. The leaning tree has been shaped by the prevailing south-westerly winds. The design of a modern building, which now occupies the site, echoes aspects of the original complex.

Traditional farmyards were usually of the courtyard type, consisting of a rectangular space surrounded by farm buildings, with the farmhouse gable and the outhouses on one side of the yard, in some cases located on the roadside boundary. The gate was very often hung on the solid cylindrical stone piers with conical tops which are still a feature of the south Wexford area. In most instances where improvements have been carried out, the original farmhouse has been upgraded but the courtyard complexes have usually disintegrated, being

Fig. 10 A substantial, two-storeyed farmhouse, with central doorway and gable chimneys, overlooking Waterford Harbour at Churchtown.

Fig. 11 The status of the blacksmith in the community is reflected in the quality of this abandoned house, probably extended to the right at some stage, beside the forge (on the left) at Little Graigue crossroads. The house has iron windows, in keeping with the trade of the owner.

B. COLFER

Fig. 12 A typical vernacular house in Churchtown. This type of house typically had a central door and chimney, two ground-floor rooms lit by two front windows with two loft rooms lit by gable windows. This house has a semi-circular decorative feature over the doorway in the small porch. Concrete barges protected the slated roof from winter storms.

superseded by buildings more suited to modern agricultural practices. In the 1950s, the introduction of a newly designed County Council cottage added another feature to the landscape. The design of these bungalow-type houses with a red-tiled hipped roof was quite successful and sat easily in the landscape; a later modified version was not as satisfactory. From the 1970s onwards, the County Council, abandoning its previous policy of erecting isolated cottages, located public housing schemes at Fethard, Duncannon and Ballyhack.

Between 1965 and 1995, 500 private houses were built in the region. Of these, 60 (12%) were holiday homes, concentrated mostly in the vicinity of Fethard-on-Sea. Since 1995, the thriving national economy has resulted in an exponential increase in both the price of houses and the construction of private dwellings in the region, with obvious landscape and infrastructural implications. New

B. COLFER

Fig. 13 Rounded beach stones were commonly used in the Hook for cobbling yards and the floors of outhouses. During the late twentieth century, most of these have been removed or smothered in concrete.

private housing is pervasive throughout the area, with concentrations at Duncannon, Fethard and Arthurstown. While the pressure placed on the planning authorities and the landscape by the housing boom has inevitably led to an uneven application of design and environmental standards, many new dwellings (with the inevitable exceptions) fit reasonably well in the landscape. On the sensitive landscape of the point of Hook, which is subject to stringent planning requirements, new development is concentrated in the villages of Slade and Churchtown. Recently there has been a welcome tendency towards restoration, perhaps due to stricter planning requirements for new houses as well as an appreciation of the aesthetic qualities of vernacular buildings. On the point of Hook, twelve traditional houses have been restored as holiday accommodation and at least ten other derelict buildings would benefit from similar treatment.

FR. HOLLAND

Fig. 14 Thirty-foot sailing yawls were used for lobster fishing. Each boat carried twenty-five lobster-pots which were checked twice a day. Pots were made of sallies or wood, and baited with salted fish. A season's fishing could be ruined if pots were lost in a summer storm. In the 1930s, boats were fitted with engines, but for a while, most fishermen, with an instinctive mistrust of mechanisation, retained their sails (as shown here in the 1950s) to be used in case of engine failure. On fine days, children were sometimes allowed to go along to watch the hauling of the pots.

FISHING

Fishing was an integral part of the lives of coastal communities in the Hook. The skills and crafts connected with fishing were widely practised. The tradition of building small boats covered with tarred canvas, known as 'punts,' survived until recent times. In these, men rowed long distances to fish the 'marks' which had been discovered over the years, and to set lobster pots made from pliable sallies. Boats were kept at Slade and at Bá Bheg (bá bheag: little bay) in Churchtown, as they are at the present time. The 'marks,' identified by using natural and man-made features in the landscape as co-ordinates, allowed fishermen to create a micro-navigation system

Fig. 15 In the late nineteenth century, women from the Hook travelled by ass and cart and ferry to the quay of Waterford, where they sold the family catch of lobsters, kept alive by a covering of wet seaweed.

which gave them a mental map of their movements on the sea. This maritime geography included a nomenclature for different parts of the sea, particularly areas where certain species of fish could be caught. These names, which sometimes referred to prominent landmarks or to underwater features, included 'the Lump,' 'the Lock,' 'the Old Grounds,' 'the Big Rock,' 'the Race,' 'Jim's Gut,' 'the West'ard Ground' and 'Short Head.' Fish were also caught in the food-rich 'scarf' created by the meeting of two currents, such as the well-defined meeting of river and sea off the point of Hook. As well as intuitively navigating the surface of the sea, generations of accumulated knowledge also gave fishermen an instinctive knowledge of seasonal variation and enabled them to understand fish ecology by visualising the sand and rock of the sea floor.

Apart from fishing, other traditional occupations depended on the sea. Men who competed for work on

Fig. 16 Lobster-pots were made to a traditional design using willow, timber, netting or any other suitable material. The 'neck' was protected by a 'trigger', which allowed the lobster to enter but not to leave. The success rate of unlikely-looking pots was a source of some wonder.

ships while they were in port came from up-river in small boats, propelled by sail and oar. These hardy individuals, known as hobblers, came mostly from the ports of Ross and Waterford, where there was keen competition for the right to work on the incoming ships. Hobblers were prepared to endure considerable hardship to secure employment, including sleeping overnight in their small boats; traditionally, the work went to the men in the first boat to reach an arriving ship at the mouth of the harbour. Fish-buyers, known as 'joulters,' were a familiar sight in the small harbours around the peninsula. The fishermen depended on these individuals to buy their daily catch of

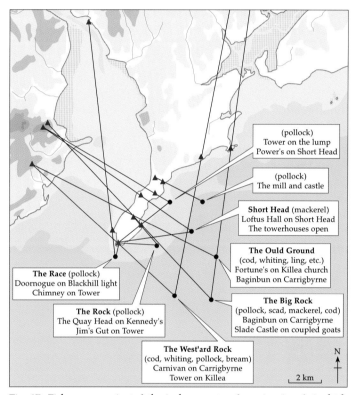

(pollock)
Tower on the lump
Power's on Short Head

(pollock)
The mill and castle

Short Head (mackerel)
Loftus Hall on Short Head
The towerhouses open

The Ould Ground
(cod, whiting, ling, etc.)
Fortune's on Killea church
Baginbun on Carrigbyrne

The Race (pollock)
Doornogue on Blackhill light
Chimney on Tower

The Big Rock
(pollock, scad, mackerel, cod)
Baginbun on Carrigbyrne
Slade Castle on coupled goats

The Rock (pollock)
The Quay Head on Kennedy's
Jim's Gut on Tower

The West'ard Rock
(cod, whiting, pollock, bream)
Carnivan on Carrigbyrne
Tower on Killea

N

2 km

Fig. 17 Fishermen navigated the inshore waters by using 'marks' which were established by referring to prominent landscape features. This system allowed seafarers to calculate precisely where they were on the surface of the sea and to return at will to long-established fishing locations. The sea around the Hook was particularly suitable for this type of navigation, as the low-lying nature of the peninsula allowed fishermen a clear view of distant landmarks on high ground.

mackerel, pollock or cod; and if only one joulter arrived the price hit rock bottom. Joulters usually sold the fish from door to door in the adjacent hinterland, but some sold from stalls, principally on the quay of Ross.

Although fish was a basic element of diet, particularly in the vicinity of harbours, only the lucky few had access to boats. However, this did not mean that people without boats could not avail of the huge numbers of fish that shoaled close to the rocks in late summer and early autumn. These fish, mostly mackerel and pollock, were

John Trotter, Churchtown, Hook, 15 August 1812

One of our party has become a very good fisher, from the stupendous rocks on the east side, and sallies out frequently before dawn with the large long rod and strong line they use here. He relates to me an extraordinary and interesting piece of natural history, with which he became acquainted yesterday morning. He set out to fish while twilight was going and he scarcely discerned his path. Arrived at the rocks, he waited further light, as he had come so early. In some time, the sun peeped over the waves! This mighty orb began faintly to redden the sleeping waves, when suddenly a vast play of fish, not far distant from shore, startled and delighted our fisherman. There was instantaneously an innumerable concourse in motion, beating the surface of the water, playing their gambols, their silvery sides glistening in the rays of the dawn! The sun slowly emerged from his bed, and when he was a few moments risen, this 'play' (as it is termed by sea-faring people) suddenly ceased. This singular mark of adoration to Heaven, paid by animated and reviving nature, when dawn appears, is not commonly known, unless to early risers, who frequent or fish on solitary rocky shores like those of Hook. I regret greatly that I never witnessed this peculiar and pleasing phenomenon. It may occur but rarely.

FR. HOLLAND

Fig. 19 Until the 1950s, locals fished from the rocks using a 'great long rod,' mentioned by Trotter in 1812, and home-made lures. Mackerel and pollock, the principal species caught, were salted or dried for winter use.

expertly caught in great numbers from the rocks, using home-made rods and lures, and were preserved for winter consumption. Most were salted in wooden barrels and some were split open and dried, usually by exposing them to the sun on a flat roof but also by hanging in the chimney to be smoked. For fishing at the rocks, a lure called a 'goat-hair' was made by tying a wisp of white goat-hair to a hook. Goat-skin was used to make an eel-like lure called a 'torgan.'

John Trotter, a visitor to the Hook in 1812, described what he thought was the unusual occurrence of fish 'playing'.[7] Contrary to Trotter's belief, the scene described by him in 1812, including the 'large long rod,' was commonplace at the Hook until the 1950s, when fish

R.S.A.I.

Fig. 18 Seaweed, or 'woar,' was prized as a fertiliser and, in spring and early summer, when the fresh crop of seaweed was washed ashore by storms, the bays were alive with horses and carts as farmers rushed to get their share of the valuable crop from the sea. In some places, tracks were quarried through solid rock to make cart roads. Land beside the sea could be more expensive to rent, as it was adjacent to coastal 'manure banks'. This watercolour sketch by G. Du Noyer of seaweed-collecting in south Wexford in 1849 captured the urgency of the task as collectors rushed to beat the incoming tide.

ULSTER MUSEUM

Fig. 20 Fish buyers, or joulters, came to the fishing villages to haggle with the fishermen over the purchase of the daily catch. The joulters sold the fish from door to door and in nearby villages and towns. The illustration also shows the type of fishing boat in use in the nineteenth century.

B. COLFER

Fig. 22 Periwinkles now fetch a considerable price as a gourmet food and are still picked, on a small scale, on the rocks around the Hook at low tide.

stocks began to dwindle. In July and August it was usual to see huge shoals of mackerel 'playing' on the surface of the sea near the shore as they fed on sprat. The crude fishing equipment and lack of fishing skill of large numbers of 'outsiders,' attracted by the abundance of fish, was viewed with considerable amusement by locals! In season, mackerel can still be seen 'playing' on the surface but on a much smaller scale.

The seashore between the high-water and low-water marks, known as the strand, was also an important resource, most of the gathering being done by women. Bárnachs (limpets) and peehauns (piothán: periwinkle) were collected as food for humans and ducks. Bárnachs were removed from the rocks with an implement called a scian trá (a strand knife). Crabs were found in 'crab holes,' which could be searched at low tide. Dilisk (duileasc), an edible seaweed, was also collected and carrigeen moss was gathered as a cash crop. An early summer storm was

welcomed, at least by farmers, as it brought the first crop of seaweed (called woar) on to the beaches, where it was collected for use as a fertiliser. The value of the seashore as a source of fertiliser is also evident in nineteenth-century Grand Jury Presentments, where there were frequent mentions of roads leading to coastal 'manure banks.'

The importance of the seashore to the community was reflected in the complicated system of coastal place-names which evolved over the years. Many of these were in Irish, an indication that their origins go back to at least the mid-eighteenth century when Irish was still spoken in the region. These place-names, now in danger of being lost, contain considerable information of a social and cultural nature. Examples include Carraigahoy, which originated as Carraig an Aith (limekiln rock), Tobar na Staighre (the well of the steps) and Pol na gCaoraigh (a pool where sheep were washed). Other names preserve the names of former residents; these include Charlie's Chan (a 'chan' is

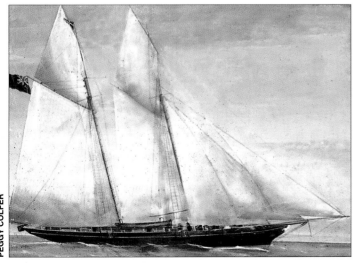

PEGGY COLFER

Fig. 21 This yacht belonging to the Marquis of Ely of Loftus Hall was crewed by sailors from the Hook. Crew members were presented with (or bought) pictures of the craft, a few of which still hang in local houses.

R.S.A.I.

Fig. 23 A sketch by G. Du Noyer, c. 1850, of fishing boats in the sheltered inlet of Bá Bheg (Little Bay) in Churchtown. Until the late twentieth century, small boats continued to be kept here by local fishermen.

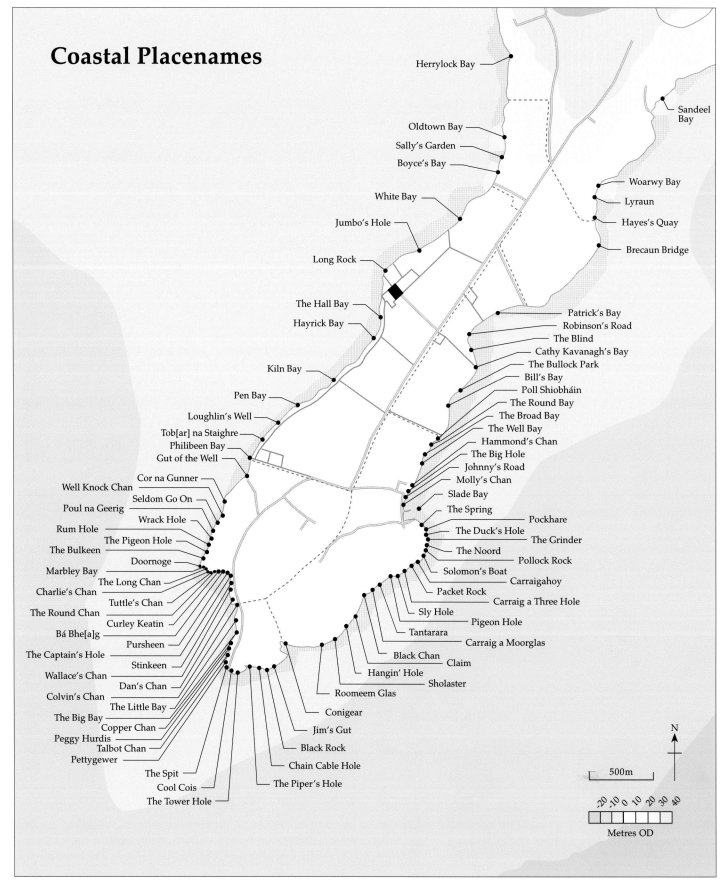

Coastal Placenames

Herrylock Bay

Sandeel Bay

Oldtown Bay

Sally's Garden

Boyce's Bay

Woarwy Bay

Lyraun

White Bay

Hayes's Quay

Jumbo's Hole

Brecaun Bridge

Long Rock

The Hall Bay

Patrick's Bay

Hayrick Bay

Robinson's Road

The Blind

Cathy Kavanagh's Bay

The Bullock Park

Kiln Bay

Bill's Bay

Poll Shiobháin

Pen Bay

The Round Bay

Loughlin's Well

The Broad Bay

The Well Bay

Tob[ar] na Staighre

Hammond's Chan

Philibeen Bay

The Big Hole

Gut of the Well

Johnny's Road

Cor na Gunner

Molly's Chan

Well Knock Chan

Slade Bay

Seldom Go On

The Spring

Poul na Geerig

Pockhare

Wrack Hole

The Duck's Hole

Rum Hole

The Grinder

The Pigeon Hole

The Noord

The Bulkeen

Pollock Rock

Doornoge

Solomon's Boat

Marbley Bay

Carraigahoy

The Long Chan

Packet Rock

Charlie's Chan

Carraig a Three Hole

Tuttle's Chan

The Round Chan

Sly Hole

Curley Keatin

Pigeon Hole

Bá Bhe[a]g

Tantarara

Pursheen

Carraig a Moorglas

The Captain's Hole

Black Chan

Stinkeen

Claim

Wallace's Chan

Hangin' Hole

Dan's Chan

Sholaster

Colvin's Chan

Roomeem Glas

The Little Bay

The Big Bay

Conigear

Copper Chan

Peggy Hurdis

Jim's Gut

Talbot Chan

Pettygewer

Black Rock

The Spit

Chain Cable Hole

Cool Cois

The Piper's Hole

The Tower Hole

N

500m

Metres OD

Fig. 24 The value of the seashore as a communal resource led to the creation of an intricate system of coastal place-names, of complex origin, many of them in Irish. As an intimate knowlege of the seashore is no longer necessary, the names are now largely irrelevant and will eventually be forgotten.

Fig. 25 In July and August, anglers are attracted to the rocks around the Hook by the shoals of mackerel that come close inshore to feed on sprat. Although some fish are still caught, the shoals are not as extensive as in former years, presumably because of increased commercial fishing.

the local name for a deep narrow inlet), Solomon's Boat, Peggy Hurdis and Colvin's Chan. Names like Kiln Bay, Gut of the Well, Pollock Rock and the Spring refer to activities of various kinds. The origins of enigmatic names like Pursheen, Tantarara and Pettygewer are obscure but bear testimony to the imagination and inventiveness of past generations.

Most coastal features were named for intimate local reasons, but the name given to one beach had wider implications. In 1765, a brig called the *Earl of Sandwich* sailed from the port of Tenerife in the Canary Islands with a cargo of wine, silk and cochineal and a large quantity of Spanish dollars to the value of £106,000.[8] The lure of the dollars was too much for four of the sailors, who conspired to seize the ship and steal the treasure. In the English Channel, they took the ship and murdered the rest of the crew, including the wife and two daughters of the captain, and set sail for Ireland. Arriving off Waterford Harbour, they loaded the treasure into the ship's boat and opened the ports to scupper the ship. The four men then

Fig. 26 The name Dollar Bay, on the west coast of the peninsula, records an incident that occurred in 1765, when a hoard of dollars, pirated by mutineers from a ship called the *Earl of Sandwich*, was hidden in the bay.

rowed up the harbour and landed on a beach just north of Broomhill. Having taken as much of the money as they could carry, they hid the rest on the beach and continued on up-river as far as Fisherstown, where they abandoned the boat. They stayed briefly at an alehouse at Ballybrazil, where 1,200 dollars was stolen from them. They hired horses in Ross and set out for Dublin, where they lodged at the Black Bull Inn in Thomas Street. Meanwhile, the abandoned *Earl of Sandwich* beached on the coast of county Waterford and suspicion fell on the four men. They were eventually arrested, confessed to the crime and were hanged. For years afterwards their skeletons hung in gibbets on Dalkey Island as a warning to potential pirates. The four had disclosed the whereabouts of the hidden dollars, which were subsequently found by revenue officers among the rocks on the beach. Mr Allen of Ballystraw was presented with a snuff-box containing one hundred guineas as a reward for his assistance. The event is remembered in the name of the beach, which became known as Dollar Bay.

As could be expected, there was always a great seafaring tradition in the Hook. P. J. McCall's song 'The Lowlands Low' has a line 'crew all from Bannow, Fethard and the Hook' and, in the days of sail and up to the middle of the twentieth century, the majority of houses had someone at sea. The fatality rate among sailors was high: gravestones at Churchtown have inscriptions such as 'lost at sea' or 'drowned at sea' and many men left their homes never to be seen again. During the 1850s and '60s Lord Ely kept a private yacht, crewed by local men, for cruising in the Mediterranean; pictures of the yacht can still be seen in a few houses where crew members once lived.

SHIPWRECKS

The huge investment in the initial construction of the Tower of Hook, and its maintenance over the centuries, underlined the hazards which the rock-bound peninsula presented to shipping. In the days of sail, wrecks occurred frequently and even in more recent times there have been numerous tragedies at sea.[9] Among the best-remembered wrecks are: the *Kinsale* and *Alfred D. Snow*, both lost at Broomhill; the gunboat *St Patrick*, driven ashore at a place called the Wrack Hole; the *M. C. Beale* and the *Royal Arthur*, both of which foundered near the lighthouse. The *Royal Arthur* was carrying a cargo of walrus tusks and hides from San Francisco to Liverpool and, for many years after the wreck, harnesses were hung on ivory pegs in local stables. The bodies of shipwrecked sailors were sometimes buried on the cliff edge where they were found. From time to time these hastily constructed graves, some lined with stone

BRENDAN POWER

Fig. 27 On 3 January 1888, an American sailing ship, the *Alfred D. Snow*, carrying wheat from San Francisco to Liverpool, was wrecked on the shoals of Broomhill with a loss of twenty-nine lives. Timber and other objects salvaged from the ship can still be found throughout the district.

B. COLFER

Fig. 29 The *Merchant Vanguard*, a steam trawler from Wales, ran aground in a heavy fog about 1km north of Loftus Hall, in June 1956. The crew got safely ashore but the vessel was subsequently broken up by heavy seas.

slabs, have been exposed by winter storms. In a few known instances where recovered bodies were buried in the cemeteries at Churchtown and Old Templetown, they were buried to the north of the church, a location that was traditionally regarded with superstition.

In the days of sail, wrecks were commonplace and were regarded with mixed feelings by local inhabitants. The first priority was to save lives if possible, but whatever could then be salvaged from the wreck and its contents made a vital contribution to the economy of the area. In

GEORGE COLFER

Fig. 28 This photograph was taken in 1967 of a German trawler shortly after she was driven on to the rocks in a storm at Doornogue Point, in Waterford Harbour, just north of the lighthouse. Fortunately, the crew managed to get ashore but the ship was completely wrecked.

B. COLFER

Fig. 30 The bodies of shipwrecked sailors were often buried on the cliff-top, near where they were found. These graves, usually lined with limestone slabs, have occasionally been exposed by winter storms. The one shown here was found in the 1970s at Patrick's Bay in Galgystown.

the days of wooden sailing ships, wrecks were frequent and ships' timbers were used in the construction of many houses and outbuildings in the Hook. Sometimes, shipwrecks had unexpected impacts on the social life of the area. A story is still told in Churchtown of how people leaving a wake at midnight in the 1860s believed that they were having a paranormal experience when they heard survivors of a shipwreck speaking in a foreign tongue.

The wreck of the *Mexico*

It is difficult to imagine the extent of the horror and suffering experienced by the victims and survivors of so many shipwrecks. The following account of a particular tragedy graphically portrays the confusion and trauma. Of all the shipwrecks that occurred around the Hook, the *Mexico* had the greatest impact on folk memory because of the loss of local lives.[10] On Friday 20 February 1914, the *Mexico*, a Norwegian, steel-hulled, three-masted schooner carrying a cargo of mahogany from South America to Liverpool, was driven ashore by a strong south-westerly gale on the Keeragh Islands, seven kilometres east of Fethard. Two members of her nine-man crew managed to scramble ashore, but the rest were trapped on the stricken ship. In spite of the terrible weather conditions, the Fethard lifeboat, the *Helen Blake*, was launched in an attempt to rescue the men before the ship was pounded to pieces by the heavy seas. As the *Helen Blake*, a thirty-five-foot self-righting boat with a crew of fourteen, under coxswain Christopher Bird, approached the Keeraghs, it was swamped by a huge wave and dashed to pieces on the rocks. Nine of the crew were drowned but the other five, with the crew of the *Mexico*, succeeded in reaching the safety of the island.

As word of the tragedy spread, attempts were made to rescue the survivors. The Kilmore lifeboat was launched but could not make headway against the howling south-west gale and was forced back to its station. The Dunmore lifeboat battled around Hook Head and reached the Keeraghs and the Rosslare Fort boat was towed to the wreck by the Wexford tug. They were joined by the Kilmore lifeboat, which had made a successful second attempt to reach the scene. However, on Saturday evening, after failed attempts to reach the men, the atrocious weather forced the lifeboats to take shelter; the Kilmore men returned to base, the Dunmore boat rowed to Fethard, while the Rosslare boat was towed around the Hook to Cheekpoint. The spirits of the men on the storm-swept Keeraghs, with no shelter and almost no food and water, must have reached a low ebb as they watched the lifeboats disappear into the darkness. As news came of bodies being washed ashore, a black mood gripped the

---

THE FETHARD LIFE-BOAT CREW
Matthew Barden

You feeling-hearted Irish sons, I hope you will draw near:
This is the worst disaster that ever you did hear.
On the twentieth of February, at the hour of two o'clock,
A schooner called the Mexico *struck on the Keeragh Rock.*
As the people watched her from the beach, they saw she was no more,
She lay three miles off Fethard quay, and a mile from Bannow shore.

The weather it was stormy, and the sea ran mountains high,
When the coxswain of the life-boat, the schooner he did spy.
At a glance he saw that she was doomed, to the life-boat house he ran,
And fired the signal for his crew, the life-boat for to man.
In less than forty minutes she was manned and on her way;
Those heroes fought most gallantly all through the raging sea.

With courage bold they braved the seas, till at the Keeragh Point,
A mountain wave capsized their boat and she vanished from our sight.
Those fourteen gallant heroes into the sea were tossed;
No assistance could be rendered and nine of them were lost.
But four of these brave fellows, by chance they got on shore;
The fifth he drifted by the ship and safely got aboard.

Poor fellows, it was hard to think when they came to, to see
Their comrades' lifeless bodies and their boat smashed by the sea.
When they saw their comrade, Kelly, had got aboard the ship
They roared to him with all their might, to them a line to get,
This line they got and when made fast, 'twas then their joy was great,
As they hauled those foreigners on the rock and then their own shipmate.

Three nights and days they did survive upon that rocky shore,
Their only shelter being the sky while the seas around them roar.
They had to cling high on that rock, to keep clear of the tide,
Where one of the foreign sailors from cold and exposure died.
On the third day they were rescued and safely brought to shore,
By the life-boats and their gallant crews from Wexford and Dunmore.

The names of the survivors I'm now going to pen down:
There's Handrick, Crampton, Mac and Bird and Kelly from Ramstown,
Of those other brave nine fellows, as you all can plainly see,
There were seven bodies washed ashore and two were washed to sea.

Now to conclude and finish, I've got no more to say.
May the Lord have mercy on the soul of each we humbly pray.
These were the men of Fethard, that gallant little band,
Who launched their boat and went afloat to give a helping hand.

B. COLFER

Fig. 31 The Tower of Hook in silhouette, dimly seen in the salt-laden air and atmospheric light of the storm-swept headland.

Fig. 32 The Fethard lifeboat, the *Helen Blake*, returning to base with a full crew, possibly after a training exercise, as the sea is very calm.

Fig. 34 The crew of the lifeboat from Dunmore, the *Fanny Harriet*, which helped in the rescue, returning to Fethard with some of the survivors.

despairing community around Fethard as distracted relatives waited in fear and hope.

On Sunday, the weather was still dreadful and an attempt made by the Dunmore lifeboat to reach the

Fig. 33 The survivors of the tragic wreck of the Fethard lifeboat. From the left: John MacNamara, Garry Handrick, John Kelly, George Crumpton and Richard Bird. The nine men who lost their lives were: Christopher Bird, William Bird, George Bassett, William Banville, Patrick Cullen, James Morrissey, Pat Roche, Thomas Handrick and Patrick Stafford.

Keeraghs had to be abandoned. Monday morning brought a slight improvement in conditions and it was decided to attempt a rescue. The Dunmore boat reached the Keeraghs first and, by getting a line ashore attached to a rocket, succeeded in pulling two of the stranded men to safety. The Rosslare lifeboat, towed by the Wexford tug, then arrived on the scene and the coxswain, Ned Wickham, decided on the hazardous plan of letting a small dinghy, with two courageous volunteers aboard, downwind to the island, at the end of a strong line. The small boat was repeatedly swamped, but the strategy proved successful and, although a hole in the boat had to be plugged with a loaf of bread wrapped in canvas, all of the men were rescued from the rock in five courageous trips. The arrival of the survivors at Fethard was greeted with conflicting emotions, as relatives of the crewmen became aware of their various fates. Relief funds were set up for the bereaved relatives and the heroic lifeboat men were showered with awards. The traumatic impact of the tragedy was immense and continues to resonate in the Fethard community to the present time.

THE MODERN LANDSCAPE

On a global level, the first half of the twentieth century witnessed two world wars and the growth of Communism, as well as spectacular advances in transport and communications. It was a time of widespread social upheaval and extraordinary technological advances. In Ireland, dramatic change was epitomised by the transfer of ownership from landlord to former tenants and the formation of the Irish Free State in 1923, following the War of Independence and three years of bitter Civil War. The sweeping changes initiated by the Land Acts had particular relevance for the Hook, as the three large estates into which the area was divided passed into private ownership, with profound implications for the community. The acquisition of the land by former tenants introduced a new social order and led to a shift in the balance of society. At a local level, the selling of Loftus Hall to a community of nuns brought a new element to life in the Hook. The disintegration of the estates had other implications, as the loss of traditional jobs inevitably led to an increase in emigration by both men and women. Some benefits

followed from the acquisition of better boats by local fishermen and the beginning of mechanisation on some farms but, in general, life remained unchanged during the first half of the century. The split from Britain had a crucial influence on the subsequent development of Irish society. Initially, agriculture prospered, but, following the election of a Fianna Fáil government in 1932, de Valera's policies resulted in an economic war with Britain. This led to widespread unemployment and a slump in demand for livestock, with a consequent move from grazing to tillage. Economic growth was further delayed by the World War II and it was not until the 1950s that gradual improvements in living conditions and infrastructure began to percolate through to the Hook. In the last quarter of the twentieth century improvements in transport and technology reduced the isolated nature of the peninsula. An increase in tourism related initiatives and other developments began to impact on the landscape. Accelerated change brought about by the 'Celtic Tiger' ecnonomy inevitably raises protection and conservation issues.

B. COLFER

Fig. 1 The construction of the Rosslare to Waterford railway in the early twentieth century required the building of a bridge over the Barrow estuary. The Barrow Bridge was a major feat of engineering, especially as a central section was required to open to give shipping access to the port of New Ross.

ELLEN CURTIS

Fig. 2 Emigration was facilitated by the arrival of the railway. This photograph shows Bob and Mary Ann (nee Wade) Sinnott, leaving Wellington Bridge station in the 1930s as emigrants to the United States.

B. COLFER

Fig. 4 Wellington Bridge station at the present time. Along with the metal rails of the permanent way, the signal huts, station houses, bridges and level-crossings introduced a new layer of features to the landscape.

A CHANGING SOCIETY

The beginning of the century saw significant social changes in the Hook. The opening of the Rosslare to Waterford railway in 1906 was the first major infrastructural initiative in south-west Wexford since the new line road from Duncannon to Wexford in the early nineteenth century. The railway opened up the area, facilitating access by emigrants to the newly established ferry at Rosslare. The construction of the railway had considerable landscape implications: the laying of the track required the building of an impressive red-brick viaduct over the valley of the Owenduff river at Taylorstown and the spanning of the Waterford estuary by the Barrow Bridge. Stations were built at Wellington Bridge, Ballycullane and Campile; Wellington Bridge and Campile subsequently developed as commercial and economic hubs.

The transfer of the land into tenant ownership was of fundamental social significance. In 1912, to mark the

purchase of holdings in the Hook, the tenants on the Marquis of Ely's estate presented an illuminated address to Cornelius Furlong of Kilcloggan Castle, in appreciation of his efforts on their behalf. Ownership of holdings generated a new spirit of enterprise within the farming community. In 1919, farmers, many of them from the Hook, established the Shelburne Co-operative Agricultural Society at Campile, making it the principal business centre in the area.[1] This was followed by the setting up of Campile Creamery in 1927. The growing of sugar-beet was encouraged by the establishment of a depot beside the railway at Wellington Bridge. However, the revolution in land ownership did not benefit all members of the community equally; the disappearance of traditional jobs on the estate accelerated emigration among labourers and very small farmers.

The turbulent impact of World War I and the War of Independence in Ireland had some repercussions in the Hook. At least one young man, Matthew Breen of

B. COLFER

Fig. 3 One of the larger Irish bridges built of red brick, Taylorstown Viaduct was constructed by Sir Robert McAlpine in 1906 to carry the railway over the Owenduff valley. The brick used in its construction was landed at St Kearns pier and transported from there by horse and cart. The viaduct was damaged by an explosion during the Civil War.

SHELBURNE CO-OP

Fig. 5 The manufacture of animal-feed in Shelburne co-op at Campile.

Fig. 6 This aerial perspective, looking west towards the confluence of the Barrow and Suir, graphically portrays the impact of the railway on the landscape. Other landscape features are also illustrated. Dunbrody Abbey is shown in the foreground beside the winding Campile stream (cam: winding; poll or pill: an estuary) and the chimneys of Great Island power station can be seen in the distance beside Barrow Bridge.

B. COLFER

Fig. 7 This monument at Saltmills commemorates five men who died and six others who were injured during the War of Independence in 1920, as a result of a massive explosion resulting from bomb-making activities.

Herrylock, died in the trenches at Ypres in 1918. A sailor from Slade who 'jumped ship' in Australia was later conscripted into the army and fought at Gallipoli. During the War of Independence, men from the south-west of the county were on active service with the South Wexford Brigade.[2] They were involved in various incidents, principally the burning of the R.I.C. barracks in Fethard and Arthurstown. There was considerable military activity in the area in 1920, following the deaths in an explosion of five men involved in bomb-making near Saltmills. Six survivors sentenced to three years in Dartmoor prison were released in January 1922.[3] A contingent of Black and Tans from Duncannon Fort, accompanied by police, occasionally raided houses in the district, but no arrests were made. During the Civil War that followed the Treaty, the railway was targeted, resulting in damage to the viaduct at Taylorstown.

THE 'EMERGENCY'

As well as the usual scarcity and rationing of food and other commodities, the impact of the World War II was felt in other ways in the Hook. The threat of invasion again

LARRY BIRD

Fig. 8 Fethard in 1914. The R.I.C. barracks on the left, with three constables standing outside, was burned by the I.R.A. during the War of Independence.

focused attention on the strategic significance of Waterford Harbour. In 1940 the Irish Army occupied Duncannon Fort and remained there until the end of the war. There was constant anxiety among families with a relative at sea, as many sailors from the district were in the British Merchant Navy, on ships which were in continuous danger of attack by German submarines. A number of men from the area were on ships that were torpedoed and some lost their lives. The war at sea was brought home to the people of the Hook in a dramatic way, as during and after the war many mines from off-shore minefields broke adrift and were washed up on the rocks around the peninsula. The army was frequently summoned to carry out the dangerous job of dismantling these mines if they were close to dwellings or blowing them up if it was

KELLY COLLECTION

Fig. 9 On 26 August 1940, four bombs were dropped by a Heinkel aircraft of the German *Luftwaffe* on the village of Campile. Extensive damage was caused to Shelburne Co-op and, tragically, three women were killed. The reason for the bombing has never been established. It is possible that the off-course bomber may have mistaken the Co-op complex and the railway for a British target. The German authorities accepted full responsibility and paid compensation for damage and loss of life.

thought safe to do so, and the normal tranquillity of the area was frequently shattered by a violent explosion. On one occasion, there were so many mines floating about in the bay of Slade that the village was evacuated by the army to the nearby village of Churchtown. This event was commemorated in a humorous song written by Willie Breen, a ballad-maker from Churchtown.

Because of the scarcity of trees on the peninsula, every scrap of timber washed up by the sea was eagerly sought after. 'Wreck-hunting' was always a popular and competitive pursuit and flotsam was claimed by the person who succeeded in getting it above the high-water mark. All timber was put to use, for firewood, furniture or boat-building. During, and shortly after, World War II, the amount of flotsam increased dramatically, because of the number of cargo ships that were being sunk in the Atlantic, and 'wreck-hunting' became a constant and

B. COLFER

Fig. 10 A use was usually found for all objects washed up by the sea. This shell of a World War II mine survived demolition and was converted for use (as others were) as a water container in a Churchtown farmyard.

TOM MURPHY

Fig. 11 The concrete coastwatching hut built at the point of Hook during the World War II. The uniformed coastwatcher in the foreground is outlining the shape of a harp on the cliff-edge with white stones. The wooden structure behind the hut was the gun-house where a gun, fired as a warning signal in fog, was stored. Both structures have been removed.

rewarding activity. It was not only timber that came ashore, but a variety of goods including boxes of candles, butter and coffee, all of which were welcome at a time of scarcity and rationing. Bales of rubber were particularly coveted, as the finder was sure of a substantial financial reward due to war-time demand. Deflated barrage balloons, which were flown over ships as a deterrent to enemy aeroplanes, were eagerly sought after, as the silver-coloured material made excellent waterproof clothing.

THE COASTWATCHING SERVICE AT HOOK HEAD 1939–45

In addition to the installation of a garrison in Duncannon Fort, the strategic nature of the estuary and headland was acknowledged by the location of a coastwatching unit at Hook Head. At the outbreak of the war in 1939, Ireland had no coastal look-out service, as the coastguards had been abolished by the government in 1923. When the war broke out, eighty-four look-out posts were established around the coast, manned by 750 men.[4] Volunteers were called up by the army and appointed to look-out posts near their own homes. These coastwatchers, as they were called, were initially accommodated in bell tents but were

provided with concrete huts early in 1940. Each team was made up of a corporal and seven or eight men, who were put through crash courses in signals, aircraft recognition, semaphore and morse code. They also did rifle drill but were not armed when on duty. They were required to do a month's refresher course each year. The men were dressed in army uniform and were subject to army pay, training and discipline. The station was inspected periodically by a district officer, who travelled by motorcycle. The men lived at home and were given a subsistence allowance of 3s 6d per week. Working three shifts of eight hours, the two men on watch logged everything that moved on or above the sea, mainly shipping and aircraft but also

B. COLFER

Fig. 12 Two members of the World War II coastwatching unit at the Hook standing outside the 'Gun House' with a visiting priest. The members of the unit were: Matt Murphy and Paddy Murphy, Ballygow; John White and Paddy Banville, Conna; Tom Colfer, Galgystown; Willie Colfer and Dick Fortune, Slade; Thomas Colfer and Jack Colfer, Churchtown.

The Evacuation of Slade
Willie Breen, Churchtown

It was on a Saturday morning, the weather it was wet,
The 24th of January, a date I'll ne'er forget,
I had slept soundly through the night till in the morning late
When a friendly voice aroused me saying 'arise and evacuate.'

I leaped up to the window, the warning voice was gone,
While hunting for my cash box, my garments I put on,
I could not find my stockings, I being in an awful state,
When I heard that dreadful warning, 'arise and evacuate.'

The morning it was dismal as I rushed through the street,
The sight that I beheld caused my poor heart to beat,
As I gazed on the ocean blue, where angry billows roar
Scores of mines were floating from Slade Bay to Carnsore.

Women they were screaming and rushing everywhere,
I saw a crowd emerging round the castle from the Square,
I took compassion on them saying 'hurry before it's late,
The mines are fast approaching, you must evacuate.'

As I gazed on my little home, my eyes filled up with tears
The loss of all my property, the scraping-up of years.
They told me not to worry, the law would compensate,
That I must go and leave it all, I must evacuate.

I harnessed up my pony, he is my joy and pride,
As I watched the mines draw closer on the incoming tide,
I said 'I cannot leave you here whatever might be your fate,
You will come with me this morning and we'll both evacuate.'

The road that day to Churchtown it seemed so awful long,
My pony seemed to understand as he bravely jogged along,
I thanked God for the warning, it had not come too late,
Or we'd both have been blown to atoms if we didn't evacuate.

If the wind does chance to change what will poor Churchtown do,
The houses all will tumble down, all will be killed that's true,
The Sladers will not let them in, they will leave them to their fate
God help the Churchtown people if they must evacuate.

And now the mines have vanished and gone for evermore,
We pray they'll never float again around our native shore,
For we never wish to see them till the year of '98
Then if Hitler bombs our little isle we won't have to evacuate.

aid kit. Coal for the fire in the hut at Hook Head, as well as cigarettes, was supplied by the military from Duncannon Fort. During the war the coastwatchers observed 'dog-fights' between aircraft over the sea off Hook Head and also a few attacks on ships by aircraft. On one occasion they reported twenty-four floating mines which were all simultaneously visible. In 1943, at the request of the American airforce, the men at each station were required to make a thirty-foot 'ÉIRE' sign, with an identification number, on the ground near the post, which was to be used as a navigational aid by patrolling aircraft. At Hook Head, the remains of the letters, formed of limestone slabs and originally whitewashed for better visibility, can still be identified on the cliff edge. The concrete hut used by the coastwatchers was removed in the 1980s.

POST-WAR DEVELOPMENTS

During the second half of the twentieth century, unprecedented advances in transport and communication technology transformed society in the Hook peninsula. Change was accelerated by a vastly improved educational system and greatly enhanced living standards. These influences opened up the area, so that the community lost the intensely local character of previous generations. This globalisation brought with it a welcome self-confidence and a broadening of horizons, but it also led to a less intimate connection with the landscape, place-names and traditions. Ironically, in 1957, just as the prospect of major social change was on the horizon, the tenacious survival of historical influences was demonstrated by the eruption of 'the Fethard boycott.'[5] In April 1957, because of a dispute in a mixed marriage about the education of the children, a Protestant wife left her Catholic husband and took the children, first to Northern Ireland and then to Scotland. The Protestant community was accused of complicity and Catholics, at the instigation of their clergy, boycotted local Protestant businesses. This sectarian activity attracted widespread media attention and on 4 July was condemned

wreckage and drifting mines. Their duty was to report any unusual or suspicious shipping or aircraft activity. The telephone was their most important piece of equipment. Before the hut was built, the telephone in the lighthouse was used to contact GHQ at the Curragh. The equipment also included a telescope, charts, signal flags and a first-

Fig. 13 During World War II, the busy shipping lanes off south-east Ireland were heavily mined by the German navy. After the war the mines were cleared by Royal Navy minesweepers. This photograph from c. 1946 shows a fleet of these minesweepers sheltering in the lee of Baginbun Head.

B. COLFER

Fig. 14 The oil-fired powerstation built in the 1970s by the E.S.B. on Great Island. Deep-water berthing for tankers was crucial to the choice of location.

in Dáil Éireann by the Taoiseach, Eamon de Valera, as 'ill-conceived, ill-considered and futile.' The boycott was ended in August by the parish priest making a purchase of cigarettes in a Protestant-owned shop. The family at the centre of the affair was reunited, educated their children at home and subsequently played a prominent role in community affairs. The shocking nature of the boycott possibly motivated the improved interdenominational links which developed in Fethard in later years. During the 1798 bicentenary commemorations, Bishop Brendan Comiskey apologised publicly for the hurt caused by the Catholic Church during the episode. In 1999, the events

B. COLFER

Fig. 15 As part of a 1970s rationalisation programme, the small National Schools of Loftus Hall and Templetown were closed; the pupils are now brought by bus to the remaining school at Poulfur, which was extended to serve the entire parish. The old schools are used as private residences.

B. COLFER

Fig. 16 For over a century, Ramsgrange has been the focus of church and school development. The opening of a Community School there in the 1970s, served by a school bus system, brought second-level education to the Hook and was fundamental to the development of the whole region.

B. COLFER

Fig. 17 Hauling a full net on a 1970s fishing trawler. The depletion of fish stocks has led to a reduction in this kind of fishing.

surrounding the boycott were portrayed in the feature film *A Love Divided*, providing a degree of closure on the event for the local community.

In the 1950s, rural electrification and a public water scheme introduced profound lifestyle improvements with significant longterm benefits. While the availability of piped water brought obvious advantages, the abandonment of numerous wells, pumps and springs, which had provided water and social contact for many centuries, had considerable social implications. In the 1970s and 1980s, demographic and economic factors led to the closure of the Garda barracks at Fethard and the post office at Slade. The small National Schools at Loftus Hall and Templetown were closed in the 1960s and amalgamated with a large central school at Poulfur. The Church of Ireland community in Fethard suffered the closure of its National School and the loss of a full-time rector. However, the provision of school transport and the establishment of a second-level Community School at Ramsgrange in the 1970s was of major significance. An increase in private transport, communications and education has removed many barriers as well as developing an awareness of the region's many attractions.

People are still leaving to find employment, but workers also commute to surrounding towns, aided by the introduction in 1982 of a modern car ferry plying between Ballyhack and Passage.

Inshore fishing has also developed in the villages of Fethard, Slade, Ballyhack, Arthurstown and particularly Duncannon. Better-equipped boats and expanding mar-

B. COLFER

Fig. 18 Catches of lobster and crab are kept alive in large storage boxes and are bought weekly at Slade and other harbours by buyers with refrigerated trucks, some of which transport the catch directly to the continent.

B. COLFER

Fig. 19 This well on the seashore at Churchtown was one of many water sources that supplied the needs of the community before the arrival of piped water in the late 1950s. The canopy helped to prevent the sea-spray from contaminating the spring water in stormy weather.

kets have increased catches, resulting in a depletion of stocks, particularly of lobster and salmon. The once renowned salmon fishery on the Barrow, based on the harbours of Ballyhack, Arthurstown, Duncannon and Passage, has declined drastically. In 1995, in an attempt to improve stocks, lobster fishermen on the south coast of Wexford agreed to take part in a re-seeding programme promoted by W.O.R.D. (Wexford Organisation for Rural Development). However, fishermen are still operating from harbours with limited facilities developed during the last century. The 1990s saw new ventures, with the introduction of mariculture to Bannow Bay (where oysters and mussels are being farmed) and a mussel-seeding project in the Waterford estuary in the vicinity of Passage and Ballyhack. With the exception of the traditional

activities of agriculture and fishing, there has been no significant employment-generating development in the region, apart from the construction in the 1960s of an oil-fired power station on Great Island.

FARMING

Over the centuries, farming activities such as woodland clearance, enclosure and drainage have modified the environment and created many aspects of the present-day cultural landscape. Aerial photography indicates that the removal of archaeological sites has also occurred, probably from as far back as the late Middle Ages. From the middle of the twentieth century, increased mechanisation made agriculture less labour intensive while at the same time greatly increasing the capacity for landscape change. During the second half of the century, the intensification of agriculture led to the removal of some hedgerows, an increase in pollution and an escalation in the loss of archaeological sites, resulting in an increasing imbalance between farming practice and the environment. Rapid change inevitably resulted in the creation of new features and the removal of old ones, including modification in the style, scale and siting of dwellings, and rationalisation of the layout of farmyards, fields and other rural infra-structure. Grant-aided land improvement posed an increased threat to archaeological sites and vulnerable wildlife habitats were damaged by reclamation and drainage schemes.

In the middle of the last century, there were 180 farmers in the modern parish of Templetown; a survey carried out in 1995 showed that this number had dropped to forty, with a further fifteen farming on a part-time basis. However, agriculture continues to play a vital role in the social and economic life of the Hook; in the early 1990s,

CHARLIE COLFER

Fig. 20 In the Hook, up to about 1950, small fields of corn continued to be cut by scythe and bound by hand. However, this picture of a reaper and binder pulled by three horses, taken at Churchtown in 1918, shows that mechanisation was being introduced early in the twentieth century.

FR. HOLLAND

Fig. 21   A 1940s threshing scene at Slade. Until the advent of the combine-harvester in the 1950s, the ritual of annual threshing at harvest time was a communal affair, as the 'drum' and elevator travelled from farm to farm with an attendant *meitheal* of workers. School holidays extended into September so that older pupils could work and excited younger children could follow the circuit of threshings to chase mice and eat bread and jam.

forty per cent of people at work in the modern parish of Templetown were involved in agriculture. The demographic profile of the farming community has changed dramatically over the past fifty years, partly influenced by the introduction of an early retirement scheme. The quotas on production and other restrictions introduced by the EU as part of a Common Agricultural Policy, have decreased farmer numbers and increased farm size. The small farming units created by the Land Acts of a century ago are now proving non-viable and are being relentlessly added to bigger farms, either by purchase or temporary leasing. This trend towards more intensive production on larger farms seems likely to be the pattern for the forseeable future.[6]

B. COLFER

Fig. 22 Cauliflower harvesting at Slade. The early years of the twenty-first century has seen a marked increase in vegetable growing in the Hook, sometimes harvested by migrant workers from eastern Europe.

TOURISM

An over-dependence on traditional farming and fishing led to the development of tourism as a significant component in the region's cash economy. Because of its maritime location, the Hook has been a popular holiday destination since the eighteenth century. In 1837, it was noted that there were 'numerous comfortable farmhouses and bathing lodges in the parish which is frequented for the benefit of sea-bathing. The sands are firm and smooth; the surrounding country is pleasant, and the air salubrious.'[7] The emphasis on 'bathing' indicates that the sea was the main attraction and, until quite recently, holiday-makers in Fethard were invariably referred to as 'bathers.' Tourists continue to be attracted to the Hook, and particularly to the main centres of Fethard-on-Sea and Duncannon, by the many quiet, safe beaches and the scenic peninsular location. In recent times, there has been an effort to capitalise on the region's other attractions, particularly activity holidays and heritage-based pursuits. The natural

PADDY BROWNE

Fig. 23 The distinctive Tower of Hook has become a symbol of the region; in the 1980s, the Hook Tourist Association brought a model of the tower to the St Patrick's Day parade in Dublin to publicise holidays in the area.

heritage of the area has much to offer, especially in the fields of geology and ornithology. The clear waters and varied sea-life make Hook Head an ideal destination for scuba-diving clubs and led to the foundation of the Hook Sub-Aqua Club in the early 1980s. Other water sports are catered for by the Outdoor Education Centre established at Shielbaggan in the 1970s and now based in Ramsgrange. The rocks around the point of Hook, which at one time provided locals with a precious supply of fish, are now used extensively by angling clubs and sport fishermen. One undesirable aspect of this has been the defacing of the rocks by painting indelible numbers to facilitate the organisation of angling competitions.

THE HERITAGE INDUSTRY

The last quarter of the twentieth century witnessed a general upsurge in the 'heritage' industry as tourism interests realised that historical and archaeological sites could have economic value as tourist attractions. As early as the 1970s, the Hook Tourism group, by using a working model of the Hook Lighthouse as a symbol of the region in the St Patrick's Day parade in Dublin, showed an awareness of heritage attractions in the promotion of an area. The development of sites was frequently facilitated by the availability of EU money for conservation and interpretation. In some cases, a limited awareness of the inclusive nature of heritage, combined with a tendency to present features in isolation, delivered only a limited appreciation of past experiences and their relevance to modern society. The rich cultural landscape of the Hook is

ORDNANCE SURVEY

Fig. 24 Following the assassination of J. F. Kennedy, a memorial arboretum was established by the government on the slopes of Slieve Coiltia. The mature park is a major amenity for locals and tourists alike.

now recognised as a resource to be utilised in the heritage tourism market, particularly the many monuments and settlement features surviving from the medieval period. The recycling of former centres of power as amenities for tourism and leisure activities, giving general access to what had been the exclusive domain of the privileged few, provides a symbol for the transformation that has taken place in Irish society during the past century. One nineteenth-century building, the former convent for St Louis nuns at Ramsgrange, is now the headquarters of South-West Wexford Community Development.

Of thirteen national monuments in Wexford, five are located in the south-west: the Cistercian abbeys of

Fig. 25 The county Wexford crest, as suggested by Kevin Whelan for the Heraldic Office in the late 1980s, features the Tower of Hook as a symbol of Anglo-Norman south Wexford. The Gaelic north of the county is represented by the Mac Murchada lion. The two parts are divided by the river Slaney along which Celtic groups, represented by spear-heads, entered south-east Ireland. The motto, *Exemplar Hiberniae* (an example for Ireland), is derived from the county's reputation as 'the model county.' The crest receives extensive media exposure as it appears on the jerseys of the county G.A.A. teams, as in the above example.

Dunbrody and Tintern, Rathumney Hall and the castles of Slade and Ballyhack.[8] Two other monuments, the Tower of Hook and Duncannon Fort, are operated as visitor attractions. Extensive conservation works have been carried out by Dúchas (The Heritage Service) at Tintern Abbey, where there is a visitors' centre with guided tours

B. COLFER

Fig. 26 This limekiln in Graigue Little, adapted as a feature in a modern garden, provides an example of the re-use of a protected heritage structure.

B. COLFER

Fig. 27 A view of Bannow Bay from Saltmills bridge. The former island of Bannow is on the horizon at the left of the picture.

Fig. 28 An extensive Colclough family museum has been installed by Dúchas (The Heritage Service) over the south transept of Tintern Abbey.

visitors' centre were officially opened to the public in 2000. The unique nature of the medieval tower combined with the spectacular location has proved to be a successful tourism venue, attracting 60,000 visitors in 2003.

However, not all heritage sites in the district are accessible as cultural assets. The striking remains of the medieval town of Clonmines, at the head of Bannow Bay, is regarded as being of major importance but has not received any official recognition or status. If the challenge of conserving, interpreting and presenting these and other heritage features can be responded to with sensitivity and imagination, they could become an important ingredient in the economic and social regeneration of the Hook. The relative lack of development in the district can be considered an advantage, as it presents an opportunity for a sensitive, restrained approach, respecting the integrity and requirements of both monuments and society. In the Hook, these monuments exist not in isolation, but in relation to each other and to the environment. If the interpretation of these heritage features can be presented in a cohesive way, it will lead to a more profound appreciation of the complex origins of the modern landscape. The implementation of a broader marketing strategy emphasising environment, heritage and lifestyle should generate a new kind of tourism that would be sustainable in the long term.

TOURISM DEVELOPMENTS

Until recently, tourism developments in the region, catering for relatively low-key modern tourist activity originating in the 1960s, was not excessively intrusive. As well as catering for visitors, two small family hotels established in the 1960s in Fethard and Duncannon also serve an important function as centres of community

and a museum devoted to the Cistercian and particularly the Colclough occupation of the building. Conservation work has also been carried out at Ballyhack Castle, where there is a more limited guiding service. When the army decided to withdraw from Duncannon Fort in the 1980s, a committee made up of local and statutory interests was formed to develop the fort as a community amenity. This project has enjoyed considerable success and the historic fort, which now houses a museum and art centre, is one of the high-profile tourist destinations in the county. In 2001, its historic and visual attractions were highlighted when it was chosen as one of the settings for the film version of *The Count of Monte Cristo*. Following automation of the Hook lighthouse in 1996, the Commissioners of Irish Lights, with Wexford County Council, initiated the opening up of the medieval tower as a visitor attraction. A trust, made up of local and statutory representatives, guided the project to completion and the tower and

Fig. 29 The car-ferry, operating on the traditional ferry route between Passage and Ballyhack, a modern expression of the link between the Hook region and Waterford, is a significant addition to the infrastructure of the region.

B. COLFER

Fig. 30 Many heritage sites are now used as tourism venues. The Old Rectory with an extensive garden has been developed as a public attraction within the monastic enclosure of Kilmokea. The small stream that drove the Early Christian horizontal mill has been utilised as a decorative feature in the garden.

activity. Other developments consisted of three quite unobtrusive caravan parks, a holiday chalet complex and a scheme of reasonably well designed holiday homes beside the castle at Fethard-on-Sea, the main tourism centre. Duncannon, with a caravan park beside its blue-flag beach and a complex of self-catering apartments, was relatively undeveloped. A fifth caravan park overlooked the sea at Houseland. Visitors were also catered for in the many bed-and-breakfast establishments scattered throughout the region.

The situation was changed dramatically by the 'Celtic Tiger' economy of the 1990s, as an increase in living standards led to a significant rise in tourism numbers with a corresponding increase in the demand for accommodation. There was also a noticeable increase in the purchase of new and traditional houses in the region as holiday homes. This encouraged the development of schemes of holiday homes, usually driven by government-sponsored economic incentives for both developer and purchaser. Over 250 of these 'second' homes have been built in the region, principally in Duncannon, Fethard and Arthurstown. Two other developments are located on

'green field' sites in a rural setting, overlooking the sea at Sandeel Bay on the east coast of the peninsula.

This introduction of a new settlement element within a very short time-span represented a major addition to the

B. COLFER

Fig. 31 As part of the promotion of heritage features, the medieval Tower of Hook has been opened to the public. The history of the building is presented on panels; tours are accompanied by guides who tell the story of the tower and the keepers of the light down through the centuries. The keepers' houses contain a craft shop and restaurant. This development is a fine example of the careful use of a unique medieval structure as a modern attraction while retaining the integrity and visual appeal of the building.

Fig. 32 Elements of traditional design have been successfully utilised in this scheme of houses called Cois na Mara, on the east coast at Templetown.

landscape of the region, the first since the construction of estate villages in the early nineteenth century. The 'second-home' phenomenon brought economic benefit to the region, as the seasonal influx of people makes a considerable contribution to local businesses. However, the sudden imposition of alien housing estates on the landscape in this manner has implications for the scenic and cultural environment and could contribute to the erosion of the unique landscape at precisely the time when an increasingly affluent society is seeking contact with a more varied environment. The increased pressure on essential services, as infrastructure has not been developed to cater for the extra demand, is the most obvious drawback. Although some attempts were made to take local vernacular styles into account in the design of houses, the results were not always satisfactory. In some of the developments, the greatest pressure on the cultural landscape comes from the sheer volume of houses, which has the effect of creating an incongruous suburban environment in a rural setting.

Apart from the landscape implications, second homes also have implications for the local community. As opposed to being organic developments closely integrated with local society, holiday-home complexes are built in response to external socio-economic demands. Some owners spend too little time in their properties to become involved in, or contribute to, local affairs. This diminishes the advantages of possessing a second home and creates an artificial grouping, within the community but separate from it. However, it is too soon to assess the longterm impact that a seasonal influx will have on the demographics of the region. These second homes can be regarded as another indication of the revolution that has taken place in society, as it was customary in the eighteenth and nineteenth centuries for the landlord class to have

houses in the fashionable parts of Dublin and other towns; for example, the Loftus and Colclough families had houses in Wexford town. Second-home developments should be seen in the context of the globalisation of society, which inevitably leads to a dilution of regional culture and identity. However, landscape quality should be recognised as a vital social and economic resource and all second-home developments should not be developed in isolation but in the context of broader environmental and community requirements.

FUTURE TRENDS: CONSERVING THE LANDSCAPE

The unique landscape of the Hook retains the superimposed imprints of successive settlement influences.[9] Place-names, many of them dating to the Early Christian period, identify features in the landscape and continue to provide a vital cultural link with the historical process. The character of regional landscapes emerged because of the necessity for communities to use local resources and to adapt to the surrounding environment. Advances in living standards and technology have made these restrictions irrelevant and maintaining the integrity of the landscape becomes a

Fig. 33 The increased affluence of the 1990s brought a transition from caravan parks to holiday homes. Two housing schemes aimed at the second-home market, Hookless Village (bottom) and Cois na Mara (top), have recently been developed above Sandeel Bay in the townlands of Houseland and Templetown respectively.

change, when local developments are motivated by external influences, a failure to take broad environmental considerations into account can have serious implications for the longterm benefit of the landscape.

The safeguarding of regional identity is intimately linked with the conservation of the cultural landscape. If the character of the environment and the value of regional distinctiveness are to be protected, projects should reflect a real sense of local character and evolving tradition. This can be achieved by ensuring that developments are planned in harmony with existing features and settlement layout. If this is allied with the use of appropriate building materials and the development of the essentials of traditional building forms, the new can blend succesfully

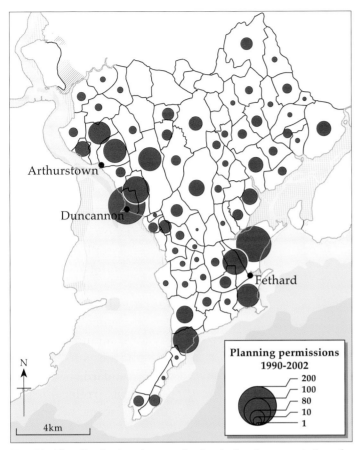

Fig. 34 The distribution, by townland, of planning permissions for dwelling houses in the Hook region, 1990–2002 according to statistics provided by the Planning Department, Wexford County Council. There are marked concentrations in the resort centres of Duncannon, Fethard and Arthurstown. Apart from Hookless Village in Houseland, the spread throughout the rest of the region is fairly even. Some of the approved houses have yet to be built.

question of conscious decision rather than necessity. Until recent times, the remote and relatively sparsely populated nature of the Hook constrained developments to follow traditional lines in sympathy with the existing environment. However, in the present period of rapid

ORDNANCE SURVEY

Fig. 36 The boom in the holiday-home market has led to the rapid expansion of the village of Fethard-on-Sea in the recent past. These new houses now out-number the homes of long-established residents and radically change the centuries-old character of the village.

with the old.[10] Other initiatives should also be considered as a means of maintaining regional identity, including the restoration of distinctive heritage features. The unique stone walls on Hook Head, for example, built over several centuries on the Loftus Hall demesne, are now in a state of dilapidation and urgently need conservation. The identity of the region could also be maintained by integrating the restoration of ruined vernacular houses in the region with a promotion of local crafts, particularly the tradition of stoneworking, which has enjoyed a welcome revival in recent years.

B. COLFER

Fig. 35 A fine example from Ballyvaroge of an old stone building that has been imaginatively restored as a comfortable modern dwelling.

B. COLFER

Fig. 37 Seagulls, by feeding on the waste produced by fishing activities, play a vital role in the maintenance of a clean maritime and coastal environment.

In an era of growing globalisation, the future protection of regional identity is closely related to the concept of a broad environmental heritage rather than the promotion of individual features in isolation. An inclusive approach to the management of heritage would recognise the interdependence of all elements in the landscape and ensure that no development should damage or diminish the environment in any way. A review of the county's environmental heritage and the implications of sustainable, integrated development is explored in a handbook produced in 2001 by County Wexford Partnership.[11] The aim should be to achieve economic growth without compromising environmental quality, to promote sustainable development by simultaneously utilising and protecting the landscape. Apart from a reference to 'sustaining the rural character of the countryside' and 'protecting environmental assets and resources,' a recent report commissioned by Wexford County Council makes no mention of broader environmental issues.[12] Development policy depends on many related factors and is officially set out in the detail of the County Wexford Development Plan. It is of fundamental importance that all members of the local community appreciate the value of their environment and share a common concern for its protection. Everyone has a role to play, but the farming community in particular, as custodians of the land, will become more involved in the protection and conservation of cultural landscapes. The Rural Environment Protection Scheme (REPS), introduced by the EU in 1992, encourages farmers to farm in harmony with the environment and signals that agriculture cannot continue to operate without regard to the environment and the principle of sustainability.[13] As Natura 2000 sites (SACs and SPAs) are identified in accordance with EU directives, the government is committed to compensating farmers and other landowners for losses arising from any restrictions on existing activities.[14] However, the expected tendency towards larger farms and more intensive cultivation potentially poses a threat to the cultural and natural environment. The absorption of traditional farms into larger units, leading to a less intimate relationship between farmer and landscape, could put even more pressure on 'unproductive' and unprotected natural and cultural environmental features.

The agricultural sector is not alone in its responsibilities towards the environment. Waste disposal is becoming an increasingly contentious issue on the political and social agenda. As the cost of refuse collection increases, there are malign indications of increased illegal dumping in the Hook. Unless this is dealt with efficiently, the unsightly effects will cause serious environmental degradation. The area has also been involved in the political aspect of waste disposal, as the proposed building of an incinerator on Great Island has generated a 'heated' debate and much public opposition. Activities related to environmental assets have the potential to cause damage if engaged in without consideration for broader issues. The visual pollution caused by large numerals painted on the rocks around the Hook by heedless anglers is an example of this narrow approach. This thoughtless activity diminishes the enjoyment of the many who use the area for walking and other leisure activities. The removal of fossils by professional fossil hunters for financial gain is another example of environmental exploitation that needs to be regulated. The Geological Survey of Ireland is concerned about this problem and consideration is being given to designating the rocks from Booley Bay aound the point of Hook to Sandeel Bay as a protected area. The full value of environmental heritage depends on continued access by the public to the enjoyment of natural amenities. The importance of this was emphasised in 2001 by the removal of a laneway that gave public access, since at least 1841 and probably much longer, to a beach known as Liú na Scooth in Templetown. Ironically, this important amenity, which was available to the community when the region was under the control of the Loftus regime, has been removed just a century after the land passed into private ownership.

THE PERSONALITY OF THE HOOK

Muir mas, nem nglas, talam ce.

Beautiful sea, blue heavens, eternal earth.

Over the centuries, diverse elements have combined to give the Hook a distinctive character and person-ality. The present inhabitants are descended from disparate groups of people who, for various reasons, were attracted into the region over two millennia. The societal mix was greatly influenced by the location of the region on vital sea routes, principally the strategic Waterford Harbour. The confined, peninsular nature of the region produced an intimate, integrated society, with a distinctive accent and personality. Family names are deeply rooted in the region, many of them first recorded locally in late medieval times as tenants on the three estates. Always a dominant presence, the sea is frequently glimpsed from unexpected vantage points some distance from the coast. Ever visible from land and sea, the iconic Hook lighthouse epitomises the maritime connection. The surrounding sea and low-lying topography combine to create low horizons and vast skies, with distant views of places such as the Saltee Islands, Creadan Head and Brownstown Pillars, frequently seen but seldom visited. The rhythm of the year is reflected in the ever-changing moods and colours of sea and sky; the Hook is at its most spectacular during a winter storm, when the headland is necklaced by white foam. Sadly, in all its moods, the sea inevitably causes loss of life; the sound of a low-flying helicopter invariably causes twinges of alarm as a possible harbinger of tragedy at sea. The unique balance between land, sea and sky created by the topographical character of the Hook peninsula generates a heightened awareness of these elements and an appreciation of changing moods and colours.

Fig. 1 The atmospheric colour and hazy light of a still summer morning sunrise, captured in the reflections of a full tide in Slade Harbour.

B. COLFER

Fig. 2 Sea foam at Pursheen near Hook lighthouse. The clear bright air after a storm emphasises the contrasting vibrant colours of rocks, sea and sky.

PEOPLE AND PLACE

The dependence of maritime activities on climate has given those involved in fishing and other seafaring activities a keen weather sense, with an ability to predict changes by interpreting signs in the sky and sea. Partial rainbows, regarded as a sign of broken weather, were known as 'wind-dogs' and wispy clouds, traditionally an omen of windy weather, were referred to as 'Tom Murphy's beard.' Generations of accumulated experience combined to give fishermen an intimate knowledge of the sea, as the currents, shoals and areas of turbulence were relevant not only to fish catches but also to their own safety. The constantly changing slack water (referred to as a 'scarf') at the meeting of two currents was regarded as good fishing ground, particularly for mackerel, as various organic material held in suspension in the 'scarf' attracted feeding fish. This is particularly true of the very pronounced 'scarf' off the Hook, where the brown estuarine water meets the blue water of the sea, and the sea's surface goes unusually flat in calm weather. As fish catches often relate to underwater terrain, fishermen's knowledge also included an understanding of the rock,

sand and seaweed on the sea floor. The experienced fisherman viewed the sea off the Hook as being as varied as fields would be for a countryman. He always knew by a quick glance to shore exactly where he was; inshore navigation was an instinctive activity, as experienced boatmen determined their location on the sea by referring to prominent landmarks.

Fig. 3 A lobster boat leaving Slade Harbour at dawn for a day's fishing.

PETER COX

Fig. 4 As society becomes more open to external influences, local customs and characteristics inevitably become diluted. The three fishermen shown in this early 1960s photograph (Paddy Kennedy with his dog, Martin and Tom Fortune), surrounded by boating and fishing gear from the days of sail, belonged to an era when society in the Hook was of a more local and well-defined nature. A visitor from Dublin is enjoying their company.

Although fishermen follow a set routine, the work is constantly changing and is subject to disruption from storms. Seasonality based on weather and the availability of species dictates a yearly rhythm, while a daily tempo is controlled by tidal changes, particularly in harbours like Slade that are dry at low water. Vastly improved boats and equipment have introduced new techniques, rendering traditional sea lore obsolete and in danger of being lost. However, even though modern technology and methods impose their own requirements, the code of the sea still applies. Despite the demanding lifestyle and the vagaries of weather and catch, fishermen remain attracted to their way of life. The part played by luck may be one facet of this attraction: one veteran fisherman in Churchtown liked to comment that hauling lobster-pots was like buying lucky-bags – you never knew what might be in the next one! The luck element in fishing, as well as actual survival at sea, also encouraged rituals of propitiation; even the most cynical boatowner had his craft present for the annual blessing of the boats and kept a small bottle of holy water and a religious medal on board. The presence of women, particularly with red hair, was regarded as unlucky in a boat; the women's role was usually confined to collecting shellfish (bia trá) 'on the strand' and processing fish for winter consumption by gutting and filleting and either drying them in the sun or salting in wooden barrels.

In spite of the rigours of the fisherman's life, or perhaps because of them, an implicit code of behaviour regulates

activity at sea. The practice of helping other seafarers in time of difficulty or tragedy is sacrosanct and is universally observed. Respect for boats and fishing gear is paramount, if only because it is a matter of vital mutual interdependence. Traditionally, a loose system of territoriality applied to the fishing grounds close to different ports, but this has been diluted by the advent of bigger and more powerful boats. Usually, farming and fishing were separate occupations, but some men who had a small amount of land were forced to follow both occupations in order to make a precarious living. In the Hook, the cultivation of land to the very edge of the cliff epitomises this close connection between land and sea, as well as giving a distinct appearance to the coastal landscape.

Because of the peninsula's location, the people of the Hook have been exposed to a conflicting mixture of isolation by land and exposure to the broad maritime world. This dichotomy resulted in a tight-knit community from which men departed to join ships, principally in Liverpool, and sailed to ports around the world. In the eighteenth and nineteenth centuries, seafaring expertise allowed many to cross the Atlantic to the Newfoundland fishery and ultimately to colonise the island. Until the mid-twentieth century, a continuous exodus of young men was facilitated by contacts with the many friends and relations who were already established seamen. Visits home resulted in the unexpected presence of exotic pictures and ornaments in houses throughout the area. Returned sailors also brought with them a more worldly attitude, which at times was manifested as a sceptical attitude towards religious practice. Women also left, to work as housemaids in cities as far afield as London or New York. Sometimes, the speech of people who returned on holiday contained a

B. COLFER

Fig. 5 For decades, 'searcing for baits' has been a popular summer activity at Slade. Members of the younger generation scour the rocks at low tide to recover fishing tackle lost by anglers. The finds are then painstakingly restored and returned to eager fishermen for a nominal charge.

Fig. 6 For centuries, quarrying and stoneworking played a significant part in shaping the society and landscape of the Hook. Skilfully carved initials in the Otter Hole, a cave in the Old Red Sandstone beside the mill-stone quarry at Herrylock, are a poignant link with the stonemasons who used the cave as a base. The initials probably record the names Fardy, Tweedy and Breen, all former residents; the Devereux family, now the only residents of the former farmhouse cluster, is also represented.

tinge of their new life, but most retained the distinctive local accent of their native place. The sea even seeped into the houses: pride of place over the mantelpiece was often given to maritime themes – ships in bottles, pictures of ships in which members of the household had served, and exotic shells from far-off places.

Waterford Harbour has had a fundamental influence on the evolution of society and settlement in the Shelburne area. Rather than presenting a barrier, the estuary served to connect the communities on its shores by facilitating contacts of a commercial and cultural nature. Because of these links, the personality of the Hook has traditionally been more influenced by Waterford and Kilkenny than by the rest of county Wexford. This association manifests itself in a number of ways in the Hook, including a distinctive estuary accent, the presence of Munster surnames (particularly Power and Foley), the prevalence of farmhouse clusters (a typical south Kilkenny settlement type) and the late survival of the Irish language. A story (perhaps apocryphal) formerly told in the Hook about a man who travelled a long distance in a vain search for a lost cow serves to illustrate this point: on his return, to emphasise the extent of his travels, he said that he had been as far as the bridge of Saltmills and had looked into county Wexford!

Because of the peninsularity of the Hook there are no passers-through. Anyone who travels by road to the headland comes for business, social or recreational purposes. This isolation by land was balanced by accessibility by sea, as the Hook defined the entrance into the busy shipping lane of Waterford Harbour, the key to the whole south-east and the richest part of Ireland from the

medieval period onwards. The classic peninsular shape, gradually narrowing to a slender point with the ubiquitous sea on all sides, is an attraction in itself. The low-lying nature of the Hook is best seen from the higher ground at Herrylock, with the view converging on the lighthouse, which dominates the peninsula. The banded column is highly visible by day, while its flashing light pulses rhythmically across the peninsula at night. Even in dense fog, the lighthouse makes its presence felt, as the sonorous foghorn compensates for the temporary loss of the most prominent visual feature in the Hook. The low, horizontal headland generates a feeling of being close to the sea, while the waves breaking on the rocky coastline provide a powerful visual connection between land and water. The very shape of the peninsula focuses attention on the lighthouse, as the vertical element is emphasised by the flat landscape, its visual and symbolic aspect being heightened by the antiquity of the building. Of their very nature, the architecture of lighthouses is amphibious and liminal, representing the threshold between land and sea. The almost inevitable definition of the extremity of a peninsula by a lighthouse creates a universal link between them. The ever-present threat of the sea is symbolised by the existence

Fig. 7 An enduring sense of the past can be demonstrated in unexpected ways. Once a year, the people of Horeswood parish attend the mass-rock in the former Loftus townland of Killesk to honour the memory of ancestors who were forced to practise in secret during penal times.

Fig. 8 International best-selling children's author Eoin Colfer, creator of the *Artemis Fowl* series, has close family links with the Hook, which is the setting for one of his early books, *Benny and Babe*. The coastal feature known as Black Chan features in the book and is used as the cover illustration for the German edition.

A Hook Childhood
by Eoin Colfer

As a boy, I often imagined that our family was tethered to the town of Wexford, and as soon as the bond of school was cut, we would snap back to the Hook for the summer. Often our father could not wait that long to get back to his native place. Towards the end of June he would begin to make luggage runs to Slade until there was more household equipment in the Hook than in Wexford town. This rendered any argument of staying in town untenable.

The final luggage run required the most planning as there were people involved. Five sons and two parents to be precise. One might think that a Renault 4 would have reached capacity with that amount of bodies. Perhaps there might be room for a dozen or so tightly packed playing cards, but somehow the clothing, kitchen utensils, reading material, cereals and gallons of pasteurised milk that had been laid out on the footpath were all swallowed by the Renault. The actual trip to the Hook often seemed dreamlike. Perhaps it was the lack of oxygen.

There was no gradual urban fadeout as there is today. Ten seconds after leaving the house, the countryside was everywhere. I would press my forehead to the window and see the roadside ditches jitter along with us. If the trip was at night I watched the stars hop and cartwheel, imagining that they were satellites keeping an eye on the Renault in case roof-rack overload caused it to tip over.

There was a particular moment that signified that the holiday had officially begun. After forty minutes of are we there yet, the Renault would crest the hill before Porter's Gate and the entire peninsula of Hook would be stretched before us. A jagged triangle of rock and field dotted with history. Slade Castle, Loftus Hall, Hook lighthouse. The triangle was roughly bisected by a black ribbon of road. The road that killed the beggarman. Legend has it that a robust tramp hiked the length of Ireland until the sight of the ruler-straight road stretching into the sea stopped him dead.

Our holiday home was above the bend in the road between the village of Slade and Hook lighthouse. Over the years our accommodation morphed from tent to caravan to family home. But my bunk was in a hardboard hut. When the family outgrew the caravan, Dad built a hut out back for my brother Paul and myself, connected to the main building by an extension cord umbilical. If the music got too loud or too late, we were plugged out. The hut was our den, sanctuary and studio. We tattooed its walls with album covers and cartoon characters. We slept late undisturbed by younger brothers, and we hid anything that needed hiding behind hardboard panels. If there is a better way to spend the summer than by the sea in a hut, I have yet to find it.

The Hook has something for every age. As under-tens, my brothers and I learned to swim, fished for crawlies on the slip and jumped into the sea from increasingly high walls. We explored the medieval hidey holes of Slade Castle and foul-hooked our first fish. As pre-teens we occasionally rose at dawn to haul lobster pots, scoured the rocks for lost baits and cycled to nearby beaches for long days of idleness. We jumped into the sea from higher walls and slept dead sleeps, skin blasted by sun, sand and salt water.

The Hook is a perfect place to unleash an adolescent. There are local dances, but they are six miles away in Fethard-on-Sea. So by the time we had cycled the distance, much of our angst driven fever had dissipated leaving us almost serene, until the first slow dance.

And now finally as an adult, I anticipate my own children's happiness as they, year after year, peel back another layer of Hook Head.

One way to measure the importance of a place in your personal history is to calculate how many of life's seminal moments occurred there. With even the briefest contemplation, several incidents spring vividly to mind. I remember our first boat, an old lifeboat with a Seagull five horsepower strapped to the back. I remember the engine failing during a storm, and black wedges of wave rising on all sides, with the hard blocks of a foam life-jacket wedged under my chin. It is the rocky stretch between Slade and the Hook that I remember best. A black ragged curve, winding around the peninsula like the results of a guilty man's lie detector test. Perhaps a thousand times I retraced my own steps across the bait traps. Searching beneath hanks of weed, below sharp outcrops, at the bottom of shadowy channels for lost lures. This walk was something that could always be done. A guardian against boredom, even in the rain. I felt something like ownership for those rocks and even now can repeat the mantra of their names. The Spring, the Noord, Solomon's Boat, Carraig Ahoy, Black Chan, Boyce's Bay. And behind each name a story. Walking those rocks made me feel a part of the Hook. Almost a local.

I became a fisherman on the Hook. Something to be envied in town. I could tie knots, bait pots, gut fish, and hold a lobster in such a way that its tail wouldn't slice through my fingers. I had oilskins, a knife and the permanent glisten of scales on my fingers. I grew up on the Hook. I sold baits to a man who never came back to his car, swept away by a sly creeping wave on the green rocks. I watched my father don his wetsuit to retrieve the body. I remember the man's white face and purple lips after an hour beneath the water. The rope lassoed beneath his armpits as they dragged him from the sea.

A boy grows up in other ways too. I brought my girlfriend camping on the Hook, and our tent amplified the sounds of nature and the foghorn. We were married shortly after. But the Hook is not all about the past. Present and future are there too. My son recently caught his first pollock, and was disgusted when someone cut his prize into fillets. I watch him sit at the kitchen table, distracted by his grandmother's stories as she feeds him something he does not want to eat. He is embarking on a lifetime of summers, that have been tried and tested by generations of our family.

I write books for children now. The Hook has to date been the source of one complete book, several characters and a few incidents that I have relocated to other settings. There is no doubt that I will revisit the Hook in future books. Children all over the world have a fascination with it, and often ask me if these things really happened. Can you actually sell baits to unwitting Dubliners? Is there really a ghost in Loftus Hall? If you throw fish guts into the air, will a seagull really catch them before they hit the water?

Yes, I tell them. All of these things are true.

Fig. 9 Late in 2003, immense shoals of sprat occupied Waterford Harbour for up to six weeks. This rich harvest attracted fishermen, whales, porpoises, seals and a great variety of sea birds. This picture shows seagulls and gannet feeding on a shoal of sprat at Boyce's Bay in the townland of Porters Gate.

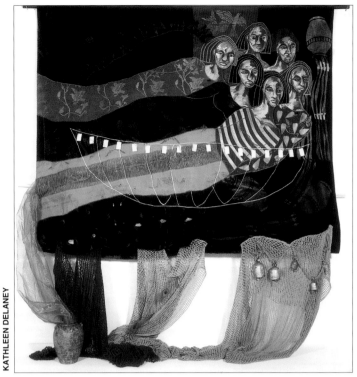

KATHLEEN DELANEY

MARK NASH

Fig. 10 As part of a scheme sponsored by Wexford County Council, this textile, created by artist Kathleen Delaney, was installed in Hook lighthouse visitor centre in 2003. Dedicated to all lost at sea, the work is specifically inspired by a bizarre event that occurred in Fethard Bay on Sunday 3 June 1787. According to local tradition, after Divine Service in St Mogue's church, six young men accompanied by six young women went for a boating trip in the bay. Later that day, the boat returned with the six men, who claimed that the women had fallen overboard and drowned. An official investigation followed but reached no conclusion due to lack of evidence. The young men are said to have left the area soon afterwards. The mysterious nature of the tragedy inevitably led to various rumours including dark stories of white slavers and Barbary pirates. The true story may be more mundane. A contemporary account in *Finn's Leinster Journal* stated that three men, accompanied by six women, went for a boating trip to the Keeragh Islands where their boat struck a rock and sank; the six women were drowned but the three men managed to swim ashore. Whatever the truth of the matter, a monument was erected shortly afterwards to the memory of the six girls. The inscription reads: *Sacred to the remains of Ellinor Lumsden, 22; Ann Winskill, 21; Mary Winskill, 20; Catherine Winskill, 19; Ellinor Clegg, 18; and Sarah Boyce, 17, who were drowned in the Bay of Feathard on Sunday 3rd June, 1787, after having attended Divine Service. They were lovely in life and in death not divided.*

Fig. 11 Despite the excellence of modern boats and technology, an unexpected mishap can be a forceful reminder of the hazards of the sea. Unlike shipwrecks of the past, the rescue services can now respond immediately to distress calls. In December 2003, these fishing boats were grounded at Herrylock while trawling for sprat. The Dunmore lifeboat and the search-and-rescue helicopter were quickly on the scene and the men were taken off. Fortunately, the crews suffered no injury and the boats were successfully refloated at high tide.

of a lighthouse and this hint of danger contributes to an intrinsic visual attraction.

Since the colonisation and organisation of south-west Wexford in medieval times, the landscape has changed in an organic way. The successive influences impacting on the Hook were absorbed and collectively constitute the physical and cultural character of the modern environment. The impact of the Anglo-Norman settlement on the landscape in the late medieval period is pervasive, as

Fig. 12 The beaches in the Hook region are a major attraction during the summer season. Because of the peninsular nature of the area, it is always possible to find a sheltered beach on windy days. Duncannon beach, overlooked by the historic fort, is one of the finest in the south-east and has been awarded blue flag status by the EU. In spite of obvious drawbacks, the unusual custom of parking cars on the beach continues.

GILLIAN BARRETT

Fig. 13 Tony O'Malley, one of the most eminent Irish twentieth-century artists, did some painting in the Hook at the end of the 1950s, based in a house called Ashgrove in Fethard, which was loaned to him by a friend. This painting from that period is entitled *The orchard at Ashgrove.*

and rocky localities in which they were erected.'[1] Wexford builders erected striking churches based on Pugin's neo-Gothic design, including those at Ramsgrange and Templetown in the Hook region.

In spite of the strong medieval emphasis in the formation of society and landscape, the area is not a homogeneous unit, as topographical, environmental and historical differences produced variations in lifestyle, customs, occupations and even accent. Much of the diversity can be linked to the legacy of the three large estates that dominated the area for almost eight centuries. Examples of settlement variety are provided by the estate villages of Fethard, Saltmills and Arthurstown, the fort village of Duncannon, the farmhouse clusters of Broomhill and Churchtown and the chapel villages of Ramsgrange and Ballycullane. These often evolved from earlier centres of occupation: for example, Fethard was a medieval episcopal town and Ramsgrange grew from a monastic agricultural centre. Some population centres had an industrial base: Ballyhack as a ferry and fishing village, Slade as a fishing village, and the farmhouse cluster of Herrylock as a centre of stoneworking. Isolation and stability allowed traditional practices and values to survive in tandem with estate improvement and other external influences. Varying agricultural practices are echoed in the difference between the complex fieldscapes of Churchtown, Grange and Broomhill and the large, regular fields of the estate demesnes and the big farmer. The contrast in lifestyles within the region, between landlord and tenant, farmer and labourer, fisherman and stonemason, contributed to the cultural and social amalgam. Another layer of difference, arising from social, religious and political factors, contributed a potentially frictional element to community life.

much of the modern infrastructure of road, village and farm, as well as the surnames of many inhabitants (Banville, Barry, Browne, Chapman, Codd, Colfer, Cullen, Devereux, FitzHenry, Lewis, Meyler, Moran, Neville, Parle, Power, Redmond, Roche, Sinnott, Stafford, Sutton, Wall, Walsh, Whitty), originated in that period. Medieval architecture also had a somewhat unexpected impact on churches in the modern landscape, as the design of Catholic churches built during the Devotional Revolution in the second half of the nineteenth century had a medieval connection. A. W. Pugin, the renowned English architect, was so impressed by the architecture of Dunbrody Abbey that its influence dominated his Wexford churches, now regarded to be among his best work. He believed that the clergy should 'revive and restore those solemn piles of buildings,' which were 'rude and simple but harmonised most perfectly with the wild

Fig. 14 An impressionistic drawing of Slade by Tony O'Malley (1959).

B. COLFER

Fig. 15 In the Hook, different weather conditions and seasonal variations present continually changing aspects of sea and land. This view of a sultry sun over the Hook with Slade Castle silhouetted in the background was captured on a balmy August evening from a boat in an oily calm Slade Bay.

Inevitably, the opening up of society in the Hook has resulted in a less intimate involvement with the exclusively local, leading to a dilution of the distinctive nature of the region. Place-names of fields and coastal features, formerly an essential part of everyday conversation, are now in danger of being lost due to lack of usage. Similarly, vernacular speech, at one time highly idiomatic and liberally sprinkled with Irish words and phrases, is more homogenised and less colloquial. Some new houses fail to acknowledge established building designs and the traditional settlement landscape. The growth of tourism and an ever-increasing number of second homes is dividing the year into two phases: an increasingly longer summer season with crowded roads, beaches and amenities, balanced by a quieter, more relaxed winter season. Although the region is now much

more open and accessible, no significant modern changes, apart from holiday-home developments, have been imposed on the cultural and physical environment. Because of the secluded, cul-de-sac nature of the area, older cultural features have frequently survived intrusive forces, creating a remarkable landscape and society of complex origin. This continuity, combined with an individual topographic personality, has generated an environment with a unique character. This applies in particular to the narrow, rock-bound point of Hook, where the flat, treeless landscape emphasises the vertical prominence of the Tower of Hook, Slade Castle and Loftus Hall. Stone walls and large fields recall estate organisation. The estate entrance, still referred to as 'the piers of Porter's Gate,' was also the symbolic limit of the Hook and people from beyond that point were referred to as 'outsiders' by the natives, who preferred to stay inside the 'piers' as far as possible, their sense of identity reinforced by the well-defined boundaries of the headland. The small fields of Slade and Churchtown, created by repeated sub-division, point to the pressure put on available land by a rising population. Subsequent emigration reduced the community to a quarter of its former level and left a melancholy legacy of ruined houses, still often poignantly known by the names of the original occupants. The distinctive personality of the Hook can be attributed to the many historic influences concentrated in a compact, well-defined landscape. This combination creates a distinct space, dominated by sea, sky and the elements, with an exceptional quality that is appreciated, perhaps subliminally, by the inhabitants and by the many visitors who are attracted by the lighthouse, winter storms and peninsular location.

This is the sense of landscape as cultural memory evoked by Seamus Heaney in 'Squarings' (xix):

> So that the mind's eye could haunt itself
> With fixed associations and learn to read
> Its own contents in meaningful order,
> Ancient textbooks recommended that
> Familiar places be linked deliberately
> With a code of images. You knew the portent
> In each setting, you blinked and concentrated.

APPENDIX 1: CISTERCIAN TENANTS AND LANDS 1541

Tintern Abbey

Farmers and tenants who carried out the survey of the lands and possessions: David Power, John FitzWater, Maurice McNicholas, Donald O'Duff, Philip McWilliam, David Mctege, Thomas Mctege, Nic. McRychard, William Mcpeers, John Fleming

Tenant	Acres	Type of land	Rent and services	Location	Townland
Demesne land	40	30 ac. arable, 10 ac. underwood pasture and moor	value 10s	Tintern	Tintern, Saltmills Castleworkhouse
—		Mill (le see mylle)	10s		
—		Mill (le overshot mill)	20s		
—	60	arable, pasture, wood	value 20s, 2 hookdays 2 weeding days, 1 sheep waste because of Irish wars	St Keran	St Kearns
—	60	arable, pasture, wood	value 20s, 2 hookdays 2 weeding days, 1 sheep, waste	Kermore	Curraghmore
—	60	arable, meadow, pasture, wood	value 13s 4d, waste	St Leonards	St Leonards
—	120	arable, pasture, wood, moor	value 16s worth 11s 8d because of war, 8 hookdays 8 weeding days, 1 sheep	Naysshe and Gaynestown	Nash not known
—	60	20 arable, 40 wood and pasture	value 10s, 2 hookdays 2 weeding days, 1 sheep	Dommain and Flemyngston	Dunmain not known
David Power	60	arable, meadow, moor, wood	16s and customary services	Rathnegeeragh	Rathnageeragh
David Power	30	arable, pasture, wood	value 10s but returning 4s customary services	Balligarwy	Ballygarvan
David Power	60	arable, pasture, wood	value 16s p.a., worth 6s because of war customary services	Bole	Boley
David Power	20	arable, pasture, meadow, wood	4s, customary services	Scarte	not known
David Power	10		value 4s, waste because of war with the Irish	Coyndowe	Owenduff (river - not townland)
David Power	30	arable, pasture, wood	16s 8d, customary services	Tobbyrnassan	?Nash
David Power	60	arable, moor, pasture, wood	10s, customary services	Ballytarssyn	Ballytarsna
Shane McConner			60s 8d	farmer of demesne lands and mills	Tintern
William McLaghland			10s	St Keran	St Kearns
—			6s 8d	St Leonard	St Leonards
John Broun [Browne]			3s 4d	Cormoren	?Curraghmore
Walter Talbot			53s 4d	Ballygarven	Ballygarvan
David Power			46s 8d	Naissh	Nash
Nicholas Power			3s 4d	Donmayan	Dunmain
Moriartagh Okeley [O'Kelly]			8s	Ranekeraght	Rathnageeragh
John McLaghleyn			8s	the Bole	Boley
William Duff			2s	Scart	not known
William Leghlan			2s	Coyndowe	Owenduff
John McComen			8s 4d	Tobirnassan	?Nash
David Power			3s 4d	Ballyscarfyn	not known

Outside of the study area, Tintern Abbey held lands in Killann in the barony of Bantry and St Mullins in county Carlow, both 'waste' because of war. The abbey also owned lands in the vicinity of Bannow and Kilmore in Bargy and in the towns of Ross, Wexford and Waterford, as well as tithes from the following rectories: Bannow, Kilcowan, Kilmore (Grange) and Kilturk in Bargy; Nash and Ballygarvan in Owenduff; Clonmines, Tintern, St Mullins and Whitechurch.

Dunbrody Abbey

Tenants and farmers of the lands who carried out the survey: Stephen Devereux, Redmond Rean, Nicholas Rean, John Phillippe, Philip Colmin, William Tege, John Hey, Nichol Crehin, Thady Managhan, Thomas Dermote, Maurice Davy, Edmund Thee, Edmund Burghe

Tenant	Acres	Type of land	Rent and services	Location	Townland
Demesne lands	20	arable, meadow, pasture	6s 8d, tithes 5s 4d	Grange	Grange
Four tenants	4 messuages 20	arable meadow, pasture	40s, 15 hookdays, 15 weed days 15 hens, 60 gals of beer, 5 sheep tithes 22s 8d	Dunbrody Saltmills	Dunbrody Saltmills
Nics. Key		fishing weir (Scarre ware)	66s 8d (40s returned)		
James Lumbert		weir (Goddiswere) weir (le ebbe weir) mill (le Shaltmille)	60s (3s 4d returned) 5s 10s		
Richard Sutton	1 messuage 60	arable pasture, moor	10s 1 sheep, tithes 9s 4d	Coule	Coole
Richard Sutton	120	arable, meadow, pasture	25s, 1 sheep, tithes 34s 8d	Shylbekan and Ballyvadre	Shielbaggan not known
Stephen Devereux	120	arable, meadow, pasture	26s 8d	Baylestown	Battlestown
Countess of Ormonde	60	arable, meadow, pasture, moor	5s, 1 sheep	Clonard	Clonlard
Matthew Devereux	60	arable	9s	Kylbryde	Kilbride
David Sutton		meadow, pasture			
John Inglysshe [English	80	arable, meadow, pasture 1 fishing weir	26s 8d, 2 hookdays	Duncanan	Duncannon
John Power	60	arable, meadow, pasture	13s 4d, 1 sheep, tithes 10s	Clonsharragh	Clonsharragh
James Cullen	180	arable, meadow, pasture	13s 4d	Ballygowyn	Ballygow
John Pursell	20	arable, pasture, wood	13s 4d, 1 sheep, tithes 10s	Newegge	Nook
9 fishermen	9 tenements 2 boats 8 cottagers		73s, tithes of fish 20s	Ballyhack (let to Countess of Ormonde)	Ballyhack
John Devereux	60	arable, meadow, pasture	13s 4d, 1 sheep, 2 hookdays, tithes 2s	Kylheyle	Kilhile
John Devereux	120	arable, meadow, pasture	23s, 1 sheep, tithes 16s	Ramysgrange	Ramsgrange
Countess of Ormonde	60	arable, meadow, pasture	10s, 1 sheep, tithes 10s 8d	Boderambusse	Boderan
Walter Devereux	40	arable, pasture, meadow	13s 4d, tithes 10s 8d	Rowestown	Rosetown
Thomas Fyn Thomas Smith			34s 4d	demesne land	Tintern
Richard Sutton			10s	Cowle	Coole
William Sutton			8s 4d	Shilbegan	Shielbaggan
William Sutton			6s 8d	Kilhoil	Kilhile
Stephen Devereux			13s 4d	Battailstown	Battlestown
Walter Sutton			2s 6d	Clonard	Clonlard
Matthew Devereux			5s 4d	Kilbride	Kilbride
Thomas Forlon [Furlong]			13s 4d	Donkanan	Duncannon
Oliver McNicholas			6s 8d	Clonessharraght	Clonsharragh
Peter Earl of Ossory			26s 8d	Ballyhak	Ballyhack
John Purcell			6s 8d	Le Newge	Nook
Shane McNicholas			3s 4d	Rathcrowen	Monacahee
Philip McWater			12s	Ramesgrange	Ramsgrange
Philip McWater			5s	Bonderan	Boderan
Philip McWater				Rathcrowan	Monacahee
Philip McWater				Boyse	not known
Walter Devereux			6s 8d	Robestown	Rosetown
Thomas Jonys			1s	Grange	Grange
David Sutton			3s 4d	Galtram	not known

No profits from waste lands in the following places: Newhaggard (Haggard), Callaghton (?Coleman), Ballymadder (not known), Ballydoman (not known), Knockansawn (not known), Polmolowhe (? Poulmaloe, parish of Whitechurch)

Outside of the study area, Dunbrody Abbey had possessions in the city and county of Waterford and in New Ross. Lands in Connacht were waste because of wars with the Irish.

[At the end of the seventeenth century, the commercial potential of estates was being developed. Robert Leigh of Rosegarland compiled a survey of south Wexford detailing the quality of land, the type of crops grown and other remarks on a variety of topics. The following extract relates to the Hook region. The text and spelling has been modernised. Editorial comments are in square brackets]

A description of the southern part of the barony of Shelburne, written in 1684 by Robert Leigh of Rosegarland

Barony of Shelburne: The Barony of Shelburne lies towards the south sea along upon the River of Ross and Waterford, and is devided into quarters or peeces [presumably pieces] (as they are termed in that country), and is the same thing with hundreds in England, viz., the Peece of Dunbrody, and the Peece of the Hook, the Peece of Sleuculter [Slieve Coiltia], and the Peece of Tintern.

Sleu Culter Peece: The Peece of Sleu Culter lies southward of the Barony of Bantry, joining thereunto, and is indifferent good land for the County of Wexford, yields wheat, barley, pease, and oats, and is a deep soil, but very cold. It belongs to several proprietors of a new acquisition, except the Lordship of Terraragh, which belongs to Mathew Forde of the same County, Esq. There is a parish church now in repair called White Church and there is another also in this Peece called Carnagh, that is ruinated. Sleu Culter, from whence the peece takes its name, is a large hill very good for grazing, and lying not far from the River of Ross.

Tintern Peece: The Peece of Tintern lies southward of Sleu Culter, and eastward of the Peece of Dunbrody; it is indifferent good land, and a large scope, and yields wheat, barley, pease, and oats, but it is shallow ground; it has 8 or 9 castles, and several farm houses. It belonged (except some few small parcells), before the dissolution of monasteries, to the Abbey of Tintern which was enjoyed by monks of the order of St Bernard [Cistercians] and is now the inheritance of Sir Caesar Colclough, of Tintern. Clonmines is a very ancient corporation, there remaining only four or five ruined castles and an old church called St Nicholas, and a monastery, also ruined, which did formerly belong to the order of Augustine and is called St Augustins. Yet it sends two burgesses to Parliament still, and was governed by a Portrieve and Burgesses; but the charter and contents thereof is worn out of memory long since. Clonmines lies upon a river composed of the rivers of Rosegarland and the Blackwater (called in Irish Owenduff) which meet together at a place called Ballylannan, about a quarter of a mile to the north-east of Clonmines, and so go together into the main sea, by the name of the River of Bannow, within a league or less of Clonmines, at a narrow passage between the Bannow Island in the Barony of Bargy, and the lands of Fethard, in the Barony of Shelburne. It is confidently reported that this Clonmines was a place of great trade in times passed, and a harbour for shipping of indifferent bulk until the sand filled up the ancient passage near the town of Bannow (another ancient Corporation lying in the Barony of Bargy, on the other side of the island of Bannow) which was the destruction of both these towns, so that now there is only a narrow passage for boats on the west side of the Island, between it and the lands of Fethard; for on the east side towards the town of Bannow, where the ancient passage was, and ships used to come in, it is now a perfect dry strand, and may be walked over from the Island to the town. It is believed that Clonmines (called in Irish Clonemeene), took its name from the silver or royal mines formerly dug there; and on the other side of the river, over against it in the Barony of Bargy, there are still to be seen five or six deep pits or mines, and some of the ore that was cast up, which seems to contain more lead than silver [Although there was mining at Clonmines the name derives from the Irish Cluan Mín: a level meadow]. There lived in these parts within a few years a very old man, that said he remembered to have seen miners at work there, but that the river water (near the banks of which those mines are) came in upon the workmen so fast, when they were deep in ground, as that they were forced to quit the undertaking for good and all. The townland of Clonmines is now for the most part the inheritance of the Earl of Anglesey. The river thereabouts yields good fish, as bass, mullet, and abundance of flukes, and (from Michaelmas tide till after Christmas) salmon in very good season, and so doth the river of Rosegarland, and the Black Water that falls into it, whereas few other rivers in Ireland affords any salmon at that time of the year.

Tintern House: Tintern Castle, being the aforesaid Sir Caesar Colclough's dwelling-house, lies south-west of Clonmines, at two miles distance, and is seated upon a rising ground or rock, but sheltered on all sides, at some small distance, by higher grounds, and several groves of oak and ash trees. Under the house, at a pistol's shot distance, in a valley running through a small grove of ash trees, and pleasant clear river, or stream, whereon stands a corn mill, and runs along the valley to a place called the Salt Mills, where it falls into the river of Bannow. On the west bank of the which river of Bannow (on Tintern side), there is an oyster bed, belonging to the said Sir Caesar Colclough, which is extraordinary large, and accounted the best oyster in that county (if not in all Ireland). They were brought thither about 70 years ago, in a barque from Milford-Haven, by order of Sir Thomas Colclough of Tintern, and sunk there, where the soil proved so natural to them that they grew much bigger and better tasted than those now had at Milford-Haven. Tintern was a large abbey of St Bernard's order, which had about £1,200 a year in lands and tithes belonging to it. It is said to have been founded soon after the English were masters of those parts, under Strongbow, Earl of Chepstowe, and that it took its name from an Abbey in Wales, called also Tintern, which abbey I have seen described in some maps of England, and so the [sic.] rather believe this may be true. There is at Tintern a large church, that belonged to the abbey, called St Bernard, and another which is now the parish church, wherein stands a large marble monument, or tomb, of Sir Anthony Colclough, Knight, the first of that family that settled in Ireland in the reign of King Henry 8th, whose guards (called the gentlemen pensioners) he commanded, and who gave him for his great services the Abbey of Tintern, with its possessions. As to his parentage and esteem at that time, as well as to his issue, I refer you to the inscription on the tomb. Sir Caesar Colclough, Bart., who is the present possessor of Tintern, is great-grandson to the aforesaid Sir Anthony Colclough.

Dunbrody Peece: The Peece of Dunbrody lies westward of Tintern, along the river of Waterford and Ross, and is counted the best land both for grazing and plowing in that side of the county of Wexford. It yields wheat, barley, pease, and oats, and is a deep, myrye [miry], dark soil.

Abbey: There is at the place called Dunbrody, on the aforesaid river, a large abbey, or ruinated monastery, that belongs to the order of St Bernard; the walls whereof are still standing. It is a pleasant seat, and has on the east side a shrubby kind of wood, which formerly was good timber, and is now an ornament only. This place has great convieniency of fishing and fowling, and has several weirs for taking of salmon. Belonging to it, a little distance from these old ruins, stands a good large house of lime and stone built before the Rebellion of Ireland [1641] by John Ichingham, Esq., but was not finished, and stands ever

since waste in a manner [Dunbrody Castle]. Over against the abbey, to the westward, lies, in the river of Ross, the island belonging to my Lord Duke of Ormond, called the Great Island, containing about 700 ac. of land, and a little below it the rivers of Ross and Waterford join, and bear the name of that of Waterford, till it loses itself in the sea near the Tower of Hook.

Ballihack: About 2 miles from Dunbrody, to the seaward, upon the River of Waterford, there is a creek and an old key [quay] at the bottom of a steep rock, called Ballihack; it is a sad place to look upon, and has not about half a dozen houses, and an old pile of a castle, besides a few cabins; but it is a place much frequented by passengers that ferry over there into Munster, to a place on that side called Passage, as also by seamen and the like, for ships often lie thereabouts in the River. There are two considerable fairs kept at Ballihack (for black cattle and hogs), in the year, the one at Michaelmas, the other upon St James' day in summer; and out of the rock that hangs above the village and quay, is wrought a number of very good millstones, which with no small skill or less danger are rolled down a very high precipice to the key, and so carried by water as occasion requires.

Duncannon Fort: About a mile from Ballihack to the south-east, nearer the mouth of the aforesaid River of Waterford, lies the fort of Duncannon, accounted of considerable strength, and well manned and furnished with a sufficient number of great guns and other armour, and commands the mouth of the river of Waterford, so that no ship can go in or out, but shall be called to account by those in the fort. The fort itself belongs to the King, who has settled about £300 p.a. land of inheritance, for maintaining the same in repair, and defraying other charges there; but none of these lands lie near the fort; all the land thereabouts to the very wall, belonging to the Earl of Dunnegal. The Peece of Dunbrody did formerly belong to the Abbey of Dunbrody till it was dissolved, as the rest were; it belongs now to the said present Earl of Dunnegal, in right of the countess, his mother, who was daughter and heir to Ichingham of Dunbrody, aforesaid.

The present governor of Duncannon is his grace the Lord Duke of Ormonde; his deputy is Sir John Ivory, knight, who commands a company of foot lying there; also Sir John bought both commands from Col. Edward Rosscarrock, a loyal ancient servitor to the crown.

Hook Peece: The Peece of the Hook lies next the sea. The Parish of Hook [the old medieval parish ended at Porter's Gate] is a narrow tract of land, jetting southward into the sea, surrounded with great shelves and rocks; upon which uttermost point whereof stands a high tower, called the

Tower of Hook, which is made use of now as a lighthouse to direct ships into the river of Waterford and Ross. The soil within this parish of Hook is good lime and stone ground, though out of it no limestone is to be found in eight or ten miles going; it yields good wheat and excellent white pease and good pasture, and is naturally inclined to yield furze, but no trees of any kind will grow there, except preserved with great cost and art, by reason of the sea winds and bleak situation. The parish belong at present to Henry Loftus, Esq., who has repaired the old mansion house there, lying on the east shore of the river of Waterford aforesaid, and added other considerable buildings of lime and stone thereunto, and enclosed his gardens with high stone walls, to preserve some fruit trees newly planted there, and dwells in that house now. It was formerly called Redmond's Hall, from the old proprietor; it is now called Loftus Hall. Mr Loftus is now building a key for fishing boats on the east side of the said tract of land or peninsula, near a place called the Slade.

The Loftuses: Mr Henry Loftus is second son to Mr Nicholas Loftus, of Fethard, in the county of Wexford, which Nicholas was brother to Sir Arthur, or Sir Adam Loftus, of Rathfarnham, in the county of Dublin. The rest of the Peece of the Hook, belonging (for the most part) to Sir Nicholas Loftus, lies joining to the parish of Hook, and northward of it, and is good land for plow, black cattle and sheep; the soil is deep and there is good pasture for the aforesaid kind (some in one place and some in another) and affords meadow land in some places also, but it is generally very free to produce furze if seven years untilled, and yields no trees but with difficulty, by reason of sea winds, and is very bad riding in winter. It yields wheat, barley, pease, oats and beans.

Fethard Peece: Fethard town, in the said Peece of Hook, is a small straggling town, containing two or three small castles, and also a stone house, and a brick house, built by Mr Nicholas aforesaid, father to Sir Nicholas Loftus, also a large parish church called St Idanus [Aidan, i.e. Mogue] which is now unroofed, and about 30 or 40 cabins or thatched houses. It has been an ancient corporation, and one of the seats of the bishop of Ferns. The Corporation consists of portrieve and burgesses, and is now the inheritance of Sir Nicholas Loftus, who dwells in the stone house or castle that was the bishop's seat

formerly. It sends two burgesses to parliament. [Fethard sent two members to parliament until the Act of Union in 1800. These were controlled by Loftus, who received £15,000 in compensation.] As for their charter, I suppose it is lost, or consumed with age long since, and a new one is not requisite. This Corporation had anciently several petty freeholders, whereof there is not at present above one or two that enjoy their freeholds. There is a convenient creek for fishermen at Fethard, but no quay; yet they make full use of it, and take good seafish thereabouts.

Bagg and Bunn: Within two miles of Fetherd, or less, is the place called Bagg and Bunn, where (as the common saying in that country is) 'Ireland was lost, and Ireland was won'; that is to say, where the Irish, under their monarch O'Connor, lost it, and where Strongbow, Earl of Chepstow, won it for the English, assisted by Mac Murrough, king of Leinster [Raymond le Gros, not Strongbow, landed at Baginbun]. The place where he landed is a small creek, between two cliffs, lying open to the sea on the east, and was called Bagg and Bunn (as the story there goes) by reason the two ships in which the English landed were called, the one, Bagg, and the other, Bunn, and which they presently after set on fire [The origin of the name is not known. It may contain the Norse word *Bec*, a promontory; perhaps Bec an bann (as in Bannow), the river promontory]. Soon after landing (within a musket-shot of the place) they cast up a strong sconse or ditch across that neck of land where they came ashore, which ditch is still to be seen there. When they came as far as Fethard, into the land, they met a party of the natives, that were in the nature of a forlorn hope (or the like) to the army that came to resist the invasion, and there skirmishing with the Irish were put to great stress, but fought it out with great courage, and made their way through, for which reason (it is said) that place was called Fighthard, now corruptly called Fetherd [Fethard comes from the Irish *Fiodh ard*: the high wood]. There is another place about a mile and a half from Fetherd, called Battlestown, where it is said the English fought the first battle, after there landing. There is now standing there an old tower and some cabins only [Battlestown gets its name from the Battaile family, who were tenants of the Cistercians on the Dunbrody estate].

APPENDIX 3: SIGNATORIES TO THE APPLICATION FOR THE CONSTRUCTION OF SLADE PIER 1846

Slade 18th of April 1846
William Fortune
John W. Breen, Occupier
John Wallace, Occupier
Richard W. Boyce, Occupier
Hugh Duffy, Occupier
Patrick Duffy, Fisherman
John W. Breen, Occupier
Hugh Duffy Junr., Occupier
Thos. Duffy, Fisherman
Philip Kennedy, Fisherman
Thomas Kennedy, Fisherman
Patrick Kennedy, Fisherman
John Kennedy, Fisherman
Philip Kennedy Junr., Fisherman
Michael Kennedy, Fisherman
Laurence Moran, Occupier
Michael Moran, Fisherman
Patrick Fortune, Fisherman
James Duffy, Fisherman
Thomas Duffy, Fisherman
Michael Colfer, Fisherman
Patrick Colfer, Fisherman
Nicholas Fortune, Fisherman
John Rossiter, Fisherman
Patrick Rossiter, Fisherman
Peter Rossiter, Occupier
Richard Duffin, Fisherman
James Bird, Fisherman
Christopher Bird, Fisherman
Andrew Revial [Reville], Fisherman
Patrick Revial, Fisherman
George Chapman, Fisherman
Patrick Chapman, Fisherman
Nicholas Chapman, Fisherman
John Chapman, Fisherman
Patrick Colfer, Occupier
William Colfer, Fisherman
Thomas Colfer, Fisherman
James Power, Fisherman
John Power, Fisherman
Patrick Colvin, Fisherman
John Colvin, Fisherman
Patrick Colvin Junr., Fisherman
William Ryan, Fisherman

Edward Ryan, Fisherman
James Power, Fisherman
William Power, Fisherman
Thomas Power, Fisherman
Patrick Bird, Fisherman
George Bird, Fisherman
Dick Bird, Fisherman
Thomas White, Fisherman
John White, Fisherman
John White Junr., Fisherman
John Tobin, Fisherman
Thomas Tobin, Fisherman
Michael Tobin, Fisherman
Thomas Power, Fisherman
Patrick Kavanagh, Fisherman
Edward Kavanagh, Fisherman
James Kavanagh, Fisherman
Thomas Dwire [Dwyer], Fisherman
James Dwire, Fisherman
John Dwire, Fisherman
Richard Dwire, Fisherman
Thomas Dwire Junr., Fisherman
Thomas Colfer, Fisherman
Patrick Colfer, Fisherman
John King, Fisherman
William Breen, Fisherman
Watt Breen, Fisherman
Thomas Kennedy, Fisherman
Michael Kennedy, Fisherman
Edward Kennedy, Fisherman
Michael Bryan, Occupier
Thomas Bryan, Fisherman
Patk. Colfer, Fisherman
John Colfer, Fisherman
Peter Rossiter, Fisherman
John Wadde [Wadden ?], Fisherman
Michael Breen, Occupier
John Wadden [Wadding] Junr.,
    Occupier
James Breen, Fisherman
Robert Wadden, Fisherman
Moses Murphy, Occupier
William Fortune, Fisherman
Michael Power, Fisherman
David Power, Fisherman

Nicholas King, Occupier
Patrick King, Fisherman
William Breen, Occupier
John Breen, Fisherman
Edward Syms, Occupier
Thomas Fortune, Occupier
Patrick Laughlin, Occupier
Michael Fortune, Occupier
Thomas Drew, Fisherman
William Drew, Occupier
John Drew, Occupier
Nicholas Moore, Fisherman
John Walsh, Occupier
John Power, Fisherman
William Power, Fisherman
Mick Power, Fisherman
John Power, Fisherman
Thomas Power, Fisherman
James Fortune, Fisherman
Luke Kavanagh, Fisherman
James Kavanagh, Fisherman
Richard Kavanagh, Fisherman
Thomas Kavanagh, Fisherman
James Power, Fisherman
Patrick Evoy, Occupier
Darby Evoy, Fisherman
Patrick Chapman, Occupier
James Chapman, Fisherman
Nicholas Chapman, Fisherman
George Tuttill, Occupier
Thos. Tutthill, Fisherman
Richard Canaly [Connolly], Fisherman
Thomas Fortune, Fisherman
James Kavanagh, Occupier
Mathew FitzGerald, Occupier
James FitzGerald, Fisherman
John Doran, Fisherman
William Fitzcharld, Fisherman
Patk. Fitzcharld [gerald], Fisherman
John Whelan, Fisherman
John Power, Fisherman
William Kavanagh, Fisherman
James Kavanagh, Fisherman
James Colvin, Occupier
Patrick Kavanagh, Fisherman

ENDNOTES AND BIBLIOGRAPHY

The abbreviations listed here are used for sources that occur frequently; other sources are given in full.

AFM	Annals of the Four Masters	**P.R.O.N.I.**	Public Records Office, Northern Ireland
Arch. Ir.	Archaeology Ireland		
Cal. Doc. Ire.	Calendar of Documents relating to Ireland	*R.I.A. Proc.*	*Proceedings of the Royal Irish Academy*
		R.S.A.I. Jn.	*Journal of the Royal Society of Antiquaries of Ireland*
N.A.I.	National Archives of Ireland		
N.L.I.	National Library of Ireland	**S.M.R.**	Sites and Monuments Record
O.P.W.	Office of Public Works	**T.C.D.**	Trinity College Dublin
O.S.	Ordnance Survey of Ireland	*Wex. Hist. Soc. Jn.*	*Journal of the Wexford Historical Society*

THE HOOK PENINSULA

1. *The Civil Survey of the county of Wexford*, (ed.) R. C. Simington (Dublin, 1953), p. 167.

2. W. J. Smyth, 'Society and settlement in seventeenth-century Ireland' in Smyth and Whelan (eds), *Common ground* (Cork, 1988), p. 61.

LANDSCAPE AND ENVIRONMENT

1. Geological information is extracted from D. Tietzsch-Tyler and A. G. Sleeman (eds), *Geology of south Wexford* (Dublin, 1994).

2. T. B. Crimes, A. Insole and B. Williams, 'A rigid-bodied Ediacaran Biota from Upper Cambrian strata in Co. Wexford' in *Geological Journal*, xxx (1995), pp 89–109.

3. For additional information on fossils at Hook Head see L. Smyth, 'The carboniferous rocks of Hook Head, county Wexford' in *R.I.A. Proc.*, xxxix, sect. B (1930), pp 523–68.

4. For a detailed account of glacial activity in the region see E. Culleton, *The south Wexford landscape* (Dublin, 1980); R. Carter and J. Orford (eds), Irish Association for Quaternary Studies Field Guide No. 4, *The south and east coasts of Wexford* (Dublin, 1982).

5. M. J. Gardiner and P. Ryan, *Soils of county Wexford* (Dublin, 1964).

6. J. Hurley, *The south Wexford coast* (Kilmore, 1994); J. K. Lovatt, *Birds of Hook Head* (Irish Wildbird Conservancy, 1983); *Tintern Abbey visitors' guide* (Dúchas The Heritage Service, no date).

PREHISTORIC AND EARLY CHRISTIAN LANDSCAPES

1. M. Moore, *Archaeological inventory of county Wexford* (Dublin, 1996), p. 85, no. 876.

2. G. Stout, 'Wexford in prehistory 5000 BC to 300 AD' in K. Whelan (ed.), *Wexford: history and society* (Dublin, 1987), pp 11–22.

3. G. Stout and M. Stout, 'Early landscapes: from prehistory to plantation' in F. Aalen, K. Whelan and M. Stout (eds), *Atlas of the Irish rural landscape* (Cork, 1997), pp 41–3.

4. Quoted in Raftery, *Pagan Celtic Ireland*, p. 204.

5. G. Orpen, 'Ptolemy's map of Ireland' in *R.S.A.I. Jn.*, xxiv (1894), pp 21–97; J. Andrews, *Shapes of Ireland* (Dublin, 1997), pp 26–9.

6. Moore, *Archaeological inventory*, p. 26, nos. 225, 226, 228; T. J. Westropp, 'Five large earthworks in the barony of Shelburne, county Wexford' in *R.S.A.I. Jn.*, xlviii (1918), pp 1–18.

7. E. Culleton, *Celtic and Early Christian Wexford* (Dublin, 1999), p. 38. See also pp 128–9 for Alloc and Dubhán.

8. M. Clinton, 'Settlement patterns in the early historic kingdom of Leinster' in A. P. Smyth (ed.), *Seanchas: studies in early and medieval Irish archaeology, history and literature in honour of F. J. Byrne* (Dublin, 2000), p. 277.

9. M. Stout, *The Irish ringfort* (Dublin, 1997), p. 32.

10. Stout and Stout, 'Early landscapes' pp 44–7; Stout, *The Irish ringfort*, p. 24.

11. Moore, *Archaeological inventory*, pp 28–43. The identification of removed sites by aerial photography is discussed in G. F. Barrett 'Recovering the hidden landscape' in Aalen, Stout and Whelan (eds), pp 64–6; also G. F. Barrett, 'Flights of discovery: archaeological air survey of Ireland 1989–2000' in *Journal of Irish archaeology*, xi (2002), pp 1–29.

12. P. H. Hore, *History of the town and county of Wexford*, 6 vols (London, 1900-11),ii, p. 147.

13. Moore, *Archaeological inventory*, p. 117, no. 1163; Culleton, *Celtic and Early Christian Wexford* , p. 210.

14. D. Kelly, 'Irish high crosses: some evidence from the plainer examples' in *R.S.A.I. Jn.*, cxvi (1986), p. 56.

15. A. Lucas, 'The horizontal mill in Ireland' in *R.S.A.I. Jn.*, lxxxiii (1953), pp 39–41; T. McErlean, 'Tidal power in the seventh and eight centuries AD' in *Archaeology Ireland*, xv no. 2 (Summer 2001), pp 10–14.

16. Hore, *Wexford*, iii, p. 224.

17. Culleton, *Celtic and Early Christian Wexford*, pp 128–9.

18. The first known mention of the name was in the late fourteenth century; Hore, *Wexford*, iv, p. 405.

19. Moore, *Archaeological inventory*, p. 124, no. 1213.

20. T. Breen, 'St Brecaun's church, Portersgate' in I. Bennett (ed.), *Excavations* (Dublin, 1988), pp 30–1.

21. For a discussion on townlands see W. Reeves, 'On the townland distribution of Ireland' in *R.I.A. Proc.*, vii (1857–61), pp 473–90.

22. Viking activity in county Wexford is examined in B. Colfer, *Arrogant trespass: Anglo-Norman Wexford 1169–1400* (Enniscorthy, 2002), pp 12–24.

23. D. Cowman, 'The German mining operation at Bannow Bay' in *Wex. Hist. Soc. Jn.*, xi (1986–87), pp 67–82.

24. J. A. Graham-Campbell, 'The Viking Age silver hoards of Ireland' in *Proceedings of the seventh Viking congress* (Dublin, 1976), p. 64.

25. J. Bradley and A. Halpin, 'The topographical development of Scandinavian and Anglo-Norman Waterford' in W. Nolan and T. Power (eds), *Waterford: history and society* (Dublin, 1992), p. 105.

26. *AFM*, i, p. 543.

27. Graham-Campbell, 'Silver hoards,' p. 64.

MANOR AND MONASTERY: THE MEDIEVAL LANDSCAPE

1. A comprehensive account of the Anglo-Normans in Ireland can be found in G. Orpen, *Ireland under the Normans*, 4 vols. (Oxford, 1911–20); a broader analysis of the period is given in S. Duffy, *Ireland in the Middle Ages* (Dublin, 1997).

2. A detailed analysis of Anglo-Norman settlement in county Wexford is presented in B. Colfer, *Arrogant trespass: Anglo-Norman Wexford 1169–1400* (Enniscorthy, 2002).

3. Contemporary accounts of Anglo-Norman activity in the south-west Wexford region are given in A. B. Scott and F. X. Martin (eds), *Expugnatio Hibernica, the conquest of Ireland, by Gerald de Barry* (Dublin, 1978), pp 31–66, and G. Orpen (ed.), *The song of Dermot and the earl* (Oxford, 1892), ll. 441–60, 1404–8, 1500–15.

4. *Expugnatio*, p. 35; *Song*, l. 3070.

5. The significance of the part played by Baginbun in the Anglo-Norman campaign is reviewed in K. O'Conor, 'A reinterpretation of the earthworks at Baginbun, Co. Wexford' in J. Kenyon and K. O'Conor (eds), *The medieval castle in Ireland and Wales* (Dublin, 2003), pp 17–31.

6. Orpen, *Normans*, i, p. 393.

7. Land grants made by the Anglo-Norman regime in the barony of Shelburne are detailed in Colfer, *Arrogant trespass*, pp 98–102.

8. A knight's fee was the amount of land given to a knight in return for forty days in the service of his lord. A payment of £2, known as scutage, could be substituted for a knight's service. The knights' fees of county Wexford are detailed in E. St John Brooks, *Knights' fees in counties Wexford, Carlow and Kilkenny* (Dublin, 1950).

9. J. Bradley, 'Planned Anglo-Norman towns in Ireland' in H. Clarke and A. Simms (eds), *The comparative history of urban origins in non-Roman Europe* (Oxford, 1985), pp 414–21.

10. H. S. Sweetman (ed.), *Calendar of Documents relating to Ireland*, 5 vols. (London, 1875–86), i, no. 1872.

11. Hore, *Wexford*, iii, pp 201–19.

12. *Cal. Doc. Ire.*, ii, no. 1330.

13. G. Orpen, 'Charters of earl Richard Marshal of the forests of Ross and Taghmon' in E. St John Brooks (ed.), *R.S.A.I. Jn.*, lxiv (1934), p. 56.

14. Colfer, *Arrogant trespass*, pp 72–4.

15. Hore, *Wexford*, ii, pp 211–62.

16. H. F. Hore (ed.), 'A choreographic account of the southern part of the county of Wexford, written anno 1684: by Robert Leigh, esq., of Rosegarland, in that county' in *R.S.A.I. Jn.*, v (1858–9), p. 455.

17. Moore, *Archaeological inventory*, pp 153–4.

18. J. N. Brewer, *The beauties of Ireland, being original delineations, topographical, historical and biographical, of each county*, 2 vols. (1826), i, pp 362–3; M. Byrne, 'The results of a resistivity survey undertaken at Clonmines, county Wexford' in *Wex. Hist. Soc. Jn.*, xv (1994–5), pp 67–73.

19. S. Lewis, *A topographical dictionary of Ireland* (1837), i, p. 372.

20. Research on manorial villages in Ireland is summarised in T. Barry *The archaeology of medieval Ireland* (London, 1987), ch. 4.

21. R. Stalley, *The Cistercian monasteries of Ireland* (London and New Haven, 1987).

22. J. T. Gilbert, *Chartularies of St Mary's Abbey, Dublin*, 2 vols. (London, 1884), i, p. 357.

23. Hore, *Wexford*, iii, p. 60.

24. *Cal. Doc. Ire.*, i, no. 1993.

25. The founding charter is given in *Chartul. St Mary's*, ii, pp 151–4; Hore, *Wexford*, iii, pp 34–44.

26. N. B. White (ed.), *Extents of Irish monastic possessions 1540–1* (Dublin, 1943) pp 353–7.

27. *Chartul. St Mary's*, ii, pp 307–8.

28. J. Bernard, 'The foundation of Tintern Abbey, county Wexford' in *R.I.A. Proc.*, C (1917), pp 527–9; Orpen, *Normans*, ii, p. 207.

29. Hore, *Wexford*, ii, p. 16.

30. *Irish monastic possessions*, p. 358.

31. J. B. Sheppard (ed.), *Letter books of Christ Church, Canterbury*, 3 vols. (London, 1887–9), iii, pp 248, 363.

32. *Chartul. St Mary's*, ii, pp 17–20.

33. A. Gwynn and R. Hadcock *Medieval religious houses Ireland* (Dublin, 1970), p. 177.

34. R. Bartlett, *The making of Europe: conquest, colonization and cultural change 950–1350* (London, 1993), p. 264.

35. P. P. Read, *The Templars* (London, 2001), pp 283–301.

36. For a general background, see H. Wood, 'The Templars in Ireland' in *R.I.A. Proc.*, xxvi, C (1907), pp 327–71; C. Faulkner, 'The Hospital of St John of Jerusalem in Ireland' in ibid., pp 275–317.

37. *Cal. Doc. Ire.*, iii, no. 666.

38. Hore, *Wexford*, iii, p. 83, n. 2.

39. *Chartul. St Mary's*, ii, p. 305.

40. *Irish monastic possessions*, pp 100–3.

41. *Cal. Doc. Ire.*, ii, no. 1447, 1448, 1541; iii, no. 20, 622, 666.

42. *Chartul. St Mary's*, ii, p. 183.

43. Moore, *Archaeological inventory*, p. 144, no. 1364; p. 184, no. 1583.

44. *Chartul. St Mary's*, ii, p. 336.

45. Wood, 'Templars,' p. 350.

46. *Memoranda roll*, p. 350.

47. *Calendar of the ancient deeds and muniments preserved in the Pembroke estate office, Dublin* (Dublin, 1891), pp 11–13.

48. Colfer, *Arrogant trespass*, pp 202–5.

49. *Calendar patent rolls James I (1618)*, p. 422.

50. Hore, *Wexford*, iv, p. 281.

51. *Letter books of Christ Church, Canterbury*, iii, pp 248, 363.

52. Hore, *Wexford*, ii, p. 27.

53. Hore, *Wexford*, iv, p. 312.

54. *39th Rep. D.K.I.*, p. 43.

55. J. Otway-Ruthven, 'The character of Norman settlement in Ireland' in *Historical Studies*, v (1965), p. 80.

56. Stalley, *Cistercian monasteries*, pp 34–7.

57. G. Mac Niocaill, *Na Manaigh Liath in Éirinn 1142–c. 1600* (Baile Átha Cliath, 1959), pp 45–8.

58. Fr. Colmcille, *The story of Mellifont* (Dublin, 1958), pp xxiv–xxxiv; Stalley, *Cistercian monasteries*, p. 20.

59. Moore, *Archaeological inventory*, p. 121, no. 1187; p. 168, no. 1503; p. 134, no. 1283; p. 177, no. 1539; p. 184, no. 1583.

60. D. Sweetman, *The medieval castles of Ireland* (Cork, 1999), pp 95–6; 'The hall-house in Ireland' in Kenyon and O'Conor (eds), *The medieval castle in Ireland and Wales*, p. 128.

61. Moore, *Archaeological inventory*, p. 98, no. 989; p. 114, no. 1155; p. 41, no. 371.

62. G. Mac Niocaill, *Na buirgéisí* (Baile Átha Cliath, 1964), ii, p. 528.

63. *Irish monastic possessions*, p. 195.

64. *Chartul. St Mary's*, ii, p. 155.

65. Hore, *Wexford*, iv, pp 275–7.

66. For an account of the construction of a moated site see Hore, *Wexford*, i, p. 31.

67. *Irish monastic possessions*, pp 100–3.

68. Ibid., Dunbrody, pp 358–63; Tintern, pp 358–63; Kilcloggan, pp 100–3.

69. J. Burtchaell, 'The south Kilkenny farm villages' in Smyth and Whelan (eds), *Common ground*, pp 110–23.

70. Moore, *Archaeological inventory*, pp 170–83; nos. 1512, 1553, 1554, 1572; W. Jeffrey, *The castles of county Wexford*, E. Culleton (ed.); typescript produced by Wexford Historical Society (1979), pp 166–7.

71. Moore, *Archaeological inventory*, p. 134, no. 1283; p. 168, no. 1503; p. 177, no. 1539.

72. Hore, *Wexford*, iv, p. 6.

73. H. Leask, 'Slade castle, county Wexford' in *R.S.A.I. Jn.*, lxxxi (1951), pp 198–202; D. Sweetman, 'The hall-house in Ireland', p. 130.

74. R. Roche, *Tales of the Wexford coast* (Enniscorthy, 1993), pp 33–4.

MEDIEVAL BUILDINGS

1. Stalley, *Cistercian monasteries*, p. 244 and *passim*; H. Leask, *Irish churches and monastic buildings*, ii, pp 83–4.

2. Stalley, *Cistercian monasteries*, pp 111–12.

3. *Tintern Abbey visitors' guide* (Dúchas The Heritage service).

4. E. Eames and T. Fanning, *Irish medieval tiles* (Dublin, 1988), pp 105, 119, 121, 124.

5. Stalley, *Cistercian monasteries*, pp 189, 198.

6. Ibid., p. 233.

7. *Tintern Abbey Visitors' guide.*

8. Grose, *Antiquities*, i, p. 51.

9. Moore, *Archaeological inventory*, pp 153–4.

10. R. Glasscock, 'Moated sites and deserted boroughs and villages; two neglected aspects of Anglo-Norman settlement in Ireland' in N. Stephens and R. Glasscock (eds), *Irish geographical studies* (Belfast, 1970), p. 170.

TURMOIL AND CHANGE: THE IRISH RECOVERY

1. Orpen, *Normans*, iii, p. 291.

2. Colfer, *Arrogant trespass*, pp 71–82.

3. J. Lydon, 'The impact of the Bruce invasion' in *New history of Ireland*, ii, pp 3–37; A Gwynn, 'The Black Death in Ireland' in *Studies*, xxiv (1935), pp 25–42.

4. W. Smyth, 'Society and settlement in seventeenth-century Ireland: the evidence of the '1659 census" in *Common ground*, p. 61.

5. Hore, *Wexford*, v, pp 412–13.

6. W. Jeffrey, *Castles of county Wexford.*

7. Hore, *Wexford*, ii, p. 217.

8. Ibid., vi, p. 204.

9. S. Cloney, 'Some stone artifacts of south-west Wexford' in *Wexford Hist. Soc. Jn.*, xii (1988), pp 92–7.

10. Hore, *Wexford*, iv, p. 312.

11. B. Murtagh, Fethard Castle, county Wexford: an architectural and archaeological report (1993).

12. J. O'Callaghan, 'Fortified houses of the sixteenth century in south Wexford' in *Wex. Hist. Soc. Jn.*, viii (1980–1) pp 22–6.

13. Hore, *Wexford*, iv, pp 322–4.

14. Hore, *Wexford*, ii, pp 217–18.

15. T. W. Moody and F. X. Martin (eds), *The course of Irish history* (Cork, 1967), pp 174–82.

16. Hore, *Wexford*, ii, pp 72–3.

17. M. J. Haren (ed.), *Calendar of papal letters relating to Britain and Ireland*, xix, p. 240.

18. *Med. rel. houses*, pp 131–2, 142–3, 297.

THE TOWER OF HOOK

1. *Cal. Doc. Ire.*, i, nos. 2811, 2872.

2. D. Hague and R. Christie, *Lighthouses, their architecture, history and archaeology* (Llandysul, 1975), p. 14.

3. D. Crouch, *William Marshal: court, career and chivalry in the Angevin empire 1147–1219* (London, 1990), p. 51.

4. R. Avent, 'William Marshal's building works at Chepstow Castle' in Kenyon and O'Conor (eds), *The medieval castle in Ireland and Wales*, pp 50–71; T. E. McNeill, 'Squaring circles: flooring round towers in Wales and Ireland' in ibid., pp 96–106.

5. Hore, *Wexford*, i, p. 219. Twelve medieval acres was equivalent to c. thirty statute acres; approximately the same acreage beside the tower is still referred to as 'the tower lands.'

6. Hore, *Wexford*, i, p. 407.

7. T.C.D. Ms. 1209, no. 64; E. Hogan (ed.), *Description of Ireland in 1598* (Dublin, 1878), p. 57.

8. Hore, *Wexford*, iv, p. 407.

9. Ibid., p. 408.

10. *Fifteenth annual report of the keeper of public records* (1825), p. 649.

11. Hore, 'Choreographic account,' p. 459.

12. New Ross Corporation minute books.

13. B. Long, *Bright light, blue water: the story of Irish lighthouses and their people* (Dublin, 1993), p. 65.

14. Hore, *Wexford*, iv, pp 409–11.

15. Barralet, *Tour through Wicklow and Wexford* (1780), p. 75.

16. New Ross Chamber of Commerce minute book.

17. *Waterford Chronicle*, 6 September 1791.

18. 'A tour through the county of Wexford' in *Walker's Hibernian Magazine* (1792), p. 487.

19. J. S. Sloane, *Manual for lightkeepers* (Dublin, 1873).

CONFLICT AND CONFISCATION: THE SEVENTEENTH-CENTURY LANDSCAPE

1. Comprehensive accounts of this period can be found in P. Lenihan, *Confederate Catholics at war* (Cork, 2001); M. Ó Siochrú, *Confederate Ireland 1642–1649: a constitutional and political analysis* (Dublin, 1999). For a concise overview see J. Lydon, *The making of Ireland* (London, 1998), pp 163–96.

2. Lenihan, *Confederate Catholics*, p. 49.

33. J. Ohlmeyer, "The Dunkirk of Ireland': Wexford privateers during the 1640s' in *Wex. Hist. Soc. Jn.*, xii (1988–89), pp 23–49; N. Furlong, 'Life in Wexford port 1600–1800' in Whelan (ed.), *Wexford*, pp 150–72.

4. Details of the Confederate war of the 1640s and the subsequent Cromwellian campaign in the Hook region are taken from Hore, *Wexford*, iv, pp 57–225. An analysis of the Confederate seige of Duncannon Fort is given in Lenihan, *Confederate Catholics*, pp 40–4, 178–89.

5. An account of the attack on Tintern is given in Hore, *Wexford*, ii, pp 133–44.

6. R. C. Simington (ed.), *The Civil Survey of the county of Wexford* (Dublin, 1953), p. 167.

7. Ibid.; Down Survey maps (1655), N.L.I. ms. 725.

8. K. Whelan, 'A list of those from county Wexford implicated in the 1641 Rebellion' in *The Past*, xvii (1990), pp 24–54; Depositions Trinity College, Dublin, T.C.D. Ms 818, Wexford, i; T.C.D. Ms 819, Wexford, ii.

9. W. Smyth, 'Society and settlement in seventeenth-century Ireland: the evidence of the '1659 Census" in Smyth and Whelan (eds), *Common ground*, pp 55–83; J. Ranson, 'A census of Ireland c. 1659: baronies of Bantry and Shelburne' in *The Past*, v (1949), pp 150–60.

10. Lewis, *Topographical dictionary*, ii, p. 616.

11. *An express from Ross, 1707*, Dept. of early printed books, T.C.D.

12. L. Cullen, *The emergence of modern Ireland* (London, 1981), p. 87.

DUNCANNON FORT

1. This account of the development of Duncannon Fort is based on documents published in Hore, *Wexford*, iv, pp 3–256.

2. 'Choreographic account,' p. 453.

3. P. Kerrigan, *Castles and fortifications in Ireland 1485–1945* (Cork, 1995), p. 41.

4. Ibid., pp 59–60.

5. Ibid., p. 458–9.

6. Hore, *Wexford*, iv, p. 233.

7. Kerrigan, *Castles and fortifications*, pp 114–17.

8. S. Lewis, *Topographical dictionary*, i, p. 569.

9. S. Cloney, 'Martello towers' in *On the Hook* (Templetown Parish Magazine), x (1995), pp 14–15.

10. Kerrigan, *Castles and fortifications*, pp 251–2.

11. P. Power,'The royal and ancient fort of Duncannon' in *On the Hook*, vii (1992), pp 54–5.

A NEW REGIME: THE DEVELOPMENT OF THE ESTATE SYSTEM

1. E. M. Johnston-Liik, *History of the Irish parliament 1692–1800*, ii (Belfast, 2002), p. 355.

2. Hore, *Wexford*, ii, pp 85.

3. Details of the Colclough family are outlined in S. Cloney, 'The Colclough family' in *Wexford Hist. Soc. Jn.*, x (1984–5), pp 44–54; S. Cloney, 'The Colcloughs' in K. Whelan (ed.), *Tintern Abbey county Wexford* (Saltmills,[1991]), pp 19–40.

4. McPeake papers; Colclough letters, P.R.O.N.I., T.3048/C.

5. Hore, *Wexford*, iii, pp 131–4; an account of the Etchingham and Chichester families is given in S. Pierce, *Dunbrody Abbey county Wexford: monastery and monument* (Arthurstown, 1994), pp 18–23.

6. Hore, *Wexford*, iv, p. 293.

7. D. Sweetman, 'The fortified house in Ireland' in Smyth (ed.), *Seanchas*, p. 448.

8. Information on the Loftus family is taken from J. Lodge, *The peerage of Ireland*, vii (London, 1789), pp 246–70; B. Burke, *Peerage and baronetage* (1906), pp 590–1.

9. A. Malcomson, 'A house divided: the Loftus family, earls and marquesses of Ely, c. 1600–c. 1900' in D. Dickson and C. O'Grada (eds.), *Refiguring Ireland: essays in honour of L. M. Cullen* (Dublin, 2003), p. 188.

10. *Calendar patent rolls James I* (1618), p. 422.

11. Lodge, *Peerage*, p. 264.

12. J. Ainsworth (ed.), 'Loftus papers' in *Analecta Hibernica*, xxv (1967), no. 85.

13. Whelan, 'A list of those from county Wexford implicated in the 1641 rebellion', pp 24–54.

14. *Book of Survey and Distribution.*

15. J. Ainsworth (ed.), 'Loftus papers,' no. 89.

16. J. Ainsworth (ed.), 'Colclough papers' in *Analecta Hibernica*, xx (1958), pp 12–13.

17. Lydon, *The making of Ireland*, p. 237.

18. *Faulkner's Dublin Journal*, 4–7 June 1763.

19. D. Goodall, 'The freemen of Wexford in 1776' in *The Irish Genealogist*, v (1973), no. 1, pp 103–21; no. 2, pp 314–34; no. 4, pp 448–63.

20. Johnston-Liik, *Irish parliament*, ii, pp 355–9.

21. Hore, *Wexford*, ii, p. 148.

22. Grose, *Antiquities*, i, p. 50.

23. Pierce, *Dunbrody Abbey*, pp 20–2.

24. T. Reeves-Smyth, 'Demesnes' in Aalen, Whelan and Stout (eds), *Atlas*, pp 197–205.

25. Hore, 'Choreographic account,' pp 454–61.

26. 'Maps of the lordships and manors of Loftus Hall in the county of Wexford, 1771,' N.L.I., Ms 4153.

27. Possibly from the Irish 'ingir,' an anchor, or 'inghiúr,' a harbour or haven.

28. J. V. Gahan, *The secular priests of the diocese of Ferns* (Strasbourg, 2000), pp 352–3.

29. S. Cloney, 'South-west Wexford in 1798' in *Wex. Hist. Soc. Jn.*, xv (1994–5), p. 91.

30. T. Fanning and J. C. Hurst, 'A mid seventeenth-century pottery group and other objects from Ballyhack Castle, co. Wexford' in *R.I.A. Proc.*, xv, C (1975), pp. 103–24.

31. 'Loftus papers,' no. 124.

32. J. Rutty, *Natural history of Dublin*, ii (Dublin, 1772), p. 135.

33. R. Frazer, *Statistical survey of county Wexford* (Dublin, 1807).

34. 'Colclough papers,' p. 15.

35. Lewis, *Topographical dictionary*, i, p. 78.

36. *Wexford Independent*, 9 March 1864.

37. J. Burtchaell, 'The south Kilkenny farm villages' in Smyth and Whelan (eds), *Common ground*, pp 110–23.

38. K. Whelan, 'The modern landscape: from plantation to present' in Aalen, Whelan and Stout (eds), *Atlas*, pp. 80–1.

39. Loftus estate maps, 1872.

40. 1841 Census.

41. K. Whelan, 'Towns and villages' in Aalen, Whelan and Stout (eds), *Atlas*, pp 187–91.

42. J. Pierce, *Arthurstown: the story of a village* (Arthurstown, no date).

43. R. Griffiths, *General valuation of rateable property in Ireland: county Wexford* (Dublin, 1853),p. 90.

44. I. Ward, 'A note on the Scottish Presbyterians of Duncannon' in *Wex. Hist. Soc. Jn.*, xvi (1996–7), pp 167–70.

45. J. B. Trotter, *A walk through county Wexford in 1812* (Dublin, 1819); quoted in Whelan (ed.), *Tintern Abbey, county Wexford*, pp 45–6.

46. Lewis, *Topographical dictionary*, ii, p. 543.

47. Hore, *Wexford*, iv, p. 328.

48. Hore, *Wexford*, iv, pp 333–4.

49. Hore, 'Choreographic account,' pp 460–1.

50. Loftus maps, 1771.

51. Lewis, *Topographical dictionary*, i, pp 627–8.

52. W. Smyth, 'Flax cultivation in Ireland: the development and demise of a regional staple' in Smyth and Whelan (eds), *Common ground*, pp 234–52.

53. N.L.I., Ms 29735 (3).

54. R. Stephenson, *Report on the state of the linen trade* (1762), pp 18–20.

55. Whelan (ed.), *Tintern Abbey*, pp 45–6.

56. P. Corish,' Two centuries of Catholicism in county Wexford' in Whelan (ed.), *Wexford*, p. 222. For a general background see P. Corish, *The Catholic community in the seventeenth and eighteenth centuries* (Dublin, 1981).

57. P. Corish, 'The diocese of Ferns and the Penal days' in *The Past*, viii (1970), p. 6.

58. 'Report on the state of popery in Ireland, 1731' in *Archivium Hibernicum*, iv (1915), pp 166–71.

59. Loftus estate maps, 1771.

60. N. Furlong, 'The times and life of Nicholas Sweetman, bishop of Ferns (1744–86)' in *Wex. Hist. Soc. Jn.*, ix (1983–4), pp 1–19.

61. W. Grattan Flood, 'The diocesan manuscripts of Ferns during the rule of Bishop Sweetman (1745–1786)' in *Archivium Hibernicum*, ii (1913), pp 100–5.

62. G. Fitzgerald, 'Estimates for baronies of minimum level of Irish-speaking among successive decennial cohorts' in *R.I.A. Proc.*, C, lxxxiv (1984), p. 132 and map 7.

63. R.I.A. MS 23 B 38; S. de Vál, 'Oidhreacht Ghaelach Loch Garman,' *Irisleabhar Mhá Nuad 1992*, pp 96–100.

64. Trotter, *Walks*, p. 84.

65. *Commission of public instruction, Ireland*, 1st Report, 1835, p. 64b.

66. Hore, *Wexford*, vi, p. 269–70.

67. J. V. Gahan, *The secular priests of the diocese of Ferns* (Strasbourg, 2000), p. 353.

68. Gahan, *Secular priests*, p. 23.

69. S. Cloney, 'Poulfur church' in *On the Hook*, vi (1991), p. 4.

70. Cullen, *Modern Ireland*, p. 94.

71. J. Mannion, 'The Irish migrations to Newfoundland' (unpublished lecture, 1973); 'A transatlantic merchant fishery: Richard Walsh of New Ross and the Sweetmans of Newbawn in Newfoundland 1734–1862' in Whelan (ed.), *Wexford*, pp 373–421; 'The maritime trade of Waterford in the eighteenth century' in Smyth and Whelan (eds), *Common ground*, pp. 208–33; 'Vessels, masters and seafaring: patterns of voyages in Waterford commerce' in W. Nolan and T. Power (eds), *Waterford: history and society* (Dublin, 1992), pp 373–402; C. Byrne, 'The Waterford colony in Newfoundland' in Nolan and Power, *Waterford*, pp 351–72.

72. Patrick Kennedy, *The banks of the Boro* (Dublin, 1875; reprinted by Duffry Press, Enniscorthy, 1989), p. 151.

73. John Mannion, personal communication.

74. K. Whelan, 'County Wexford priests in Newfoundland' in *Wex. Hist. Soc. Jn.*, x (1984–5), pp 55–68.

75. A description of Tilting, an Irish village on Fogo Island off Newfoundland, is given in R. Mellin, *Tilting: house launching, slide hauling, potato trenching, and other tales from a Newfoundland fishing village* (New York, 2003); see also P. Devine, *Devine's folklore of Newfoundland* (St John's, 1937).

76. Reeves-Smyth, 'Demesnes' in Aalen, Whelan and Stout (eds), *Atlas*, pp 197–205.

77. Loftus estate maps, 1771.

78. Jobson's map of Waterford Harbour, 1591, Ms dept. T.C.D.

79. Hore, 'Choreographic account,' p. 459.

80. Hore, *Wexford*, iv, p. 379.

81. Loftus estate maps, 1771.

82. O.S. Wexford, sheets 49, 54.

83. 1841 Census.

84. J. Otway-Ruthven, 'The organisation of Anglo-Irish agriculture in the Middle Ages' in *R.S.A.I. Jn.*, lxxxi (1951), pp 1–13.

THE EVOLUTION OF SLADE

1. Details taken from a manuscript history of the Mansell family, pp 160–4.

2. *Wexford Chronicle*, 28 July–4 August 1777.

3. C. Smith, *The antient and present state of the county and city of Waterford* (Dublin, 1746), pp 250–1.

4. Loftus estate papers.

5. *First report of the commissioners of education* (1826), pp 826–7.

6. 'Tour in Wexford' in *Walkers Hibernian Magazine*, 1790.

7. Lewis, *Topographical dictionary*, ii, p. 561.

8. N.A.I.; O.P.W. 8 337/2; 337/3.

AN EVOLVING SOCIETY

1. For an analysis of eighteenth-century Ireland, see K. Whelan, *The tree of liberty* (Cork, 1996). The dispersal of Wexford families is mapped in Whelan, *Fellowship of freedom*, p. 18. The eighteenth-century status of the Redmond family is documented in the Stuart papers, vol. 152 f. 126; vol. 261 f. 96.

2. Cullen, *Modern Ireland*, p. 251.

3. The background to the rebellion is discussed in ibid., pp 193–233.

4. A narrative account of the rebellion is given in D. Gahan, *The people's rising* (Dublin, 1995).

5. McPeake papers; Colclough letters.

6. Activity in the Hook region during the 1798 Rebellion is summarised in Cloney, 'South-west Wexford in 1798', pp 74–97.

7. D. Gahan, 'New Ross, Scullabogue and the 1798 Rebellion in southwestern Wexford' in *The Past*, xxi (1998), pp 3–37; 'The Scullabogue massacre 1798' in *History Ireland* iv, no. 3 (Autumn, 1996), pp 27–31.

8. R. O'Donnell, ''Liberty or death': the United Irishmen in New South Wales, 1800–4' in T. Bartlett, D. Dickson, D. Keogh and K. Whelan (eds), *1798: a bicentary perspective* (Dublin, 2003), p. 610.

9. K. Whelan, *Fellowship of freedom* (Cork, 1998), p. 104.

10. P. Kerrigan, *Castles and fortifications in Ireland 1485–1945* (Cork, 1995), p. 276.

11. Kerrigan, *Castles*, pp 182–3.

12. Jones Hughes, 'Continuity and change' in Whelan (ed.), *Wexford*, pp 369–70; L. O'Connor, *Parish of Tintern* (Ballycullane, no date), p. 9.

13. B. Colfer (ed.), *Templetown Church 1899–1999, Centenary souvenir booklet* (Templetown, 1999).

14. *First report of the commissioners of education* (1826), pp 826–7.

15. *Commission of public instruction* (1835), p. 54b.

16. Lydon, *The making of Ireland*, p. 299.

17. K. Whelan, 'The Catholic parish, the Catholic chapel and village development in Ireland' in *Irish Geography*, xvi (1983), pp 1–15.

18. Whelan, 'The modern landscape' in Aalen, Whelan and Stout (eds), *Atlas*, pp 87–92.

19. For an overview of the Famine, see Lydon, *The making of Ireland*, pp 301–5.

20. An account of the Famine in county Wexford is given in A. Kinsella, *County Wexford in the Famine years* (Enniscorthy, 1995).

21. M. Gwinnell, 'The Famine years in county Wexford' in *Wex. Hist. Soc. Jn.*, ix (1983–4), p. 50.

22. Census of Ireland 1841 to 1911.

23. Grand Jury Presentments for county Wexford (1846).

24. Gwinnell, 'Famine years in Wexford,' p. 48.

25. N.A.I., O.P.W. 8/337/2; 337/3.

26. Whelan, 'The modern landscape,' pp 90–2.

27. *Evidence taken before the commission appointed to inquire into the occupation of land in Ireland* (1844), p. 469.

28. M. Gwinnell, 'Some aspects of the economic life of county Wexford in the nineteenth century' in *Wex. Hist. Soc. Jn.*, x (1984–5), pp 21–2; Jones Hughes, 'Continuity and change in rural county Wexford' in Whelan (ed.), *Wexford*, p. 363.

29. McPeake papers; Colclough letters.

30. *Evidence taken before the commission appointed to inquire into the occupation of land in Ireland* (1844), pp 467–8.

31. *The Watchman* (Enniscorthy), 24 July 1869.

32. S. De Vál, 'Father Tom: the Land League priest' in *The Past*, xii (1978), pp 23–30.

33. *The People* (Wexford), 1881.

34. O'Hanlon Walsh's involvement in the Hook is detailed in M. Urwin, *A county Wexford family in the Land War: the O'Hanlon Walshs of Knocktartan* (Dublin, 2002).

35. *The People* (Wexford), 17 August 1881.

36. N.A.I., CSO RP 188/1882.

37. Ibid.

38. *The People*, 26 April, 21 June, 1882.

39. *The People*, 21 January 1885.

40. *The People*, 10 February 1886.

41. *The People*, 2 September 1886.

42. N. Furlong and J. Hayes, *County Wexford in the rare oul' times*, ii (Wexford, 1987), pp 13–16.

43. An account of the sale of the Loftus estate to the tenants is given in *The People*, 9 July 1913.

44. Whelan, 'Modern landscape,' p. 95.

LOFTUS HALL

1. A. Malcomson, 'The Loftus family,' p. 187.

2. Ibid., p. 210.

3. T. Walsh, 'The history of Loftus Hall' in *Wex. Hist. Soc. Jn.*, v (1974–5), pp 32–8.

4. D. Rowe and E. Scallan, *Houses of Wexford* (Whitegate, 2004), no. 671.

5. *The People*, 9 July 1913.

6. Sr M. O'Connor, 'The Rosminian sisters in Loftus Hall' in *On the Hook* (1988), p 14.

TRADITIONAL LIFESTYLES

1. From documents in the possession of Jim Cullen, whose family owned the mill in later years.

2. Hore, 'Choreographic account,' p. 458.

3. Personal communication from his nephew, Aidan Devereux.

4. Loftus estate maps, 1872, N.L.I.

5. J. Parle, *Mumming in county Wexford* (Wexford, 2001), pp 155–63.

6. *The Watchman*, 23 June 1906.

7. J. B. Trotter, *A walk through county Wexford in 1812* (Dublin, 1818). In 1813, Trotter was arrested at Porter's Gate for non-payment of debts and sentenced to two weeks in prison. Trotter, a former secretary to the liberal politician Charles James Fox, claimed that his arrest had been instigated by the right-wing Loftus–Tottenham faction because of his support for Catholic Emancipation (*Wexford Herald*, 15 March 1813).

8. N.L.I. Ms 14,038.

9. R. Roche, *Tales of the Wexford coast* (Enniscorthy, 1993), pp 102–23.

10. Details of the event are taken from J. Doyle *The Helen Blake: the last Fethard lifeboat* (Fethard, no date).

THE MODERN LANDSCAPE

1. C. Deacon, *Wexford's co-operatives, 1895–1989* (no date).

2. P. Cummins, 'War of Independence' in *On the Hook*, no. 10 (1995), pp 28–9. Peter Cummins was an active member of the South Wexford Brigade of the old I.R.A.

3. *The People*, 23 October 1920; *The Free Press*, 12 February 1921, 21 January 1922.

4. O. Quinn, 'The coastwatching service' in *The Irish Sword*, xix (1993–5), pp 91–2.

5. H. Butler, *Escape from the anthill* (Mullingar, 1985), pp 134–40.

6. *Templetown: profile of a peninsula* (Templetown Parish Development Group, 1995), pp 28–30.

7. Lewis, *Topographical dictionary*, i, pp 627–8.

8. P. Harbison, *Guide to the national monuments of Ireland* (Dublin, 1970), pp 245–50.

9. F. Aalen, 'Contemporary challenge' in Aalen, Whelan and Stout (eds), *Atlas*, pp 236–43; 'Management of the landscape' in ibid., pp 255–9.

10. Guidelines for suitable house designs are given in P. Geoghegan, *Building sensitively in the landscape of county Wexford* (Wexford, 1998).

11. A. Divall, *Wexford heritage and the challenge of change* (Enniscorthy, 2001).

12. P. Bacon and associates, *County Wexford: a rural development strategy* (Wexford, 2001).

13. 'Better farming for a better environment' in *REPS 2 Conference Proceedings* (Teagasc, 2001); 'Delivering for farming and the environment' in *National REPS Conference Proceedings* (Teagasc, 2002).

14. *REPS 2 Conference Proceedings*, pp 30–40.

THE PERSONALITY OF THE HOOK

1. P. Stanton, *Pugin* (New York, 1972), pp 70–2.

BIBLIOGRAPHY

Manuscript sources

Books of Survey and Distribution, vol. 12.

Colclough Papers, P.R.O.N.I. T3048/C

Colclough Papers, N.L.I.; Ainsworth report on papers in private keeping, pp 3097–3114.

Depositions Trinity College, Dublin. T.C.D. Ms 818 Wexford, i; T.C.D. Ms 819 Wexford, ii.

Down Survey maps (1655), N.L.I. Ms. 725.

Dunbrody Estate Maps, 1803, N.L.I. 21.F.20.

Dunbrody Estate Maps, 1825 (Wexford County Library).

Maps of the lordships and manors of Loftus Hall in the county of Wexford, 1771, N.L.I., Ms. 4153.

Tithe Applotment Books, N.A.I.

Valuation survey of the Ely estate in county Wexford, 1872, N.L.I.

Printed primary sources

Ainsworth, J. and MacLysaght, E. (eds), 'Colclough papers' in *Analecta Hibernica*, xx (Dublin, 1958), pp 3–16.

An express from Ross (Dublin, 1707), Dept. of early printed books, T.C.D.

Annals of the kingdom of Ireland by the four masters, ed. J. O'Donovan, 7 vols. (Dublin, 1848–51).

Brooks, E. St John (ed.), *Knights' fees in counties Wexford, Carlow and Kilkenny* (Dublin, 1950).

Commission of public instruction, Ireland (Dublin, 1835).

Gilbert, J. T. (ed.), *Chartularies of St Mary's Abbey, Dublin*, 2 vols. (London, 1884).

Grand Jury Presentments for county Wexford.

Gwynn, A. and Hadcock, R. N., *Medieval religious houses Ireland* (Dublin, 1970).

Hore, H. F. (ed.), 'A choreographic account of the southern part of the county of Wexford, written anno 1684: by Robert Leigh, esq., of Rosegarland, in that county' in *R.S.A.I. Jn.*, v (1858–9), pp 451–67.

Hore, P. H., *History of the town and county of Wexford*, 6 vols. (London, 1900–11).

Lewis, S., *A topographical dictionary of Ireland*, 2 vols. (London, 1837).

'Loftus papers' in *Analecta Hibernica* xxv (Dublin, 1967).

McNeill, C. (ed.), *Registrum de Kilmainham*, 1326–50 (Dublin, 1932).

Meadows, H. L., *Alphabetical index to the townlands and towns of the county of Wexford* (Dublin, 1861).

Moore, M., *Archaeological inventory of county Wexford* (Dublin, 1996).

O'Flanagan, M., (compiler), *Letters containing information relative to the antiquities of the county of Wexford collected during the progress of the Ordnance Survey in 1840*, 2 vols. (Bray, 1933).

Orpen, G. (ed.), *The song of Dermot and the earl* (Oxford, 1892).

Scott, A. B. and Martin, F. X. (eds), *Expugnatio Hibernica, the conquest of Ireland, by Gerald de Barry* (Dublin, 1978).

Sheppard, J. B. (ed.), *Letter books of Christ Church, Canterbury*, 3 vols. (London, 1887–9).

Simington, R. C. (ed.), *The Civil Survey of the county of Wexford* (Dublin, 1953).

Stout, G. et al., *Sites and monument record, county Wexford* (Dublin, 1987).

Sweetman, H. S. (ed.), *Calendar of documents relating to Ireland*, 5 vols. (London, 1875–86).

White, N. B. (ed.), *Extents of Irish monastic possessions 1540–1* (Dublin, 1943).

Secondary works

Aalen, F., 'The origin of enclosures in eastern Ireland' in N. Stephens and R. Glasscock (eds), *Irish geographical studies in honour of E. Estyn Evans* (Belfast, 1970), pp 209–23.

Aalen, F. (ed.), *The future of the Irish landscape* (Dublin, 1985).

Aalen, F., 'The re-housing of rural labourers in Ireland under the Labourers (Ireland) Act, 1883–1919' in *Journal of Historical Geography*, xii (1986), pp 287–306.

Aalen, F., 'Buildings' in Aalen, Whelan and Stout (eds), *Atlas*, pp 145–79.

Aalen, F., Whelan, K. and Stout, M. (eds), *Atlas of the Irish rural landscape* (Cork, 1997).

Andrews, J., 'Land and people, c. 1780' in Moody and Vaughan (eds), *New history of Ireland iv, eighteenth century* (1986), pp 236–64.

Andrews, J., *Shapes of Ireland* (Dublin, 1997).

Andrews, J., 'Landmarks in early Wexford cartography' in Whelan (ed.), *Wexford* (Dublin, 1987), pp. 447–66.

Barrett, G. F., 'Recovering the hidden archaeology of Ireland: the impact of aerial survey in the River Barrow valley 1989–9' in J. Konow (ed.), *Aerial archaeology in eastern and central Europe/Luftbildarchaologie in Ost- und Mitteleuropa, Forschungen zur archaologie im Land Brandenburg 3* (Potsdam, 1995), pp 45–59.

Barrett, G. F., 'Recovering the hidden landscape' in Aalen, Stout and Whelan (eds), *Atlas*, pp 64–6.

Barrett, G. F., 'Flights of discovery: archaeological air survey of Ireland, 1989–2000' in *Journal of Irish archaeology*, xi (2002), pp 1–29.

Barry, E., 'On ogham-stones seen in Kilkenny county' in *R.S.A.I. Jn.*, xxvi (1896), pp 127–9.

Barry, T., *Medieval moated sites of south-east Ireland* (Oxford, 1977).

Barry, T., *The archaeology of medieval Ireland* (London, 1987).

Barry, T., Cleary, R. M. and Hurley, M. (eds), *Late Viking age and medieval Waterford*, (Waterford, 1998).

Barry, T. (ed.), *A history of settlement in Ireland* (London and New York, 2000).

Barry, T., 'The defensive nature of Irish moated sites' in J. Kenyon and K. O'Conor (eds), *The medieval castle in Ireland and Wales* (Dublin, 2003), pp 182–93.

Bartlett, T., Dickson, D., Keogh, D. and Whelan, K. (eds), *1798: a bicentenary perspective* (Dublin, 2003).

Bennett, I., 'The settlement pattern of ringforts in county Wexford' in *R.S.A.I. Jn.*, cxix (1989), pp 50–61.

Bernard, J., 'The foundation of Tintern Abbey, county Wexford' in *R.I.A. Proc.*, C (1917), pp 527–9.

Bradley, J., 'Planned Anglo-Norman towns in Ireland' in H. Clarke and A. Simms (eds), *The comparative history of urban origins in non-Roman Europe* (Oxford, 1985).

Bradley, J. (ed.), *Settlement and society in medieval Ireland* (Kilkenny, 1988).

Bradley, J., 'The interpretation of Scandinavian settlement in Ireland' in Bradley (ed.), *Settlement and society*, pp. 49–78.

Bradley, J. and Halpin, A., 'The topographical development of Scandinavian and Anglo-Norman Waterford' in W. Nolan and T. Power (eds), *Waterford: history and society* (Dublin, 1992), pp 105–30.

Brewer, J. N., *The beauties of Ireland, being original delineations, topographical, historical and biographical, of each county*, 2 vols. (1826).

Burke, B., *Peerage and baronetage* (London, 1906).

Burtchaell, J., 'The south Kilkenny farm villages' in W. Smyth and K. Whelan (eds), *Common ground* (Cork, 1988), pp 110–23.

Butler, H., *Escape from the anthill* (Mullingar, 1985).

Butler, T. C., *Near restful waters: the Augustinians in New Ross and Clonmines* (Dublin, 1975).

Byrne, F., *Irish kings and high kings* (London, 1987).

Byrne, M. E., 'The results of a resistivity survey undertaken at Clonmines, county Wexford' in *Wex. Hist. Soc. Jn.*, xv (1994–5), pp 67–73.

Carter, R. and Orford, J., *Irish Association for Quaternary Research, Field guide no. 4: the south and east coasts of county Wexford* (Dublin, 1982).

Clarke, H., Ní Mhaonaigh, M. and Ó Floinn, R. (eds), *Ireland and Scandinavia in the early Viking age* (Dublin, 1998).

Clarke, H., 'Proto-towns and towns in Ireland and Britain in the ninth and tenth centuries' in Clarke, Ní Mhaonaigh and Ó Floinn (eds), *Ireland and Scandinavia*, pp 331–80.

Clinton, M., 'Settlement patterns in the early historic kingdom of Leinster (seventh to mid twelfth century)' in A. P. Smyth (ed.), *Seanchas: studies in early and medieval archaeology, history and literature in honour of F. J. Byrne* (Dublin, 2000), pp 275–98.

Cloney, S., 'The Colclough family' in *Wex. Hist. Soc. Jn.*, x (1984–5), pp 44–54.

Cloney, S., 'The Colcloughs' in K. Whelan (ed.), *Tintern Abbey*, (Saltmills, [1991]), pp 19–39.

Cloney, S., 'Some stone artifacts in south-west Wexford' in *Wex. Hist. Soc. Jn.*, xii (1988–9), pp 92–7.

Cloney, S., 'A Fethard sea-mystery' in *On the Hook*, viii (1993), pp 54–5.

Cloney, S., 'South-west Wexford in 1798' in *Wex. Hist. Soc. Jn.*, xv (1994–5), pp. 74–97.

Cloney, S., 'Martello towers' in *On the Hook*, x (1995), pp 14–15.

Colfer, B., *The promontory of Hook* (Wexford, 1978).

Colfer, B., 'The tower of Hook' in *Wex. Hist. Soc. Jn.*, x (1984–5), pp 69–78.

Colfer, B., 'Anglo-Norman settlement in county Wexford' in Whelan (ed.), *Wexford*, pp 65–101.

Colfer, B., 'Medieval Wexford' in *Wex. Hist. Soc. Jn.*, xiii (1990–1), pp 5–29.

Colfer, B., 'The Hook, county Wexford' in Aalen, Whelan and Stout (eds), *Atlas of the Irish rural landscape*, pp 262–76.

Colfer, B., *Arrogant trespass: Anglo-Norman Wexford 1169–1400* (Enniscorthy, 2002).

Colmcille, Fr., *The story of Mellifont* (Dublin, 1958).

Corish, P., 'The diocese of Ferns in the penal days' in *The Past*, viii (1970), pp 5–17.

Corish, P., *The Catholic community in the seventeenth and eighteenth centuries* (Dublin, 1981).

Corish, P., 'Two centuries of Catholicism in county Wexford' in Whelan (ed.), *Wexford* (Dublin, 1987) pp 222–47.

Cowman, D., 'The German mining operation at Bannow Bay' in *Wex. Hist. Soc. Jn.*, xi (1986–7), pp 67–82.

Crimes, T. B., Insole, A. and Williams, B. P. J., 'A rigid-bodied Ediacaran Biota from Upper Cambrian strata in Co. Wexford, Eire' in *Geological Journal*, xxx (1995), pp 89–109.

Croke, F. (ed.), *George Victor Du Noyer 1817–1869: hidden landscapes* (Dublin, 1995).

Crookshank, A. and Knight of Glin, *The painters of Ireland c. 1600–1920* (London, 1978).

Crouch, D., *William Marshal: court, career and chivalry in the Angevin empire 1147–1219* (London, 1990).

Cullen, L., *The emergence of modern Ireland 1600–1900* (London, 1981).

Cullen, L., 'Economic development: 1691–1750' in Moody and Vaughan (eds), *New history of Ireland iv, eighteenth century* (Oxford, 1986).

Cullen, L., 'The 1798 Rebellion in Wexford: United Irishman organisation, membership, leadership' in Whelan (ed.), *Wexford*, pp 248–95.

Cullen, L., 'Man, landscape and roads: the changing eighteenth-century landscape' in W. Nolan (ed.), *The shaping of Ireland* (Dublin, 1988), pp 123–36.

Culleton, E., *The south Wexford landscape* (Dublin, 1980).

Culleton, E., *Early man in county Wexford 5000 BC–300 BC* (Dublin, 1984).

Culleton, E., *Celtic and Early Christian Wexford* (Dublin, 1999).

Culleton, E. (ed), *Treasures of the landscape: county Wexford's rural heritage* (compiled by B. Culleton for the Wexford Organisation for Rural Development) (Wexford, 1994).

Deacon, C. F., *Wexford's co-operatives, 1895–1989* (Enniscorthy, no date).

Devine, P., *Devine's folklore of Newfoundland* (St John's, 1937).

De Courcy Ireland, J., 'County Wexford in maritime history' in Whelan (ed.), *Wexford*, pp 490–506.

de Paor, M. and de Paor, L., *Early Christian Ireland* (London, 1961).

de Vál, S., 'Father Tom: the Land League priest' in *The Past*, xii (1978), pp 23–30.

de Vál, S., 'Oidhreacht Ghaelach Loch Garman' in *Irisleabhar Mhá Nuad*, 1992, pp 75–107.

Doherty, C., 'Exchange and trade in early medieval Ireland' in *R.S.A.I. Jn.*, cx (1980), pp 67–89.

Doherty, C., 'The Vikings in Ireland: a review' in Clarke, Ní Mhaonaigh and Ó Floinn (eds), *Ireland and Scandinavia*, pp 288–230.

Doyle, I., 'The foundation of the Cistercian abbey of Dunbrody, county Wexford and its historical context' in *Wex. Hist. Soc. Jn.*, xiv (1992–3), pp 81–91.

Duffy, S., *Ireland in the Middle Ages* (Dublin, 1997).

Eames, E. and Fanning, T., *Irish medieval tiles* (Dublin, 1988).

Edwards, N., *The archaeology of early medieval Ireland* (London, 1990).

Estyn Evans, E., *The personality of Ireland* (Belfast, 1981).

Falkiner, C. L., 'The Hospital of St John of Jerusalem in Ireland' in *R.I.A. Proc.*, C, xxvi (1907), pp 275–317.

Fanning, T. and Hurst, J. G., 'A mid seventeenth-century pottery group and other objects from Ballyhack Castle, co. Wexford' in *R.I.A. Proc.*, lxxv (1975), pp 103–18.

Feehan, J. (ed.), *Environment and development in Ireland* (Dublin, 1992).

Ffrench, J., 'Dunbrody and its history' in *R.S.A.I. Jn.*, xxvi (1896), pp 336–48.

Ffrench, J., 'Group of bone and ivory objects from the Hook peninsula' in *R.S.A.I. Jn.*, xlii (1912), pp 67–8.

Finn, M., *A Wexford childhood 1915–30* (Dublin, 1998).

Flanagan, M.-T., *Irish society, Anglo-Norman settlers, Angevin kingship* (Oxford, 1989).

Frame, R., *Ireland and Britain 1170–1450* (London, 1998).

Fraser, R., *A statistical survey of county Wexford* (Dublin, 1807).

Furlong, N., *Dermot, king of Leinster and the foreigners* (Tralee, 1974).

Furlong, N. 'The times and life of Nicholas Sweetman, Bishop of Ferns (1744–85)' in *Wex. Hist. Soc. Jn.*, ix (1983–84), pp 1–19.

Furlong, N. and Hayes, J., *County Wexford in the rare oul' times*, ii (Wexford, 1987).

Furlong, N., *A history of county Wexford* (Dublin, 2003).

Gahan, D., 'The estate system of county Wexford 1641–1876' in Whelan (ed.), *Wexford* (Dublin, 1987), pp 201–21.

Gahan, D., 'The Scullabogue massacre' in *History Ireland* iv, no. 3 (1996), pp 27–31.

Gahan, D., 'New Ross, Scullabogue and the 1798 Rebellion in south-western Wexford' in *The Past*, xxi (1998), pp 3–37.

Gahan, J. V., *The secular priests of the diocese of Ferns* (Strasbourg, 2000).

Gardiner, M. J. and Ryan, P., *Soils of county Wexford* (Dublin, 1964).

Geoghegan, P. and Culligan, D., *Building sensitively in the landscapes of county Wexford* (Dublin, 1988).

Gillingham, J., 'Conquering the barbarians: war and chivalry in twelfth-century Britain' in *The Hoskins Journal: studies in medieval history*, iv (Woodbridge, 1993), pp 67–84.

Glasscock, R., 'The study of deserted medieval settlement in Ireland' in M. Beresford and J. Hurst (eds), *Deserted medieval village studies* (London, 1971), pp 279–301.

Goodall, D., 'The freemen of Wexford in 1776' in *The Irish Genealogist*, v (1973), no. 1, pp 103–21; no. 2, pp 314–34; no. 4, pp 448–63.

Goodall, D., ''All the cooking that could be used' – a county Wexford election in 1754' in *The Past*, xii (1978), pp 3–22.

Graham, B., 'The towns of medieval Ireland' in R. A. Butlin (ed.), *The development of the Irish town* (London, 1977), pp 28–60.

Graham. B., 'The definition and classification of medieval Irish towns' in *Irish geog.*, xxi (1988), pp 20–32.

Graham-Campbell, J. A., 'The Viking-age silver hoards of Ireland' in B. Almquist and D. Greene (eds), *Proceedings of the seventh Viking congress* (Dublin, 1976), pp 39–74.

Grattan-Flood, W. A., *History of the diocese of Ferns* (Waterford, 1916).

Graves, J. and Tuomey, J. C., 'The bay and town of Bannow' in *Transactions of the Kilkenny Archaeological Soc*iety, i, part 2 (1850), pp 187–210.

Graves, J., 'Notes on the topography and history of the parish of Hook, county of Wexford' in *R.S.A.I. Jn.*, iii (1854), pp 194–9.

Griffith, R., *General valuation of rateable property in Ireland: county Wexford* (Dublin, 1853).

Gwinnell, M., 'The Famine years in county Wexford' in *Wex. Hist. Soc. Jn.*, ix (1983–4), pp 36–54.

Gwinnell, M., 'Some aspects of the economic life of county Wexford in the nineteenth century' in *Wex. Hist. Soc. Jn.*, x (1984–5), pp 5–24.

Gwynn, E. (ed. and trans.), *The Metrical Dindshenchas*, 5 vols. (Dublin, 1924).

Hadden, G., 'Some earthworks in county Wexford' in *Cork History and Archaeological Society Journal*, lxviiii (1964), pp 118–22.

Hague, D. and Christie, R., *Lighthouses, their architecture, history and archaeology* (Llandysul, 1975).

Harbison, P., *Guide to national and historic monuments of Ireland* (Dublin, 1992).

Haren, M. (ed.), *Calendar of papal letters relating to Great Britain and Ireland*, xix (Dublin, 1978), p. 240.

Holland, C. H., *The geology of Ireland* (Edinburgh, 2001).

Hurley, J., 'The Keeragh Islands: a review' in *Wex. Hist. Soc. Jn.*, xii (1988–9), pp 86–91.

Hurley, J. *The south Wexford coast* (Kilmore, 1994).

Johnston-Liik, E. M., *History of the Irish parliament 1692–1800*, ii (Belfast, 2002).

Jones Hughes, T., 'Town and baile in Irish place-names' in Stephens and Glasscock (eds), *Irish geographical studies*, pp 244–58.

Jones Hughes, T., 'Continuity and change in rural county Wexford in the nineteenth century' in Whelan (ed.), *Wexford*, pp 342–72.

Journal of the Shelburne Co-operative Agricultural Society, 1958-61.

Joyce, P. W., *The origin and history of Irish names of places*, 3 vols. (Dublin, 1910–13).

Kavanagh, A. and Murphy, R., *The Wexford gentry*, i (Bunclody, 1994); ii (Bunclody, 1996).

Kavanagh, A., *The Kavanaghs: kings of Leinster* (Dublin, 2003).

Keogh, D. and Furlong, N., *The mighty wave: the 1798 Rebellion in Wexford* (Dublin, 1996).

Kelly, D., 'Irish high crosses: some evidence from the plainer examples' in *R.S.A.I. Jn.*, cxvi (1986), pp 51–67.

Kelly, E. P. and Maas, J., 'Vikings on the Barrow' in *Archaeology Ireland*, ix, no. 3 (Autumn, 1995), pp 30–2.

Kennedy, P., *The banks of the Boro* (Dublin, 1875; second edition, Enniscorthy, 1989).

Kerrigan, P., *Castles and fortifications in Ireland 1485–1945* (Cork, 1995).

Kinsella, A., *County Wexford in the Famine years 1845–49* (Enniscorthy, 1995).

Leask, H., *Irish castles and castellated houses* (Dundalk, 1941).

Leask, H., 'Slade Castle, co. Wexford' in *R.S.A.I. Jn.*, lxxxi (1951), pp 198–202.

Leask, H., *Irish churches and monastic buildings*, 3 vols. (Dundalk, 1977).

Lenihan, P., 'Aerial photography: a view on the past' in *History Ireland*, i, no. 2 (Summer, 1993), pp 9–13.

Lenihan, P., *Confederate Catholics at war* (Cork, 2001).

Leroux-Dhuys, J.-F., *Cistercian abbeys: history and architecture* (Paris, 1998).

Leslie, J., *Ferns clergy and parishes* (Dublin, 1936).

Lewis, S., *Topographical dictionary of Ireland*, 2 vols. (London, 1837).

Lodge, J., *The peerage of Ireland* (Dublin, 1789).

Loeber, R., *The geography and practice of English colonisation in Ireland 1534–1609* (Athlone, 1991).

Long, B., *Bright light, blue water* (Dublin, 1993).

Lucas, A., 'The horizontal mill in Ireland' in *R.S.A.I. Jn.*, lxxxiii (1953), pp 39–41.

Lydon, F. J., *The lordship of Ireland in the Middle Ages* (Dublin, 1972).

Lydon, F. J., *Ireland in the later Middle Ages* (Dublin, 1973).

Lydon, F. J., *The making of Ireland* (London, 1998).

Macalister, R., 'The ogham inscription of Hook Point, county Wexford' in *R.S.A.I. Jn.*, lx (1930), pp 52–5.

MacNeill, T., *Castles in Ireland* (London and New York, 1997).

Mac Niocaill, G., *Na Manaigh Liath in Éirinn 1142–c.1600* (Baile Átha Cliath, 1959).

Mac Niocaill, G., *Na buirgéisí* (Baile Átha Cliath, 1964).

Mac Niocaill, G., 'Documents relating to the suppression of the Templars in Ireland' in *Analecta Hibernica*, xxiv (Dublin, 1967), pp 181–7.

Maddock, F., 'The cot fishermen of the River Nore' in Nolan, W. and Whelan, K. (eds), *Kilkenny: history and society* (Dublin, 1990), pp 541–66.

Malcomson, A. P. W., 'A house divided: the Loftus family, earls and marquesses of Ely, c. 1600–c. 1900' in D. Dickson and C. O'Grada (eds), *Refiguring Ireland: essays in honour of L. M. Cullen* (Dublin, 2003), pp 184–224.

Manning, C., 'Delusions of grandeur: the pictorial forgeries of Sheffield Grace' in J. Kirwan (ed.), *Kilkenny: studies in honour of Margaret M. Phelan* (Kilkenny, 1997), pp 112–28.

Mannion, J., 'A transatlantic merchant fishery: Richard Walsh of New Ross and the Sweetmans of Newbawn in Newfoundland 1734–1862, in Whelan (ed.), *Wexford*, pp 373–421.

Mannion, J., 'Vessels, masters and seafaring: patterns in Waterford voyages, 1766–1771' in W. Nolan and T. Power (eds), *Waterford: history and society* (Dublin, 1992), pp 373–402.

Martin, C. and Parker, J., *The Spanish Armada* (London, 1988).

McErlean, T., 'Tidal power in the seventh and eight centuries AD' in *Archaeology Ireland*, xv, no. 2 (Summer 2001), pp 10–14.

Mellin, R., *Tilting: house launching, slide hauling, potato trenching, and other tales from a Newfoundland fishing village* (New York, 2003).

Mitchell, F., *Shell guide to reading the Irish landscape* (Dublin, 1986).

Mitchell, F. and Ryan, M., *Reading the Irish landscape* (Dublin, 1997).

Moody, T. and Martin, F. (eds), *The course of Irish history* (Cork, 1967).

Mullarney, K., Svensson, L., Zetterstrom, D. and Grant, P., *Collins bird guide* (London, 1999).

Murphy, H., *Families of county Wexford* (Wexford, 1986).

Nicholls, K., *Gaelic and Gaelicised Ireland in the Middle Ages* (Dublin, 1972).

Nolan, W., *Tracing the past: sources for local studies in the Republic of Ireland* (Dublin, 1982).

O'Callaghan, J., 'Fortified houses of the sixteenth century in south Wexford' in *Wex. Hist. Soc. Jn.*, viii (1980–1), pp 1–51.

O'Conor, K., *The archaeology of medieval rural settlement in Ireland* (Dublin, 1998).

O'Conor, K., 'A reinterpretation of the earthworks at Baginbun, co. Wexford' in Kenyon, J. and O'Conor, K., *The medieval castle in Ireland and Wales* (Dublin, 2003), pp 17–31.

O'Connor, L., *Parish of Tintern* (Ballycullane, no date).

Ó Corráin, D., *Ireland before the Normans* (Dublin, 1972).

Ó Corráin, D., 'The Uí Chennselaig kingdom of Leinster 1072–1126' in *Wexford Hist. Soc. Jn.*, v (1974–5), pp 26–31.

Oftedal, M., 'Scandinavian place-names in Ireland' in B. Almquist and D. Greene (eds), *Proceedings of the seventh Viking congress* (Dublin, 1976).

O'Grada, C., *Ireland: a new economic history* (Oxford, 1994).

O'Keeffe, T., *Medieval Ireland: an archaeology* (Charleston, 2000).

Ó Muirithe, D. and Nuttall, D. (eds), *The folklore of county Wexford* (Dublin, 1999).

O'Neill, T., *Merchants and mariners in medieval Ireland* (Dublin, 1987).

On the Hook, Templetown parish magazine.

Ó Riordáin, S., *Antiquities of the Irish countryside* (London, 1953).

Orpen, G., 'Ptolemy's map of Ireland' in *R.S.A.I. Jn.*, xxiv (1894), pp 115–28.

Orpen, G. H., 'Site of Raymond's fort, Dundonnolf (Baginbun)' in *R.S.A.I. Jn.*, xxvii (1898), pp 155–60.

Orpen, G. H., 'The Carew, Baginbun and Fethard Castle inscriptions' in *R.S.A.I. Jn.*, xxxiv (1904), pp 261–70.

Orpen, G. H., *Ireland under the Normans*, 4 vols (Oxford, 1911–20).

Ó Siochrú, M., *Confederate Ireland 1642–1649: a constitutional and political analysis* (Dublin, 1999).

Otway-Ruthven, J., *A history of medieval Ireland* (London, 1968).

Parkes, M. A. and Morris, J. H., 'Earth science conservation in Ireland: the Irish geological heritage programme' in *Irish Journal of Earth Sciences*, xviiii (2001), pp 79–90.

Parle, J., *The mummers of Wexford* (Wexford, 2001).

Pender, S. (ed.), *A census of Ireland circa 1659 with supplementary material from the poll money ordinances 1660–61* (Dublin, 1939).

Pierce, S., *Arthurstown: the story of a village* (Arthurstown, no date).

Pierce, S. *Dunbrody Abbey* (Arthurstown, 1994).

The Past, the organ of the Uí Ceinnsealaigh Historical Society.

Power, P., 'The royal and ancient fort of Duncannon' in *On the Hook*, vii (1992), pp 54–5.

Quinn, O., 'The coastwatching service' in *The Irish Sword*, xix (1993–5), pp 91–2.

Raftery, B., *Pagan Celtic Ireland* (London, 1997).

Ranson, J., 'A census of Ireland c. 1659: baronies of Bantry and Shelburne' in *The Past*, v (1949), pp 150–60.

Redmond, G. O'C., *The history and topography of the parish of Hook, county Wexford* (Waterford, 1898).

Reeves, W, 'On the townland distribution of Ireland' in *R.I.A. Proc.*, vii (1857–61), pp 473–90.

Roche, R., *The Norman invasion of Ireland* (Tralee, 1970).

Roche, R. and Merne, O., *Saltees: islands of birds and legends* (Dublin, 1977).

Roche, R., *Tales of the Wexford coast* (Enniscorthy, 1993).

Rowe, D. and Scallan, E., *The houses of Wexford* (Whitegate, 2004).

Shaffrey, P. and Shaffrey, M., *Irish countryside buildings: everyday architecture in the rural landscape* (Dublin, 1985).

Simms, A., 'Core and periphery in medieval Europe: the Irish experience in a wider context' in Smyth and Whelan (eds), *Common ground*, pp 22–40.

Smith, C., *The antient and present state of the county and city of Waterford* (Dublin, 1746).

Sleeman, A. (ed.), *Geology of south Wexford* (Dublin, 1994).

Sloane, J., *Manual for lightkeepers* (Dublin, 1873).

Smyth, A. P., *Celtic Leinster: towards an historical geography of early Irish civilisation AD 500–1600* (Dublin, 1982).

Smyth, A. P. (ed.), *Seanchas: studies in early and medieval Irish archaeology, history and literature in honour of Francis J. Byrne* (Dublin, 2000).

Smyth, L., 'The carboniferous rocks of Hook Head, county Wexford' in *R.I.A. Proc.*, xxxix, sect. B (1930), pp 523–68.

Smyth, W., 'Society and settlement in seventeenth-century Ireland: the evidence of the '1659 census'' in Smyth and Whelan (eds), *Common ground*, pp 55–83.

Smyth, W., 'Flax cultivation in Ireland: the development and demise of a regional staple' in Smyth and Whelan (eds), *Common ground*, pp 234–52.

Spencer, K., 'Pugin and county Wexford' in *Wex. Hist. Soc. Jn.*, viii (1980–1), pp 77–90.

Stalley, R., *The Cistercian monasteries of Ireland* (London and New Haven, 1987).

Stanton, P., *Pugin* (New York, 1972).

Stout, G., *et al*, 'The sites and monument record for county Wexford, an introduction' in *Wexford Hist. Soc. Jn.*, xi (1986–7), pp 5–13.

Stout, G., 'Wexford in pre-history: 5000 BC to 300 AD' in Whelan (ed.), *Wexford*, pp 1–39.

Stout, G., *Newgrange and the Bend of the Boyne* (Cork, 2002).

Stout, M., *The Irish ringfort* (Dublin, 1997).

Stout, G. and Stout, M., 'Early landscapes: from prehistory to plantation' in Aalen, Whelan and Stout (eds), *Atlas*, pp 31–63.

Swan, L., 'Enclosed ecclesiastial sites and their relevance to settlement patterns of the first millennium AD' in T. Reeves-Smyth and F. Hammond (eds), *Landscape archaeology in Ireland* (Oxford, 1983), pp 269–80.

Sweetman, D., *The medieval castles of Ireland* (Cork, 1999).

Sweetman, D., 'The fortified house in Ireland' in Smyth (ed.), *Seanchas*, pp 448–53.

Sweetman, D., 'The hall-house in Ireland' in Kenyon and O'Conor (eds), *The medieval castle in Ireland and Wales*, pp 121–32.

Templetown parish development group, *Templetown: profile of a peninsula* (Fethard, 1995).

Tobin, M., 'The population of county Wexford in the seventeenth century' in *The Past*, vi (1950), p. 134.

Vigors, P., 'Notes on three inscribed stones (1) at Baginbun Bay, co. Wexford (2) at Fethard Castle, co. Wexford (3) at Carew Castle, Pembrokeshire, south Wales' in *R.S.A.I. Jn.*, xxvii (1897), pp 150–63.

Walsh, D., *100 Wexford country houses* (Enniscorthy, 2001).

Ward, I., 'A note on the Scottish Presbyterians of Duncannon' in *Wex. Hist. Soc. Jn.*, xvi (1996–7), pp 167–70.

Watt, J., *The church in medieval Ireland* (Dublin, 1972).

Went, A., 'Irish fishing weirs' in *R.S.A.I. Jn.*, lxxvi (1946), pp 176–94.

Went, A., 'The Duncannon weir' in *R.S.A.I. Jn.*, lxxviii (1948), pp 1–4.

Went, A., 'Sprat or white-fish weirs in Waterford Harbour' in *R.S.A.I. Jn.*, lxxxvii (1959), pp 91–108.

Westropp, T. J., 'Five large earthworks in the barony of Shelburne, county Wexford' in *R.S.A.I. Jn.*, xlviii (1918), pp 1–18.

Whelan, K., 'The Catholic church, the Catholic chapel and village development in Ireland' in *Irish Geography*, xvi (1983), pp 1–15.

Whelan, K., 'County Wexford priests in Newfoundland' in *Wex. Hist. Soc. Jn.*, x (1984–5), pp 55–68.

Whelan, K., 'The regional impact of Irish Catholicism 1700–1850' in Smyth and Whelan (eds), *Common ground*, pp 257–77.

Whelan, K. (ed.), *Wexford, history and society* (Dublin, 1987).

Whelan, K., 'A list of those from county Wexford implicated in the 1641 rebellion' in *The Past*, xvii (1990), pp 24–54.

Whelan, K., *The tree of liberty* (Cork, 1996).

Whelan, K., 'The modern landscape: from plantation to present' in Aalen, Whelan and Stout (eds), *Atlas*, pp 67–103.

Whelan, K., 'Towns and villages' in Aalen, Whelan and Stout (eds), *Atlas*, pp 180–96.

Whelan, K., *Fellowship of freedom* (Cork, 1998).

Wood, H., 'The Templars in Ireland' in *R.I.A. Proc.*, xxvi, C (1907), pp 327–71.

Unpublished theses, papers and reports

Andrews, J., The Wexford Civil Survey as a source for historical geography (private circulation, 1956).

Colfer, W., Anglo-Norman settlement in medieval Shelburne, unpublished M. Litt. thesis, T.C.D. (1986).

Colfer, W., Anglo-Norman Wexford 1169-1400, unpublished Ph.D. thesis.

Doyle, I., The medieval borough of Hervey's Island, Co. Wexford, 1169–1654, unpublished moderatorship thesis, T.C.D. (1994).

Jeffrey, W. H., *The castles of county Wexford*, ed. E. Culleton; typescript produced by Wexford Hist. Soc. 1979.

Hart-Davis, H. V., Mansell family history.

Mannion, J., Irish migrations to Newfoundland, unpublished lecture (1973).

Murtagh, B., *Fethard castle, county Wexford: an architectural and archaeological report* (1993).

Murtagh, B., *An archaeological survey of the Tower of Hook* (1999).

INDEX